PENGUIN BOOKS

BEHIND THE WALL

Colin Thubron was born in London in 1939, a descendant of John Dryden. He left publishing to travel – mainly in Asia and North Africa, where he made documentary films that were shown on BBC and world television.

Afterwards he returned to the Middle East and wrote five books on the area. In 1984 the Book Marketing Council nominated him one of the twenty best contemporary writers on travel.

Colin Thubron is also the author of four highly praised novels, including *A Cruel Madness* (Penguin 1985), which won the 1985 Silver Pen Award and *Falling* (1989). His travel books include *Journey into Cyprus*, *The Hills of Adonis* and *Among the Russians*, and are all published in Penguins. *Behind the Wall* is winner of the Hawthornden Prize and the Thomas Cook Travel Book Award for 1988.

BEHIND THE WALL

A journey through China

COLIN THUBRON

PENGUIN BOOKS

PENGUIN BOOKS

Published by the Penguin Group
27 Wrights Lane, London w8 5TZ, England
Viking Penguin Inc., 40 West 23rd Street, New York, New York 10010, USA
Penguin Books Australia Ltd, Ringwood, Victoria, Australia
Penguin Books Canada Ltd, 2801 John Street, Markham, Ontario, Canada L3R 1B4
Penguin Books (NZ) Ltd, 182–190 Wairau Road, Auckland 10, New Zealand

Penguin Books Ltd, Registered Offices: Harmondsworth, Middlesex, England

First published by William Heinemann Ltd 1987
Published in Penguin Books 1988
10 9 8 7

Made and printed in Great Britain by
Richard Clay Ltd, Bungay, Suffolk
Filmset in Ehrhardt

For my Father
with love and admiration

Contents

1. The Capital 1
2. The Power Circles 38
3. Over the Yangtze 67
4. To the Nine-flower Mountain 109
5. Shanghai 138
6. To the South 162
7. Canton 176
8. Mao Slept Here 193
9. The Land of Peacocks 210
10. Through the Gorges 226
11. China's Sorrow 247
12. To the Last Gate Under Heaven 282
    Index 303

Author's Note

The identity of several people in this book has been disguised, in case harsher times return. The journey recorded here took place over a single autumn and early winter, but incorporates a few episodes from an earlier, briefer visit to China. So the book is a compression of experience, and inevitably omits many encounters made barren by people's reticence or by my poor Mandarin.

The spelling throughout follows the modern, *pinyin* system of romanisation, except for a handful of names with well-known English equivalents (such as Tibet, Canton). So Peking becomes Beijing, Mao Tsetung and Chou Enlai become Mao Zedong and Zhou Enlai, etc.

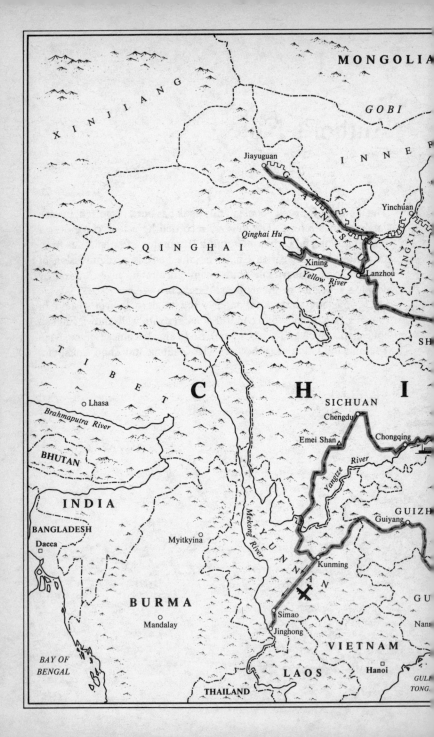

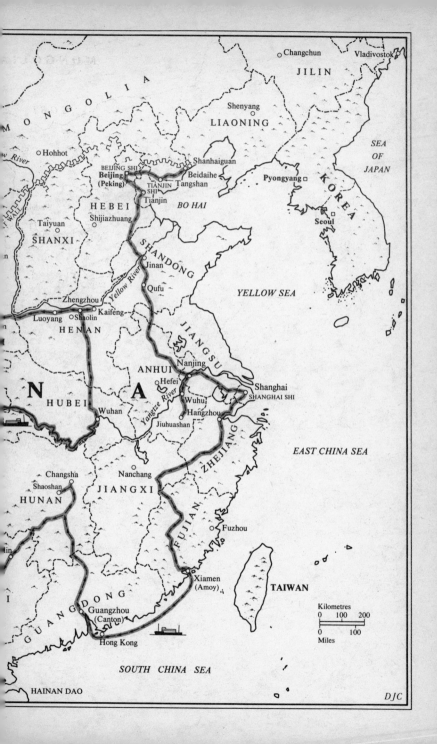

1. The Capital

AFTER THE SHORT night, the sun rose upon a country of such desolate strangeness that the woman sitting beside me leaned forward with her hands tensed over her stomach and let out a constricted 'Ohhh!' For three hours we sat craning at the aeroplane window while the Karakoram and the western Himalaya glimmered and died among camel-coloured mountains, the mountains merged into hills and the hills burrowed at last into the Taklimakan Depression, the deepest waterless region on earth. Momentarily to the north the blades of the Tian Shan erupted from cushions of cloud, turned pink and harmless by the climbing sun. Then these too vanished, and we were flying along the southern fringes of Mongolia and the Gobi desert. And still, in this country of a quarter of mankind, we saw no sign of life.

Her nation's vastness seemed slightly to have appalled the woman. She said: 'Are you travelling *alone?*' She was young, conventionally pretty. Only her stained teeth suggested some history poorer than her dress. She wondered where I was going in China, and – covertly – why.

But I could scarcely answer why. The opening-up of China had stirred me unbearably. It was like discovering a new room in a house in which you'd lived all your life. Five years ago the country had been almost inaccessible. Today nearly the whole land could be penetrated by a traveller going alone. More than two hundred and fifty different regions and cities had fallen suddenly open, and the traffic of trains, boats and buses between them offered ways of vanishing into the wilds. I had plans for criss-crossing classical China (no Tibet, no Manchuria) almost at random for over ten thousand miles, of plunging into the tribal regions abutting Burma along the Mekong river, of reaching the eastern Himalaya and following the Great Wall to its end in the far north-west.

But to the woman I only said, a little ashamed (since no Chinese could see so much of her country): 'I want to visit Beijing and

[1]

Shanghai, and maybe I'll go up the Yangtze, then to Canton and. . . .'

She smiled her set smile. Perhaps she was wondering what the foreigner could ever understand of her nation – this Westerner with his boorish rucksack (I'd dropped it on her feet) and his failure to travel in a group. What could he ever learn?

Even in childhood – that time of intense, dissociated images – my idea of China had been contradictory and distorted. Its colours even then were subtle. It lay embalmed in distance and exotic etiquette. Chinese atrocities were chattered about at my prep school during the Korean War. 'Have you heard the latest Chinese torture?' my classmates would demand, before twisting somebody's arm or neck in a novel direction. The Chinese, after all, were stunted and yellow and looked alike. Their multitudinous numbers lent them anonymity. They weren't quite human. Yet for me their landscape resolved into a mist of waterfalls and twisted pines – the Shangri-la of the scroll-paintings – and the idea of a Chinaman harboured a paradoxical element of the ridiculous (something to do with pigtails and *The Nutcracker Suite*, I think). In any case, China was too distant to be threatening. It was – and remained – a luminous puzzle.

People's images of countries are rich in such buried sediment, which goes on haunting long after experience or common sense has diluted it. And by now – as we floated above the wrung-out steppes of the Gobi – other strata had overlaid the first. In the anarchy of the Cultural Revolution, between 1966 and 1976, the Chinese people had not merely been terrorised from above but had themselves – tens of millions of them – become the instruments of their own torture. The land had sunk into a peculiar horror. A million were killed; some thirty million more were brutally persecuted, and unknown millions starved to death. Yet it was less the numbers which appalled than the refinements of cruelty practised – in one province alone seventy-five different methods of torture were instituted – and I never thought of the country now without being dogged by a tragic question-mark.

The woman was rummaging in her handbag. In the seats behind us a conclave of Beijing businessmen sprawled, their shirt collars open, their eyes closed. I was seized by the foolish idea that each one of them was withholding some secret from me – some simple, perfect illumination. Because that is the foreigner's obsession in China. At every moment, round every corner, the question *Who are they?* erupts and nags. How could they be so led? How could they do what they had done? And had they ever changed – this people of exquisite poetry and refined brush-strokes, and pitilessness?

A billion uncomprehended people.

Beneath us now, where the last hills tilted south-eastward out of Inner Mongolia into the huge alluvial basin of the Yellow River, I could see the divide between plateau and plain, agricultural hardship and sufficiency, drawn vertically down the earth's atlas with the precision of a pencil-stroke. To the west brown, to the east green.

Within half an hour we would be landing in Beijing – old Peking – and as if these last airborne minutes might liberate us from inhibitions, I started talking with the woman about the Cultural Revolution. She turned quizzically to me and asked: 'What do you think of Mao Zedong in the West?'

I said we thought him a remarkable leader, but inhumane.

She said coldly: 'Yes. He made mistakes.'

Mistakes! He had caused more than sixteen million deaths. Sometimes he had acted and talked about people as if they were mere disposable counters on an ideological gameboard. And she talked of mistakes. It was how the Russians spoke of Stalin. I said tightly – I felt this might be my last (and first) chance to vent anger in China: 'All that suffering inflicted on your people! How can you forgive that?' Then I added: 'I think he became a monster.'

She went quiet and stared somewhere beyond me. The fact did not seem to have occurred to her before. Then she said simply: 'Yes.'

For some reason I felt ashamed. Whatever she meant by her 'Yes', its tone – distant, as if admitting something irrelevant – signalled that I did not understand. She fastened her seat-belt. I said: 'Of course it's hard for us in the West to imagine. . . .'

Us in the West. We must seem outlandish, I thought, with our garish self-centredness, our coarse opulence, our sentimentality. Somebody had told me that the Chinese found our big feet and noses preposterous, and that to them we smelt. The next moment I had asked the woman penitently: 'Do we smell?'

Her fragile face smiled back at me. 'Yes, of course.'

I baulked. 'Very much?'

'Oh yes. All the time.'

I suppose that her bemused smile was there to cover embarrassment. But I asked finally, edging a little away: 'Do I smell?'

'Yes.'

It was too late to go back now. 'What of?'

'What?'

'What of? What do I smell of?'

'Oh!' She plunged her face into her hands in a sudden paroxysm of giggles. '*Smell*. I thought you said smile!' The tinkle and confusion of her laughter sabotaged the next few sentences, then she said: 'Only in the summer. Westerners sweat more than Chinese. That's all, that's all. No, you don't . . . smell. No, really . . . no. . . .'

We were coming in to land.

*   *   *

Something impersonal and unfinished pervaded the whole metropolis of Beijing. Often I felt as if I was not in a city at all, but on a building-site where a city might one day be created. I tramped its streets in disorientation, looking for a core which was not there. Across the tarmac desert of its roads the flat-blocks and Soviet-style institutions rose as featureless as cardboard, and the sycamores and silver poplars planted along them paled beneath too vast an expanse of sky. I was feeling displaced from some other capital perhaps, an imagined city – imperial Peking, whose walls and temples had been hacked away.

Along the quiet streets commuters moved in unisexual flocks, jacketed in olive green and boilersuit blue. The boyish hair and tobacco-stained teeth of a million factory workers bobbed and grimaced from jam-packed trams and buses, while sallow girls, their plaits and pony-tails bound in elastic bands, bicycled solemnly all together down special lanes in regimental shoals. Staring at passing faces, I wondered if I could ever come to know them. They conspired to fulfil Western clichés of themselves: inscrutable and all alike. The pavements fell noiseless under the uniform tread of their canvas shoes and black cloth slippers. I smiled at the gentler faces. They looked bemused, smiled slowly back. Nobody approached me.

Even the city's plan was vaguely estranging. The medieval Chinese, who invented the magnetic compass, laid out their capital according to an intricate geomancy, so that its dead-straight streets and gates inscribed a sacred force-field out from the emperor's inner palaces to the farthest reaches of the empire. So wide and tall were they, wrote the astonished Marco Polo, that 'you can see all the way along from end to end and from one gate to another'.

The walls and gates had almost gone now, pulled down in the

Revolutionary ferment, but they had left behind them this mystic gridiron fattened to six or eight lanes with scarcely a motor on them. Its roads sliced through the mesh of alleys and courtyards like the imposition of some unrepealable law, a giant idea driven through the throbbing softness of private life.

Such roads are the city's public face. But their expression is blank. Nothing shakes their desolate serenity. It is as if the whole city were composed of enormous but near-bloodless arteries, fuelling some heart invisible over its horizons. A few trams and Russian-style taxis clatter by, with an occasional Chinese-made 'Shanghai' or Japanese saloon (but never privately owned), while here and there a black Mercedes or lumpish 'Red Flag' conveys its officials between residence and ministry, concealed by curtains. For the rest, the roads are given up to a drifting river of five million bicyclists.

But as I approached the city's centre, I noticed differences. They came in apparent trivia – girls wearing skirts and tentative lipstick, markets spilling over the pavements with sacks of bananas, improvised stalls piled with cheap clothes. Arguments flared, and reticent tenderness: women walking arm in arm, a man's hand drifting to his workmate's shoulder. Compared to the Beijing of ten years ago – a city still frozen in the puritanism of Mao's Revolution – all this was unimaginable. But the changes now were everywhere. Window-dressing had appeared, with hairstyles, fashion, advertisements – all the messengers of a gentler, more self-centred, more humanely varied life. Among the streetside hoardings, pleas for modernisation or family planning ('that the Motherland may be Strong and Flourish') were interlarded with the praises of 'Bee and Flower Liquid Soap' or 'Queen Huang Pearl Cream' or 'Flying Fairy Brand Fireworks'.

I abandoned the avenues and slipped down side-streets into a maze-world of alleys and courtyards. These *hutong*s are still the living flesh of Beijing, and once you are inside them it shrinks to a sprawling hamlet. The lanes are a motley of blank walls and doorways, interspersed by miniature factories and restaurants. Each street is a decrepit improvisation on the last. Tiled roofs curve under rotting eaves. The centuries shore each other up. Modern brick walls, already crumbling, enclose ancient porches whose doors of beaten tin or lacerated pinewood swing in carved stone frames. Underfoot the tarmac peels away from the huge, worn paving-slabs of another age, and the traffic thins to a tinkling slipstream of pedicabs and bicycles.

Sometimes, as I stepped under one of the porches, I found its door ajar and peered into a courtyard littered with panniers, potted shrubs, bicycles, bird-cages. Three or four families would be living there. Their windows offered grime-dimmed visions of bare living-rooms and kitchens. Their walls of glass and latticed wood were thin as paper. I imagined a gust of wind clearing the whole *mise-en-scène* away. But in August the wind scarcely found them. Instead, smells of urine and rotted fish hovered in a sultry air.

In these lanes, too, the inhabitants drifted into solitude and became individual. As they gossiped or bartered at little stalls of private enterprise, they looked mysteriously cleaner and trimmer than the houses from which they came. And they no longer seemed alike. Already I was mentally separating the dark southern immigrant from the taller Beijingnese, and identifying the deep chestnut hair of northern girls. People detached themselves into portraits – a bright-cheeked tomboy skipping with a frayed strand of rope; a man pulling his wife on a hand-cart, to work; while beside me an old woman hobbled on feet crippled by binding – they were less than six inches long, and their broken bones rose in a pained hillock close to the ankle. She smiled weakly at nothing.

I, too, had lost my anonymity here. Sometimes, at the head of narrow lanes, the nonplussed eyes of street committee members scrutinised me from kiosks. I tried to talk to three old men who had set up a counter piled with second-hand books, but they stared back at me dumbly. When I joined a queue outside a milk stall, the women I addressed only simpered and covered their mouths with their little blue residency permits.

A suspicion that these people would remain forever inaccessible was filling me with suppressed alarm. Like an insecure child, I began to crave for any kind of contact, even abuse. The ordinary people call themselves *Laobaixing*, 'Old-Hundred-Names' (an allusion to the hundred commonest surnames among them) and the quaint title suddenly seemed formidable in its anonymity. I lingered by open doors and windows – any perforation in the intestine of these alleys. But I encountered only silence, emptiness or bemusement. Westerners who had lived many years in south-east Asia often said that the Chinese were unknowable. I had not believed them. But perhaps I had been wrong. In England my haphazard researches had filled me less with knowledge than with mounting curiosity. For the past year I had spent several hours every day learning to speak (but not write) Mandarin. Yet now I often could not understand the dialect in the streets around me.

In Russia, once the surface grimness has been penetrated, you find yourself in a human maelstrom; but here in China, I sensed, there was no identical world. The people were more opaque, more inhibited, more disciplined, through and through, filled with an ancient *politesse* which was too internal to be so quickly pierced. I felt a prick of panic. At some point, I imagined, my separate images of China must align themselves like the different screens of a printed illustration, to produce unblurred lines and real colours. But I was no longer sure.

The alleys flood into Tiananmen Square as streams vanish into the sea. No urban space I had ever seen struck me with the same sense of aridity. Even the Chinese groups here were whittled to meandering centipedes. Its paving-slabs were painted with numbers for the regimentation of official demonstrations, more than five hundred to a row. It could hold half a million. It was less a square than a stone field – a hundred acres of emptiness, distantly fringed by the scarps of public buildings. To its east and west (and the inhabitants of this geomantic city are always describing things by compass-point), the Great Hall of the People and the Museum of Chinese History and Revolution spread in a functional wall of colonnades – leftovers from the years of Sino-Soviet *entente*. Sculptured red banners and yellow stars drooped across their pediments. They had become architectural dinosaurs, numbed in their own enormousness. Their blank rectangles, like the city enclosing them, seemed to await an identity.

To the north rose the giant gate from which Mao Zedong, on 1 October 1949, proclaimed the birth of a new China. Entranceway to the secret precincts of the Forbidden City, this was the gate from which the emperor's edicts used to be lowered to the outer world in the beak of a gilded phoenix, and beyond it the yellow-tiled roofs of that timeless sanctity still shone and multiplied among their trees. But the gate was hung now with a portrait of Mao – the last emperor – and the imperial ramparts were exorcised by Communist slogans.

It was here that the million-strong legions of Red Guards had worshipped him in a delirious ocean of red flags and brandished booklets, then rushed away to make revolution. And here, ten years later, defiant crowds – sickened with Mao's despotism – had flooded into the square to raise a hillock of wreaths to the memory of Zhou Enlai, then, when the wreaths were removed overnight, had surged angrily back in an outbreak of rioting, which was brutally suppressed.

As I lingered near one of the deep entrances, I was approached by a sad-looking man whose eyes peered at me so myopically from behind their spectacles that I thought he must have mistaken me for somebody else. His English came halting and quaint.

'Excuse me, sir.' He delved into his pockets. 'Do you wish a purchase?' Even when standing still he looked dangerously uncoordinated; his legs seemed on the point of buckling. 'I wish to study in America.' He pulled out a trio of coins, joined with grubby string through their perforated centres. 'These are Tang dynasty,' he said. 'Do you buy antiques?'

'How did you get them?'

'They provenate from Luoyang in Henan province.' His face came close to mine, death-white. 'They come from old tombs.'

I stared back at him. He looked all but broken. Beneath their bones his cheeks were cratered into two starved crescents. He was thirty-eight, perhaps, but already old.

I said gently: 'I can't buy them.' I didn't want them (and their export was illegal).

He thrust his face still closer to mine. His breath was asphyxiating. 'I must go to America. There's a special course there. I need $250. I need. . . . These coins are genuine.' He juggled them miserably in his fingers. 'The peasants dig them up. The peasants are my friends.'

'From school?'

'Yes. Old classmates.'

I understood now. He was one of that lost generation of youth whom the Cultural Revolution tore from its high schools and colleges. Some were left stranded in the countryside for ever; others had come back to haunt the cities with unemployment and petty crime. Millions strong, they embodied the memory of a deep, collective madness, and will perpetuate this hiatus among the generations until they are gone.

This man had fared better than most. He had become a low-grade mathematics teacher in Luoyang, while his classmates had gone on ploughing that grave-filled soil. He clung to a dream of university. 'Ten dollars for these three. Would it trouble you?'

'But I haven't got any dollars.'

There was growing on his face a beaten, defensive look which reminded me of Western dropouts. But in China nobody voluntarily dropped out. It was the system which had dropped out, from under him. I glanced down at his baggy trousers and frayed sandals. I had a few Chinese coins on me, but felt ashamed to offer them. 'Perhaps you can find an American. . . .'

'I can't.'

He came down to $2. I began to distrust him. What was he really? Not a teacher at all, perhaps, but simply one among thousands of illegally returned ex-students, no longer young, from country exile, unable to get work permits, peddling fake antiques, anything. There was a kind of maimed gentility about him.

All at once he bowed faintly, said 'I'm sorry', and before I could say anything, his thin legs had wobbled into strides and he had gone.

My boarding house was typical of the cheapest places into which Westerners were allowed. Beijing had been subsumed by tourism, and the more opulent hotels were packed with groups. The few lone travellers – mostly student backpackers from Australia, Scandinavia and America – had been crammed into a run-down hostel in the southern suburbs. But an ancient apartheid still divided us from Chinese travellers. There were none here. In fact it would be possible to travel through this whole country and never sit beside a Chinese. The divisions reappear on boats and trains (where foreigners occupy softer seats and berths), in restaurants (where they are ushered up to grander, isolated rooms), on boats and even in some shops. It is as if the hated distinctions laid down by colonising Westerners in the last century were being reimposed – through some masochistic reflex – by the Chinese on themselves.

In fact these barriers spring from an old superiority complex mixed with its opposite, a deep-laid Chinese instinct for guarding their cultural uniqueness, mingled with pride of hospitality and a timeless fear of ridicule, a knowledge that the West – by some fleeting chance – has materially surpassed them. But in the face of the lone traveller, as he wanders the local restaurants and tea-houses and barges onto the poorest class of railway carriage, the system collapses, until in the land's obscurer reaches there is no sign of it at all.

It was halfway to collapsing even in my hotel. The halls and corridors resounded like those of some defunct monastery, and files of ants commuted across the walls. A boiler panted out steam in a room beside my dormitory, gibbering and roaring through a broken door. The place was pervaded by an indefinable but peculiarly Chinese smell, which was to follow me all round the country. It might have emanated from years of accumulated grease.

Nothing eased my sense of displacement. The lethargic staff – two girls giggling behind a desk on every landing – waged a passive war with the clientele. They mutually despised one another. Most of the backpackers behaved as if Beijing were a suburb of Sydney or Hamburg, and seemed angry and incurious at the difference. The conversations in my dormitory revolved around the price of things, not their strangeness or interest. We seemed as insulated as the most self-sufficient tour-group. Even the dining-hall had succumbed to poor Western cooking.

Outside, the city was sunk in a village-like stasis. There were no telephone directories, few street plans. Taxis were scarce or reluctant to move, the buses crammed to bursting. The gathering of train tickets could consume a morning. It was as if some conspiracy were afoot to immobilise the whole population. The only simple thing was to remain where you already were.

I hired a bicycle and escaped into the streets, wobbling down lanes where other cyclists moved in huge, torpid drifts, all together. Some bicycles had been adapted with side-cars for babies or rear-cars for grandmothers, or had been built as bicycle rickshaws. But most were near-identical. There were no lamps, no pumps, no gears (mine had no brakes either). Their dreamy flood became addictive. All was slow motion. At intersections we glided across each other's bows with the placid deliberation of fish, or oozed out *en masse* to submerge the roundabouts and drown jaywalkers in a slow tinkling of bells.

The younger women went in patches of timid colour. Jeans had arrived, and jaunty straw hats. Beneath their split skirts the sedately pedalling legs betrayed knee-length stockings. Spangled hairnets were the rage.

At early morning and dusk the flow of cyclists swelled to a clogged torrent and the bus queues enlongated into worn-faced hundreds. Yet in these first days the streets struck me as curiously unpeopled. Men curled in random sleep on any patch of grass or shade, or spreadeagled in the backs of parked trucks. In the heart of this puritan city, beneath the walls of the imperial palace, a woman squatted with her shirt wrenched back from her shoulders and dangled her baby first at one breast, then at the other. Beside her a beggar slept with his blackened hand still cupped for alms – an inverted claw twisted open by decades of pleading. Beside them a notice-board gave warning of traffic accidents. Its photographs showed a line of corpses in the civic mortuary, laid out rather casually on trolleys, and a girl cyclist lying dead in a puddle of blood and crumpled iron. There were close-ups of her face. In my recoil I dimly saw that these warnings belonged to an unfamiliar balance in things: the service of the individual to the mass, even in death.

I met Chen on the cable-lift which travels up the Fragrant Hills on the north-west fringes of the city. By chance we were hoisted into the air together on twin chairs, and so found ourselves in forced intimacy. The dappled slopes passed softly below, while ahead of us the summit rose in a thin mist.

What did people do in this parkland, I asked (hauling my Mandarin into life)?

They didn't do anything much, he said, then added: 'It's a place to go with your girlfriend on Sundays. Perhaps they kiss a little.'

He turned a boyish face to mine. He might have been any age between twenty and forty. Above his glasses his eyebrows jerked up and down in nervous spasms. He looked paradoxically impish. He had walked here with his girl himself, he said, before they were married. 'You see those birds down there?' – he pointed to a flash of green in the trees – 'Those are the happiness birds. They're meant to bring you luck.'

'Did they?'

He smiled a hard, temporary smile. 'I don't know yet.'

In the chairs descending past us, other couples sat like portraits, immobilised. A young girl was clasping her man's arm, while he chewed sunflower seeds and looked away, hawking and spitting over the edge. Two old men floated by from an earlier world, gazing down and laughing nervously. Another couple sat bolt upright. His hands were severely interlaced, while she clutched a little bag and umbrella, and presented him with a clear, smiling profile. But on her other cheek a birthmark flamed. 'The Blue Danube' lilted from loudspeakers above.

Meanwhile, I was trying to piece Chen's life together. Suspended in quiet, our words seemed not precisely ours. He spoke as if to the hills in front of us, and I felt that once we had reached the summit he would be gone. He had returned from exile in the Cultural Revolution to become a clerk in provincial government. 'But many of my friends, more gifted than me, never recovered at all,' he said. 'They stayed in the country for as long as seven years. Now they're just factory workers.'

We were travelling low over the ground. Purple convolvulus and forget-me-nots passed just under our feet. Chen kept pressing his fingers through a fine dust of hair. 'But those days have gone. It's better to forget them.'

His boyishness seemed to lie only thinly over an emotional permafrost. Even his smiles seemed on loan. He lived with his wife and child in one room; they shared a kitchen and sink with three other families and a telephone with a hundred. He took his baths in his office. Yet it was not only necessity which dictated his habits. In him the softer needs seemed to have remained stillborn, as if the Cultural Revolution had brutally reinforced a natural asceticism, and personal desire was in itself a peril. Yet I think he was ambitious. These repressions surfaced in staccato bursts of talk. At such moments the spasm of his brows was less comic than a violent, self-torturing tic.

'We Chinese are an inward people. We don't show much.' He bunched his fingers against his chest. 'Foreigners express a great deal which we never could.'

'And you find that ugly?'

'Sometimes, yes. Chinese who work with foreigners talk about their – excuse me – arrogance. It's not that aliens are exactly resented here, but sometimes when people see the special privileges they're granted, they think: *This is our country. Why should others be preferred in it?*' He hated the special hotels and 'Friendship Stores', which were open only to tourists and élite Chinese, together with the foreign exchange certificates by which they bought exclusive goods. 'It's not that I want those things myself. I don't. I've been inside those Friendship Stores, and I don't want a thing. It's not my taste.' A jerk of his hands ejected all that garish luxury. 'I prefer practical things. Just practical. Isn't that better?' His voice had turned high and tense. 'I think all these privileges and differences will be swept away in a few years, and we'll see the end of this . . . this . . .' – his teeth bared – 'unequal system.' He stopped, teetering on the edge of something dangerous, or perhaps just discourteous.

I began uneasily: 'Perhaps when we're more alike. . . .'

'We're already more alike. Our young people have become more cynical. They just want to get on with their own lives. The slogans have mostly gone from our streets. The Party has turned from politics to economics.'

'Are you in the Party?'

'Yes, and I'm proud of it.' For some reason he laughed. 'There's a danger of our forgetting ideology altogether. That's why we need the Party.' The hill's summit was no longer in mist. We were almost there.

'You said you were a writer, didn't you? So write that. *Our country needs the Party*. Make sure you say that. . . .'

* * *

The curious name of Wangfujing Street, 'Well of the Princes' Residences', betrayed that this motley collection of brick and concrete – the shopping centre of Beijing – was once an artery of palaces; and the alleys round about – 'Pig Market Street', 'Lantern Market Street' – were redolent of trades long changed or gone.

Wangfujing was now animated and styleless, jostling with supermarkets and foreign shops. The toy counter of 'Number One Department Store' was piled with dolls like surrogate babies swaddled in pink or blue fur and an expressionless regiment of pandas. A few tanks and tinny pistols were the only military toys. The little phalanxes of buses, vans and trains included no cars. A crowd of small boys was gazing in hopeless fascination at a 'sonic-control electronic beetle', which cost more than half a normal monthly wage.

In the Eastwind Market cosmetics department, women clustered three deep around a few sticks of lipstick and mascara. The lipsticks came in two violent, simple colours. Nobody dared touch them. Customers bought talcum powder and face cream instead, and watched the shop assistant demonstrating how to use mascara, gazing at her in mesmerised silence.

In the electrical department a crowd of men was staring at two display televisions which kept breaking down. The shelves groaned with Chinese-made cassette-recorders, music centres, transistors. Many of the customers were farmers in from the country, and they bought with deep caution. One old man at last thumbed out a wad of 50-kwai notes for a black and white television which cost more than six months' industrial wage. A blank-face shopgirl tied it up with string, but the old man uncoiled a length of rope from his waist and bound up the television again before tottering away with it.

Nearby I entered Beijing's nuclear shelter network. Its digging had started in 1969 during fears of Soviet invasion, and had continued for ten years. Now, beneath every large Chinese city, the earth is perforated like a rotten cheese. One moment I was standing in a styleless clothes shop, the next – at the touch of an electric button – the tiled floor behind the counter glided away and I descended a stair into a maze of fetid corridors. The way was wanly lit by neon lights and an

[13]

occasional, outlandish chandelier. Iron doors slid back in Ali Baba silence at the flick of a switch. Further on still, a second dummy floor dropped away, separating into iron steps, and I descended into a deeper warren which beetled into darkness. Walls gleamed with damp, and water-pipes squirmed along the passageways. The air came suddenly cold.

I reached a chamber where a guide was delivering a lecture. Occasionally she referred to a fluorescent map standing against a wall. The whole city, she said, was riddled with underground tunnels. In the event of a nuclear strike its nine million people could bolt underground like gophers, and survive there for five days. This section, she said, served all the shops in the street above, with their two thousand staff and an estimated ten thousand visitors at a time. The shopkeepers had dug it themselves, without machinery. Air conditioning had been fitted, an electricity-generating plant installed, wells sunk. Ninety different concealed entrances led into the labyrinth, one from each shop, and she reckoned the street could be cleared of people in six minutes. Seven other entrances led from here into the greater network, where people could flee down tunnels from the city centre for ten miles, or reach the underground railway which would carry them fifteen miles to the Western Hills.

These prodigies of mass coercion or will always struck me into numbed credulity. The past brimmed with them. The huge lakes by the Forbidden City and the Summer Palace were scooped out purely by manpower, and the 200-foot Coal Hill – the highest point in Beijing – was raised by an army of nameless conscripts. The 1,100-mile Grand Canal between Beijing and Hangzhou was dug by a workforce of five and a half million in the seventh century; the tomb of China's first emperor engaged 700,000 craftsmen and slaves who laboured from the beginning of his reign to its end; the Great Wall. . . .

But I stared back at the woman with a tentative, growing dismay. The upper corridors of the fall-out shelter lay a mere eight metres underground. A nuclear explosion would reduce the labyrinth to a mass tomb, too atrocious to contemplate.

'But we have air-tight doors to keep out radioactive dust and light,' she said. 'The walls are shock-resistant.' Her serene expression had turned into one of slightly boorish simplicity. 'Our slogan is "preparedness against calamity". . . .'

Perhaps she was right. I didn't know. But I heard with relief that since 1979 this stone jungle had been turned to other uses. Now it contained restaurants, hospitals, libraries, more than a hundred hotels, a roller-skating rink, cinemas, while the shops above had appropriated thousands of rooms for warehouses and ateliers.

I asked: 'Are you still afraid of nuclear attack?'

She hesitated, then said formally: 'No.'

Yet somewhere beneath this city's surface, I felt, a vivid life was going on and I was missing it. That evening I noticed a door from which men were emerging with washing-bags and plastered-down hair: a public bath-house. Feelings of ostracism made me enter. I had an idea that the stripping of clothes might strip away mental barriers too. Formality would be harder in the nude.

I entered a hall lined with wooden beds. Its colours were those of school: buff and pale green. The cubicles smelt like school too – each one narrow as a plank, and each holding a locked cupboard. I was aware of eyes following me from numberless bunks – steam-drowsed eyes shaded by towels. Spectacles were being lifted and wiped and re-adjusted to focus the intrusion; confused murmurs of astonishment arose.

I found a cubicle and slipped off my clothes. By now the whole hall was gazing at me. Swathed heads jostled and ogled along the tops of the partitions. Opposite me sat an old man, his senile breasts and stomach converging in three oil-smooth folds. When he caught sight of me, his hand had been extended to grasp a mug of tea, but now it remained outstretched before him in meaningless semaphore, while he froze bolt upright and stared. Could this foreign body be real – white, hairy (comparatively) and mosquito-bitten?

I joined a shuffling queue, seized a towel from a pile of others, and entered the bath chamber. In its white-tiled hall some hundred men were soaping themselves under showers or lying like drug-addicts in steamy pools. Naked, they looked more than ever like a nation of boys. They showed none of the accumulated muscle or flab of the Westerner, nor the passive Russian bulk. Their skins were creaseless and unblemished. There was something lapidary, almost polished, about their hairless chests and narrow shoulders. Their limbs were slender, unshaped. Many looked malnourished.

The bath-ritual involved a slow self-broiling in three connected tanks, each hotter than the last. I slid hesitantly into the coolest of them, then submerged myself until I presented no more than a small, dazed head, and hoped for anonymity. All around, the heads of the pool's other denizens gyrated to look at me – disembodied faces whose eyes were all but closed. We were spaced like prawns around the basin's sides, sitting feebly on an underwater shelf.

Soon the steam-filled air induced a luxurious indolence. My head tilted back to stare unthinking at the glass-panelled ceiling. My feet lifted sybaritically from under me. Time stopped. Everything was blurred to a ghost of itself. As for the others, even their eyeblinks had slowed into torpid flutterings, and their conversation dwindled to sleep-talk.

I stared at those outside the water. Some men squatted along the tiled pool-sides, soaping their armpits or crutches with an odd, matter-of-fact delicacy as if flushing out extra small fleas. Others scrubbed themselves under the showers, chatting in staccato bursts, or scraped at their feet with hunks of black pumice-stone. Among them a few old men stood thin as storks. Their shoulder-blades stuck out like those in famine posters. They shuffled over the tiles with a terrible, pained caution and lowered themselves into the baths as if into their graves.

I remained for a long time plucking up courage to slide over the lip of my bath into the deeper swelter of the adjoining one. When I did, the water felt incandescent. For a moment I lay gasping against its tiles. The steam ballooned about me while a new conclave of heads turned to inspect. They murmured conspiratorially together. But their lips were parted by seraphic smiles, and their heads thrown back in a depersonalised ecstasy. Everything here – even astonishment – had slowed to a dream.

Then little by little, these faces came circling round me. They were grinning. One of them suddenly spoke: 'Welcome. We are very pleased that you are in our bath.'

'I'm very glad to be in your bath.'

The mouths widened. Level gleams of teeth appeared. The heads oscillated a little. All down the edges of the pool they were now aligned in concourse, adding their greetings to his. In a moment, I felt, a formal committee would be voted in, drinks produced, toasts proclaimed. My hope for informality was turning grotesque.

I insinuated a leg over the pool-side and into the hottest tank which was subdivided into three bath-sized basins of pure anguish. I wanted to withdraw, but the floating heads were watching my progress. Inch by inch I lowered myself into a liquid inferno and stood there, not daring to move.

In the bath beside me an old man was swimming unconcernedly. He glanced at me and closed his eyes in disbelief. Then we stared at each other out of our mutual incomprehension. Through the steam he reminded me of those photographs of Mao Zedong swimming the Yangtze. Perhaps he wasn't really there. My eyes misted over, probably in pain. His head was no more than two feet from mine, but soon he became merely an expression in the ether, like the smirk of the Cheshire Cat. There was nothing to be heard but the slop and gurgle of water. In the bath beyond, another old man was lying with his legs splayed and his toes gripping the bath's sides, like a woman in childbirth.

I don't know how long I lay immolated there, but eventually I became alarmed by my own dizziness, and lifted myself out. I was burnt raspberry pink from the neck down. I walked with the raw delicacy of something new-hatched. The warm tiles slid cold under my feet. Near the door two masseurs in galoshes were scouring men's chests and armpits with wooden blocks wrapped in towels. The dirt was runnelling off them in solid, black tidemarks. I slunk past them, and out.

The dressing-room was like a morgue. Exhausted bathers stretched inert under sheets, their heads covered, their legs projecting limply. Some were asleep, others had lapsed into limbo. From time to time a spate of coughing or hawking announced their imminent resurrection. Then voices rose in confabulation, and a convivial tinkling of teacups sounded. In China, where public conversation is often carried on in declamatory shouts, these collusive mumblings fell on the ear like a subterfuge. Knots of men gathered sleepily around the tin spittoons, where ash and phlegm mingled in a tobacco-coloured pool. Others summoned the attendant for metal trays with enormous scissors attached, then assiduously sliced the dead skin from the soles of their feet and dropped it on the floor.

Two beds to my left, I noticed the most solemn of the water-browsing heads which had welcomed me. I followed him out. Coveys of young women were emerging from another door as we passed, and were combing out their long black hair in the hall mirror.

'In the West,' said the man in English, turning a heavy face to mine, 'there is a bath in almost every house, isn't there? You've given up places like this.'

I wondered how he knew: knowledge of the West is so thin in China.

'I was three months in your country,' he said.

We entered a restaurant, where dumplings were soon mounded on our table in putty-coloured heaps. When I asked what he had been doing in England, he thought for a long time. Everything about Dengming, even the set of his shoulders, was painfully deliberate. Stupendous pauses gaped between my questions and his answers.

At last he said: 'I was studying computers. In our country, you see, technology is just a baby' – he cupped his hands round a dumpling – 'a very *little* baby.'

Even his expression changed only slowly, after the sanction of long thought, so that humour or regret came welling up from behind his face long after the remark which had caused it had gone. 'We must copy your technology. But in other things – human things, organisation – we have to stay ourselves. Western systems don't exactly work here. They don't fit our mind.' He looked vaguely puzzled. 'We need to evolve some pathway of our own. That's the question-mark over our whole future. We can't just borrow bits and work them in to a jigsaw. No.'

'You've tried that?'

'Yes. When I came back from England, for instance, I tried implanting some Western management ideas. But our people didn't grasp them. I've tried so many changes . . . but. . . .'

Here the machinery of his thought or language broke down. He picked open a dumpling in exasperation.

I said: 'What went wrong?'

Another immeasurable interval fell. Then he said: 'Life is different with us. Everything slows down.'

'Why?'

'People.'

Bureaucracy, of course, the immemorial curse of China. This is still an old man's country. And Dengming was barely thirty. In his ponderous caution it was hard, at first, to see him as the harbinger of change, or of anything. But I think I was confusing slowness with stupidity.

I said: 'Is there anything about England that you miss?'

He took so long to answer that I thought he hadn't heard. Then a look of happy remembrance suffused him. 'Yes,' he said. 'Milk deliveries.'

'What?'

'*Milk deliveries*. I thought that was marvellous. How you get up in the morning and there's milk on the doorstep!' His voice accelerated into positive animation. 'And taxis! You can get a taxi anywhere. Wonderful.'

'Anything else?'

'Yes. Politeness. Order. Everybody's very polite with you, whereas our officials are rude.' Some bitterness undermined his voice. 'Most people hate them. They're arrogant and lazy. Shop supervisors, ticket-sellers, office cadres, all of them. . . .'

I said: 'I don't know how you stop that.' I could envisage only generations of cultural change, another history.

But Dengming said with (for him) unnerving speed: 'We'll stop it by . . . what do you call that in the West? . . . Material incentives. That's it. If bosses are made responsible for performance, they'll ensure their workers are courteous. That's how it will be cured.' His fingers met smugly over a third dumpling. For a moment he seemed a parody of the cynical Chinaman, advocating the manipulation of people by self-interest.

I stared across the table into his dark-thatched face. Perhaps he was, after all, the herald of the new China – a nation emerging from the nightmare idealism of Mao into a more pragmatic and disillusioned world. Even as he spoke, his government was completing plans further to loosen its grip on industry and to foster competition.

'It's coming,' he said. 'It's coming very soon. You know our expression "the iron rice-bowl"? It means you have a secure salary, like I do. There are millions like me, and it's hopeless. Sometimes I'm sitting at my desk for days with nothing to do.'

'Many Westerners,' I said, 'envisage the Chinese as worker ants.'

'Workerance? What's that?'

'Ants. You know. Ants which do nothing but work.'

A burst of laughter hit him, high pitched in its astonishment. 'Ohoho! No, no . . . no . . .' – I waited a full minute while this chortling evaporated – '. . . worker-ants . . . no . . . ohoho. . . . Most of us sit about. . . . But this slackness is changing now. People are being made responsible for making their firms pay. Many people are going to get rich.'

I said: 'It's becoming like Britain. . . . Capitalist.'

A frown settled between his eyes and percolated upwards. 'But you in Britain have made mistakes.'

I wondered which ones he meant, which ones a Marxist would mean. Uncaring government? Exploitation of the working classes? The tyranny of private enterprise? 'Yes?'

But he said astonishingly: 'Nationalisation. It doesn't work. It doesn't pay. Your railways and other things. They should go private.'

I stared back at him. Dimly I sensed that I was listening to a very old China, a China in whose millennia-long voice Marxism was no more than a sigh. My own voice sounded querulous and prim: 'But your country isn't used to the modern economic world. If you adapt you'll take on all our Western pushiness . . . stress and . . . all that.'

He was now watching me in the faintest mockery. Suddenly I seemed (to both of us, I think) younger than him, more naïve, more Communist. But I rushed on: 'You'll release all sorts of forces. Individual needs and ambitions. Industrial unrest, crime. You remember England?'

'Oh yes.' A momentary smile – the bliss of milk deliveries – crossed his face. 'But crime here isn't due to individualism. It's due to boredom, just like with you. Many young people have no proper jobs. They just wander about. Thousands and thousands of them. I know a family of six youths, all unemployed, who used to be in and out of the police-station all the time. They had nothing to do. But now our policies are changing and they've got a business licence and have started trading in watermelons. They're doing fine, getting rich. A mass of people are doing the same thing. They buy all sorts of stuff – clothes, food, even books – at the wholesale exhibitions, then sell it at a profit like that. So their minds are full of making money now. It's all changing.'

Already I had sensed this. A proliferation of commerce could be felt all over the city. Parts of it seemed to have become one enormous free market, and the pavements and station platforms swarmed with men selling toothbrushes, crabs, bananas, anything. Where would it end?

Dengming pondered. I nagged. Could his country take on Western systems without the attendant Western diversities, corruption, freedom?

But he only swayed his head from side to side with snail-like patience, and said: 'We must find our own way.'

But history did not suggest – I wrangled on – any Chinese immunity to Western ills. Nobody who saw his country's poverty could resent Westernisation, but it would carry its price.

Dengming said: 'But we in China don't expect as much as you do. We're used to sacrifice.' He brooded for long seconds. 'It horrifies your people, for instance, that we can't move about like you do, or have as many babies, or that husbands and wives can be separated by their work. But millions of us are.' If any new expression embalmed his face, it was one of placid enduring.

I asked: 'Are you?'

'My wife works for a government office near Shanghai. We haven't seen each other for five months.'

I said foolishly, forgetting: 'Can't you change jobs?'

'You can't change jobs in China. You follow your prescribed path.'

'You have children?'

'One. One is allowed. He lives with my wife's parents now, but he'll board in kindergarten.'

'Board in kindergarten?' I was remembering my own distress at prep school (the sight of Berkshire heaths still makes me sick). I said: 'How old will he be?'

'Two.'

'*Two?*'

'It's old enough,' said Dengming.

'What about his holidays?'

'He won't have holidays. We'll see him at weekends sometimes. If we can teach him right and wrong, that will be enough.'

'Will it?'

'Yes.' He started tearing at another dumpling. 'That's life.'

'Yes.' My voice sounded sadder than his. A lot of things are 'life' in China.

Later I saw one of these boarding kindergartens: a scattering of concrete dormitories and classrooms round a plot of asphalt. Although I had arrived during school holidays it was full of children. Their clothes were assertively bright – their trousers jaunty with Mickey Mouse patches, and the girls' hair a mass of muslin ribbons. They played on a steel chute and roundabout. A few of them fought or cuddled one another, but listlessly. At lunch they sat on benches at long, clean tables, while lamb and rice were spooned into their tin bowls from a bucket. They whispered together.

I was ushered into a classroom where the pupils sat on little wooden chairs. The floors were of baked earth, but the walls covered with children's pictures of monkeys and pandas. In front of them a teacher struck up tunes at a tinny harmonium, and nodded their cues, while the children chorused back. They sang like mechanical birds: vivacious and dead.

A moment's silence fell. Then, all together, they chanted at me: 'Hello – welcome! How – do – you – do?'

I thanked them, and they replied in treble concord: 'Not – at – all!'

Their faces – perhaps because of the faint decline of their eyes outward – looked anxious and melancholy. They had been trained to speak – with near-perfect unity – these heartbreaking, disembodied anthems of greeting or farewell.

I asked what they had been doing.

The teacher gave them their cue and they chorused: 'We – have – had – lunch.'

'Did you enjoy it?' I asked.

The teacher called: 'It was tasty?' and back came the treble roar: 'It – was – tasty!' – a consensus shared by everybody except a little girl who was gazing dumbfounded at my outsize feet.

Perhaps my desolation at these children was misplaced. I couldn't tell what they were feeling. Their faces, in repose, were frail, mask-like, sometimes beautiful. Their black eyebrows arched across their foreheads with the delicacy of wings. Already they had imbibed the mannerisms ritually considered sweet in Chinese children. In the playground they jumped up and down with their feet together, clapped their hands coyly or splayed them in front of their peeping eyes in a parody of bashfulness. Meanwhile the bespectacled teachers stood by with maternal watchfulness, bestowers and withholders of all love.

Half an hour later the children settled in their dormitories for afternoon rest. Thirty blue-painted cots stood end to end in every room. Each was piled with a quilt, a towel and a pillow stuffed with barley-husks in order (said a teacher) to prevent them from sleeping in incorrect postures. They swivelled back little doors in the beds' sides and climbed in apprehensively. The teachers filled the rooms with a crossfire of scrutiny. The tiniest divergence of behaviour drew staccato orders and pointed fingers. One girl hadn't laid her towel precisely enough over her pillow. A five-year-old had folded his jacket wrong. For a minute or two the flurry of correction blew and subsided. Then the teachers were gone.

I waited a little, watching to see what would happen. Momentarily a few faces peered over the cot-sides with a residue of mischief. A lone giggle echoed. Then they lay back in utter silence. Their legs buckled against their bedrolls. For a minute or two their eyes stared upwards from their barley-husk pillows, then they shut.

Before I left, the children of another class – seven or eight years old –

were ordered on to the playground to entertain me. Heavily made-up and dressed in traditional costume, they waited in a self-conscious line while I was positioned before them on a stool and served green tea. Then music crackled from a loudspeaker overhead, and all together, like those figures which waltz to the dust-softened tinkles of old musical-boxes, they began to dance. They lilted over the asphalt in an arc of quaintly turning heads and hands and a trail of tinselled sleeves. They were immaculate as porcelain. Under round caps or a burst of ribbons their rouged cheeks fanned into set smiles. They performed odd, gnomic pavans. They mimicked flower-picking and horse-riding. The asphalt rang with the kicking of their booted feet. Even in mimed warfare their droll faces remained stamped with obligatory grins. Only once a small boy in a blue Mongolian gown became so bemused by my presence that he forgot his steps altogether. For an instant he stood stock-still and stared – a fuddled expression with sticking-out ears – then broke into a dissident cakewalk of his own, throwing everyone else into confusion.

When I left, the diminutive dancers flooded to the compound gates after me, waving. Even for them, perhaps, the spontaneity of their farewell was impossible to gauge (the teachers were urging them from behind) but eventually they spilled into the street altogether, waving still – a disciplined blaze of colour against their grey home. It was impressive, vivid and somehow terrible.

In the zoo everything unusual seemed to be asleep. A herd of square-lipped rhinoceroses had foundered like battleships into the dust, and three pandas lay on iron benches in the sun, their fur discoloured and their arms wrapped over their faces. The visitors tried to goad the animals into action, but the sour-faced gorillas only went on chewing at their grasses; the big cats yawned as if reality stopped at their bars; and the Yangtze alligators focused on nothing through burnt-out eyes.

But the place of people's greatest fascination was the aquarium. In these dark corridors, hung with their illumined panels, the crowds banked six deep to investigate the goofy-faced paradise fish or watch the *Santamariae* fluttering across their tank in a silver diagonal of sparks.

I was looking for creatures special to China: the white-lipped deer, the wild Tibetan donkey, golden-hair monkeys. I found the deer swatting insects out of their eyes with casual rotations of their ears.

Their white lips lent them a painted calm and seemed faintly to smile. But the golden-haired monkey turned out to be a recluse. A man was standing at its cage with his small daughter, shouting for it to emerge from its hutch. But nothing happened. We joined our voices in a comical request to it – first courteous, then cajoling, finally rude. But it turned away in its shelter, so that we glimpsed only a moody, black-streaked back and disconsolate ears.

The man was humorously disappointed. He had spent years in the wilds of the northern provinces, he said, and had never spotted a monkey – and now here he was, within shouting distance of one, and it wouldn't even look round.

Some reticent difference of dress or manner distinguished him (I never defined it) and he was tall for a Chinese, gangling even.

There were greenish-furred apes in the north, I'd heard, which looked as if they were covered in lichen. Had he never glimpsed those?

'I don't remember any wildlife at all.' His hand dropped to his daughter's, as if they were about to go, but instead he leant back against the cage. We were alone. 'Up there in Shanxi province the peasants have stripped all the trees, they're so poor. They kill and eat anything that moves. There's scarcely even wood for building materials.' His lips enacted the tasting of something bitter, and this fleeting expression all at once seemed natural to him, and his suavity just a temporary concession. He asked suddenly: 'Why are you speaking Mandarin? Are you a teacher?'

'No. I'm just . . . interested.' I was uneasily aware of the monkey stirring in its shelter behind us. The man smiled.

'Out there in the north-west life is much harder,' he went on. 'You can't imagine. So little food, fuel. And terrible winters. I remember seeing ancestral tablets reused as timber in the walls. The ancestor cult had been banned by then – so there they were, just stuffed into the walls like bricks.'

'Really forgotten?'

'Well, not really. They stayed in the peasants' memories even if they weren't on their altars' – he tapped with his fingertips at his forehead – 'and as soon as new policies came in they started returning. Not the old tablets, I mean, those were burnt or lost. But the peasants made new ones. It was all in their minds, you see. It never left.'

I asked: 'Do you come from the north-west?' But I had guessed, already, that he did not, and why he'd been there. He was in his mid-thirties, the age of China's lost generation: seventeen million youths exiled to the country.

'No.'

I blundered on: 'Were you away long then? I mean during the' – I hoisted the name gingerly – 'Cultural Revolution.'

'I had seven years. I was young then. I should have been able to bear it.' Between one sentence and another the urbane veneer had slipped from his face. Its flesh had stiffened. He said incongruously: 'I see you're interested in our history.' That turned my questions – and his experiences – impersonal. 'I was sixteen when I was banished. I lived with another youth – an ex-Red Guard like me – in a peasant's two-room cottage. We took over one room while the farmer and his four children moved into the other. Half theirs was occupied by a brick bed heated from beneath, where they all slept. That was all there was. With a pig-sty and a closet for night-soil in the courtyard. That was us.' By now he was speaking with slight theatricality. 'But of course the peasants didn't welcome us. We were just extra mouths to feed. We knew nothing about farming. Some years the family came near starvation and the man thought of selling one of his daughters – the sickly one. Quite a few from our village were sold off like that, as cheap future brides. That way a peasant could get a bride for 1,000 yuan, perhaps, instead of paying 2,000. They were sold off while they were still young.'

I glanced down at his daughter. Her face held an empty clarity. She was tying her hair-ribbon. 'How young?'

'I can't remember. One was eight, I think, another only five.' They went to distant villages, he said, these brides for £200. It was better than being killed in infancy. 'I heard of them being killed in other villages. It was quite common. The peasants would just drop them in the water and drown them.' His lean hands lobbed an imaginary baby into a pool: his gestures had grown constricted, filled with histrionic revulsion. 'You see, they don't think. They just drop it in. They just say "It's a girl! It's worthless!" Girls are not *descendants*, you understand. They're not viewed that way. It's boys who continue our line.'

He stopped, as if at some ghastly logic in the thing. His little girl's hand was still in his, but she was gazing behind us, waiting for the monkey to emerge.

'What do the other villagers say about it?' I asked.

'They probably say nothing. They understand. They're peasants

[25]

too, after all. They don't denounce them. Only if officials hear, then the man will go to prison.'

'And the woman?'

'The woman maybe not. It's the men who get the long sentences. Five years for a man – one for a woman! Perhaps, I don't know.' He glanced up suddenly – like someone just waking. A few people were walking near us. 'You're interested in Chinese animals? I'll find a takin for you. . . .'

His smile relaxed him into somebody else again, somebody pleasant, studiously courteous. We ambled away up a slope to a new line of enclosures. Half unconsciously, perhaps, he had chosen somewhere lonely. His daughter ran ahead of us to find the takin (whatever that was) while I asked him tentatively about the Red Guards. The year 1966, when they were unleashed upon the country, still touched me with a faint, naïve regret. I remembered Mao Zedong's belief that the Chinese were a blank sheet of paper on which could be written a poem of creative and unending revolution.

But men turned out to be different, of course. Between 1966 and 1968 China sank into a terrified collective madness. Nobody was safe. Officials, doctors, teachers, scientists – all the élite of the professions and the arts, anybody tinged with privilege or the West (and millions who weren't) – were ritually humiliated, ingeniously tortured, exiled, beaten to death. In the peculiarly Chinese 'struggle sessions', the victim was subjected to a remorseless psychological and physical battering by hundreds of jeering co-workers over days or weeks, his every word contradicted, his past shredded by accusation, his will broken, until he had groaned out confession. A hysterical xenophobia reigned. Cultural life was laid waste. Variety and beauty in themselves became criminal. Even pet cats and dogs were slaughtered (producing a plague of rats). Ornamental trees and flower-beds were dug up. Stamp-collecting, chess, keeping goldfish – nothing was innocent.

The man had the feeling that he had been somebody else at that time. 'Yet I remember it very distinctly. Everything. We only had one idea then. Whatever Chairman Mao said was right, God-given. Our heads were empty. Perhaps we had gone mad. We didn't think at all.' He was staring into vacant cages. 'And now it seems like a nightmare.'

I didn't answer, because I didn't really understand. He was deeply bewildered at his own past. Once authority had sanctioned violence, no monitor inside him had called a halt. Such a pattern, I realised, ran far back in China's history: a recurring cycle of constraint broken by sudden ungovernable savagery.

And what had he done?

As he spoke about it, the tension crawled back into his voice. But instead of silencing him, it seemed to be this which made him speak – a tension created simply by recollection, by re-entering a past in which (he now felt) he had been a sleepwalker, another man.

'I was at high school then, when some of us attacked our teacher. Those whose work he'd criticised were out for revenge, of course, and others joined in, but not me. They starved him of food and water, then "struggled" him for being a revisionist until he confessed.' The essence was to humiliate, to break a man's image and remake his thoughts – or to create the illusion of this. 'But he didn't die. For years he was forced to clean out the school lavatories. His hair was shaved in a criss-cross pattern over his skull, so that he was made to look ridiculous, terrible.' He added in the same tone: 'He's principal of the school now. I go to see him sometimes.'

'Did people believe their own confessions?' I had no idea of the answer.

'No, not often, no. This is a very old and complex thing. Perhaps a few of the academic ones thought they'd had wrong ideas. But mostly people just accepted criticism and bent.' He leaned forward and cupped his hands pathetically in front of his face as if to drink from them, then gazed up with beseeching eyes – a picture of supplicating helplessness. 'This confessing is our custom, you know. You choke down what you really feel.' Now he curled a finger down his neck as if swallowing pain, swallowing until it nestled deep inside. He made the whole rigmarole of confession seem like a perverted charade, at once sophisticated and tribal – and as I loooked at him I had the confused idea that the breathy cabaret of his talk belonged to the same order: an archaic theatre of signs.

'And this is the takin.' We had reached an enclosure labelled *Budorcas Taxicolor*, and there it stood. 'I believe it's exclusive to China,' he said. With its droll, equine head, it did indeed look like the member of some old and exclusive club, possibly China. A drizzle of tufts fell from its chin, and it was crowned by a pair of short, useless horns, set between its ears like a little anvil. The girl was trying to feed it sweets.

The man ignored it. 'I've never talked to my teacher about these things. And he's never asked me. It's difficult.'

Why then, I wondered, could he talk to me? But perhaps a foreigner, with his outlandish rules and values, didn't count.

Then some violence of nerves erupted in the man again. 'That year we beat up several people in the street,' he said. 'If our leaders said "He's a reactionary! Beat him!", we beat him.' His lips squirmed back from his teeth and he lifted his interlaced hands and chopped the air with an imaginary club. 'We didn't know – we didn't ask – why this or that man was bad. People said hit him, so you hit him. It was simple. It wasn't even personal.' He was re-enacting the past with an odd fear, yet without a trace of guilt. In his own eyes he was no more to blame than the splinter of a bomb which somebody else – the guilty one – had exploded. I was reminded of what anthropologists said about 'guilt cultures' and 'shame cultures': that a 'guilt culture' is characterised by an internalised sense of sin, whereas a 'shame culture' stresses only outward social values, and that once these are gone, all is havoc. Next year, doubtless, the theories would be different. But this man would be the same, enigmatic even to himself.

I found it hard to meet his gaze. I kept my eyes on the outlandish face of *Budorcas Taxicolor*. Its presence was ludicrous, reassuring. The man went on: 'We found a porter who had been reading novels with a love interest. I don't mean porn. Just a personal story. This was decadent. We beat him unconscious, and burnt the books. Then he died.'

I looked at him in astonishment, mesmerised, for some reason, by his immaculately pressed trousers. Once the armour of social constraint had been stripped from him, the person inside had been exposed as a baby: conscienceless. Was that China, I wondered bleakly, or just him? Or perhaps it was no longer him. In any case, where was that feeling of pity which Mencius said was common to all men?

'We were just the tools of the others,' he said. 'We were children. We didn't know a thing.' Yet his face was a rack of bones and tightened skin.

A little later he walked off with his daughter's hand in his, and I was left gazing at the calm herbivorous movements of the takin.

*　　　*　　　*

Ever since the thirteenth century, when Kublai Khan spread his palace on the site of the Forbidden City, imperial China had been ruled with scarcely a break from these once-impenetrable walls. During the early fifteenth century two hundred thousand men laboured for more than a decade to create the sanctum in its present shape – a giant rectangle of courts and palaces locked in two miles of moated ramparts.

Even today it resembles no other place on earth. Through multiple ranks of walls, and gates of beaten clay, I burrowed down entrance tunnels fifty yards long into courtyards like paved meadows. Their stone acres were glazed with weeds. Five bridges spanned the arc of a marble-banked stream. The painted wooden halls surrounding them looked evanescent, almost domestic. All their colours were unfamiliar. The scarlet pavilion façades and colonnades had darkened to Pompeian red or discoloured purple, and their tiled roofs rose in tents of saffron yellow.

But the marble terraces on which this flamboyance rested shone in a dazzling, white-grey permanence. Their stone glinted with metallic lights. The carvings of the balustrades were fine and shallow. No paint disturbed them. And up the long, carved ramp to each hall, where the emperor's palanquin used to glide in the hands of bearers to either side, a commotion of sculptured dragons swarmed up the marble slabs.

As I followed the Imperial Way, the palaces and enclosures succeeded each other in ever more intense barriers and deeper privacies. The balance and pairing of the buildings, and the level profile of their shrouding roofs, spread an unearthly peace. Their symmetry and repetition suggested some immutable order. Every ensemble played a subtle variation on the last, until the whole palace resembled a maze of echoes and reflections. Nothing astonished, except the tranquil and mysterious sameness of the whole.

I came to where a triple terrace ascended in marble stairways to the Hall of Supreme Harmony. Behind it lay the Hall of Perfect Harmony, and behind that again the Hall of Preserving Harmony. The names perhaps betray an ancient fear, the holding of a precarious balance. For here was the epicentre of the world. Along the central axis from the emperor's throne, the light of his divinity radiated out to the limits of his dominion and of the earth. A cosmic equilibrium rested delicate in his hands. Just as the God of Heaven lived at the heart of the universe in a polar constellation called the Purple Protected Enclosure, so his earthly counterpart ruled from the Purple Forbidden City, and in his person united heaven and men.

On certain days – the winter solstice, New Year or the emperor's birthday – the ritual rose to a mystic clamour. Shortly before dawn, when oil-filled cisterns lit the Hall of Supreme Harmony, the imperial bodyguard of Manchu and Mongol bannermen was marshalled beneath it in ranks of crimson satin. Squat in their padded armour, studded and plumed, they assembled like an army of monstrous chessmen, grasping pennants and ceremonial spears. Down the stairways the princes of the blood were ranged in precedence, while in the court below, the nine grades of mandarins clustered between eighteen double ranks of officials – civil in the east, military in the west. The coloured bobbles which crowned the mandarins' caps, their precious girdle-clasps and the insignia on their ceremonial robes – birds for civilians, beasts for military – disposed them in a rigid and jealous hierarchy. Buckles of jade set with rubies ranked above those of sapphire, gold above crystal and buffalo horn. The heraldic military unicorn marched with the ministerial Manchurian crane; the lion took precedence over the bear, the golden pheasant over the mandarin duck, until every blazoned creature had found its appointed station and settled in a glimmering ocean of silk under pointed caps dangling peacock feathers.

At last the voices of the criers would ring out: 'He comes, he comes, the Lord of Ten Thousand Years!' and the whole vast assembly, in their appointed groups and order – the Grand Secretaries, the Presidents of the Boards, the noblemen of the Council – stepped forward each to his number engraved in the flagstones, and kowtowed before the empty throne. Then the unearthly chanting of a eunuch choir arose. Punctuated by sounding-stones and bell-chimes, it slid between tone and tone in a mist of gongs and cymbals. At last, from an inner chamber, the yellow sedan chair of the emperor appeared, and the whole company fell to its knees. Their eyes fixed the ground, but their voices lifted in a plea for imperial longevity: 'Ten thousand years! Ten thousand! Ten and ten thousand years!' Centuries later the same shout was to greet the appearance of Mao Zedong.

When the prostrate ministers looked up they saw the open throne-hall surrounded by the guardians of imperial insignia – standard-bearers, officials cradling a symbolic sun and moon and the banner on which the emperor's five-clawed dragon rampaged among clouds. But now, high and far away at the zenith of the hall, hedged about by guards and dimmed in a pall of incense, the Son of Heaven sat enthroned and utterly still, sashed and robed in gold.

As the music gave its cue, the court lowered itself into the Great

Obeisance. The few Europeans who witnessed the ceremony – a ninefold kneeling and touching of the forehead to the ground – did not describe a grovelling of slaves so much as a timeless celestial ballet. Each mandarin, sunk in the shining circle of his silks, seemed to abase himself to the pulse of the music in a strangely mingled stateliness and humility. Meanwhile the emperor sat facing south on his throne at the axis of the Earth. His hands reposed on his knees. Dragon-painted columns and Coromandel screens glittered and swam around him. But he, 'The Lord of all under Heaven', remained motionless, maintaining the world's equipoise without the flicker of an eye.

It was bewildering to peer into the halls now. I felt I was spying behind stage scenery. The thrones still stood on their daises, thronged with sacred furniture and statuary – the cranes and tortoises symbolising longevity. But they were grimy and faded. The coffered ceiling a hundred feet above them loomed in tarnished green and gold. The heraldic rumpus of dragons over the throne-backs appeared more whimsical than frightening. Round the columns their orange and silver coils had darkened into obsolescence, and their heads were only disclosed by the glare of their white eyes. A level pall of dust seemed to have settled over everything. Here and there the painted parchment was peeling away from the pillars, where the dragons had damp-rot.

Outside, Chinese tourists were tramping the palaces in the same astonishment as I was, but a sense of something familiar must have touched them. For these courtyards were colossal replicas of their own traditional living-quarters. Even the bronze lion-dogs which flanked each hall were copies of the little Dogs of Fo – male and female hearth-sentries which still attend the entrances to some old homes. But as palace-guardians they had become formidable. Their terrible riverine manes were swept back from pop-eyes and tufted eyebrows, and their jaws yawned with fangs. The male lion patted a ball like an evil kitten at play, while beneath one paw of the suckling female her tiny cub sprawled helplessly on its back.

As I climbed and descended the terraces, I began to feel bemused, as if this elaborate succession of masks concealed a specific face, which had eluded me. But at last the palaces passed into private quarters – rooms haunted by the shuffle and gossip of seventy thousand eunuchs and the yawns of concubines. I wandered through a honeycomb of memorial halls, storehouses, pavilions, archives, a theatre (complete with windlass for winding gods up to heaven), rockeries and obscure altars where the last Manchu emperors, true to their nomad origins, presided over shamanistic rites. The names around me grew ever more grandiloquent. I ambled out of the Palace of Earthly Tranquillity through the Gate of Sunbeams to the Hall of the Most Exalted and the Palace of Pure Affection. The loudspeakers declaiming against litter and spitting softened to music. I left the Hall Where the Heart is Nourished and failed to find the Pavilion of Literary Profundity or the Palace of Vigorous Old Age. Then the paths twisted into courts ancient with ginko trees, and the palace shrank at last to the little rooms of the emperors' reality (if that is what it was), dark with their black marble and ricepaper windows. The furniture reduced to man-size. The pier-glasses in their blackwood frames, the beds laid on platforms heated from beneath, the jade ornaments and lanterns – all became the *mise-en-scène* for domestic bickerings and conspiracy. Here the imperial family dwindled to sickly boys and despotic old women, and the Son of Heaven reverted to common day.

North-east of the Forbidden City a long bridge separates two lakes. Nobody lingers here, except a pair of sentries. The surface of the northern lake is choppy with pleasure-boats, and pavilions erupt among the trees. A Tibetan shrine stands on a nearby peninsula, and the lantern-hung kiosks beneath it swarm with sightseers buying trinkets and photographing one another.

But close to the bridge, something happens. A line of stakes prevents the battered pleasure-boats from approaching it, and its arches are walled up. Life seems to stop here. Beyond, the waters smooth into solitude and the roofs of villas poke up behind a screen of willow trees. The whole compound is walled impregnably, its few gates heavily guarded. Scarcely a vehicle goes in or out.

This is Zhongnanhai, today's forbidden city, where China's rulers live. Here the Politburo and the Communist Party have their headquarters, and their leaders occupy villas along the shore. But the low roofs and sheen of water give nothing away. When I peered down from the bridge into the brown-green waters of the lake, my stare was met by the enormous eyes of numberless grey carp, soundlessly opening and closing their mouths.

On the lake of the living, to the north, the only fish are goldfish for sale – the delight of old men. Such goldfish, which once swam wild in China's rivers, are intensively inbred until their eyes become grotesquely protuberant, while their bodies fan into fins like sleeves of muslin, and bridal trains of tails.

The entrance fee for this lake is less than a penny. The other you may not enter.

*   *   *

When Western dance reached China after the Second World War, it did so in the tiny shape of Dai Ailian, an overseas Chinese woman who returned from Trinidad to fight in her country's civil war and to found Chinese ballet almost single-handed.

I sought her out on a chance introduction from England, but became lost in the district where she lived – a tundra of five-storey apartment blocks. Their balconies dangled onions and caged finches, and were crammed with potted ferns as if their occupants still dreamt of *hutong* courtyards. Here and there between the blocks, old men sat on benches, and grandmothers wheeled babies through the sunlight in bamboo prams.

She was scarcely five feet tall, and in old age her body had thickened. But her heart-shaped face with its wide-spaced eyes, her pinned-back hair and unconscious poise, betrayed her as belonging to the frontierless community of ballet. She lived in modest comfort now, in a concrete-floored flat whose bed-sitting-room was lined by photographs from her disparate worlds – Nureyev, Zhou Enlai, Merle Park.

The ballet company she founded is almost the largest in the world, with 180 dancers. But the Cultural Revolution had severed its continuity like an axe-blow. Her eyes still winced when she spoke of it. 'Mao Zedong's wife Jiang Qing, that terrible woman, had theatrical pretensions – she'd been an actress herself – and she imposed absurd restrictions on us. She got it into her head that certain ballet movements – *frappés* and *jetés*, for instance – were Capitalist, and so she simply eliminated them!' Her laughter was still tinged with incredulity. 'Actually, I think she was a bit mad.'

Only the slight colour-changes in her voice disclosed the strength of these memories. 'The repertory we'd built up was reduced to two Revolutionary ballets – *The Red Detachment of Women* and *The White-haired Girl*. My whole company – dance and administration – collapsed into chaos.'

The evening before, I had seen a fragment from one of these ballets. Her company had performed it in a run-down theatre with canned music instead of an orchestra, and somewhere in the auditorium's dark a Maoist claque had greeted its announcement with cheers. Dai Ailian, too, had been surprised by the cheering. 'But I don't believe it was political, no, I don't think so. They must have cheered simply because they hadn't seen that ballet for so long. And of course it was well danced' – her face softened – 'since my dancers performed it so much in those years, when I wasn't there.'

'You weren't there?' It was hard to press people about what they had done or suffered in those years. But Dai Ailian looked sturdy, even buoyant.

'Jiang Qing hated me,' she said. 'At the beginning of the Cultural Revolution I was employed to clean out the lavatories, wipe the mirrors and stitch the dancers' shoes. I was made to work for ten days on end, then allowed twelve hours' sleep, then another ten days' work. . . . They were trying to kill me.' Her hands touched her cheeks. 'But I survived and was sent to work in the fields for four years. At first I was a farm labourer, then I fed pigs. That was the worst time. My hands became infected through being plunged into the pig food to test its temperature, and I caught fever. Once my pulse failed altogether and the doctors thought I'd gone. I kept regaining consciousness and wondering if I was dead. It's strange, but I didn't wonder this with any alarm – just with curiosity.'

Her tone had turned cold, as if – even now – nothing could ever again matter as deeply as it once had. Then she began to laugh. 'Actually, I rather like pigs. They're intelligent. In fact they compare quite well with. . . .' She half lifted her hands. I noticed how slender and smooth they were as they recomposed in her lap: still a dancer's hands. 'It was after this, when I became physically weak, that I contemplated suicide. I only had a daughter-in-law alive to think of, and we didn't even know where one another was. Then I recovered and was put to work in the fields again. I had to sleep in a cupboard-size room with one other woman, because we both snored. I don't usually snore, but I must have grown thin. We kept each other awake.' The tinkle of her laughter turned the ugly ludicrous, exorcised it. 'But it was then that I got very weak. I'd had a bad back since sleeping in the open during the Sino-Japanese war, and when I worked in the vegetable plots they wouldn't allow me to straighten up. I became a near-cripple. I had to walk with a stick. And I thought of suicide again. I'd even worked out how to kill myself.'

She paused, inviting the question *How?*, then added: 'But I'm not telling you! It's my secret! Just in case I need it!'

I couldn't laugh with her. Even my smile was uncertain.

'In the end,' she said, 'it was remembering my dancers that prevented it. I felt they needed me.' So the will to survive had looked round for an object, and had found this surrogate family. At last she had returned. 'Then came 1976, our year of terror. First Zhou Enlai died. Then our great marshal Zhu De died. Then came the earthquake which obliterated Tangshan. Houses were flattened all over Beijing too. My lamp swung so hard it hit the ceiling from side to side.' She glanced up where a cracked lampshade dangled. 'Then Mao Zedong died, and the whole country was prostrate. I believe that if the Russians had invaded us then. . . .'

But the year also saw the defeat of the Gang of Four and the slow dawn of sanity. 'My dancers had split into factions long before, and these were remembered even after I returned,' she said. 'It wasn't their fault. They were led astray. But there were those in the company's administration who were guilty, people who have mostly gone now.'

It was impossible to tell what bitterness underlay this. Many of those who survived the Cultural Revolution were still working cheek-by-jowl with those who persecuted them, and the whole nation lives on in a limbo of remembering and distrust. I asked her: 'How could you return to working there?'

'Oh my dancers!' she said. 'That was all right! I'd known them as children! I'd nurtured them and trained them up and handed them their diplomas at prize-giving. As for the trouble-makers I told them: I'll treat you as equals whatever the past, but never let me catch you ladling out injustice to anybody else! But of course our continuity was broken. Our footwork was awful, and many roles were barely remembered.' She got up suddenly. 'Now I'll show you something.' She took me to where a small, mirror-lined studio was being built out into the yard in front. 'I mean to train a handful of dancers in my retirement here. The special ones.'

We caught sight of the two people standing together in the mirrors: she compact and small, he gangling and awkward. We laughed involuntarily. 'We Chinese have trouble with self-projection, you know,' she said. 'We're reticent. Sometimes I think I should remove these mirrors altogether. They make the dancers self-conscious, so they just alter their *épaulement* or instep instead of their inner feelings.' She frowned at her feet. 'Either they won't express themselves at all, or they overdo it, as if acting licensed something extravagant in them.'

It seemed, at that moment, a deeply Chinese problem.

'But everything will get better,' she said. 'Out there in the countryside an enormous audience is waiting for us. We were touring the provinces one year and I realised how deep this response can be. When the heroine of *The White-haired Girl* grew despairing on the stage, old ladies would stumble out of the audience and push their stools on to the boards for her to sit on. "There, there, my dear," they would say. "It will all be all right." They simply couldn't distinguish between the role and the person. And several times, when the ballet's villains were recognised in the streets, they were stoned and had to run for shelter.'

She was relaxed now. She was imagining ballet as a force for beauty, as it had briefly been a force for revolution. For now the pistol-wielding ballerinas of *The Red Detachment of Women* had faded from the ideal image of the dance. In their place, on advertisements and biscuit-tins – and chocolate-boxes – there has reappeared the familiar classical princess crowned or white-feathered: a stubborn pictogram for ideal grace.

The dead catalyst of China's past vision and terror lies in a vast mausoleum in Tiananmen Square. Several times a week a serpent of pilgrims, four abreast, wraps itself quarterway around the square, curls beneath the granite Monument to the People's Heroes and approaches the tomb of Mao in sudden quiet. They are dowdy in green and blue, and most have come in from the provinces. They number many thousands.

Whatever may have happened since Mao's death, the poetry of Revolution still sings around his tomb. Massed sculptures of Struggle and Plenty rear to either side in a surge of soldiery and sheaf-waving land-girls. The *Little Red Book* is held aloft. Yet even here, like some ineradicable disease, tradition has leaked in. The 120-foot Monument to the People's Heroes resembles nothing so much as a Confucian memorial stele, the terraces of the mausoleum mimic those of the emperors' halls and its yellow roof-friezes are haunted by the saffron canopies of the Forbidden City.

As the pilgrims trickled under the dwarfing colonnades, their tread slowed to a shuffle and their caps were cautiously doffed. What they were feeling as we entered the cenotaph of their dead god and tormentor, I could not tell. I tried to listen to their muttered conversations, as if they might yield up some posthumous key. But the only remarks I caught were about children and train-tickets.

We entered a hall where a marble colossus of Mao gazed at us from behind a bank of flowers. Our feet turned silent on the crimson carpet. Two military policemen with fixed bayonets and fiercely polished boots (the only ones I ever saw) stood rigid to either side. Then we passed into the mausoleum.

It was airy and spacious, lit evenly from pale lights in the coffered ceiling. Somewhere a fan whirred. In the centre, roped off all around, the crystal coffin looked small, almost temporary. Here was none of the violently illumined, claustrophobic theatre of Lenin's tomb in Red Square, but a simple lying-in-state. The crowd bifurcated round it and was forbidden to stop walking. We were in its presence for barely half a minute.

The embalmed body lay stiff and shapeless under its mantle, only the head exposed. I did not feel as if I were looking at anything that had been a man. Nestled in its jowls and double chin, the face held a sheen like discoloured ivory. Its eyes were closed, the hair swept back from the high forehead, thin and barely greyed. All that distinguished it were the wide convexities of the cheeks, and a faint, ashy discolouration which spread around the nose and upper lip. Otherwise it presented a heaped enigma. And those who passed by on either side were expressionless too, hurried on by plain-clothes security men. The whole uneasy ceremony seemed to have no heart at all, as if this corpse now belonged only to the terribleness of history. China was already moving away from it. I told myself: this man wreaked havoc and change on a quarter of mankind. Yet I passed in and out of that awesome presence as if through a void. He looked altogether smaller than that. It was strange.

2. The Power Circles

BEFORE SUNRISE, AS the smog-tinged haze thins from the city, the public gardens fill with students, factory workers, old men, women in slippers and hairnets, all bent on *taijiquan*, 'ultimate supreme boxing'. Along every path and clearing their arms and legs lift and rotate in grave shadow-play, while the faces above them look closed away. The motions of the most expert unfurl in a rhythmic flow. Their breath comes steady and deep. Their gaze follows their elbows or fingertips. In another country they would be taken for mad. Whereas Western callisthenics are charged and strenuous, *taijiquan* looks more like the slowed-down film of a lost martial art. Its aim is not to turn the body more slim or dynamic, but more flexible and poised. In it the national mind seems to be concentrated for the day ahead, as if the people were in training for a subtle passive resistance. Self is achieving equilibrium.

Nearby, old men stroll with their bird-cages, and hang them up in the trees. The air is filled with the warble of finches, orioles and Mongolian larks, while the men retire to benches and listen, their faces crossed by watery smiles. Then they take down the cages again and cradle them on their knees, gazing through the varnished bamboo bars.

The orioles carol here with little competition. In the 1950s, in one of those mass feats of which the Chinese are peculiarly capable, the whole population of the country turned out to destroy its birds, which were thought to be consuming too much grain in the fields. For twenty-four hours on end the people beat tin cans and blew whistles, so that the startled flocks took off and found nowhere to alight, until they fell from the sky in their millions, dead of heart failure.

Unconsciously I must have missed this wild birdsong, because when I heard a mob of sparrows singing in the gardens of the Lama Temple, I eavesdropped on them as if they were nightingales. 'I think the city people eat them,' said a droll-faced man who chanced into conversation with me. 'The birds come here because the monks are vegetarians.'

He pronounced this in a tone of absolute solemnity, but the corners of his mouth were twitching. This, I discovered, was his habit. Just as others had faith in God or predestination, Ziyang believed in the absurdity of things. His spiky fuzz of hair epitomised him; it refused quite to sit down. 'When I was a child this place was full of Tibetan monks,' he said. 'Very holy, or at least I thought so. But now look.'

Almost within memory the temple had been the seat of a Living Buddha, fourth in rank beneath the Dalai Lama, patronised by emperors and served by fifteen hundred priests. But it had been transformed from a princely palace in the eighteenth century, and a gaudy hedonism still clung about it. In the courtyard where we walked the monks' cells had been converted into tea-houses and souvenir stalls, and the porticoes rang with the shouting and bickering of Old-Hundred-Names. In court after court, desanctified by the tramp of tourists, the roofs tilted and swung above synthetic blue and green eaves.

But once inside the temple halls, this glamour darkened into a heady chaos. Here the godlings and demiurges of Tibetan and Mongolian Lamaism mingled promiscuously with Chinese Buddhas and an underworld of Hindu demons. Their altars rose in zones of guttering candle-flame and a trashy magnificence of offerings. Conch-shell trumpets and cloisonné vases, faded peacock feathers, mantras, plastic flowers and liturgical rattles all jostled together in syncretic medley and dust. A lurking animism haunted the side-chapels, where statues of unexplained beasts lumbered. Rare tapestries dangled above offerings of sour apples. 'An unwholesome moral atmosphere', concluded a decent-minded Englishwoman earlier this century, and it was still here. Above their gifts of cakes and sweets – 'Banana soft fruit centres' wrapped with cellophane – the Buddhas sat fattened in their haloes, and lifted gold hands to dangle tribute-scarves of dirty orange muslin.

In this mongrel confusion a few remaining lamas lived, their brown habits topped incongruously by matching slouch caps. They sat ignored in gloomy corners of the temples, or busied about the altars with workaday intimacy. Beneath one altar an old priest guarded a crammed offertory and harangued Chinese tourists and believers for alms. His voice grew high and perplexed at their reluctance.

'Give a little money. Look what the Hong Kong faithful give!' He pointed a quavering finger at a glass cabinet fluttering with notes. His voice filled with hurt. 'They give five yuan and the Buddha answers them. The money goes on offerings. To feed the Buddha. Pay

[39]

something and feed him incense.' But they only stared at him in silence.

All at once he seemed to grow desperate; his mouth opened on a querulous oval studded by three sulphur-coloured teeth. 'Why don't you feed the Buddha?' His pathetic gaze searched the young crowd in front of him. Nobody moved. On the altar a last joss-stick died into the ash where a hundred others had expired like grey worms, undisturbed. The priest's voice rose to a neigh of disbelief, at once threatening and bewildered: *'Why don't you feed the Buddha?'*

A young man said: 'I've paid my ticket to look round this place. I don't have to give any more.'

'But this is different!' The priest glared from face to face. They began to titter. 'You young people . . . you're far younger than me. But you don't want to give. . . .'

Formally, as if he were making a statement, an elderly man detached himself from the crowd and placed a small note in the box. Muttering, punctured, the people filtered away.

I approached the priest gingerly, but the fire had left him. He looked small and exhausted. Over his thin nose and cheekbones the flesh stretched frail as tissue-paper, almost translucent. When Ziyang asked him about his work, he said it was little: just upkeep, with two hours' prayer and recitation a day. Years ago there were Tibetan monks here as well as Mongolian, he said, but they had gone away in the Cultural Revolution and never returned. Of the eighty-three monks left, only two were Tibetan, and all the prayers were in Mongolian now, and the holy books.

We trudged into a further temple, where the Buddhas of the past, present and future stood together in a mandorla of tarnished gold. Ziyang observed their offerings of fruit with a faint, subversive lip-smacking. On the prayer-mat before the altar three loutish-looking youths were kneeling in succession, lowering their foreheads to the floor before burning incense to the Buddha of the present.

'We Chinese aren't really religious, you know,' Ziyang said. 'People just come in here to ask for something.' His eyes closed in mock prayer, and his face became a beseeching boy's; then he lifted supplicating hands and whispered: 'Oh please, Buddha, let me go to university. *Please.*' He turned his back on the altar. 'I think it's true what Mao said: that we're a practical and secular people. We only pray when we want something. It's not like India or South-East Asia. I know a woman who never once visited a temple before she married, and now she's in and out all the time. And I can guess why.' He rubbed a hand vigorously around his stomach, and raised his head in prayer again: 'Here are some apples, Buddha, and a packet of biscuits. Now *please, please* give me a *baby*.' His plea petered into a whisper. 'Just *one* will do' – the whisper shrank to pianissimo – 'and, oh Buddha, make it a *boy*.'

I suppressed my laughter in the temple's quiet. I had heard that religion was reviving in China. But precisely what was being revived I didn't know. 'Do you have many friends who believe?'

'Not one.' He was suddenly serious. 'How can young people believe? We were brought up without gods.' He wandered into a side-chapel. 'Nobody knows anything about this Buddha anyway. I've seen huge statues of him lying down – they pretend he fell asleep. But of course he just died.'

I said vaguely: 'Did he?'

'Yes. Just dead.' He pointed to the earth. 'Nothing.'

We found ourselves in a shrine where the dark impurities feared by early visitors broke out in a riot of copulating Hindu gods. Their supple bodies and multiple arms abandoned them to an inventive bliss, but their activies were saved from scandal by swathes of silk from which only delirious heads and a few rare disengaged arms stuck out. We were confronted by a dog-headed divinity impregnating a fragile, blue-faced goddess. In his coal-black head, crowned with a tiara of skulls, the eyebrows spurted in gold flames and his jaws gaped on a level arsenal of fangs. Ziyang said: 'I don't know what she sees in him.' Their two confronted heads, and her ambiguously supplicating hand, were all that showed.

An old farmer was murmuring and bowing to each pair. 'The peasants will worship anything,' Ziyang muttered. 'When I was a factory-worker during the Cultural Revolution, we lived in poor country in the middle Yangtze. Half the people still believed in spirits – fox-demons, fox-sisters and so on. Every house had a phantom warden, and many old people said they'd actually seen these gate-keepers, armoured like old mandarin warriors.' He plucked a ghostly helmet out of the air and clamped it on his head. 'Then some rumour got about that a nearby spring had healing properties. The villagers said it could cure anything, and within a few weeks you couldn't see the place for people fighting and struggling up to it with little bottles to collect water. The whole way there was littered with broken glass.'

We wandered into the sunlight. 'Just before the Spring Festival,' he said, 'the family I was living with went into a panic trying to placate the oven-god. They told me he was a sooty-faced type who lived in the kitchen and rushed up to heaven once a year to report them to God. So they put out offerings six days before he went, to bribe him against giving away their secrets. All the families around were doing the same. They even selected sticky sweets to gum up his mouth.' His lips began their insidious fidgeting. 'And this in the middle of a Marxist revolution!'

So that was what had happened, I thought. The galaxy of spirits which once swarmed over the country had merely gone underground, driven to fighting an obscure guerrilla warfare against the Communist invader. I enquired after them rather tenderly. They were old in Chinese lore. Where now, for instance, were those minor pranksters – the urchins and hoydens of the spirit-world, who banged your skins on doorposts or drenched you while washing vegetables? And what of the beneficent ones – the friendly, ham-fisted giants, and those deified monks and emperors who rode to the rescue at the last moment?

They were still alive, Ziyang assured me, even if he had never come across them personally. So were all those ugly-minded demons – the stranglers and drowners, the leaders astray on dark nights, and the bringers of plague with the blown red sands of the Gobi. Hardy but remote, they lived on in the villages of the hinterland. They were born reactionaries.

As we entered the last of the temples, we found it raised tall and narrow to house the Tibetan Buddha of the future. This statue rose seventy-five feet high – the mystical height attained in paradise – and was carved out of a single trunk of sandalwood. From a monstrous navel ringed with dust, the dimly jewelled body lifted to a voluptuous negroid head pressed close against the ceiling.

'It's ridiculous,' Ziyang said. 'You can't even see it.'

The native Chinese conceive the future Buddha quite differently: as a paragon of laughing obesity. He had his shrine near the temple entrance, where Ziyang had said: 'That's the only Buddha I like.'

No wonder, I thought. This jester does not absent himself in contemplation, but guffaws level with your chest. He is a gross optimist. His belly explodes out of his robes, and his eyes are not closed in prayer but screwed tight shut by a burst of uncontrollable merriment.

But in the presence of the Tibetan Buddha, Ziyang was nonplussed, distrustful. It loomed above us in a mote-filled cylinder of light, and gazed far away through a clouded window, dreaming of eternity.

*   *   *

The marriage introduction bureau occupied a prefabricated shed where two officious women sat behind desks, and strands of tinsel sagged from striplights along the ceiling. A group of young men dithered in an unnatural hush, filling in registration forms and scanning those of potential wives. They looked anxious and unimportant, wearing their best clothes. On a line of chairs against the wall three girls clutched and unclutched their handbags and each other's arms.

I had slipped in unnoticed. Beside me a man was loitering nervously. His face tapered to a shrew's thinness and some adolescent wisps of beard; but he was twenty-nine. 'Getting late for marriage,' he said. 'It all gets more difficult after thirty. You haven't got much choice.'

We huddled against one wall, facing the drab girls. He was dressed in jeans, with planned casualness. His shirtsleeves eased back from a digital watch.

'What is it you most want?' I said.

He glanced at his registration form, as if he couldn't remember. The questions on it were practical: family background (official, worker, peasant), school background, health, height, salary, age. There was a space at the bottom for his conjugal requirements. He read from it in a pat, dead voice. 'I want three things. She must have good health, be reasonably educated – at least up to graduate level – and be attentive to her man.' He shook an admonitory finger. 'Above all she must be attentive. She must work hard in the house.'

I said: 'And you? Will you be attentive?'

His face went subtly blank. He answered formally: 'Yes, of course.'

'And what about her character?'

'That's what I've said.'

'Her looks?'

'I want big eyes – but not lethargic eyes, that's no good. She must look vital and spirited, with long legs and . . . oh yes . . . not too dark a skin.'

The old mandarin prescription for beauty – the perfect oval face pricked with tiny eyes and lips – seemed to be fading. Only the lure of white skin reflected the timeless prestige of indoor pallor for a labourer people.

I glanced round the room, then back to his pointed face with its dry, small eyes and pubic beard. 'Do you think you'll get what you want?'

'Yes, I think I should. I have a good education, you see. I've been four years in an electronics firm.' He weighed his chances as coldly as a broker. 'Most of the people who come to these places aren't officials like me.'

'What do women want then?' I sounded rudely surprised.

'T ney want a man with status – a good salary, prospects. Women like a man's educational level to be high, higher than theirs.' He spoke as if status not only superseded character, but defined it. 'And he must come from a good family.'

'You mean a worker's family?' I straightened my expression.

'A worker's? Oh no!' His mouth fell open, closed again. 'Nobody wants that. Not now. I mean an executive's family, a cadre's family.' His tone wobbled with disgust. 'Not a *peasant* or a *factory* worker. No, no.' He shook his head. '*No.*'

I watched the other clients. None seemed younger than the government's minimum age for marriage – twenty-five for men, twenty-three for women – but several appeared far older. Two gauche factory workers couldn't fill out their forms, and a melancholy-faced woman, dressed up in high boots and a pink skirt, blushed continually and looked down at her hands. She was waiting for somebody who hadn't come.

One of the dragons behind the desks suddenly called out. 'Your passport!'

She was staring at me. I fumbled in my pockets automatically, then stopped. She had looked away. I supposed I was not allowed to be there, but I slid a little further down the wall and hoped to be forgotten.

'Passport!' Her voice was irritated now. I came sheepishly forward. Somebody pushed a chair towards me while she riffled uncertainly through my documents, unable to read them. Then she said: 'What is your profession? And what is your cultural level?'

I echoed feebly: 'Cultural level?'

She snapped: 'Yes.' She seemed to be screening me for imbecility. 'And we'll want a photograph.' She thrust a form at me. 'What is your reason for wishing to meet a Chinese girl?'

As the truth dawned, I felt a faint, erotic regret.

'I'm sorry, there's a mistake. I'm leaving Beijing in two days.' In the instant before I rose from my seat a troupe of lemon-skinned beauties (like none I'd seen in Beijing) swept across my innner eye, then dwindled away. 'I was just . . . interested. . . .' The woman's face puckered into realisation. She looked relieved, kindlier. I slithered foolishly towards the door.

Momentarily I wondered whom I would have met. Would we have walked in the People's Park together or watched black and white television in her parents' flat? (Somehow the romance was in the drabness.) Or would. . . ?

But the line of girls sitting by the wall returned me to reality. Their hands were lifted to their faces like the three wise monkeys, and they were giggling uncontrollably.

Westward along Changan Avenue I passed the long curtain of grey bricks which was once Democracy Wall. Here in November 1978, a 35-year-old mechanic plastered up a poster which shook the country to its marrow: it was the first public criticism of Mao Zedong. Almost overnight the wall became the focus of spontaneous, grass-roots demands for democracy and human rights. Tolerated by Party reformists, to whom it was temporarily useful, the movement flared for four months. It spawned a mass of unofficial journals, and similar walls sprang to prominence in every provincial capital, even in Lhasa.

But it generated, too, a haunting fear of anarchy, of a new Cultural Revolution. By April 1979 its usefulness as a political weapon against the Left was over, and next winter, in the early hours of one morning a battalion of municipal workers with scrapers and twig brooms scrubbed away the last tatters of free speech.

Now, as I walked along it, I saw heavy iron shafts driven into concrete blocks all along its length. They framed advertisements which hid the entire wall in a long, seductive picture-gallery: refrigerators, scented soap, sewing-machines, face-creams, vacuum-cleaners. . . .

Staring up at them, I wondered if they had cauterised the desire for democracy more effectively than Maoism did. And I wondered, too, at the irony. For it was Mao's Cultural Revolution which instilled into its youth the idea that they could become political architects, and build a Marxist paradise.

But in the end they wanted to build freedom.

*　　　*　　　*

Guo was one of those men in whose face and body a ghost of the Cultural Revolution lingered. The rigours of ten years' rural exile

[45]

seemed to have pared away any gentling flesh from him, and it was with a slight shock that I realised he was ten years younger than me. I had been given his address by a Chinese friend in England, with a warning that he was a Communist Party secretary and had no sense of humour. But now he sat facing me less formally than I had feared, his gaunt hands furling and unfurling round a little cup of tea. He spoke with nervous compulsion, as if my foreign presence at once agitated and unfettered him. Where did I plan to travel, he asked? And why alone? He feared for me. China was so poor, he said. I could have no idea. Did I realise how different it was, out there in the countryside? The peasants' cultural level. . . . The thought hissed into silence.

All his speech was a soft tension. His own remembered exile, I think, was colouring my imagined danger. At first my gaze strayed round his sitting-room – the concrete walls, garish pictures and photographs, ornaments crammed round a colour television – but little by little I became mesmerised by his pale face and tight lips, which were saying increasingly frank things in a clear, beautiful Mandarin. He reminded me unnervingly of the man I had met at the zoo: the same innate theatricality and harrowed intensity in speaking. But Guo showed none of that suavity, nor any laughter.

How much – he asked suddenly – did I know about China? Well then, he must tell me. He peeled the glasses from his eyes – they emerged staring and wide-set – and assumed the role of teacher. China still lagged in an infant stage of socialism, he said. True Communism remained far away. Only four per cent of the people were Party members, and although everybody wished to join the Party. . . .

Did they? I asked. I'd heard not.

A rude pause fell. His mouth curled in simulated pain. He began, 'If I were to say this to a Chinese. . . .' The sentence dwindled incomplete, while a reflex swivelling of his eyes took in the room's emptiness. Then, quite consciously – the struggle and its resolution travelling flagrantly over his face – he relaxed into partial trust with me. 'You're right. It's true. After the Cultural Revolution, things changed. Three things.' He held up a trio of fingers, like a blessing. He was plunged in an old Chinese need to number, label, differentiate. 'First, young people' – he scooped his hands towards himself – 'don't believe in government any more. When the Party issues a directive, nobody cares. We've had all that. People don't believe anything now. They don't even believe one another.' The desolate implications of this were drowned in his rushing on: 'There are more than fourteen million unemployed in our cities, and these youths have no faith in the Communist Party, they don't believe in the future, not in anything.' His words came whispering towards me in dramatic collusion: 'They're lost. Some of them are turning to God, or at least to fate. A few of them have even taken to wearing crosses.'

'I haven't seen that.'

'No, of course not.' He thrust his hand inside his shirt – 'They wear them there, on the quiet.' A soft, constricted *Yueehh* intensified their duplicity. 'Some of these unemployed bribe officials for permits to set up work on their own. But most of them have nothing.'

The candour of his talking was ambiguously steeped in dramatics. His speech had become a performance for the foreigner, a play of national pain. A constricted *Weeihah!* crowned his lament on vanished trust. Explosions of *Euuhh!* maximised unemployment. Now he lifted two pedantic fingers. 'The second change since the Cultural Revolution is that young people only care about money now, how to afford a sofa or a colour television. They go to Western films and spend their time dreaming of cars' – he uttered 'cars' with uncensored longing – 'then they get dissatisfied with everything here. As for the third change, it's this: nobody wants to do a labourer's work any more.' His fingers went shredding down his chest, recreating the filth of ten years' exile. 'We all want a white-collar job. We want to be managers. No more dirt. That's the ideal now.'

'Young people': in this country the innocent-sounding phrase embraced 650 million. Those aged between fourteen and twenty-five alone outnumbered the total population of the United States.

'Nowadays if they join the Party,' said Guo, 'it's just to get a better job.'

He made it sound natural, almost moral, so that I asked: 'Is that why you joined?'

He answered unperturbed: 'Yes.'

I wondered how deeply I could trespass into this delicate region of the Party. It was only his high-strung need to communicate, I sensed, his frustration with his world, which stopped him withdrawing. Between one sentence and another, this might change. I asked tentatively: 'What if you'd refused the invitation to join the Party?'

'I'd never get a senior job. Never. They'd always know. If you refuse them, they force you into shoes smaller than your feet, as we say. They cramp you.' He wrenched his mouth into a new caricature of agony. He was perversely enjoying himself. 'My younger brother was one who refused to join. So he'll never get a high post. Not now.'

'Why did he refuse?'

Guo's face became a flurry of conflict. He stared down into his empty teacup. I sensed that he was distressed not by articulating this to me, but to himself. At last he said: 'He just did refuse. Perhaps he thinks the Party's corrupt.'

I said nothing. The pause intensified.

He began again firmly: 'You'll never hear people say that the Party is deeply corrupt.' Then he added in a stage undertone 'But' – and there came a burst of pent-up air: '*that is the truth.*'

Looking at him, I wondered why I had never thought the Chinese expressive. They could be violently, histrionically so. They were used to conspiring in a public image. One moment Guo's brows would coalesce between his eyes in a furious ideogram of pain, the next his words had slowed to soft-breathed suspense or left his lips in a hiss of shattered secrecy. All this, I sensed, was an elaborate lipservice paid to the emotions, in which nothing was necessarily felt. To call it false would be too simple, but truth – with all its frightening delinquencies – had first to be channelled through this ancient masque, as through a safety-valve, and might arrive unrecognisable.

'There are people in the Party who steal from the masses,' he was saying: 'They take government grain, government televisions, anything. I hate it. Party members are privileged, you see. We have a chance to go abroad and buy luxuries or smuggle back foreign money.' His tone strayed into wonder. 'I've heard that prices with you are so cheap – colour televisions for £170 and a refrigerator for £140. Can that be right? With us they cost over twice that. . . .'

He wavered helplessly between puritan idealism and self-interest. His disgust with Party corruption was genuine, but when he talked of televisions or accepting Party membership, his eyes grew childishly round. Perhaps the only part of the system which he deeply wanted to change was the part which obstructed his advancement within it.

But now he was trying morally to distance himself from the Party. 'Party members should be above the normal level of the people, not below it. Yet some of them even take mistresses.'

For some reason I found this comforting. 'What sort of mistresses?'

'Just women with ordinary jobs. You wouldn't know. Even their wives probably don't know.'

'You have friends who do this?'

He went quiet. 'Yes.'

'Is this what your brother hates?' Unwittingly I had slipped into the role of inquisitor, had usurped his dominance. I was bullying him, and he was putting up a show of suffering.

'Yes,' he said. 'My brother thinks the Party's utterly corrupt – but he daren't say. He'd never say. If you spoke against the Party you'd be arrested.' He crossed his wrists graphically in front of him. 'Nobody here ever admits that the Party has *any defect*. At the conferences Party members all publicly agree, but in reality half of us are dissenting or angry. The trouble with us – with our whole country – is that we're feudal. That's at the root of everything. In the Party too. Many members are just peasants in their minds. So *old*. When foreigners come here and don't understand us, it's nothing but a very old, irrational state of mind which is inexplicable to them.'

He seemed to waver towards including himself in this archaic commune, or else I unconsciously included him. He alarmed me. Perhaps it was my awareness of some deep instability rocking him which made the dark suit appear to hang on him so incongruously. His wrists projected hungrily six inches beyond their cuffs, and even his polished shoes looked temporary.

Now he pulled a blank piece of paper from his pocket and flattened it on the table between us. 'Look, I'll show you. This is how our country is.' He leaned stiffly forward and inscribed four concentric circles in red ink. In their centre he placed a handful of progressive leaders, but all around them, in the wide track of the second circle, a horde of senior cadres lingered. He said: 'These men never retire. We'll have to wait forever for them to die.' He had covered their circle with inverted Cs, like reptilian scales. 'When they are told to delegate power, they agree, but do nothing. And there are thousands of them. You can see them in every ministry. You can tell them because they're fat and old. Most of them are over sixty at least. And they walk like this – ' he stood up, inflated his stomach and floated his arms out from his body, as if they had been pushed there by the importance of the torso between. His eyes half closed in self-worship. Then, with a sanctimonious roll, he launched into a saunter. Borne along between these stuffed-out arms and pompously waddling legs, his body sailed like a tabernacle, gaseous with prestige. In two or three seconds, he had conjured a mandarin as old as Confucius, moving down the centuries with light, self-loving steps: the eternal bureaucrat. Uneasily I began to understand the fury of the young Red Guards if such men were their targets.

'Most of them are just peasants in origin,' he said. 'With us the first consideration for office is not ability but length of service. That's what counts. These men are out-and-out Marxists who came up during the War of Liberation, before 1949. They consolidate their power by picking yes-men and elevating them at will.' He pulled these sycophants into the air with his fingertips, as if drawing up worms through the floor. 'One . . . two . . . three . . . their own children too . . . four . . . five . . . so they have armies of people indebted to them. That's how the system works.' He looked unsurprised, as if all surprise was naïve. This was how things had always been.

Dimly I remembered a Chinese saying from imperial times: 'When a man becomes an official, even his dogs and chickens go to heaven.'

But now Guo had returned to his chart and was guiding his pen-tip out of the scaly inner circle and into the next one. Here, in the tertiary track, he said, were the frustrated young men of the Party, among whom he counted himself. He emphasised the circular barriers with bitter scorings of red ink. They looked like an aerial view of Dante's *Inferno*; and in the outermost circle, of course, was the blank, unspeaking void of Old-Hundred-Names. I asked: 'What happens in there?'

'Ah there. They just suffer. They may hate the bosses, but they can't say a thing. They're powerless.'

As if responding to a cue, like the materialised ghost of his words, a dark-skinned girl pushed through the door and lumbered across the room without lifting her gaze from the floor. Guo went on talking as if nobody had entered at all. I asked in surprise: 'Who was that?'

'That? That was our maid.'

I stared after her. 'Where's she from?'

'From Anhui province, very poor,' he said. 'The city's full of servants from there.'

A little later he crumpled up his scribbled *Inferno* – the feudal maze in which he was lost – and thrust it into his jacket pocket. He said: 'The force of change is with the young now. But the government's frightened of us, frightened of too much Western influence, frightened of losing control. They're afraid we'll grow to hate them.' In his mind now he was divorced from the government and even the Party. He was just a still-young man, and impatient. 'Their nightmare is that we'll break into chaos, revert to another Revolution. And if the controls slacken too much. . . .' But he stopped at the abyss.

'Does that frighten you then?'

'If things relax very much, I. . . .' He began again: 'You see, the minds of our workers and peasants are terribly . . . *old*, all their ideas so *old*. If they have too much freedom – yes, I'm afraid of chaos.'

'What sort of chaos?'

But he didn't know. He only felt that somewhere inside his heart Old-Hundred-Names nurtured a terrible capacity for violence; and when he spoke of it his thin hands came up and encased his own ribs too, as if the demon waited in him.

As I left him in his doorway, he said: 'You want to know about our country, I can tell. You must realise that if a man's alone he will talk. If he's with a friend he'll speak a little, perhaps. But if he's in a crowd he'll only joke or say nothing at all.'

It sounded like England, I said.

It was night, and the street where he lived was unlit. In the dark I overtook his maid with a parcel of blankets on her shoulder. She stared at me from behind them with a furtive wonder, then looked away again. When was she going back to Anhui, I asked? She dropped the bundle hesitantly between her feet. She hoped to go back for a few days during the Spring Festival, she said, to her husband. She spoke in a shy monotone.

'You're *married*?' She looked very young, barely adolescent.

'I was betrothed at fourteen.'

'How often do you go home?'

'I don't know.' She stared at the ground. 'I haven't been back for nine months.' She did not seem to care. Life here was not so bad, she said, not so hard as in the fields.

She picked up the blankets. Her stare never left the ground. She added in a curious tone of optimism: 'Life is hard everywhere.'

*　　　*　　　*

I sat in the atrium of the Great Wall Hotel. My shoes were dirty and I felt like a spy. All around, the foyer glittered in carpeted silence, ramifying down spotlit galleries before opening on a science-fiction clearing of forty-foot chrome pillars and plate-glass walls. I was spying on my own personality; I watched it separating into layers, like something improperly cooked. I was at once childishly ogling and puritanically disgusted. I wanted one of these feelings to engulf the other, but this did not happen.

Eventually these warring personalities sank down in a chair in the foyer's Orchid Court, hid their dirty feet under the sheltering fall of a tablecloth, and ordered a smoked salmon canapé as if this were their sole purpose in coming to China. On the cocktail list, I noticed, a single whisky cost a week of the waitress's salary, but her face was clouded in impenetrable indifference.

I was unprepared for this dislocation. Here the crush and din of urban China had been exaggeratedly repudiated. The clientele moved through rooms of spacious privacy and near-silence. Up and down the 22-storeyed walls, neon-lit elevators glided like glass beetles, without a whisper. Western and Hong Kong businessmen occupied the sofas in easy connivance, probing for business under the urbanity of casual conversation, or putting the finishing touches to a contract. The dense carpets and long, quiet vistas drank up their talk. The foyer was their familiar cosmopolis. But their Beijing counterparts entered it anxiously. They blinked about them, covertly smoothing the creases in their trousers, fingering their jaws.

The blank-faced waitress dropped a hefty bill on my table. Over an invisible tannoy came the strains of the New World Symphony. I had an ominous sensation of returning history. This place mirrored those privileged foreign ghettoes in Shanghai or Canton during the 1930s, teetering on the edge of their nemesis – enclaves incarcerated in cities of the waiting poor, blinding their expatriates in an illusion of home. Now I could not tell if the hotel were flagship or dinosaur.

I roamed the rooms in perverse fascination – the saunas and floodlit tennis courts and jogging-track, the nine restaurants and lounges, the deluxe suites costing over $1,000 a night and instilled (said the brochures) with the 'essence of prestige'. In the night-club 'The Exciting Electros live from Manila' were playing (recommended dress: chic-casual).

China was present here only in permutations and refinements. Guests in the French restaurant toyed with their *terrine de Viande trufée façon Escoffier* under painted Beijing silks, and the state rooms and corridors shone with the sacred ochre of the emperors.

At the cost of $75 million, this hotel was the largest Sino-American joint venture before 1985. It had been prefabricated in other countries – plate-glass curtain-walls in Belgium, elevators and furniture in Japan, carpets in New Zealand, crystal and silver in France, computer system in Britain, food in Hong Kong. It was its own country: eclectic, placeless. The palisades of its reflecting walls glimmered synthetically over the eastern city.

Yet inside, it was fearfully isolated. Its Chinese staff seemed hesitant, estranged. If you tried to telephone outside the hotel, the modern world collapsed. Often the lines were overloaded, permanently engaged, or went dead. Taxis left the annexe into a city which the drivers did not seem to know. Beijing and the hotel were severed from one another. It lay on the outskirts like a space-capsule discharged from another planet.

*   *   *

Twice a year, in spring and at the winter solstice, the emperor would leave the Forbidden City to make sacrifice at the Temple of Heaven. All citizens were ordered to stay indoors and to shutter their windows along the route, while the side-alleys were curtained off. Even in the twentieth century, railway traffic was banned during these sacred days, in case some distant whistle profane the air, while the procession of eunuchs, mounted archers and elephant-chariots creaked and jingled southward in silence: ghosts out of another time.

The Temple of Heaven still rises from its parklands in the southern city, flanked by green-tiled walls pierced with gates at each compass-point. Above its marble terraces it floats in a serene unity – an enormous, three-storeyed pagoda. It is, perhaps, the most beautiful temple in China. From the gold finial at its summit the roof sheds itself in a triple tier of mauve-blue tiles, like a sumptuous ritual umbrella. No Western dynamism troubles it. Its simultaneous fall and tilt create a triumphant equipoise.

Raised in 1420, at the height of the Ming splendour, it was struck by lightning in 1889 and burnt to the ground. Piece by piece the Chinese reproduced it, but by now their forests were so impoverished that its four central pillars had to be imported from Oregon. Around the drum outside, the wings and tails of inlaid phoenixes and dragons bifurcate into precious tatters and ribbons of gold. Inside, the ceiling shoots up in an inverted whirlpool of transoms and crossbeams, jointed without a nail. Circle by circle, through arcs of gilded brackets and coffered panels in vermilion and green, it turns on a narrowing spindle of light, upward more than a hundred feet to where a carved dragon hangs incestuously in its coils.

The emperor entered the temple only in spring. He was dressed in the symbolic blue of the triple roof and the sky above. In the doors and windows, curtains of glass rods filtered the sunlight to a wash of blue, and a constellation of blue-robed officials attended him as he offered sacrifice for a propitious harvest with utensils of sky-blue porcelain.

But the most sustained and delicate sacrifice of all, in which the emperor took upon himself the sins of his people at the winter solstice, was enacted on the Altar of Heaven, at the end of a long causeway to the south. I followed it with crowds of Chinese tourists, past groves of junipers and firs. At its end a wall enclosed a miniature temple. Here, where the emperors' ancestral tablets once awaited worship at the solstice, a horde of Old-Hundred-Names was clapping and bellowing to arouse acoustical effects. When they stood on three adjacent paving-slabs before the temple, they heard their yells returned in single, double and triple echoes.

I could understand why the ancients also loved the place. For these voices out of stones – posthumously returning, fading, returning again – suggested that men were not alone, and that there was life in other realms.

But the tourists were communicating robustly with one another. Their mouths and ears were clamped against the curved wall, which could circulate a whisper for over a hundred years, it was said. But nobody was whispering. Bawled questions and cacophanous greetings ricocheted along the stones. 'Wei! Little Li? Can you hear me? *Weeiah! Ai-ai-ai*, second son! Old Lao! Have you eaten today? Wooyoooh! I'm here! Where are you? Have you gone dead?'

I put my ear to the curve and started conversation with a weatherbeaten veteran fifteen yards away. 'Where are you from?'

A bleating semi-quaver arrived: 'Shanghai.'

'I'm from England.'

After a pause: 'Where's that?'

'The other side of Russia.'

A smile crept into his voice. 'Is that the same as America then?'

'*No*. It's an island. On its own.'

Silence.

I added: 'It used to control Shanghai.'

'I don't remember that.' He turned his other ear against the wall and shouted along it to somebody else: 'This foreigner says some island controlled Shanghai. . . .'

But the line was cut by a tiny man and wife. They tucked their cheeks to the wall between us, facing each other self-consciously two feet apart, and mewed the same question in thin alto voices over and over again, until it acquired a bleak symbolism: '*I can't hear you. Are you there? I can't hear you. . . .*'

[54]

I left this bedlam for the quiet spaces where the Altar of Heaven rises. Its outermost wall was a perfect square, the inner a perfect circle, and from these – conforming to a belief that the earth was square and the heavens round – the altar ascended in three circular terraces of marble, one upon the next, uncrowned by any building. It existed almost una-dorned, secure in the beauty of its faintly translucent stone. Only the lightly incised carving of the rain-vents gave out a reticent opulence.

But its simplicity was a disguise. The great altar had been laid out by mathematicians and astronomers, and was steeped in magic. Its lowest level symbolised man, its centre earth, its summit heaven. The 360 pillars of its balustrades represented the days of the lunar year, and the balustrades themselves ran in multiples of nine – the celestial number which divided the Chinese heaven. In the stairways between each terrace the steps too numbered nine. From the centre of the topmost tier nine rings of paving-stones radiated out in concentric multiples of nine, and fanned down into the lower terraces, nine rows to each, in ever-expanding manifolds of nine.

Into this haunted circle the emperor stepped at the winter solstice. Before the first glimmer of dawn, when the spirits of his ancestors gathered mystically around him, he was robed in his sacrificial vestments and approached the altar down the empty causeway. Along its terraces the shrines to the North Star and to thunder, the stations of the imperial prompter and the guardian of silks, remained unchange-able. Decade after decade nothing was altered or forgotten. The smallest ritual gesture or word had been ordained in a remote past, of which the emperor and all his court were puppets.

While the smoke of an unblemished bullcalf billowed from a furnace behind him, the emperor mounted to the topmost tier, the hub of the world. Then the flutes and singing stopped. The earth held its breath. In silence he advanced to the epicentre, alone beneath the vacant and merciless sky of his father in heaven. Then he spoke.

And his prayer, like all else, was foreordained – read from a tablet, in a solitary self-gathering of his people's guilt. For this ceremony had been refined ever since the half-legendary rule of the Perfect Emperors five thousand years ago, and under the ritual accountability for his people's sins there lurked memories from a time when the ageing emperor was himself sacrificed before his decline could magically weaken the realm.

Around my feet, where the magic flood of paving found its still centre, a famous acoustic amplified sound, and perhaps gave the emperor a sense of equal voice with that tremendous sky. Now groups of tourists were stamping and shouting to awaken it. But the feet of the emperors seemed still to brush faint on the stones, their voices small, pedantic, intoning their responsibility. I wondered what this acceptance of national guilt implied for their people, even today. Did the displacement of responsibility on to the ruler elevate obedience to him into the only virtue? And if personal liability. . . .

But the thought waned into ignorance.

I waited until the last Japanese tour-group had crocodiled away, then stepped on to the umbilical stone. I called: 'Is anybody there?' And it was true: my own voice echoed back – bigger, oddly late. But it seemed less to ascend to heaven than to fester under the earth, darkened in those marble vaults. It returned to me disembodied, soothing, someone else's: '. . . there, there, there. . . .'

*   *   *

Off the unlit corridors of the traditional medicine college the offices were all empty except for enormous desks and Associate Professor Yang. I had wandered in unannounced, but he emerged to greet me, weirdly charming. He reminded me of a gangling bird – not a living but a prehistoric one. His face tapered in a sad isosceles triangle which wavered solicitously around mine, goggled in spectacles and tendering obscure greetings and apologies. For more than thirty years, mostly spent in Inner Mongolia, he had devoted himself to herbal medicine and the study of the human tongue. Tongue diagnosis was his passion. Chinese medicine observed numerous parts of the body for diagnosis, he said – abdomen, hands, eyes – but none was quite so marvellous, so sensitive, as the tongue.

'Of course you can tell things from a patient's face or chest, and even from his speech or cough or pulse,' he said – all this seemed a faint disappointment to him – 'but there's nothing like a tongue.' His hand came to rest on the doorhandle behind him. 'Will you see my tongues?'

We entered a narrow room lined with glass cabinets. He turned a switch and there, from every wall and showcase, rank upon pink rank, two hundred disembodied tongues stuck out at us in soundless abuse. 'Wax models,' he said joyfully. 'All diseased.'

I blinked around at them. They were obscenely lifelike. I had the illusion that those on the walls belonged to people in neighbouring rooms who were sticking them through the cracks. There were stunted tongues and swollen, translucent ones, yellow-coated gastric tongues, ghoulish opaline ones and wicked little dried-up red forks – tongues filmed over, tongues cleft, tongues fissured – greenish, retracted, putrid, carbuncled.

Yang surveyed them with fatherly concern. His crooked forefinger pointed tenderly along the cabinets. 'That dark red one has liver disease . . . and these watery tongues, they mean stomach trouble.' He shook his head. 'The stomach isn't moving the water properly round the body. . . . You see this one with lopsided coating?' – he pursed his lips – 'kidney failure on the way. . . .'

We marched past derisive regiments of mulberry tongues, mutinous ranks of green ones. I became nervously conscious of my own and slithered it over my lower lip, feeling for fissures. We peered at a desiccated blue specimen – 'Heart' – and a cleft, yellow model with faint spots – 'Scarlet fever!' – then came to a halt before a blazing purple item. 'This is in the last stages of chronic hepatitis,' he said. We dithered in front of it. If I'd been wearing a hat, I would have taken it off. But the next moment the gloom had passed and Yang had swooped on a favourite wall-cabinet. 'Look at those fissures! That means the stomach is *very* bad. It could be cancer.' He was getting into his stride. 'And these vessels under the tongue – swollen and purple. Cancer!'

From time to time his voice would trickle off into high, shaking laughter. It punctuated his running talk of *Yin* and *Yang*. In these ancient concepts the feminine *Yin* produced a heavy, cold tongue; the masculine *Yang* a small, hot one. All around us the tongues were afflicted by fearful imbalances of one or the other.

'Look!' He pounced on a flaming, dragon-like tongue. 'Insufficient *Yin*, you see. . . . Hmmm . . . almost no *Yin* at all . . . that colour. . . .' He moved on to a saucy pink one. 'Ahohehoha . . . altogether too much *Yang*. . . . It's in the last stages of. . . . Ahohehohe. . . .'

By now I was neurotically conscious of the wriggling lump inside my own mouth, which I had never much considered before. Had it, I wondered, become horribly fissured or green without my noticing? Were the telltale pustules developing even as I spoke? I clamped it firmly behind my teeth.

'All these models were copied from actual patients,' Yang was saying. 'We have several models for sale. . . .'

I ignored this, and we moved on to still stranger cabinets. A nervous disorder had doubled one tongue backwards inside its mouth, and stuck out another irretractably. They lay twisted, lips and all, in their complementary agony. Beyond them gleamed a pair of cancer suspects. The benign tumour pushed up from below as a glaucous dome; the carcinoma perched in a baleful sugarloaf on top.

Then came the moment I had been dreading. Yang sat me down and asked might he trouble me, just for a few seconds, to open my mouth the tiniest bit? He'd like to glance.... He spoke as if he had no idea that a tongue might be inside.

I stuck it out submissively, and watched his expression for the first intimations. A full minute passed while his isosceles triangle hovered back and forth across my vision. 'Your tongue . . . ahoheha . . . is a little small . . . a slight surfeit of *Yang*. . . .' He started to cackle with high-pitched, uncontrollable laughter. 'Ahohehohehe. I suppose you feel your stomach is not very well? . . . Ahohahehe. . . . Are your bowel movements normal? Thick coating means the bowel movements. . . . Ahohehaho. . . .'

Slowly I relaxed. Whatever was wrong, it was embarrassing rather than deadly. For a while his pterodactyl's face went on circling about my jaw, cackling of *Yang* and diarrhoea. But I was in the clear. When I stared at the wax tongues now, smug with my reprieval, they no longer appeared to be engaged in mass insult, but to be rather pathetic. I thought of all the patients from whom they had been moulded. Where now, I wondered, was the owner of the sinister, pearly chunk labelled 172? What had happened to poor, dyspeptic 59? Had 112 been able to retract her tongue eventually, or was she still living in a state of involuntary provocation? But 88 must certainly be dead.

*   *   *

Every year at the autumn equinox, the Altar of the Moon received a choice sacrifice. As the moon rose in the twilight, white jade, white silks and pearls were laid on the altar before a pale cream tablet inscribed with the silvered characters: 'Spirit of the Light of the Night'. Then three pure white animals – ox, sheep and pig – were offered up in flames.

The temple gardens have been a public park for years. The celebrant's disrobing hall I found converted into an office, and the bell-tower had become a potted plants depot. Around the old enclosure children were driving wooden bumping-cars (which they never bumped) to the piped strains of 'Jingle Bells'. When I peered through blocked gates into the ruined inner precinct, I saw that the altar had gone. In its place, huge with its own sorcery, loomed the transmitting tower of China Central Television.

I found a labourer in the park who remembered the altar. 'It was about as high as my shoulder,' he said. 'Not as big as the one at the Temple of Heaven, but rather beautiful. It was made of . . . I can't remember, not marble exactly. . . . But in the Cultural Revolution it was smashed up. It's vanished completely.'

A young, gentle-faced man drew me aside. 'Nobody even recalls a time when that altar was used. Those things are all finished.' He seemed to be consoling me for some personal loss. We started to stroll together round the park; it was quiet and uncrowded in the dusk. 'We young people are looking to the West now.'

Such casual approaches generally developed into covert requests for foreign exchange certificates. But Liuyin was dressed with what I took to be laconic distinction: pale blue trousers and a pale grey, zip-fastened jacket.

'I suppose I'm middle class,' he said. 'My parents are teachers, intellectuals. If only they'd been high cadres, they'd have got me a job.' He laughed airily. 'Instead I'm out of work.'

We settled on a bench near the silenced bell-tower of the moon. In front of us an avenue of lamps shed down bleakness where people wandered in the evening warm. 'Half my friends are officially unemployed,' he said, 'but we find jobs all the same. You see them advertised – just stuck up on the walls. Or you get something through the grapevine. That's how things are here. I've worked as a salesman, a builder, a shop assistant. I earn more than my friends on salaries.'

He did not conform to the lost unemployed evoked by Party Secretary Guo. I asked: 'What about the future?'

'Oh, I'm training at civil engineering in my spare time. Once I've got that diploma, I mean to get on.' He added moodily: 'Meanwhile I have to live. Until yesterday I was a waiter in a tourist restaurant. I hoped to pick up some English there. But our bosses forbade everything. They warned us never to talk politics with the clientele, never to say anything detrimental about our country, never to accept tips. It was ridiculous. So I quit.'

Ever since encountering him I had been suffused by a vague dejection mixed with a relief which at first I could not define. Then I realised that I had forgotten he was Chinese at all. He might have been any twenty-year-old in London or Los Angeles or Moscow – footloose, bored, a little cynical. This notion was heightened by the blurred oval of his face in the night, and the placeless pallor of his dress. He belonged to the No-man's-land of disaffected young. Now and again his voice would drop an octave or trail into silence, and I would follow his gaze to where – in this nation without privacy – somebody had slurred to a halt opposite us or loped up inquisitively behind.

'I thought this government favoured young people. . . .'

He stared into the trees. 'No. It's better than in the past, that's all. The trouble with our leaders is they've had no education. They're old men. They live in another world.' His voice tapered whispering away. 'And there's no system of retirement except death.'

Two policemen with revolvers strapped to their waists had marched near us, slowed down, moved on. Liuyin's talk became a chastened mutter. 'I don't like those fellows. They're just peasants brought in from the country. They're clods. Only the government likes them, because they do whatever they're told, they're so thick. But of course it's the plain-clothes men who are dangerous. A few years ago I couldn't be seen talking to a foreigner like this.'

It was growing late and the park was emptying. I noticed our shadows thrown clear on the grass in front of us, and looked behind to see a small, desanctified moon hanging malevolently above the television transmitter.

'What are you looking at?' he asked.

'Nothing.'

Liuyin and his friends were bored in the evenings, he said. 'Maybe we get together in a restaurant, or go to somebody's flat and listen to pop music. And sometimes we gamble a bit. It's illegal, but harmless. There's not much else to do, unless there's a Western film on. The nude scenes are censored out, of course, which makes everybody more curious about them.'

There seemed some disjunction between the arid life he was describing and the delicate clarity with which he saw it. But perhaps it was only my mood or his passing ennui which made all this sound so desolate. What had I wanted him to say? That he was living for the Revolution? But no. The time of Westerners investing their puritan ideals in China was over.

I asked: 'What about girls?'

He smiled to himself in the dark. 'We sometimes pay to get into a factory dance and look for pretty ones. Of course when we bring them home, our parents talk about marriage – parents always think something different. But we think about having fun.'

I wondered about this fun. He made it sound childish. In the towns, I had heard, intercourse outside marriage was all but unknown. 'What kind of fun?'

'Oh, we throw our money after them,' he said. 'Restaurants are full of men showing off to their girls. The girls too, they'll spend two months' salary on just one dress . . . maybe 130 yuan, just to impress. . . . Sometimes my friends spend *half a month's* salary on one meal. That's to get the girl to do what they want.'

'You sleep together?'

His voice dropped, but nobody was near. The last old men in Mao caps and blue jackets were trudging home under the lamplight. 'Not me,' he said. 'But several of my friends borrow rooms or even slip into their factory dormitories, although that's difficult. They sleep regularly with their girls.'

I supposed it was only the oddly mixed flatness and delicacy of his speaking which turned these affairs so matter-of-fact – or my own sudden tiredness, or the moon's disembodying light.

By nine o'clock at night the city is already closing itself away. A single thread of lights glows dimly above each street and a river of lampless bicyclists. The enormous lotus-bud columns along Changan Avenue sprout stately clusters of whitish orbs, but all the alleys and *hutong*s have darkened to threads. Here and there, a lit window hangs in the night like a lantern-slide. In its rectangle of grimy glass, a family huddles with lifted rice-bowls under a naked bulb, or sits round a television beneath walls pinned with garish calendars.

As I walk across Tiananmen Square, ringed by its monstrous, soft-lit halls, I find couples sitting in the paved wastes alone, their arms circled about one another's backs or tucked-up knees. The girls bury their faces on their forearms or their partners' shins, as if in public contrition. A group of youths stands drinking orange-juice and listening to anaemic pop music on a transistor. Nearby an elderly man lies curled on the stone like a foetus, his head resting on a polythene bag, his eyes wide open and staring before him at nothing.

In the neighbouring strips of public garden, the couples have locked their bicycles together on the paths, and monopolise a nearby pine or cypress tree. There they stand motionless, leaning against one another in the same half-forbidden tenderness, their eyes not meeting, their mouths not kissing – simply stand there in a frozen embrace, while bats flitter out over the square.

*   *   *

The feeling never left me that Beijing was the wan head to a living body – the head of a confirmed worrier, racked by struggle and policy.

In the frozen polemic of its squares and avenues, its people seemed muffled or struck dumb, and I suddenly longed to get away.

I started gently. For thirty miles I took a bus northward to the valley where the Ming emperors are buried, while Beijing sprawled incontinently after me, scattering the plains with villages. Their latticed fronts and tiled roofs crowded behind mud walls, surrounded by rubble. Everything seemed to be reconstructing. I toyed with the idea that were I to return next year, all these half-built houses, walls, roads would shine complete; but I knew, of course, that I would see only new rubble, new reconstruction, new decay. Between fields of maize and sorghum plodded small chestnut horses, and bullock-carts carrying sweetcorn and stones. Some peasants trudged beside miniature tractors. Others were bent under harness, men and women together, pulling their ploughs like oxen over the earth. The torpid tempo of the city had stilled into rural quiet. Beside the poplar-sheltered roads farmers squatted all day in markets of their own, before a handful of tomatoes or peppers. Others dozed or fished or washed their clothes along the irrigation canals.

After an hour the horizon corrugated into smoke-blue mountains. They arrived with the artifice of a stage backdrop, shaped and complete, where in a tranquil valley the Ming emperors were entombed. The dynasty had been founded in brilliance during the mid-fourteenth century, but it ossified for over two hundred years until the Manchus from the north overwhelmed it in 1644. In accordance with the ancient geomancy of *feng-shui*, 'wind and water', the imperial graves were shielded from the desert winds by mountains to the north, and fringed to the south with streams which mystically carried their power into the vale of the living. Walls and huge gateways sealed off the valley. A standing garrison guarded it.

Beyond its central gate, which was opened only for the passage of a dead emperor, the 'spirit way' entered the valley between guardian ranks of stone animals. Now hedged with souvenir stalls and photographers' kiosks, it curved in a tarmac crescent under the thunder of tourist buses. But the sentinel beasts were still at their posts. Elephants, camels, horses, lions mingled with mythical monsters, standing and reclining alternately along the way in order (it is said) to permit a midnight changing of the guard. They seemed more magical than lifelike. The lions were unrecognisable, their manes permed into tight ringlets, and the elephants rested on legs buckled before them in defiance of anatomy. Children were crawling over their backs. Even the monsters had lost their terror. Their hair fell lank over their spines or sprouted around a single, incipient horn, and Time had dimpled their snarls into a comic benevolence. They were soft toys in stone.

Since the ancients believed that evil spirits could only travel in a straight line, the sacred way changed course at its centre. Here it was supervised by the scaly-bodied *chilin*, benign solitaries whose hair flamed up crankily on either side of their heads, while beyond them the final guardians were not beasts but men – mandarins civil and military, twice life size. Their sleeves dripped to the grass and they lifted their tablets of office against a flood of beards and tributary moustaches. Past them, scattered far into the valley, the imperial tombs reared lonely above the trees.

Only one has been excavated: the tomb of the profligate emperor Wan Li, who died in 1620 – so fat that he could not walk. Through its gates and courtyards, up into the vaulted sepulchre, tides of tourists pushed shoulder-to-shoulder. The Chinese mania for snapshots ran riot. A camera hung from every arm. And here I first noticed one of those small phenomena which (I thought fancifully) might unravel a whole society for me if I could only understand it: the flurry of Chinese snapshots was directed not at this beautiful and curious valley, but exclusively at one another. A place seemed to take its meaning only from a person's presence there. Sometimes I received the overwhelming impression that these snapshots were really statements of identity, and that to be commemorated within a famous site was to be touched by its mana. 'You're travelling alone?' I was later asked, *'Then how do you manage to photograph?'*

In front of the Wan Li tomb a table and chair had been raised on iron trestles so that its funerary tower formed a perfectly framed backdrop. Here, exalted by a white tablecloth and a vase of plastic flowers, clients were captured by professional photographers in postures of indolent high living, the trestles severed beneath them by the camera's tact, at home with the Ming emperors.

Other photographers' stalls were equipped for other daydreams. Their clients were lent helmets or tinsel tiaras, then they slipped into place behind headless cut-outs of warriors or concubines. I watched them in fascination. At first they tittered self-consciously, or called out to their friends. Momentarily, above the cardboard outline of a princess, there blushed a jolly shopgirl in spectacles – and the Ming general riding his cut-out horse to battle acquired hoary peasant features and was smoking a cigarette. But the moment before the camera clicked, something happened. The friends went silent. The cigarettes and smiles vanished. Suddenly the posing faces froze into the faraway look of their dream. Then I realised that they had entered this fantasy in private earnest, and that as the camera shutter came down, it was being paid to document a transfigured self. The cardboard had crawled upward to subsume the living face.

But down in the underground tomb, all was pandemonium. Little was visible but thousands of heads and thrusting shoulders above which the vaulted roofs arched in near-seamless stone. The excavators had entered in 1957 after burrowing through the tumulus mounded sixty-five feet above. They had found a series of seven-ton marble portals locked by stone bars, which had slid automatically into place when the doors were closed for the last time. These they had prised away by inserting metal rods between the door-leaves, and one by one the gates swung open on to chambers of pharaonic magnificence.

In the sacrificial hall, before the altars of the emperor and his two empresses, stood the 'everlasting lamps' whose fire had nourished their weakened spirits. But the flames had consumed the last oxygen in the sealed chamber, and the wicks now floated dead in pools of coagulated oil.

When the last doors parted on to the burial chamber, the red lacquer coffins were seen undisturbed where they had been laid. Around them on the marble podium tablets and incense-burners stood beside silk banners and jewelled armour, untouched, and wooden chests and lacquer boxes had decayed in priceless confusion. Weapons and silks had rolled out of their rotted panels, mingling with jade belts and pendants, jewels, golden chopsticks – more than three thousand objects. Inside the coffins, on quilted mattresses, the skeletons were robed in silk gowns and drawers, their shoes still on their feet, their skulls crowned, a few earrings clinging idly to the bone. The emperor's headdress was of minutely woven gold thread, twisted into dragons pursuing a flaming pearl. The phoenix coronet of the empress – a delicate cascade of blue – had been composed of kingfisher feathers and inlaid with more than five thousand precious stones.

All these had now been scattered to museums, and in the chamber a notice declared that the eight million ounces of silver used here could have fed a million people for six and a half years. I studied this, waiting to contract its outrage, but the judgement and its obese target were too separate in time. I climbed back into the sunlight.

Among the thirteen imperial mausolea in the valley, the grave of Wan Li receives thousands of visitors every day. Yet when I walked to other tombs, some less than a mile distant, I found not a soul. All over China the conformities of tourism have stifled some sites under a deadening sea of visitors, and released others into utter emptiness.

The tombs stood in solitude. Their sacred ways moved through villages and woods, rutted with cart-tracks now and shrilling with cicadas. Here and there carved dragon-tortoises – symbols of longevity – squirmed under twenty-foot commemorative tablets laden on their backs. Even in desolation, they looked indestructible. From the enclosure walls where I went the plaster had fallen in ochreous chunks. In the gateways the doors were broken in, but their frames still rose to weed-blurred roofs or were dropping friezes piece by piece into the dust. I wandered across courtyards thronged with wind-slanted pines. In the grass symbolic altars lay in solid stone, strewn with their solid stone urns and incense-burners; and here and there protective screens still blocked the way so that evil spirits, with their known ineptitude at cornering, would crash into them in a boorish charge.

But high above all, looming more than a hundred feet and topped by memorial temples, crenellated towers abutted the tumuli themselves. Their windowless strength and faintly tapering proportions steeped them in a remote, unearthly awe. They were gates to the underworld. In their crowning temples, overlooking the grave mounds, the memorial stelae stood in poignant solitude. Upon them only the name of the dead emperor, with a single attribute, was engraved in shocking isolation. The ancients believed the emperor's soul resided here, and I never looked at one without unease. For a moment the shining tablet would take on the force of existential fact. Then my gaze would stray beneath it to where the funerary way reached its end at the blank mound – the void of death – with a muffled jolt.

The tumuli were ringed by parapets which circled them for hundreds of feet in ambulatories of sad beauty. Trees thronged about them, softening the mounds in a shell of green, and squirmed between the moss-dripping stones of the stairways. And these hillocks, like the starkness of those engraved names, struck me each time with an unhinging force, as if the emperors themselves survived here in some form, dimly powerful beneath the mound.

'People don't go alone there . . . at least not at night.' The elderly peasant had stopped on the track. He peered at my guidebook map, pushing a callused fingertip along the location of each grave as he named it. 'But I can't read this script.'

Threading through the pages, he was distracted by an illustration of the Great Wall. It lay less than twenty miles to the north of us, yet he had never seen it. He ran his thumb along the line of its towers – 'Wonderful!' – then slanted his hoe across his shoulder and trudged away. It could have been the moon.

This whole valley, enclosed, poetically sombre, might have been conceived as a monument to Time and the pathos of earthly glory – and at the tomb of the emperor Tian Qi it ascended to a theatrical climax. Thuya trees twisted about the terraces, tossing the balustrades left and right into the grass. Around the stone altar the symbolic bowls of sacrifice sprawled in the scrub, spouting stone flames, and a fleet of Red Admiral butterflies seemed to have been turned loose by a stage designer. Even the light was strange, the sky unnaturally blue. I ambled among the stage-props in a fit of melancholy. Somewhere a sound engineer (surely) was relaying the prattle of magpies through concealed speakers, and alternating them with uneasy silences. It was very effective. And behind all this, in a surge of operatic kitsch, the stele-tower hoisted its temple into the air. Its roofs sagged and crashed in weed-plumed glamour, and its tiles slid off fifty feet below or dangled precariously to expose a thatch of shattered eaves, where whole trees sprouted.

And who was the emperor Tian Qi? A pathetic recluse, he devolved his power into the hands of eunuchs, spending his days in an amateur passion for carpentry and his nights in the clasp of concubines, while around him the empire stiffened into rigor mortis.

It must have been easy to think that this empire was eternal. Its changelessness is still hypnotic. Even the pattern of this necropolis – its tumuli and sacred ways, its tortoise-born stelae and sacrificial halls – was inherited from a time long before Christ. And when I visited the nineteenth-century tombs of the Manchu emperors sixty miles south-west of Beijing, nothing had deeply changed, even to the buckle-legged elephants and solid stone altar-vessels.

But its scale was immense. Its walls circled more than twenty miles. Beneath an arena of mountains the bridges curled in loneliness over lotus-filled moats. The silence was utter. The twenty-foot doors of the gateways reeled in their apertures, the bosses pilfered; and the sacred ways wandered through bosky woods, their guardian beasts roaring in emptiness. In the only excavated tomb, which had been robbed by a warlord long before – the bodies spilt from their coffins, the empress's head wrenched off – the beautiful marble gates swung free on their bronze pivots to disclose mythic sentinels, guarantors of a happy end, carved there with a failed solicitude.

3. Over the Yangtze

THE FRISSON OF solitary travel – travel in a boyish euphoria of self-sufficiency – tingles in my stomach as I march across Beijing's railway station. This feeling is perfectly individual, like homesickness or *déjà vu*, and I greet it as an old and bullying friend, who is stronger than I am, and more enterprising. My rucksack perches light on my back. The morning's zest and apprehension are both heightened by knowing that everything – the old-fashioned paraphernalia of platform guards and flags and whistles, the gargantuan queues, the duel with ticket-clerks – will be exacerbated and redoubled the further I travel from the centre.

Under the enormous vault of the station hall – a leftover colossus from Soviet *entente* in the 1950s – there resounds the tramp of a newly mobilised peasantry. I have seen them before all over the city: families arrived to buy or trade, sleeping under bridges or in shop porches with their caps over their eyes. Now they step on to the escalators as gingerly as Western eight-year-olds, laden with rope-trussed boxes, newly bought televisions, chickens in hampers, radios, bags spilling out fruit and biscuits – bearing El Dorado back to the village. They overflow the waiting-rooms and camp against every wall behind their baggage palisades, snoring open-mouthed through the din with the detachment of Brueghel swineherds, their children in their arms.

In my mind's eye there exists a delicate web of rail links by which I hope to circle and traverse the whole land south of the Wall. Yet the network, compared to India's, is thin. China entered late into the railway era. The earliest track, laid down by the Jardine, Matheson Co. in 1875, is said to have been ripped up again by frightened officials, who supervised its destruction from sedan chairs in token of their loathing of machines. The rolling stock and rails were shipped in abhorrence to a Taiwan beach, where they rusted into oblivion, and for years afterwards the railways intruded only slowly. Court mandarins objected that their reverberations disturbed the ancestral spirits in their graves. When concessions for building were finally granted or forced, the great powers laid down tracks in pursuit of their commercial and political ambitions. It was left to the Communists, who in 1949 inherited a war-shattered network of thirteen thousand miles, to extend its grid into the country's centre and far north-west.

I bought a ticket to Shanhaiguan, where the Great Wall meets the Yellow Sea. Three hundred other passengers were corralled in the waiting-room with me, and were loosed on to the platform in a scrimmaging flood as the train came to rest. China, alone in the world, still manufactures steam-engines – blackly gleaming heavyweights complete with scarlet wheels and cowcatchers – and it was one of these which carried us slowly east. In my 'hard seat' carriage – the cheapest and most common class of travel – loudspeakers no longer broadcast the patriotic music of the 1960s, but relayed lilting pop songs, neutered news bulletins and negro spirituals in Mandarin.

A fisherman idled up and down the corridors, covertly selling crabs to passengers. Peasants and soldiers sat crammed four abreast, bawling, spitting, marinated in cigarette smoke, their trousers tugged above their hairless shins. A gang of construction workers in wicker helmets was tapping hot water from one of the train's boilers into little jars of tea. They came over to finger the texture of my jacket and roared incredulously at my poor Mandarin jokes. The floor was a rink of ash-clogged spittle. From the window-rods above us swung lines of gaudy face-flannels; on the luggage-racks the bulging boxes and black bags loomed like boulders.

The peasant women looked interchangeable with their men, unsexed by the same shapeless trousers and jackets. Their hands and features had been beaten out in bronze by work and sun. Their hair fell short and lank. It was not an adornment, just something that grew there. Their voices were jungle bird cries. Yet opposite me, the face of a seven-year-old girl shone in a fragile moon, the eyebrows brushed like feathers over her crescent-lidded gaze and a tiny, exquisite mouth.

Outside the window the land pushed flat to a grey sky. Invisible kilns and factories littered the horizon with smokestacks. Over the plains between, parcelled into family-farmed strips, the maize and cabbages, sorghum and sunflowers, unfolded between canals in a million immaculate rectangles.

We rumbled through the industrial colossus of Tianjin and into Tangshan, the coal-mining city hit by earthquake in 1976 with the loss of 220,000 lives – more than twice the death-toll of Hiroshima. A wall had been built along the track to conceal its devastation from passing trains, but from the vantage-point of a six-foot Westerner, miles of ruin fell visible. Over this tragic swathe tens of thousands of houses had been reassembled out of rubble, and roofed by tarpaulins weighted down with stones. People were picking at the debris as if still in shock. They gathered like ghosts at the level crossings. Factories rose in gashed shells. Rebuilt, they veined the air with smoke like a lingering dust of dissolution. Even in the centre, no new block stood higher than four storeys; people had lost trust in that uncertain earth.

I got off at Beidaihe, the summer resort of the Party élite. The afternoon had softened under a mackerel sky. I hired a bicycle and freewheeled to the beach along leafy streets where Victorian villas and bungalows stood. The town had been built around the turn of the century as an enclave of foreign diplomats, missionaries and business-men from the Beijing legations and the concessions of Tianjin, and they must have chosen it in a sickness for Europe. Half close the eyes, and the grey descent of rocks and pines to the sea was falling to the Mediterranean, the hibiscus and oleanders blazing in Cannes or Taormina.

But something, of course, was wrong. When I wobbled flat-tyred down certain lanes, armed police waved me back. Most of the Politburo, it is said, have villas here. I had glimpses of dilapidated mansions in British colonial style with a dash of mock Tudor. Now, in early September, many showed locked gates and empty sentry-boxes along drives adrift with poplar leaves. But notices waved Old-Hundred-Names away.

These privileges sit deep in the system and in the past. The nine grades of the imperial mandarinate, whose perquisites were laid down by decree, live again in the twenty-five ranks of Communist official-dom, ascending towards prerogatives of carpeted flats and valets and limousines. In high summer these old divisions invade the beaches too. A small cove is cordoned off for top cadres, and a sandy lido set aside for foreigners, where voyeurs of the bikini-clad Western women are dispersed by lifeguards. But now the rope barriers were down, and cautious troupes of bathers overflowed the frontiers.

High on a pine-shaded bluff a grey-haired couple sat under a blue sunshade lifted in the woman's quavering hand. The man smiled and bowed to me as I passed, and they looked so settled that I asked him if they lived there.

'Not here. We're from the city.' His voice was gentle, high-pitched.

'If a man's been doing good work for twenty years without a holiday, he may be sent to the sea for twenty days.' He smiled at his wife for confirmation. 'I'm sixty now, and I've just got here.'

I could not tell if his faltering voice contained irony or gratitude. We gazed along the shore. The partitions on the beach were gone, but lines of submerged nets still quartered the sea. 'Those demarcate the diplomatic and cadres' beach in July and August.' He laughed softly, with the indifference of a man too old deeply to worry. 'You are here long in China? You will often see such things.'

Down on the shore, people were undressing in makeshift beach-huts, from which the women emerged stocky or androgynously thin in frilly, one-piece bathing-suits. They viewed the ocean with an innate distrust. A hundred yards out, the coast was ringed with safety nets which cut off the whole basin from the wider sea. Nobody could tell me their purpose (since sharks were non-existent at this latitude). Marked by a sequence of black floats, they seemed rather to be a statement of undefined fear – a dread of the undomesticated, of exposure to anything so limitless, so disordered. Notices warned bathers against trespassing beyond these nets, and demanded that dark swimsuits be worn, to avoid the illusion of nudity. Into these waters the swimmers launched out delicately on blue and pink rubber mattresses, or clutched enormous rings like motor-tyre tubes. Nobody ventured more than thirty yards out.

But mostly people did not bathe at all. Old workers, enjoying their first holiday by an ocean they had never seen before, promenaded its rim in a slow, replete wonder, still dressed as if they tramped the factory floor. Sometimes they sat speechlessly together. The sea in itself was cause enough for being here – this restless mass of water flowing nowhere, strange with its snapping waves, its sand, its landless sky-line.

Once or twice a work unit came trooping down to be photographed all together, dressed identically in striped and numbered bathing-gowns. Photographers' parasols were everywhere. Posed on rocks, their clients gazed nobly into the distance while the surf broke safely behind them, or paddled fully-clothed into the shallows – few of them had bathing-costumes – in a token liaison with the deep. They chased beach-balls or gathered edible seaweed into cellophane bags. The tiniest incident or eccentricity attracted mammoth crowds. They thronged to stare at me as I entered the water and circled in hundreds around a decomposed jellyfish washed up in heaps of blubber and red, streaming hair. At such times the whole Chinese world seemed to coalesce into a vast audience for a stage which was almost empty.

The same timelessness had seeped into my hotel. Its heavy decrepitude typified certain guesthouses surviving all over the country. It emitted a spurious atmosphere of having seen better days. In my room the dark-varnished cupboard and ponderous desk, the plush curtains and classical Chinese carpet cancelled each other out into a feeling of nowhere. Rusty water exploded from the taps. Everything was faded. The curtain-folds had been bleached by sun into cherry- and prawn-coloured columns, and the already pale carpets etiolated to pastel. Into this placeless *mise-en-scène* a leftover chinoiserie crept, its elements interchangeable in each room. The walls were hung with a regulation scroll-painting of mountains and waterfall, or a runic verse of Tang poetry. An inkstone and a relief-nib pen changed guard on the desks with a lunar-year diary giving dietary advice for the day. Sometimes a clothes-brush would appear, or a thick-toothed wooden hair-comb, suitable for grooming lions. And by the bedside, invariably, stood a thermos of boiled water, two china mugs and a tin of fragrant green tea.

Sometimes in these hotels I was chivvied out of the dining-hall and into a private room. Here, alone with the ghosts of banqueteers and a huge, off-white circle of tablecloth, I would sit like a penguin on the rim of an ice-floe, poking my chopsticks into four or five little dishes of dried meat, beancurd, cabbage or sea-cucumber, and plotting escape.

The fifty-mile journey along the coast to Shanhaiguan began with pandemonium. I stood in gawping gentility while thirty or forty men battered their way into the bus before anyone inside could disembark. Those in front muscled forward in a scrum of hacking elbows, while those behind burst into yells of 'Push!' Huge parcels were juggled above their shoulders, got stuck in the doorways, crashed to the dust. A woman was crushed against the folding door, screaming theatrically. But this savage free-for-all took place in a social vacuum. No anger followed. Everybody settled grinning and chattering into his achieved place, as if nothing had happened at all. So our bus, like most Chinese buses, set out with the women, children and old people standing wheezing in the aisle, while the seats to either side were packed by two phalanxes of lounging young men.

I secured a foothold in the well of the folding door, feeling depressed. I never forgave these brutal rushes. They banished me back into my own culture, challenged my right to travel in this world I could only pretend to share. I eased my rucksack to the floor and perched on it in a self-righteous temper. A minute later, a frail hand touched my arm. The bus conductress was asking that I take her seat. Her sallow face disclosed a conflict between duty and tiredness. She insisted. So for over an hour I occupied her cubicle, operating the push-button doors to the staunchless merriment of the passengers, while the broken teeth of mountains rose above the sea to the north.

At Shanhaiguan, 'the Pass between Mountains and Sea', the Great Wall descends from the foothills to cross the coastal plain, before crumbling into the waves of the Bohai gulf. A stumbling mass of ramparts encloses the old town like a pocked skin. They rise thirty feet in a sheath of grey brick, pierced by gates.

I trudged the streets in fascination. They belonged to a past not dogged by feudal wars – no castle or episcopal palace bullied the little town – but sunk in a changeless sleep under mandarin bureaucrats and the Will of Heaven. Their alleys fractured into intimacy. The very old and the very young seemed more prominent here than in Beijing, and sometimes poignantly alike. A woman was pushing her grandchildren in a squeaky bamboo pram, her expression lost under a whirlpool of wrinkles. She traversed the pavements on crippled pin-feet, herself like an ancient child, while the pair of babies stood up to stare about them with the impassive, uncrying gaze of patriarchs. Schoolchildren trickled behind their teachers in interconnected formations, clinging to one another's jackets or shirts, or to a rope sewn with metal rings, in adult orderliness. Along the pavements infants urinated at will through trousers ritually slit open between the legs, often tilted back in their parent's arms as they fouled roads or parks to the smiling indulgence of everyone nearby.

A young woman, stark mad, teetered on one leg, her hair flooding her shoulders in two matted rivers. One hand extended a plastic box for alms, while the other picked over and over at the ulcers on her upraised foot. In this provincial town, her lunacy struck with a chill alarm, like a breach of good manners.

Free markets had sprung up everywhere – streets pavilioned with stalls more varied than in the state emporia. The country people had spilled their wares over sacks on the tarmac – aubergines, peppers, live carp and turtles, rhubarb, quails and orioles in bamboo cages, heaps of lethargic chickens with their legs bound beneath them. Others presided over tubs writhing with yellow-green river-eels, and ripped out their spines with scissors on the spot, or spilled them into bags and beat them to death on wooden counters.

An old woman was selling marrows and bamboo-shoots. Her jet-black hair had almost withered from her brows, leaving her half bald. Her answers came hoarse to my questions. Only her gold earrings betrayed that she was not a man. Yes, she had grown these vegetables herself. The village people could grow what they liked these days. So they were better off.

'In what way?' she echoed harshly. 'In different ways.' She fondled a marrow. 'My way is here. These weren't allowed before.'

The wall behind her fluttered with pink and yellow posters: a bus timetable, a fish shop announcing new prices, a bank coaxing investors with a lottery. Amongst these, scored with a blood-red tick as if some mathematical problem had found its perfect solution, hung the announcement of an execution.

Where the Great Wall joined the city parapets, they erupted into a temple-crowned gateway blazoned 'The First Pass Under Heaven'. Once it guarded the battle-scarred road to Manchuria, and as I climbed it an angled outwork rose still formidable into view, and a half-emptied moat soggy with rice and cabbages. To the south the Wall lunged toward the sea through hovels where white-haired piglets scampered; here and there the villagers had burrowed their way clean through it, or stripped off its bricks three deep to expose a stupendous core of rubble. But to the north, after stumbling brokenly over the plain, the monster lifted bastion upon bastion into the hills, zigzagged along razor peaks and plunging declivities, scaled the furthest precipices in a megalomaniac sliver and disappeared into cloud-patterned mountains.

A swarthy girl was reading on the battlements. She asked me if I knew anything about universities. On her lap lay the application forms for a scholarship exam to the United States.

'I long to go. All of us long to go.' Her pen raced up and down the names of colleges she had compiled, each one peppered with personal hieroglyphs. What was the university of Ohio like, she asked? What of Pennsylvania (she despaired of ever pronouncing it)? How about Kansas? My uncertain answers detonated a new surge of hieroglyphs. She said: 'There's only a handful of vacancies, and I'm applicant number five thousand-and-something from my college alone. . . .' Yet she assessed her chances with stoic determination: this exam was the needle's eye into the heaven of America.

'And what are you studying?'

'Early medieval sculpture. In the West.'

I stared at her – the daughter of a factory engineer from Tianjin (she said). Below her red skirt the legs were thick and scarred. 'Why that?'

'I don't know. But when I saw those carvings, I started to have feelings about them. Everybody said it was a Dark Age in Europe then, but as I looked at the photographs, I didn't think so.' Her hands fumbled the papers in embarrassment. 'That was the time of our Tang and Song dynasties, you see, when China was very great. We like to say that the West was in darkness then. But it's not true. That's why I want to study them.'

I was still staring at her, as if waiting for her face to fall into some more aesthetic or eccentric mould. But it stayed blunt, warm, coarse, backed by the mad switchback of the Great Wall. 'You saw illustrations in books?'

'Yes, at college. Then I managed to buy *The Oxford Dictionary of Art*.'

'In Beijing?'

She nodded. 'My father found it. It cost four weeks of his salary.'

'Will you ever go to Europe, do you think?'

'Oh no!' She said it with a kind of bright hopelessness, as if I had enquired about entering paradise. 'I'd never get the money. Not for that. If I were a scientist. . . .' She looked at me in sudden earnestness. 'Have *you* seen those places? Vézelay? Aachen?'

'Yes.'

'Oh!' She smiled with a sad excitement that made me feel unbearably fortunate, smiled with no trace of envy, but simply as if to talk with me drew her magically closer to those carvings. Guiltily I remembered how I had rushed through Aachen on the way to Cologne: for a brief hour I had wandered round Charlemagne's palace-chapel, and inveigled myself on to his marble throne in the tribune above the west door. I suffered the girl's gaze for a moment, then looked away. Forty feet below us a youth in jeans was catching lizards in the rice fields, to eat.

But something about those Dark Age artefacts had fascinated the girl. When we veered into discussing other things the light drained from her voice. She simply lost interest, and suddenly broke in with: 'Have you seen Autun? . . . Toulouse?' Her future seemed to contain none of the directives which her parents must have lived by or suffered under. She belonged to the new China. Obedient still, but cautiously individual, she was innocent of zeal for any revolution, any yearning to reform mankind or build Socialism.

She just wanted to go to America.

All afternoon I followed the Great Wall into the mountains. Cracked open by farmers' tracks or half buried under the shelving earth, it crossed the plain in broken chunks then hoisted itself through the foothills. At first it went squat and straight as a causeway. I strode in its shadow over a river of debris, dotted with dead animals scarcely seen in life – rabbits, snakes, cats – and on through fields rustling with sugar-cane into a scrub-covered waste. Then the Wall rose into quiet. The sky spread in a sheet of bird's-egg blue. I realised how I must have longed for silence in this overcrowded land, and now it was all about me, deeper for the dry, insistent rubbing of cicada wings. The mercilessness of the peasants towards their environment – the land hunger, the edibility of everything alive – had spared these tall grasses and wild marguerites. They were filled with the clack and hop of grasshoppers. Small, ordinary life – the dip of swallows, the fussing of brimstone butterflies over the rocks – continued in its native radiance. My stride slowed to a dreamy loping. Bronze-red flowers dribbled from the Wall's cracks. And just where the rampart began its ascent, a praying mantis straddled the way in unearthly waiting. At my approach it unfurled serrated claws like some delicate lobster, and above its body, which I had mistaken for a sheath of folded leaves, a minute prehistoric head jerked mechanically back and forth. I lowered my hand to it. But its pointed face and jade-green eyes were beyond fear, so pale they might have been sightless, and only as I passed did it lift itself on saw-toothed arms, and lurch away into prehistory.

Beyond it the Wall hovered along stone-filled ravines, pared to a spectre of its original self, its steps crumbled, its parapet half shorn away. But on its enemy salient the crenellations survived, and for five hours it carried me into the mountains.

I was climbing in an awesome perspective, I knew – on the furthest rim of a 2,000-mile causeway to the west. In my mind's eye it snaked before me for eight hundred miles, choking off Inner Mongolia until it met the Yellow River. For another thousand miles it looped beneath the southernmost reach of the Gobi – now a rampart of compacted earth, or hacked from the living loess – then curled towards the far province of Xinjiang before it found its end astride the ancient Silk Road at the Jiayuguan Gate. At Jiayuguan too, my own journey would end at the onset of winter, and this lent a strangeness to my walking here, as if the months which would intervene were merely an interlude – a trivial burst of variety – before I returned to this grey frontier.

The Great Wall's age and dimensions almost evade analysis. Even its official builder Qin Shihuangdi, the first emperor of a unified China in the third century BC, achieved no composite creation, but linked the older defences of many warring states. He knit his bulwarks with twenty-five thousand towers, and with parapets so wide that five horsemen could ride them abreast. Men died in their hundreds of thousands constructing it, and its wreckage still litters hills and deserts north of the present defences. Over the centuries it was rebuilt, extended and partially abandoned, until today's Great Wall – mostly built by the Ming at the turn of the seventeenth century – bifurcates and doubles back on itself over more than four thousand miles. An extra three hundred miles were discovered this century, extending west even of Jiayuguan; and in the tenth century a 600-mile crescent once carried it east of Shanhaiguan to the borders of Korea.

Even the reasons for its building are touched with enigma. Its mammoth expense was undertaken at a time when the nomads of the north posed little threat; as a measure of true defence it repeatedly failed. The barbarians broke through it in the end, many times, and China conquered them by subtler means. Probably it was raised as much to contain the empire's frontiersmen as to keep out the pastoral invader. It formed, in fact, one of those definitions which the Chinese seem especially to love or need. It established the divide between the desert and the sown. Within it spread the Celestial Empire of the Son of Heaven, all the world's civilisation and harmony; outside lingered the rootless demons of the wilderness, a nameless chaos.

Its unifier, Qin Shihuangdi, was torn by fears and megalomania. Historians wrote that his 270 palaces were connected by covered tunnels, and that nobody knew where he slept. The Great Wall was his realised fantasy: less a barricade against the Hun, perhaps, than against some undefined darkness. At intervals along its length dead men were immured, to ward off evil spirits.

Now, in the goldening light, I saw my shadow wobbling tall in the ravine below, and I turned back. It was possible, I supposed, to see the whole Wall as the materialisation of a profound psychological fear. I was reminded of the safety-nets stretched across the sea at Beidaihe, dividing the inhabited calm from the unknown. But the thought lost itself in the beauty of a wild apricot tree red on the bare slopes. Far below, the Wall struggled like a giant earthwork to the shore, and a ship's siren moaned out of the haze.

* * *

South from Beijing, the land does not change for hundreds of miles. The villages maintain a northern defensiveness. There are walls everywhere: walls built against cold and the invader – brick walls, clay walls, walls of unhewn stone, walls enclosing factories, kilns, hamlets. As my train heaved southward hour after hour, the carriage window unrolled an immense panorama of allotments cross-hatched over the plains: wheat, sugar, cotton. Drying maize thickened on the village rooftops or lay beneath them in leaf-whitened heaps. Cows grazed in their cemeteries or on isolated hills of fir and scrub.

I pulled out a map and traced my imagined future. It was one of those richly coloured physical maps whose examination becomes a sensuous kind of travel. Down its green littorals, crossed by snakes of riverine blue, my finger journeyed to Nanjing, wriggled inland to the Buddhist holy mountain of Jiuhuashan, then reached Shanghai along the ancient cities of the Grand Canal and slid south over a thousand miles to the Straits of Taiwan. Across the turquoise of the China Sea I invented an ocean voyage to Canton, then climbed north where the cartographer's green turned to an arduous-looking beige, until, after two thousand miles of detour, I was drifting down the Mekong river to the Burma-Laos border.

But before I could reach it the man sitting opposite plucked the map off my lap. He was bald and simian. 'Where is your group?' he asked.

'I'm alone.'

'Alone?' He held the map so close against his eyes that I thought he was sniffing it; but he was hopelessly myopic. Then he lapsed into silence.

We were travelling in 'soft seat' luxury, our cubicles covered with lace antimacassars and bamboo matting. A potted plant and four porcelain tea-mugs stood on each narrow table, and a uniformed girl with an outsize kettle replenished the thermos beneath. In this class, senior cadres and army officers lounged spaciously, two abreast. Little signs of privilege – pens glinting along their breast-pockets, their superior watches – separated them from the factory workers jamming the carriages next door. Olive jackets and army caps swung clean from the hooks above them, and the lumpy bags and boxes on the racks were interspersed with floppy briefcases.

The man handed back my map nonplussed. He started peeling apples on to our table and tossing the segments between his outlandishly protruded lips, as if eating apples were some new and precious celebration. From time to time he would watch me, his forehead tangled in perplexity, muttering to himself: 'Alone . . . on your own. . . .', trying to come to grips with the concept. Then he would concentrate on paring another apple, only to look up and stare again for five or ten minutes on end, his eyes separated by a vexed triple-knot. 'On your own. . . .'

I returned to my itinerary. My finger started north along the edge of the chill, lavender-coloured vastness marked 'Himalaya', then 'Tibet'. The journey seemed to be sliding into fantasy. This blanched mass of plateau and mountain, trickling with tiny veins of rivers and dotted only by faint, italicised names, was unimaginable as living landscape. After almost a thousand miles I had looped east across Sichuan, a province twice as populous as Britain, then down the Yangtze gorges and into the plains. My finger was already running north again, making for the hills and steppes abutting Mongolia, when somebody said: 'Look, the Yellow River!'

Outside the window a whole muddy ocean was on the move. So flat and brown were both land and water they seemed indivisible. For two hundred miles inland the plain's altitude scarcely alters, and at its mouth men may be seen fishing far out to sea. Here the Yellow River finds the end of its 3,000-mile journey to the Pacific, and the entire coastal plain, almost twice the size of France, is nothing but the soft loess earth of the northern hills spread here by the great river. Now only the fallen sun, hovering above the near-static glass of the water, betrayed that it moved at all, gilding the eddies smudged like thumb-prints on the current's surface.

The alternation of drought with rain and melted snows makes the river's discharge violently unpredictable. Not for nothing is it called 'China's Sorrow'. Its sudden floods have drowned millions. The country's earliest civilisations grew up in its valleys, already exhibiting many of China's historic traits, and as the river fell behind us, I wondered if it were true (as some scholars believe) that the effort to master its awesome, meandering force – exacting a constant collective effort to build dikes and channels – explained the deep conformist instincts which infuse the Chinese still.

But the abstruse thought faded into disbelief as our blinds came down against the night. The scene in the carriage grew surreal. Synthetic national pop songs chirruped over the loudspeakers, with Glenn Miller hits and 'Believe Me If All Those Endearing Young Charms' in Mandarin. Beside me a grizzled army general squatted barefoot, chewing cashew nuts and picking his toes. He was reading a comic book. The man opposite had demolished his bag of apples, but still gazed at me from time to time, and I heard him repeating softly: 'Alone. . . .'

I reached my destination late at night. In the dark the town looked half abandoned. Decaying walls and bastioned gates loomed and glimmered theatrically. I wondered if they would still be there by morning. The whole inner city of Qufu looked like a moon-whitened painting.

Qufu is the unacknowledged Vatican of China. Here, more than 2,500 years ago, the sage Confucius was born, and died in disappointment; but posthumously he overawed all China, and for two thousand years its official ethos was his. The town became the patrimony of his descendants, 'the first family under heaven', and the heart of his cult. Century after century it acted either as the seat of imperial conscience or as a reliquary of sterile tradition. This benevolent, constricted and intensely conservative faith propounded a social law for man, not a conversation with God, and in its name the imperial government sank into a stasis of thought and ritual whose scholar-guardians tended it through rebellions and dynastic changes until the twentieth century. Even today, the country is shaped in its image.

The palace of Confucius's descendants partly served as a guest-house now. But only the murmuring of tourists in its low porticoes and dovetailed courts disclosed that anything had changed. I lay awake on a lacquered four-poster in a room soft with old carpets and polished woodwork. The stillness was unnerving. Somewhere a fan rattled. Somewhere else a dog howled. Dogs are so few in cities (they were exterminated as scavengers) that the sound rose and faded in shivering solitude. Out in the mosquito-whining darkness I could sense the mesh of palace colonnades boxed about me like concentric coffins. I was in the heart of something airless, gone.

I went out in early morning. The main palace alone covers thirty acres with 460 chambers and pavilions. A fusty secrecy pervades it. Its courts and audience-halls multiply one behind the next in an ever-deepening succession of barriers and privacies. Mellow walls

[79]

shelter, divide and categorise everything. Rooms are still musty with mandarin regalia – inkstones, seals, palanquins, manuscripts of ritual and genealogy. They succeed one another in a maze of splendour and discomfort. Circular moon-gates lead from one court to the next. Water-lilies float in font-like stoops. Barrel-shaped seats and tables stand in the bamboo shade of courtyards, their stone surfaces incised with dragons, flowers, phoenixes.

I trespassed here with no sense of violating. Its inhabitants might have left millennia ago. Recent renovations look subtly obscene, and I found myself lingering under those halls whose beams had been worn paintless and pale by wind, and whose tiles no longer shone.

The palace has been dying a long time. After the imperial system collapsed in 1911, its rooms closed down one by one. Its last prince – a seventy-seventh generation descendant of Confucius – could not restore it. He fled to Taiwan with the Guomindang in 1949. The stone keep became a nest of owls, its doorlocks impenetrably rusted over. The past had always owned the present here, and now the place grew haunted. A hundred long-shut rooms were said to scamper with nocturnal demons, and the sealed-up chambers where people had hanged themselves stirred into atrocious life. Even the books in the great library were said to have souls of their own, and could be heard moving at night in the shape of a delicate girl, whose wooden-soled shoes clopped eerily over the floorboards. Finally, like good Confucians, the wraiths conformed to hierarchy and fell under the control of a white-haired immortal who tippled in the moonlight and received a yearly offering from the prince.

In 1966 the temples and palaces were ransacked by Red Guards from the Beijing universities, together with local students. The philosophy of Confucius had always been a bulwark against revolution. Violence had sickened him. His whole ethos sought to build upon the past, to inculcate ancestral virtue and respect, to reconstitute an imagined golden time. All was retrospective. To be old was to be in touch. Into this long continuum the Maoist dictum 'Destroy the old, create the new!' crashed like a blasphemy.

Again, in 1974, the quaint but savage slogan was propagated to 'Criticise Lin Biao, Criticise Confucius'. Lin Biao was the Defence Minister killed in 1971 and anathematised by Mao; Confucius stood not only for his feudal self but as a codename for another supposed conservative, Premier Zhou Enlai. Such covert attacks were common even in Confucius's time.

Many of the treasures of Qufu were saved by local officials and peasants who spirited them away to the countryside. But many others – tomb stelae, hosts of memorial tablets and minor artefacts – vanished under the Red Guards' sledgehammers. Above all, a colossal statue of the Great Sage, holy with years and worship, was hauled from his temple by tractor and smashed to bits.

All this, I found, lent a mingled euphoria and pathos to what was happening in the streets that morning, the anniversary of his birth. Troupes of fancy-dressed schoolchildren were on the move. In every shop and stall the counters overflowed with statuettes of Confucius, cypresswood portraits of Confucius, Confucius key-rings, Confucius medallions. His buck teeth and elephantine ears glowed from painted plates and printed handkerchiefs and wall posters. You could wear him, light him up, blow your nose on him. He was as ubiquitous as the Virgin at Lourdes. But he was so ugly, ran legend, that his mother rejected him and he was suckled by a tigress – and his humblest figurines have reproduced this homeliness.

Today a replica of his destroyed statue was to be unveiled in his temple. To the people of Qufu, many of whom declare themselves his direct descendants, it was a moment of pure triumph. The entire town was spilling towards the temple complex, with a swarm of television crews and newsmen. For this was no ordinary ceremony of restitution but a political signal to the nation, a message transmitted in the code familiar from ancient times – the language of symbols. 'The madness is over,' it was saying. 'The old values are back.'

On several stalls I spied a little red book, blatantly mimicking that of Mao. I picked one up, and what did it contain? No Marxist exhortation – but the pedantic and kindly analects of the Great Sage.

By mid-morning, as the procession of state dignitaries started up the avenue towards the temple, the whole town was moving after it. Firecrackers burst along the shrub-tufted city bastions and stammered from the drum-tower. Archaic bands, which had come in from the countryside, were playing outside the temple walls again, as if responding to some atavistic memory. The semicircles of their hoary faces gathered about the sacred way in a rumpus of squealing and tootling. They clashed finger-cymbals and banged drums. They blew through black stone mouthpieces into bundles of reeds. They hit gongs with wooden blocks and puffed through raucous trumpets. The music they created was an immemorial music, without melody or resonance – but monodic, dry and shrill, a magic for punctuating village ceremonies.

I walked towards the temple through nine successive courts. The way had become an avenue of dancing children. Their plangent voices rose in rhythm: 'Welcome! Welcome!' Their fists were closed around plastic flowers and candy-coloured banners. In each courtyard the agitation grew sharper, the voices more pipingly insistent, the crowds thicker. Boys dressed in the blue trousers and red scarves of the Communist Youth Pioneers had slithered back a century into a world of temple acolytes. Their foreheads were bound with turbans and they struck tom-toms and danced in stylised rhythm. Girls masked as cats or monkeys jigged up and down on papier-mâché horses. And the much-loved dancing dragons were cavorting and undulating again.

I thrust on beneath stone gateways under trees themselves half turned to stone – junipers and 700-year-old cypresses. The outer halls and temples fell behind. I passed the sacred library – a galleon of a palace foundering on its terrace, its roofs stuck with weeds, its painted dragons faded to a ghostly squirming; then on again to the Apricot Altar, where the Great Sage taught, until I climbed at last to where the double roof of an enormous temple rose and spread on a forest of intricately painted eaves – the Hall of Great Perfection, the heart of all this homage.

Here, outside the deep crimson and gold doors, on the site of the Red Guards' depredations, the tumult of officials stilled into expectation. Reporters and camera crews teemed round the shut entrance. An antique orchestra hovered.

Opposite the central gates two officials supported an elderly woman by either arm. She wore black trousers and black felt slippers. They held her like a mascot or an icon, with impersonal tenderness. She was Kong Demao, a seventy-seventh generation descendant of Confucius, whose brother had fled to Taiwan.

Suddenly the orchestra struck up. For a moment the whole crowd seemed to lean forward on tiptoe. Then the gates parted and we saw beyond them, enthroned in a stifling brilliance of vermilion and gold, the half-veiled effigy of a monstrous god. Around him all the paraphernalia of sanctity was banked – incense-burners, gongs, ceremonial drums, jade chimes. Swept into the surge of the crowd, stumbling over the temple's threshold and through the hall, I arrived where the statue loomed in a recess of gold-blue curtains. Even as I looked, the chintzy pink veil was lifted invisibly from his face – and there was the Master, gazing over our heads. He was bland, fat, strange. He looked like a playing-card king. He was twice life-size, a replica in smoothest clay. His jowls flowed undisturbed into a black spade-beard, and his fingers joined like sausages over his wand of office. A glitter of robes in cinnabar and olive green parted around two prodigious, gold-embossed feet. I could see why his mother threw him out. The buck teeth and elephant ears of his infancy were worn like insignia. Two or three bats were flying unplanned around his face.

Kong Demao stood at the statue's foot in an electric storm of flashbulbs. Half a dozen microphones were pushed against her mouth. What did she think? How did she feel?

But she seemed overcome. Wisps of greying hair had escaped from her kirby-grips. Nothing in particular appeared to distinguish her; no look of inbred aristocracy (or buck teeth) – simply a 68-year-old woman, portly and rather pale.

What, in any case, could she have said – she whose youth had been incarcerated in the Confucian palace, in a tundra of etiquette and feudal brutality, whose concubine mother had been murdered by her stepmother and whose brother had gone? Her childhood had been passed in aristocratic luxury mingled with Confucian thrift and a small girl's loneliness, even while the storm-waves of civil war and Communism were beating at the palace walls. She had seen her father carried to his scented grave by a fantastical procession of pall-bearers, executioners and walking silk puppets, with paper servants to serve him in the underworld, all preceded by two cavalry platoons to hack away the evil spirits from the grave. And now a Japanese television crew was asking her what she felt.

Her hands trembled to her spectacles, as if the flashbulbs were blinding her. It was all very suitable, she said, glancing at the statue. Yes, she was glad, so very glad. . . .

Then she turned, and was helped like an invalid from the temple.

A mile outside Qufu is a quiet grove – almost a forest – where the descendants of the Master have been buried around him for two and a half thousand years. A hundred thousand tombs are scattered here, it is said, in the shadow of trees whose ancestors were planted by Confucius's disciples. Hardly anybody comes. Neglected paths converge among bamboo and juniper, meander over shrub-strangled bridges, fade away.

The graves are spread without order through the undergrowth.

Trees twist from their tumuli. Sometimes their memorial tablets are attended by altars for food-offerings and incense to the dead. But now the smells are those only of the musky forest. Here and there the funerary avenue to some grander tomb erupts from the jungle, lined by guardian animals in stone. They grimace from the undergrowth. A carved horse`stands ready under the pines, and sculpted mandarins lie toppled in a lichen-blackened tumult of robes and hats. Here are still cave-tombs more than two thousand years old, in which (according to the strange memoirs of Kong Demao) people who survived beyond the age of sixty used to be buried alive. Sometimes their children went on feeding them by lowering bamboo baskets of food and drink into their graves; sometimes not.

When I found the tomb of Confucius, I wondered if signs of worship might remain. But the site was very simple. The larger stone, topped by a ritual coil of dragons, had been overturned and split by Red Guards, and the scar showed vivid across it. I waited under the ivy-gripped trees as if something might happen. Magpies cackled in the pine branches. An incense-burner stood before the tomb; but when I peered into it I found cigarette-stubs.

It was foolish, I suppose, to look for something more. The worship of the Master has been condemned as superstition, just as he would have wished. He flows in the national bloodstream more subtly. Sometimes I felt that the Confucian belief in an overlying cosmic system pervaded the whole culture still, promoting a profound distrust of the new or various. Such a concept suggests that the basis of things is good, and man perfectible. Even the veneration for high office (and the smugness of its incumbents) may stem from an old but unarticulated feeling that hierarchies reflect a divine order.

At a press conference that morning the foundation of a Confucian Study Centre had been announced, and a Confucius Museum. Communist cadres, delivering their speeches under a scroll-painting of the Chinese God of Heaven, went on to announce the transformation of Qufu into a 'tourist town', with a move to encourage foreign investment in hotels. Ten thousand overseas tourists had come to the city that year, they said. In five years' time. . . . There was no telling how lucratively Confucius, who despised commerce, could be commercialised.

I slid over a wall to walk beside his burial-mound. Until far into this century it was said to be mysteriously trimmed, unlike the graves around it. Old people cited this as proof that his spirit still lived. But now it was covered with wild grass, and an ominous weft of shrubs and trees.

*   *   *

Southward to Nanjing, the land begins to change. The tractors and draught-horses of the north grow rare. Allotments become smaller and richer. At first the fields stretch to a horizon of poplars and kiln chimneys, or to nothing at all. Then the country starts to heave a little under its burden of maize, vegetables and lakes. Beyond my carriage window a rim of misted hills emerged, vanished, re-emerged to the west. The green of crops deepened under a waterlogged sky, then yellowing rice-fields appeared, fringed with soya and cut by canals or pools glazed with white ducks.

I wandered down the corridor to the dining-car, hoping for lunch, and found a girl in a waitress's white jacket in its doorway. Yes, she said, she would bring me a meal. It was only when she returned with two plates of indeterminate meat, and sat down opposite me, that I realised she wasn't a waitress at all. She was an economics student on her way to Shanghai. Her clothes and bobbed hair were unexceptional, but she was laughing at my confusion. Her name, she announced, was 'Morning-Sunshine'. 'I hate the name.'

'Why?'

'I don't know. I just hate it.' She added inconsequently: 'I'm homesick.'

'Your mother?'

'We both get upset when I go back to university.' She undid her jacket buttons to reveal a T-shirt with 'Up-beat' inscribed on a flat chest. 'My father doesn't mind me going much. He's a cadre. . . .'

As we pulled the scraps of meat from our platefuls of bones, I examined her appearance for any giveaway elvishness. But her face belied her. Its features might have been sketched in by an artist portraying an average Chinese girl. They were regular, minimal, unemphatic.

I said: 'What's your future after college?'

'I don't know. I think my future may be unhappy.' She gazed out of the window. I could detect no self-consciousness. She simply looked sad, and no longer quite ordinary.

'Why do you say that?'

'Because I'm different. My friends all call me mischievous. I'm fun, I

[85]

suppose. But I risk too much.' She spoke with a brittle hardiness, as if she were talking of someone else. 'I'm too independent. I don't think I'll marry. I don't want that sort of life, and I don't like children.' She glanced with distaste at the woman sitting across the aisle from us – a grandmother cosseting a squinting baby. 'I can't stand those.' As if on cue, the infant began to howl. 'You see. Disgusting.'

We had become a focus for the stares of other passengers, turned on us non-committally.

'I might not get a good husband anyway,' she said. 'Western girls seem beautiful, but I don't think I'm beautiful.' She looked at me in cheeky enquiry. 'Am I?'

'You're attractive,' I said. (She had become so.)

The next moment a fat, earnest youth in glasses dumped himself down opposite. He announced a desire to practise his English, and enfiladed our conversation with unanswerable questions. His mouth was a grinning load of crooked teeth. 'Excuse me, sir, how much do the peasants get to eat in England?'

Morning-Sunshine ignored him. 'No, I won't marry. I don't want to work about the house, not even my own house.' She lifted a fragile fist, laughing. 'I say "Down with housework!"' She looked barely adolescent, let alone marriageable, although she was twenty-one. Sometimes I could not tell if she believed herself or not. Her talk would lapse suddenly into slogans and clichés. 'I hope I will use my life to serve the people and my motherland,' she proclaimed, then added: 'I want to be a millionairess.'

The youth interrupted: 'Excuse me, sir, is England a gentleman's country?'

She rushed on: 'I want to have power over all that money' – her hands wriggled in manipulation – 'to give to the poor.'

I did not believe this charity, even if she did, but her thirst for manipulative power – those delicately wriggling hands – was certainly real. The youth smiled in slow-witted accord. He was beginning to take an interest in her.

I asked her: 'Are you a Party member?'

'No.' She said it with clear derision, and asked the youth: 'Are *you* a Party member?'

'No.'

Then, quite loudly, and surrounded as we were by a score of anonymous officials, she said astonishingly: 'I don't believe in Communism.'

My glance panicked round the other faces. I had the impression that they fell faintly out of focus, and that the chopsticks dithered at their mouths. The earnest youth looked as if he had been acupunctured in some distant part of his body.

'I don't believe in any 'isms.' She added formally: 'They cheat the people.'

I asked: 'Do most of your friends feel as you do?'

'All of them.'

I got up and we went into the corridor. She lifted her face synthetically to mine. Her boyish figure and deludingly empty features – the common-denominator eyes, nose, mouth, all perfect and characterless in the creaseless oval of her face – restored her to a troubling innocence. She seemed imperilled by believing her country's own propaganda: including the myth that she was free.

I told her so.

'Don't worry about me,' she said. 'I'm always like that.'

'I was afraid you were.' I suddenly remembered: 'I owe you for my meal.'

She answered with her mingled toughness and naïvety: 'Give me foreign exchange certificates.' These gave access to goods she could never normally buy, and could be exchanged at high profit. They were Chinese gold-dust. At the start of each term, she said, after she had paid for her college food and textbooks, she had two pounds left over. I changed a few notes with her, and trebled her income. She suddenly giggled, and called back as she vanished down the corridor: 'Would you mistake me for a waitress now?'

All this time we had been sliding across the basin of the Yangtze. The country had sunk into an amphibious lushness. Water buffalo lumbered down sodden tracks or stood submerged in ponds under a conclave of dozing eyes and snouts. As the rice mellowed toward harvest, the quilt of fields deepened into emeralds and golds, and by evening the sun was plunging toward a slough of interlocked land and water – fisheries, reed-dimmed lakes and rivers staked with fragile-looking nets.

At dusk the girders of a giant bridge crossed the carriage window like the flicker of a cine-shutter. I craned out and saw the Yangtze moving below, a mile wide, and the lights of Nanjing beyond. The air was hot and motionless. Into this valley, over many decades, the lifeblood of China had seeped down from the north, until by the twelfth century the regions south of the river, grown populous with quick-yielding rice, outweighed the older heartlands. Here, in the refined trading cities of the Yangtze delta, the vigour of the northern Tang transformed into the gentler grandeur of the Southern Song, and Chinese civilisation began silting up.

Thirty years ago no bridge crossed the river at all. Even today the Yangtze redefines the country with a subtle absoluteness. It marks the immemorial divide between a soldierly, bureaucratic north and the suave, entrepreneurial south. Men dwindle in size and integrity as they go south (say the northerners) and the clear-cut Mandarin of Beijing becomes a slushy caress. The dust of the wheat and millet-bearing plains dissolves to the monsoons of paddy fields and tea plantations. The staple of noodles becomes a diet of rice, and the low cottages and symmetrical northern streets twist and steepen into labyrinths of whitewashed brick.

At the confluence of these worlds lies Nanjing. It is known as one of the 'Four Furnaces of China', and I emerged from the railway station into a humid, utterly still night. I had scarcely tramped a hundred yards before I was filmed in sweat and my rucksack dragging like a hawser. Along the streets where I went, lugging one foot after the other as if through liquid cement, all the cottage doors stood open, and I saw into their poverty: dungeon-rooms stuck with rough chairs and beds. I found a hotel given up to overseas Chinese, its walls black with damp. Between the cracked tiles of the shower-room waved familiar ranks of feelers, and the air-conditioners hung from the windows in a mass of dishevelled wires.

I lay on my bed in torpor. Every movement – taking off shoes, turning off the light-switch – became a campaign. The challenge of crossing the room and opening the window nagged at me for ten minutes while I lay and stared at its rectangle of suffocated stars. When I at last opened it, the air outside stood hot and solid in its frame.

All night I lay naked and unsleeping, and rose exhausted. I joined the drifts of commuters on a hired bicycle through streets which became a dreamy chaos. Pedestrians meandered off the pavements with carrying-poles or babies, and two girl cyclists collided before me in slow motion and crumpled into a collage of wheels and old-fashioned summer dresses.

But I grew to like Nanjing. The main streets moved in double or triple tunnels of sycamores, which curled like candelabra overhead. From the revolving roof-restaurant of the Jinling Hotel, the tallest building in China, you may see these dense rivers of green driving through a medley of old roof-tiles and modern concrete, with here and there a Kuomintang ministry or a decaying ex-consulate from the 1920s.

The city's history is scattered pathetically about. As early as the third century it was the head of a powerful southern kingdom, and in 1368 the first Ming emperor took it as his capital. His twenty-one miles of crenellated walls – almost the longest city walls ever built – still coil in an irregular belt around the gutted past. His palace is a ruin of split pavings and crashed columns. His tomb outside the walls is overgrown. Along its sacred way the animals wait gauche and compact in the pink-red local marble: the Bactrian camel incised with an archaic smile, the ears of the elephants like lightly-carved flowers.

Nanjing's past has gone underground. Of the rich and ordered nineteenth-century capital of the Taiping Heavenly Kingdom, whose leader declared himself the younger brother of Christ and whose revolt engulfed half China, nothing is left but a stone pleasure-boat on a stagnant pond. The Manchus sacked the city hideously, and half a century later, as capital of the Guomindang, it again fell into one of its periodic bloodbaths. Chiang Kai-shek executed thousands of Communists here, and soon afterwards, in a massacre still vivid in memory, the Japanese decimated its citizens in such numbers that the conflicting estimates of death – a hundred thousand or four times as many – grow unimaginable.

I bicycled through the hills to the mausoleum of Dr Sun Yatsen, the father of modern China. With the fall of the Manchu dynasty in 1911, he had planned democracy for his country, but had been drowned by the brutality of events, and his tomb has become the pilgrimage-shrine of an unblemished national hero.

The mausoleum was as eclectic as its occupant: a *mélange* of traditional China and the classical West. The imperial furniture of lion-dogs and incense-burners (stuffed with discarded iced-lolly sticks) was all here, and the mauve-tiled roofs climbing the forested slopes lent the sepulchre, at first, the radiance of strangeness. Not the tiniest incised cross betrayed that the man was a baptised Christian. But while the nearby Ming tomb, sensitive to the laws of *feng-shui*, wriggled subtly into the hills, the nationalist shrine – gross and European in its symmetry – charged up in a bullying surge of four hundred stone steps. At their head, where a statue of the defeated idealist sat before his burial-chamber, excerpts from his 1912 constitution were inscribed in gold on the grey marble wall. Visiting peasants and workers circled it, mouthing aloud the promises of freedoms which they still did not own.

'They don't know what they're reading,' muttered a man I questioned. He was dressed in a black suit despite the heat, and I thought he must come from Hong Kong. 'They're looking at the West – Dr Sun had a Western education – and they don't understand it. You have to go to the West to understand it.'

'You've been?'

'Yes, to America, on business studies.'

He was a banker from Nanjing, dusky and slight. He exuded an indefinable precariousness. His face seemed to be expressed not by its eyes but by its sensuous mouth.

'I was brought up during the Korean War to hate the Americans. When I went there, I thought there'd be Capitalists with whips in the factories – I really believed this – who lashed the workers if they arrived late. So you can imagine. . . .' His hands unfurled from his chest in dumb revelation. 'All at once it dawned on me that everything we'd been told had been a lie. The Americans didn't want war. It was extraordinary. They were . . . well . . . *nice*.' He seemed still shaken by this. His words had lifted him on to tiptoe. 'I was invited into more than twenty private houses and I couldn't believe it . . . televisions, carpets, air-conditioning, cars. And the houses were all separate. Our leaders had said that we'd overtake the West in fifty years, but I knew then that this would never happen. Not even if the West were to stand still. And of course the West doesn't stand still.'

He had returned to a two-room shared flat in Nanjing, and an income of $22 a month. A quarter of this was spent on keeping his three-year-old son at boarding kintergarten. 'My wife was assigned a government post in Shanghai, but my own work's here. Neither of us can look after the boy.' By now his speech came in cathartic bursts. 'I don't know how long we'll be separated. That depends on the government. People can be separated here for ten or twenty years. We get forty days a year holiday together. After thirty-three years you can retire. It's hard, but that's how things are.'

He showed me a snapshot of this split nuclear family, in which he and his wife – a woman with a vivid, pale face – held up their baby like one of the government advertisements for a single, healthy child. 'We've been parted for seven years since our marriage. We wish it wasn't like that, but how can we change it?'

'Perhaps if you knew some official. . . .'

'I'm not even a Party member.' He dropped his voice, and glanced round him. But only the weary-faced statue of Dr Sun was in earshot, gazing out from the hall of his betrayed manifesto. 'I'm the black sheep of our family. I've got eleven brothers and sisters, and every one's in the Party. But I'm not a Communist, I'm not an anything. All that . . . sickens me.' His lips curled in a disgusted smile. I sensed something angrily hurt in this, as if the corruption which he left unsaid – the giving of favours and receiving of bribes across the whole of public life – had at some stage personally damaged him. 'When I was asked to join the Party, I answered *I'm not worthy, I'm not worthy*.' He laughed bitterly. 'And they believed me.'

*   *   *

Four men lay on wooden stretchers in the Nanjing hospital, while a doctor pressed acupuncture needles into them. He looked bland, matter-of-fact, too young. Tired crescent-moons looped under his eyes. Patients were often treated here if Western medicine miscarried, he said, but if acupuncture failed they would revert to pain-killing drugs.

I stood watching and ignorant, while one by one he turned the men into pin-cushions. They followed him with sultry, half-closed eyes. One man had goitre in the leg and stomach. Another, a wincing youth with long, aesthetic feet and hands, was suffering high blood pressure. They grunted and frowned as the needles went in. The doctor talked of them as if they were absent, and they seemed to conspire in this. They never spoke. The worst had a stone in his kidney – bigger than a soya bean, the doctor said. The man was grinning. He was in much pain. He would receive acupuncture for five days, to expand the ureter, said the doctor, but if the stone was still not released, they'd operate.

What were the chances of success, I asked?

The doctor pointed to a tray scattered with small dark stones. 'There.'

In the last bed lay an old peasant wearing pyjamas and a perforated cap. His toes had almost rotted away, as if from years in the paddy-fields. He stretched inert, but followed us with frightened eyes.

'This one had a blood circulation problem.' The doctor touched a needle into the man's groin. 'He was half paralysed. Western medicine couldn't do anything. We've treated him for twenty days, and he's nearly cured.'

[91]

I wondered if he were a hysteric. 'Why?'

But the doctor would not guess. He dealt in cures, not theories.

I slipped away and peered into the pharmacy. It was banked with wooden drawers for more than a thousand different herbs, and the air was pungent with hypnotic aromas, like a spice-bazaar.

A line of white-jacketed girls was fastidiously preparing mixtures for each patient, assigning them for immersion in tea or soup. As I watched them, I noticed a hole in the wall above their heads. Inside it, a pair of yellow incisor teeth had appeared. Nobody took any notice. The next moment a colossal rat came scuttling down the piping. The girl beneath it was mixing herbs with dainty exactitude. It plopped on to the counter and dashed away over her hands. I waited for her scream. But she did not emit a sound. She merely glanced up as if at some tiresome pet, then continued sorting herbs with fussy deliberations of her white fingers.

*   *   *

The only foreigner I met in Nanjing was a French businessman who said he was being shadowed by secret police. He regarded my belief that I was alone with the sarcastic pity of a school bully.

'You think you're not being followed? You do? You really do?' The fish-like bulging of his eyes implied that I was gullible beyond belief. 'Well, my friend, you may think you're not, but. . . .'

'I'm not a journalist.'

'Nor am I, but they follow me just the same. Always two of them. But the moment you notice them, they change.'

My silence, he knew, meant dissent. Perhaps they changed anyway, I thought. Perhaps they were his illusion. Or maybe businessmen were followed. We were on delicate ground. Either I was naïve or he was paranoid. I was thinking: this is how totalitarianism works – by creating dementia, a conviction of all-seeing authority. But its inhuman efficiency is an invention of its victims. While he was thinking (perhaps): this is how it works – by concealing its mechanisms so successfully from the innocent (and stupid) that they do not know what is happening to them.

I could not tell how frightened he was. His goitrous eyes swelled with a look of permanent alarm. He said: 'The rooms are all bugged too.'

'I don't talk to myself. . . .'

But he wasn't listening. He was filled by the evangelistic certainty that his own truth was universal. 'Nobody escapes these people, my friend. They are like highly intelligent children. Their short-term tactics are brilliant, but their overall strategy is nonsensical. In other words they're *mad*.' His mouth leered close against my ear. 'Last year they were executing people all over the province. Just to fulfil a quota. Several hundred a month. Some of them were shot on local television.'

This was true. In a national campaign against crime, men who would previously have received prison sentences had been executed instead. He went on: 'If you're in this country long enough you become unhinged. You start to think you're mad and they're sane.' The bulge and roll of his eyes was alarming now. 'You wonder: how can I be right and all the others wrong? Quarter of the world! But they are wrong.' He seized my arm. 'Never forget that. They *are* wrong! *All* of them. . . .'

'Yes, yes,' I said. In fact I knew that travellers were watched. A Party official had admitted to me privately that a newly formed branch of the tourist service had been set up specially for counter-espionage. A friend of his had been transferred to it straight from the security police.

So I inherited a little of the Frenchman's fear, and from time to time thereafter, whenever an agent would have been unavoidably exposed – plodding up a lonely Buddhist mountain, wandering through the forests of Yunnan – I would catch myself suddenly glancing round – and would see nobody.

Which only showed how clever they were.

Or that I was alone.

*　　　*　　　*

I gained permission to visit the city's top high school, and nobody pretended it was ordinary. The tuition and maintenance fees together cost two-thirds of an average worker's salary, and the entrance examination was gruelling.

I was met by an official with an anxious, kindly face. A little group of visitors had assembled. His introductory speech stressed the teaching of creativity and independence, parroting the current Party line. 'During the Cultural Revolution we had a wrong policy. The Gang of Four used Revolutionary slogans to lead students astray. Intellectuals were crushed. . . .' My attention strayed to the cluster of schoolgirls assigned to us as guides. They stood awkwardly together in hideous purple uniforms. The official's voice rose into formal harangue. '. . . When a nation wishes to develop, it needs intellectuals . . . the Cultural

Revolution, a tragic mistake . . . a necessary lesson. . . . Gang of Four . . . pernicious . . . mistakes. . . .'

We trooped into the schoolyard, and one of the fourteen-year-old girls came alongside me. I was not sure if she was there to guide me or to practise her English. I tested her covertly: 'Do you like your school uniform?'

'This?' Her expression crinkled into laughter. 'It's *terrible*. Don't you think?'

'Yes, it is.' I looked with relief into a brown, puppyish face, rather pretty. I said: 'Your principal talked about discussion groups. I wondered what you discussed.'

'Principal?' She grimaced comically. 'He's not our principal. He's just a yes-and-no man.'

'Propaganda?'

'Yes,' she giggled. 'There's not much political discussion any more. Luckily.'

On the tarmac in front of us several hundred lethargic little boys were drawn up in ranks for drill. They all moved at different times and speeds, listlessly. 'They're much better than usual,' the girl said. 'They must know you're here.'

From our guided tour it was hard to sense anything beyond a mind-crushing discipline, the Confucian respect for rote-learning and inherited wisdom. We were shown into classrooms whose fifty-odd students only raised their eyes from their books when ordered. The teachers' command was absolute. They were all expecting us. Model pupils delivered dead-sounding speeches: 'We think our school is lively and interesting. We all study very hard. . . .'

In this wall of formality, the only window was my guide. In her I discovered a vital but homesick girl, who found her teachers too didactic. She loved reading, she said, or just sitting alone in the dusty garden of osmanthus and pines by one of the classrooms. On Saturdays she rushed home to her parents – factory engineers living twenty miles outside the city. Her father was even smaller than she was, she said, and kept her doubled up with laughter all weekend.

As for the school, its occupants seemed frozen in pre-adolescence. Boys and girls were rigorously separated. One or two, she had heard, maintained covert friendships – a little kissing and passing of love-notes – but she was not sure. Her friends did not even talk about clothes fashions. Their worst crimes were chatting after lights-out in the dormitories (for which they were ejected into the corridors).

'What about the food?' I asked.

'Our food? It's horrible.'

'And the teachers?'

She wrinkled her nose.

Yet somehow, I thought, this system had fostered her. Her independence was more eloquent than the official's speech about nurturing it.

We wandered through the empty science-rooms and into a small biology museum lined with stuffed animals and marinated reptiles. We came to a standstill in front of a jar of chicks. They hung blind and long-dead in their amber. When the girl looked at them I thought she might joke: their nakedness was faintly ludicrous. But instead her face glazed into sadness, and she murmured: 'I feel pity for them.'

As she said this, I realised that I was still steeped in a conventional anxiety about Chinese cruelty, and that ever since entering the country I had unconsciously waited for some expression of tenderness, of empathy with pain. And now here it was, absurdly, expressed for bottled birds, and I felt a sharp, unexpected surge of warmth, as if somebody – either she or I – had been absolved. I wanted to hug her.

Instead, a few minutes later, I shook her hand in farewell, and partly because the phoney principal was hovering near us, added formally that I hoped she would build (as the slogans say) a new China. She seemed small and precarious for such construction, but perhaps the time was right.

*   *   *

Cockcrow Temple was built on an old execution-ground to appease the ghosts which howled there at night. During the Cultural Revolution, when fears of Soviet invasion were running high, its hill was quarried with passageways and rooms which still worm through it.

Now the labyrinth has been transformed into an amusement arcade. I found its iron doors painted to resemble wood, its tunnels wallpapered and decorated by moon-gates. Outside, a hoarding was advertising 'The Hindu Serpent Show'. Inside, where striplights shed their bleakness down miles of mildewed corridor, makeshift stalls were selling statuettes of the Buddha and the Venus de Milo. Further on spread a half-abandoned maze of slot-machines, miniature swings and see-saws where pampered single children dipped and swung before their nervous parents. Mao's vision had become a pinball alley.

I loitered in a gallery of distorting mirrors. Long salvoes of merriment were rolling out of the people fattened and elongated there. They were laughing at themselves as well as one another, at the ridiculousness of everything – and, of course, at the foreign devil, already obscenely tall and now turned spindly as a pine before being squashed by an adjacent mirror. In one cul-de-sac, crammed with fifty chairs, the audience for the Hindu Serpent Show sat in silence as a man introduced a snake into his mouth and drew it through his nostrils. On the stroke of every hour an androgynous-looking youth, stripped to the waist, wrapped a python like a lifebelt round his hips and reclined sleepily in its coils. Oblivious of any audience, man and serpent seemed to collude together in a narcissistic dream, as sacks of other snakes – fangless cobras and water-snakes – were poured writhing over him, pullulated languidly across his chest and dropped on to the tunnel floor.

On the summit above, twenty Buddhist nuns, ousted during the Cultural Revolution, were contentedly back in place, their temple scattered with carpenters' benches where the smashed statues and lanterns were being reconstructed. Behind one altar, mothers were teaching their children to kneel before a scroll-painting of the Goddess of Mercy, touching the infants' fists together in prayer. With every obeisance a cloudless old nun struck a bronze bowl to elicit a haunting *gong-gong-gong*.

From this hill, before the warm air thickened into dusk, I gazed down on the white mirror of lake where the Song dynasty navies had trained. Three shaven-headed novices sat nearby, gazing too, and only stirred themselves at sunset. In the riddled rock under our feet the epicene youth would be reclining again on his mattress of serpents.

*   *   *

The bridge over the Yangtze, completed in 1968 after the Soviets had withdrawn technical aid, is a showpiece of Maoist achievement, glorified by statistics (a million tons of cement, 100,000 tons of steel) and still crowned with scrums of bullying stone soldiers and workers holding aloft the *Little Red Book*.

'Those are out of fashion,' a man told me, as if they were hem-lines. 'Some people want them destroyed, but they're our history now.'

Lurking in the great hall beneath the elevator tower we found a giant statue of Mao. 'There are hardly any of these left,' said the man.

All over the country, in town squares, factory halls and commune headquarters, the Great Helmsman has come crashing down, to be replaced by dancing-girls or rocks topped by stags and storks – or by resounding emptiness.

'Do you miss them?' I asked. I was trying to imagine all the churches of Europe vanishing at a stroke.

He countered: 'Wouldn't you miss it if every statue of your Queen disappeared?'

'There aren't any,' I said. 'Statues usually go up after the person's dead.'

He looked surprised, then laughed with a dry, nervous rattle. 'That's when ours come down.'

On Sunday morning I went to the city's Protestant church, which had been reopened three weeks before. A congregation of four hundred packed its grey-brick nave. The bobbed and horsetailed girls and white-shirted men looked like a flock of clerks and students, but the scarred heads of factory workers interspersed them. There was a sermon on the meaning of the Cross from a teacherly figure whose voice vanished to a whimper when the microphones failed. A woman behind me brought out a celebratory thermos of tea and started stuffing her baby's mouth with biscuits, and further along the pew two elderly ladies began massaging the temples of the old man in front, as if the sermon were too much for him.

My neighbour turned and whispered to me in English: 'The sermon concerns Eternal Life.' He was a priest from the local seminary, who had been educated in missionary school. I remember his face only as an Identikit of middle-aged benignity – although he asked me back to his office and a glass of boiling tea.

He poured out happy statistics at me. Since the end of the Cultural Revolution 3,500 churches had reopened, he said, and some 10,000 assembly points for worship. Every day, somewhere in China, two new churches were consecrated. Four hundred students attended his seminary; ninety had just graduated into the ministry. 'But we still have difficulty in retrieving the churches. They were taken away during the Cultural Revolution and used for schools, factories and even living quarters. Recovery takes a long time. . . .'

This freedom had returned at a price, I knew. The six million Chinese Christians, even Roman Catholics, had been forced to sever official ties with churches abroad. They must be Chinese first,

Christian second. Many of them, habituated to underground worship during the Cultural Revolution and distrustful of state-controlled religion, had continued in their 'home worship churches', stubbornly outside the law.

But these were not the priest's flock (or if they were, he did not say). His path ran delicately between State and conscience. 'I'm not a Party member, of course, but I think religion can be a healthy political factor, even' – he laughed – 'a Revolutionary factor. Almost a quarter of our seminarists don't come from Christian families at all, and a few are children of Party cadres.' His tone levelled into caution. 'That's made for difficulties, of course. Some parents hold to the doctrinaire theory of religion as the opium of the people, but soon they discover that their children's training has borne moral fruit. . . .'

I was wondering, as he spoke, about the nature of this Christianity. In the church that morning there had been no prayers at all, no personal disclosures to a listening God; only the education of lessons and sermon, and the rites of hymn-singing. What had happened, I wondered, to the sacred drama of grace and atonement? To conscious-ness of sin? And now my nagging disquiet about the Cultural Revolution erupted again. He was a priest, I thought, he would understand. Constantly, when talking with others, I had felt as if there were something self-evident, something simple, which I didn't realise. I sensed that my questions were subtly irrelevant to them, my Western preoccupation with suffering and conscience merely a measure of my isolation, a sign of my not understanding.

'That sudden persecution,' he said, ' – it was unthinkable to us. We couldn't understand it at all. The personality cult had something to do with it, and crowd psychology. . . .' His voice slowed down, as if he were reading something. 'The Gang of Four took advantage of the young people's devotedness, loyalty to . . . the leaders. . . . Everything was done in the name of Revolution, then the devil, the evil in man broke out. . . .'

He stopped. He had descended into this black well and drawn up only a clutter of Marxist and Christian shibboleths. I wondered what had happened in the seminary at that time to these quiet men with their drab suits and dutifulness? What of the porter we had passed on the stairs, and the Old Testament teacher with the deaf-aid walking in the garden?

'The young people,' he was saying, 'the Red Guards . . . were good people. They simply didn't know how to make revolution.

They wanted to create something . . . different. But I think they were manipulated.' He looked perplexed, apologetic. But he avoided the name of Mao Zedong – Mao the neo-emperor who had revived his political fortunes on the hero-worship of the young, on the fantasy of a society without authority (except himself): the paradise of an ailing mind.

The priest repeated: 'Yes, the Red Guards were good at heart. They were following an ideal.' Was he, I wondered, forgiving them for something?

Or perhaps he was comparing their puritan naïvety with the cynical tumult which followed. For after they were banished, the Revolution had weltered into a more squalid chaos, every faction dubbing itself more revolutionary than any other. The original issues had disappeared into crude power-struggles at every level – village, city, province – until nothing was left but anarchy and a gas of rhetoric.

The priest was saying: '. . . Most of the ordinary people didn't join in out of their own will. They were forced to do it. If they'd refused, they'd have been accused. . . .'

'I've heard about teachers being persecuted,' I said, 'but I can't imagine . . . in a place like this . . . by their own seminarists?' He was silent. 'Did they?'

'Not me personally. But some of the teachers were . . . badly abused.'

'Even here?'

'Even here.'

So his pupils, I thought, had turned out less Christian than Chinese. They had withdrawn, perhaps, into an ethos ancient in their history – a womb-world of submission to the group, a family obedience emanating out to the largest family of all, whose father was the emperor ruling by the Mandate of Heaven. Here, at worst, a person relinquished all responsibility, all self. His conscience was stillborn. To dissent was to defect from Nature, from the very order of things. Of everything in Europe which had nurtured the individual – ancient Greece and its Renaissance, Christianity, eighteenth-century humanism – only this infant incursion of the Bible had happened here, and even in the seminary it had not been enough.

Momentarily my head filled with savage, condescending notions. The Chinese (I raged mutely) knew cruelty and squalor enough in their hierarchy-ridden families, where wife-beating was common and equality unknown. Their massed millions made the individual expendable, almost valueless. Perhaps it was strange that any imaginative sympathy survived at all. . . .

'This sort of thing isn't peculiar to my country,' the priest said: he might have been thought-reading. 'Look at Germany, Russia. Of course those countries are not old civilisations like ours, but still. . . .'

Of course. I was wading into an ocean. He was listening patiently, but I could not assemble any coherent thoughts. I wanted to explain that it was not the presence of cruelty which surprised me, but some imbalance between obedience and mercy, the collapse of domestic compassion in the face of official demand, the refinements of torture practised against teachers and friends, the denunciation of parents – but I stumbled into inarticulacy. I was juggling only with my own values, not with theirs. I knew nothing.

But I said bluntly, insultingly: 'In Europe we sometimes think of the Chinese as cruel.'

I was speaking to his faith, separating off his nationality. It was clumsy, unforgivable. At that moment I saw myself in his eyes: a spoilt Westerner, sentimentally concerned about pain, favouring an incontinent sympathy above moral decision.

'Maybe in those years you might find people lacking pity,' the priest answered levelly. 'But with us the teaching of *ren* is very old – older, perhaps than anything similar in the West.' His voice held only a shadowy reproof. '*Ren* is the Confucian "loving kindness".'

'Yes, of course.' I clung to this, but knew that in 'loving kindness' he had given *ren* a Christian wholeness. (Perhaps he was feeling sorry for me.) But *ren* belonged to the cooler realm of charity and mutual benefit in a balanced social order.

We sat in silence for a moment. I felt embarrassed and vaguely miserable. But suddenly the priest laughed, as if unsure of himself. 'You have so many questions. I don't know how to answer them. They're very revealing. . . .'

His words trailed away as I stood up to go. I didn't know what had been revealed, except myself. But that was perhaps what he meant, and why he laughed.

I was bicycling through farmland ten miles east of the city when I saw the monuments standing in paddy-fields. They rose huge in their isolation. They were all that remained of a funerary avenue from a sixth-century dynasty – a commemorative column and a guardian chimera.

I crossed sodden rice-fields towards them. The neck and back of the chimera were welted in cracks, yet its strength remained stupendous. Above its winged body the head was hurled backward from its ballooning chest in a black gully of jaws and fangs, forked tongue lolling, roaring at the clouds.

But the column was curious. I waded along the field to inspect it, past a band of grinning peasant women. It rose from a base of wind-worn creatures, indecipherable now, and was capped by an inverted lotus-flower from which a lesser chimera bellowed. But in between base and crown – eerie, unforeseen – hung a fluted classical column.

Permutation of a permutation, its ancestry lay far back in a half-remembered Hellenism filtered overland from India – the India invaded by Alexander the Great – back beyond buried Greek cities in Afghanistan and Persia, and home to the wine-dark Aegean. But by now, of course, it was only a disfigured memory, a last, ghostly heir of ancient Athens come to rest here among the paddy-fields of eastern China. I examined it with a dim homesickness. I wanted to smooth my hands over it. But instead of Pentelic marble my fingers touched a putty-coloured limestone, riddled with fissures like a fungus. One side was still smeared red with a faded Revolutionary slogan; and the inscribed tablet and cushion-like capital crowning it were irretrievably strange.

I circled it uncertainly. Its effect – stumpy, isolated – was alien too. Yet I went on gazing at its Corinthian trunk from different distances and angles, trying to resolve my bewilderment at a familiar expression on a foreign face, and I experienced, as I left it, the faintest pang.

*　　　*　　　*

Weigi, an acquaintance in Beijing, was separated by his job from his wife and parents, and had asked me to visit them when I travelled south. So one evening, carrying his gift of clothes for them, I groped down a dark street in a district of shabby flat-blocks, and prepared myself for an evening of courtesies.

Weigi's parents lived in the kind of rooms by now familiar to me: bare-floored, crudely furnished, and stark with the signs of modest privilege – a television, a refrigerator. A huge, fragmentary family had assembled to meet me – children of absent aunts, wives of husbands still at work. I could not sort them all out. They massed across the sitting-room in a wavering crowd of hesitating hands and smiles and greetings, sabotaged by an undertow of yelling babies.

The old couple were formal and reticent. They had joined the Revolution from Nanjing in the mid-1940s, and had now entered a decent retirement, cushioned by six children. Of their two daughters-in-law, one was a pert-faced girl from Suzhou, a city famous for its women's beauty. Her delicately lashed eyes looked as if they had been surgically widened, and she chattered with steely brightness. But the second woman, Weigi's wife Hua, was extraordinary. Whereas the others were dressed in workaday shirts and trousers, she wore an evening dress, flamboyant white, and from her neck dangled a quartz pendant-watch. She was darkly imposing. She intentionally eclipsed them all. She seemed not to notice them. She clasped my hand and fixed me with a face not beautiful but oddly arresting: a feral power about the heavy slope of her cheeks and bow-shaped mouth. In another society she would have been a sexual predator. Here she emanated a black charge of frustration and contempt. She seized the parcel I had brought from her husband for his parents, pulled it open, then tossed it derisively on to a sofa. 'Just men's things.'

The old people had prepared a banquet for me – an extravagant spread of cold meats and dumplings which we ate with the prestige television blaring, and nobody watching it. I had always conceived the Chinese family as a stereotype of unity and closeness. But soon I realised that the war between mother-in-law and daughter-in-law was being waged in iron silences. Compared to the old couple – conservative peasants – Hua was the daughter of a once-discredited bourgeoisie: voluble, raw, overbearing.

The Suzhou girl was unorthodox too. She could scarcely bear the sight of her own three-year-old son – an electric urchin with a sprout of chimney-brush hair. 'I think he's mad. He never stops. Not even at night. I don't think he sleeps. He just wears me to death.' Her pretty face never smiled as he sprawled yelling across her knees. She pushed him away. He came back. She pushed him away again. 'Do you have a word for this in English?'

'Hyperactive, I think.'

She thought about this word and said softly 'Hypercti,' as if it held some solution.

'Hypercti! Hypercti!' the boy screamed. He dashed the chopsticks out of her hands. She pushed him away. He thrust a fist into her rice. She elbowed him back.

At last, frustrated beyond endurance, he reached into his split pants for an ultimate weapon, discovered his penis, plucked it out and waved it derisively round the table. For a few seconds everybody pretended not to notice. The old couple developed an important conversation together. The women's gaze shuddered into their laps, and the foreigner concentrated on his dumplings. The cabaret ended with a furious slap from the boy's mother – the first and last time that I saw a child hit in China – and a volley of laughter from Hua.

I turned tactfully away. On my other side sat a shrimpy thirteen-year-old girl with long, hoydenish legs and plaits, who promised to be beautiful. She wormed against me and started practising her English. Hua tried to shut her up but she only said loudly: 'I like *Weigi*. He's really nice.'

I asked: 'Is the little boy your brother?'

'No. I'm Yulong. My parents aren't here. I haven't got any brothers or sisters, and I'm glad.' She rotated her bony shoulders. 'It means I get all the love.'

The clichés of family unity were dropping dead about me – a mother who hated her son, a niece who despised her aunt, a domineering daughter-in-law. Almost everybody was competing for my attention. Hua tried to monopolise me with a sexual tyranny which seemed second nature to her. 'I'm a singer,' she said. 'I sing for factory workers. But I'm studying Western opera too.' Her head tilted back in a silent High C. 'You'll come to my home afterwards and I will sing for you.'

Her home, in this confused family, turned out to be that of an absent sister, a divorcee whose daughter was the skinny nymphet Yulong. It was still early when the three of us wandered there along a muddy lane. In their tenth-storey flat the signs of prerogative multiplied – a Hitachi cassette-player, an electric fan, an old Chinese-made piano, central heating – but aluminium chairs scattered the concrete floors, and when I mentioned hot water they laughed.

Over this eyrie presided Hua's mother. She had been half paralysed by a series of strokes a decade before, and she looked even older than her eighty-eight years. Her hand, when I took it, was a cold hook. Her hair was coiled in a grey pigtail, clipped to the back of her head by a huge iron paper-clip, and her nose sank so flat that its bridge completely vanished, and seemed to place her eyes on collision course. Almost immobile, she navigated the tiny rooms by premeditated shuffles, often clutching the shoulder of a daughter or granddaughter in front, and heaving one dead leg after her like a club.

'I can't grip,' she said, staring at her hand in disgust. 'I'm sorry. Often . . . often I can't speak either. There are days . . . when I can't say anything at all. My voice goes. But today I can . . . say things.' The fingers of her live hand circled her throat. 'I should talk Russian with you. I used to teach Russian in . . . in Harbin. But I can't speak it now. All those consonants . . . I can't express anything clearly any more. . . .'

She settled watchfully on the sofa, smoking out of a box of two hundred cigarettes, while Hua sat at the piano in her astonishing dress as if this were a concert hall. Her voice was so good, she said, that her academy teacher had hoped she might represent China at international festivals, and she had rehearsed six show arias for over a year. She longed to go abroad; she craved Western dresses and make-up, which she called the good things of life. But the factories had refused to release her.

She turned back the lid of the piano. 'Shall I play "I love you, China"?'

Her voice was a deep contralto: astonishingly strong and sure, harshly expressive, unlovely. It drowned the untuned piano and lingered sentimentally over selected phrases, with swooping portamenti. She sang on and on: Bach's 'Qui Sedes', the 'Habanera' from *Carmen*, Strauss's 'Zueignung'. After each one she would ask: 'You like it? Really? *Really?*' She was exultant that I knew these songs. And all the time her voice grew louder and fuller. She trilled at the bare wall in front of her as if a vast auditorium – or a division of factory workers – lay beyond. I wondered what the neighbours thought. And now the cramped bareness of the room and the crippled woman hunched in the dim light had ceased to exist for her. Her face was burning with self-love. She was creating a first-night audience, an ocean of idolaters applauding her arpeggios or legati, her shimmering white dress, her fierce, momentary, masculine beauty – a clapping Festspielhaus, a cheering Carnegie Hall, a whole La Scala. But her shoes on the pedals were caked with suburban mud; one of the piano ivories had gone dead, and her old mother was suddenly, uncontrollably laughing. She rocked up and down on the sofa with short, guttural, mocking coughs. 'When I laugh I can't stop . . . I don't know why.' She massaged her throat. '. . . I just can't stop.'

Hua took no notice. She launched into *Les Huguenots*. The nymphet came in from the bedroom looking wronged and defiant, and flung out again with a groan. The old woman's laughter guttered into coughing. The last coloratura bars of 'Nobles Seigneurs' rolled dreamily from Hua's lips, and for a few seconds, while the badly tuned piano notes survived her own, she went on gazing at the wall-plaster. Then: 'You liked it? *Really?* You really did?' She was darkly radiant, touching, preposterous. 'My husband hates my singing.'

The old woman spluttered like a firecracker.

Hua said: 'Do you want to see the clothes I'm going to sing in? You'll tell me what you think.' She vanished into the bedroom and reappeared with an olive-green jacket. 'I sing in this for the workers. What do you think?'

I said it was smart, a bit stiff perhaps.

'I hate it. I long to get rid of it. I want to dress as a woman!' She disappeared back into the bedroom.

I sat down by her mother, and in the sudden quiet we started to talk.

The old lady was bitter. Her parents had been educated people from Harbin University in Manchuria, she said. They'd spoken Russian, and she'd become a teacher. But Hua, she implied, had married into a family of village farmers, and that class – in post-Mao China – carried no dignity on the old lady's lips.

'Do you know what sort of clothes Weigi sent with you? Hua told me. Just men's clothes. Poor quality shirts. Cheap ones.' She cracked into laughter, then abruptly stopped. 'He sent things for his parents, but nothing for anyone else. I suppose he hasn't any money.'

Hua emerged from the bedroom in a black *qibao* garnished with a brooch of artificial pearls. 'How does it look?' She twisted her hips outrageously. Her fingers trickled over her breasts and down her thighs. Her raven hair and eyes shone above the black curves below. My own gaze was drawn irresistibly down to her broad hips and up again to her cheeks and mouth. 'You really like it? You do?'

Her mother went on ignoring her, trickling cigarette-ash on to the floor with the ceaseless tapping of her liver-spotted hand. Hua vanished again.

'I don't like living here,' the old woman said. 'Yulong is always weeping and complaining. I hate her.' The people she hated were many. Her eldest daughter had divorced, and this had rankled for years. It was proof that the world was rotting. 'Such things weren't done by my generation. That man still comes to visit me at the New Year Festival, I don't know why.' She stared bitterly at the window. 'I hate him.'

Most of the time she sat brooding in the narcotic halo of her smoke, gazing in front of her, but then she would suddenly turn to me and I would see a kaleidoscopic face of slyness, humour and cynicism. These expressions traversed it unpredictably, so that I lost confidence that I was reading them right, and I did not always understand why she laughed or why the ancient eyes – undivided in their plain of noseless flesh – should sometimes narrow into theatrical distrust. 'I hate Hua.' She lit a new cigarette from another barely started. 'She's got a pile of money but she never shares it.' She added: 'I shouldn't have had daughters.'

In 1938 during the Japanese invasion, she and her husband had retreated with the Guomindang to Chongqing, the temporary capital, and there she'd borne her children. 'My husband died when the youngest was three.'

'In an accident?'

'No, I think he was just tired out with so many children. I think he just gave up.'

'So you brought them up yourself?'

'It was very hard. Those times.'

'You must be proud of them.'

'No,' she said stubbornly, angrily. 'I'm not proud. They're all monkeys. Just a lot of monkeys. They've no education. None of them. They don't know a thing. And none of them is pretty.'

At this moment Hua reappeared in a wine-red velvet. 'Yes? No? What do you think?'

'Just monkeys,' the old woman said.

Hua spun round. She drew the cloth in tighter at the waist, letting her hips fall into languorous disequilibrium.

'My children keep going away. They're nearly all gone.' The old woman wedged her dwindling cigarette between the fingers of her dead hand, and pulled a sprig of dirty grapes out of her pocket. 'I had one son and five daughters, but two died in Chongqing as tiny girls. They all leave me on my own. And now Hua wants to leave me too. She wants to go to Beijing. . . .'

Hua was grimacing down at her dress. Its shimmer dissatisfied her. 'It spoils everything. Look, look!' She plucked at the material, setting off a rippling sheen. Once or twice she grasped my hand to emphasise some point. Our fingers twined. The old lady was stuffing grapes into her mouth. Hua said: 'Weigi doesn't care about my dresses. Sometimes he's like a peasant.'

'. . . She just wants to get away to Beijing,' the old woman said. 'A week after Weigi went she realised she was pregnant, so what does she do? She goes to the doctor and gets it aborted. She doesn't want to have a baby here. Not here.' She bolted down the last grapes. 'Not with her old mother.'

I was surprised when they asked me to stay the night with them. But the buses had stopped and it was starting to rain in light, scuttling gusts. Hua ushered me into the bedroom. 'You'll sleep here,' she said.

But nobody slept yet. I became the object of an obscure, half-conscious duel. On the dressing-table were Hua's music-sheets and cassette-recorder, on which she played me operatic arias. Her cultural isolation was formidable. She owned four classical cassettes, acquired at random: she had never heard of Callas or Sutherland.

Then Yulong barged into the room, and Hua flounced out. Yulong had changed into a black, bare-shouldered night-dress dotted with pink flowers and her hair was loosed down her back in a glossy torrent. She stretched out on my bed in delectation, coddling a Japanese cassette-player and a pair of earphones. She sang tunelessly to herself.

'Have I taken your bed?' I asked. 'Is this your room?'

'Yes,' she said resentfully. 'But it's Hua's now. It *used* to be mine.' She clipped her earphones gently over my head. I was surprised to hear a tinny Beethoven piano sonata. 'That's what I like,' she said. She edged closer to me, spreading her homework possessively over Hua's dressing-table, and opened an English exercise book. I read: 'Mary likes to go to lessons every week. . . .'

But now Hua was back. 'I'd like you to help me with my French diction.' She lowered the score of 'Clair de lune' on to my knee, displacing Yulong's book. 'Listen. Is this right? Listen:

> Votre âme est un paysage choisi
> Que vont charmants masques. . . .'

The words whispered and fluted through her pouts. 'We can't afford proper French tuition, you see. Weigi's so poor. We've been married seven years – and look!' She extended empty fingers. 'No ring! He can't even afford that. So poor, but always working. Even when he's here, he comes home late and it's work, work, work. We never talk. No time any more. Not any more. "Au calme clair de lune triste et beau. . . ."'

Before the evening was out she had metamorphosed twice more – first into a crimson ballgown and finally into an unbecoming mini-skirt in which she eventually went to bed. She could only have acquired such clothes in the privileged Friendship Stores, but there was no opportunity for her to wear them, except secretly. Hers, I felt, was the narcissism of the emotionally deprived, an enforcement of self.

[107]

I slept in the bedroom, alone, while the three women lay in the sitting-room on sofas and camp-beds. Outside, the rain steadied, thickened. I fell into dreams haunted by the wife of Mao's ex-president Liu Shaoqi: the Red Guards had attempted to break her by decking her out in the trappings of a grotesque femininity – a necklace of ping-pong balls. . . .

By dawn the verandas of the flat-blocks opposite were a commotion of hanging bird-cages and onions and suspended bedrolls violently swinging. Potted plants were rolling along the balustrades. I woke to rain and wind beating through the mosquito meshing of my window, its flimsy curtains billowing. When I peered into the sitting-room, only Yulong was awake; she lay indolently with her dress thrown up above her thighs, staring at the ceiling. Half an hour later Hua lumbered out of her camp-bed. The glow of the night before had gone. She looked heavy and ordinary.

The old woman was sitting at the piano. 'Years ago I had another piano,' she said, 'better than this one. I bought it by scraping together a few kwai from my salary over years. But it was smashed in the Cultural Revolution, so my children wasted money by buying me this one.' Her face had softened. She lifted her dead hand fruitlessly on to the keys. 'Wasted.'

For all I knew, she was proud of her children, or even loved them.

4. To the Nine-flower Mountain

My FAVOURITE CHINESE poet, Li Bai, was drowned in the Yangtze forty miles south-west of Nanjing while leaning drunkenly overboard trying to embrace a reflection of the moon. After hearing that his grave lay on the river bank near an obscure town named Caishiji, I had a sentimental desire to visit it, and from there to circle south a hundred miles to one of the loneliest of the Buddhist holy mountains.

By his contemporaries in eighth-century China, at the zenith of the Tang dynasty, Li Bai was regarded with superstitious wonder. He passed his life in vagabondage, shockingly free from the civic duties expected of educated men, and flung off the domestic bonds of four successive marriages in favour of concubines or solitude. His poetry is filled with the desolate mountains and waterfalls of his journeying. It is the poetry of darkness and of the spirit-voyage. When he was drunk – which was often – he composed at supernatural speed, and his startling shrillness of voice and the possessed glitter of his eyes only enhanced the spell which he cast on those who met him. They believed him an immortal banished from heaven.

I did not know if Caishiji was open to foreigners, and it seemed wiser not to ask. At the central bus depot in Nanjing I was turned away, but a garrulous young salesman adopted me in the small railway station outside the southern gate, bought me a ticket and followed me on to my train in mixed fascination and concern. He had taken my quest to heart. He, also, desired to locate the tomb of Li Bai, he announced, and ensconced himself delightedly in my carriage. His name was Jianming, he said, which meant 'Build the Splendour', but there was no telling what splendour this might be. Dressed in shorts and sandals, and carrying only what appeared to be a large washing-bag, he looked unheroically nomadic. He was meant to be visiting the regional offices of his firm – an electrical trading company from the coastal province of Fujian – but he waved all this into the air. He would go wherever I was going, he said. He would protect me. He grinned at me with ugly, boyish charm. His protruding lips and shelving brows turned him into early Peking Man. I was his new friend, he said.

Our train crept painfully up the Yangtze valley. The carriage was full of soldiers, wretchedly equipped – shapeless fatigues, plimsolls, no insignia but the red star on their caps. They looked infinitely expendable. After two hours we left them and took a series of bone-jangling buses over the paddy-fields towards Caishiji. The heat was intense. My companion negotiated our itinerary in complicated bouts of enquiry, while I sank into passivity.

I started to despair of finding Li Bai. Our buses degenerated into rotting hearses bursting with peasants spitting and retching out of the broken windows. I had a deepening sense of burning my boats. Whenever we trudged between bus-stops, my rucksack bowed me like a congenital hump. But Build-the-Splendour was thrilled. He had never been in these parts, he said. We were seeing life. It slowly dawned on me that he was as lost as I was. From time to time he would turn and beam at me with a mouthload of crooked teeth, and say: 'Only one more bus!'

But where was Li Bai? The drunkard seemed to be laughing at me. He was shifting about. Some said he was in one place, some in another. Ubiquitous but unspecified, he had returned to being a god.

But beyond Caishiji we left our last bus and entered a parkland where trees grew young from the pale soil, and a temple stood under hills. Far below us, barges were hooting on the Yangtze. When we peered into the temple, expecting to encounter the obese calm of the Buddha, we saw instead – stark on a scroll-painting – the vagabond-poet toasting the moon from a mountain-top (with a pretty girl and a picnic nearby). We went in. The whole temple was dedicated to him. In hall after statued hall he stood or lolled in earthy ecstasy, wine-cup in fist, his chin tufted defiantly by a Mephistophelean beard, glaring in furious challenge at the sky.

We climbed through galleries and into courts. Where was his tomb? The pilgrimage had become a stubborn point of honour now. I imagined him wilfully eluding me. We reached the apex of the enclosure, but found only a restaurant where two waitresses lay asleep in immodest postures, as if Li Bai had positioned them.

But behind the temple rose a steeper hill, where we circled up a stone stairway roaring with cicadas. The heat groaned and throbbed in my ears. The feeling that Li Bai was playing a practical joke intensified. Then the steps hoisted us into solitude, up to the summit under a blue tent of sky. I felt a light sense of triumph. The place was perfect: crowned with a tiny tumulus like the grave of a dwarf emperor. In front of it, an inscribed stone. The Yangtze rolling yellow beyond. Nobody there, but a few old men sunning themselves.

I asked Jianming to read out the inscription. He squatted in front of it and declaimed: '"Here lie the cap and clothes. . . ."' He stopped.

'What?'

'". . . the cap and clothes of the Tang poet Li Bai."'

'Just his clothes? A tomb for clothes?'

'Yes.'

Sweating and bewildered, I consulted the conclave of old men. Dimly I remembered that in the poet's final song he described himself faltering into death but leaving a part of himself behind:

> A garment that he hung upon the rocks
> when he wandered to the Islands of the East.

But was that all? And had he really died here?

Yes, said one of the patriarchs, he had been under arrest and died of grief on his way back to the capital. He had received pardon, said another, and just died of disease. But most of them repeated the time-honoured story that Li Bai had drowned in wine and the Yangtze while trying to cuddle the moon. His body had been disinterred at some unknown time and buried. . . . But they disagreed elaborately on where, or on how I might reach the place, and only concurred in evoking an inferno of five or six more bus-drives.

From far away down the slope near the river, rose the sound of shrill laughter.

*   *   *

Sometimes in offices and shops the foreigner is treated with exaggerated politeness and aplomb. But more often he is confronted by a Great Wall of lethargy, helplessness and dissimulation. In the larger hotels the desk-clerks yawn in a coma of earphones and cigarette smoke; and above the charming photographs on the identity badges of waitresses, the real faces are a rockery of sulks and scowls. Their lidless eyes have been invented for avoiding yours. Requests for service become guilty intrusions into the intimacies of shop assistants as they chatter together or slumber over novels. Private life has eaten into business life, reversing the unhappy Western trend. Amidst these inactivities the customer is an irrelevance, who must attract attention not by discreet coughs or murmurs, but by yelling. Then, as likely as not, he will be rebuffed by a trembling handwave, palm outwards, as if his face were being wiped off an aerial blackboard, or hear the mewing negative *mei you* – a leitmotiv of all his travels. Ever since Confucius's day, the service industries had been stigmatised as menial, uncreative.

But the foreigner's trials are nothing compared to those of Old-Hundred-Names, who is locked in daily battle with a bureaucracy steeped in vanity and obtuseness, from mandarin minister to the meanest assistant. He is forever a supplicant. When his face appears at ticket-office windows, the clerk may simply go away, or strike up conversation with a fellow-worker, as if the face were a bad dream. At his approach, government or Party officials clear a little space of authority around themselves – a silence, a pretence of other business, a symbolic interval – before bending their languid gaze on the worker or peasant, whose voice has dwindled unrecognisably.

Even in our obscure hotel, the barriers were not all down. It was almost night when we found it: the only pretentious one in town. By a veteran play-act – his eyes raised pleading to the dragon behind the reception-desk – Build-the-Splendour argued down our room's price by three-quarters.

'You wouldn't have paid 30 yuan?' he asked me in horror – it was equivalent to £6 – 'for only *two* beds? Just for *one* night? That's two weeks of my salary!' His face became a sunburst of grins at the thought of the money he'd saved me, then puckered into pity. 'You have to know how to work things!'

He was right, of course. I'd never been good at working things. Now he and I were allowed to share a bedroom but not a supper table. I sat in a banqueting-hall sterilised by tablecloths and kitsch paintings, and settled to a meal which cost an extravagant 5 kwai – while he vanished into another room and ate one for a twelfth as much. The only other diners were a group of army officers outlandishly splashed in medals, celebrating their return from the Vietnam front. They kept toasting one another with relief.

No, said my waitress, I could not eat in the common part of the restaurant. It was unorthodox. And no, there was no beer after seven o'clock, *mei you*, and no butter. . . .

Her refusals were delivered in the sweet, synthetic sing-song cultivated by urban women, but underneath glinted a hornet. Whenever she returned to the kitchens, I would hear her break into staccato running arguments, before emerging to refuse me something else with her lilting indifference. But I too did not see why she should be serving me a meal that cost three days of her salary, and I obliquely told her so.

She looked surprised. There weren't many other jobs around, she said. If only she'd got to university. . . . 'I didn't know it was going to be like this.'

'That what was going to be like what?'

'That after leaving school . . . that things . . . I can't say really.'

But I knew what she meant. Was this all there was? She belonged among millions of educated young, brought up with high promises – a legion which the undiversified economy could not gratify, now pursuing forlorn hopes through correspondence courses or radio universities, or simply lapsed into boredom. She was stuck, she said, probably for ever.

But back in the bedroom I found Jianming bursting with excitement. He exulted in everything: the curtains, the television, the sheets. He played like a child with the air-conditioning, twisting its knobs into a paradise of temperatures: he never realised it was broken. Out of deference to the carpets he even stopped spitting. He dashed into the bathroom and raced out again. 'There's cold *and* hot water!'

'Yes,' I said vaguely.

He thought I hadn't understood. 'There's *hot* water! Coming out of the tap!'

I joined in his crazed delight. He doused his head singing in the bathwater. 'I'm not used to this,' he shouted. 'I'm a poor man!'

He earned £13 a month. He described to me the room where he lived with his wife and baby for fifteen pence a week, circling his arms around a quarter of the modest bedroom. They shared a communal kitchen and a lavatory on the street. 'I'm not even a Party member.' He wrinkled his forehead comically. 'It's very bad now, the Party. It's gone right down. Nobody's interested in it.'

All his luggage consisted of a flannel, a bag of dried carrots, some electric batteries and the enamel mug full of tea-leaves from which he drank when he could find boiled water. Yet his shorts were immaculately pressed, his shirt lather-white, and he carried a sheaf of visiting-cards. His business was not important, however, now that he had met me, he said. He perched cross-legged on his bed. Wherever I planned to go, he would come too. And did I know about a curious kind of money called foreign exchange certificates? He could only buy a good television with such money. . . . .

I had been waiting for this. I asked bleakly: 'What about your office?' He was meant to be travelling to the provincial capital of Hefei north of the Yangtze. 'You can't just. . . .'

'I think I'll forget it.' His jumble of teeth settled into a steady grin. 'It doesn't matter. What was that Buddhist mountain you said you were going to?'

'Jiuhuashan. It's miles away. . . .'

'I'll come with you!' He slapped his shins in delight.

'But it's very quiet.' My voice sounded querulous, pleading. 'There are only monks. . . .'

'We can talk! Then we'll go to Wuxi and on to Suzhou!'

He was thrilled with this idea – with the adventure of it, with the distinction that a foreigner's company conferred, and with the spectacle of foreign exchange certificates materialising beyond. I imagined him remorselessly chattering and hawking through these tranquil places – Suzhou, a city of gardens – and I couldn't bear it. I told him that I needed to be alone, that I was of a sad and solitary disposition. I stared at the ceiling like an anchorite.

He said: 'I'll cheer you up!'

'But I may be weeks in Jiuhuashan,' I said perfidiously. I conjured days of study and dumb self-communings, lonely in gong-tormented monasteries, attendance at ceremonies dragging into the night. After a while he crawled dejectedly into his bed and turned out the light. I went on in the dark about the interminable rituals of Mahayana Buddhism, about the beauty of silence and contemplation, and about bad monastic food.

'I think I'll go to Hefei,' he said at last. 'The office needs me. . . .'

After a while he started to snore.

Our double-jointed bus bowled along crumbling verges and jack-knifed over rocks between a changing quilt of paddy-fields and lotus ponds and neat, bursting vegetable patches. The temperature had dipped to 90°F, but the humidity was stifling. Tall brick houses scattered behind their village walls in a tentative new prosperity, and the bus was filled with peasants wearing metal-strapped watches on their skinny wrists.

'They don't like people thinking they're poor. For one thing, they want to marry off their children well.' Jianming differed from them only in the bag he carried and by the pallor of his face. When they spoke, their exchange of news or greetings came in a harsh bellow of challenge and counter-challenge. 'Most of them are getting richer now. That's what the new agricultural policy's done.'

Jianming had turned sober this morning, and kept scanning the balconied and double-storeyed houses sprouting in the fields, their courtyards chaotic with haystacks, chickens, wandering goats. He said: 'Before, we all used to eat out of the same bowl, as we say, but that's changed now. So there's more poverty about too. . . .'

By mid-afternoon we had arrived in Wuhu, a town distinguished by little but its bird-brained name. Here Jianming was to go north to Hefei, and I south to Jiuhuashan, but the station was empty of buses. We were approached by a woman who looked as Morning-Sunshine might thirty years hence. The wrinkles on her face could have been touched in by some spiritless draughtsman as a convention of 'middle age'. 'You'll only get buses tomorrow at dawn,' she said. She wore no expression at all. She was cleaning out her ears with a matchstick. 'Come to my hotel.'

Jianming announced that he would inspect it on my behalf, and I was left sitting before a mounting audience of fascinated townspeople. They trickled through the doors and filled the seats in front of me. Then they banked up behind – standing two, three, four ranks deep, jostling for the best view – until they choked the whole building. But over the past weeks I had become inured to this relentless staring. Even in shops and offices I would turn to find layers of noses squashed at the glass behind me. Now the hoary faces came circling a foot or two from mine, as if examining the detail in a statue. When I affected to read, one man wordlessly lifted the book from my hands to inspect it. To some of them I was probably the first foreigner they had ever seen, and as they gazed I found myself marvelling at the enclosed conformity of this land – infinitely more impressive than its differences – now mirrored in the still, unblinking focus of the crowd. Their stare lingered down from my face and over my clothes, my shoes, my rucksack – not with the acquisitive glitter of the Arab but with a dull, hopeless disconnection, as they might stare at fish.

What were they seeing? I rediscovered myself in their eyes. I became grotesquely gangling, with skin the colour of their grey rock and a proboscis of a nose. My hair flared obscenely pale around aggressively protuberant features, and my eyes, instead of being modestly almond-shaped and external like theirs, were burrowed inexplicably into my temples like frosted saucers.

Later, after returning from the countryside to the tourist sites and Friendship Stores of a large city, I would encounter my own kind with an inkling of the shock which they administered to the Chinese. Opulence turned us uglier than poverty could. To this trim, slender, homogeneous people we could seem a waxwork collection of coarse and distorted variety. Barbarically hairy, often luridly fat or tall, and made-up as if life were a Beijing opera, we passed our time buying and spending in a disordered display of individual grossness. We sweated under a stupefying hodgepodge of gear and hairstyles. We went in for unseemly shows of affection, and were even seen publicly to kiss our big-breasted girls with their eerie light eyes. Many of us seemed like giants or albinos. And a few were disturbingly, untouchably beautiful.

Sometimes, so unrelenting is the crowd's stare, that the foreign devil's face glazes out of focus, unable to meet the intrusion. He ceases to see anything at all. Perhaps he remains very still for long minutes in the hope that the spectators will tire – and slowly they do. But should he pull out a notebook, for instance, or merely blow his ant-eater nose, the interest around him will instantly reintensify, and the entertainment start all over again.

It may also happen that the foreign devil, if he is resilient, will look up and smile – and hesitantly, in the confusion of surrounding faces, there dawns the realisation that the creature is reciprocal. At first, when he speaks, nobody responds, because he must surely have uttered something incomprehensibly foreign. Then a nervous epidemic of smiling breaks out and trickles through the whole crowd. Somebody asks a tentative question. . . .

But now Build-the-Splendour was elbowing self-importantly through the throng to take me away.

The hotel turned out to be little more than a *hutong* cottage – a hostel of the kind he knew well, the kind foreigners never see. Its six iron beds were matted in straw and pavilioned with discoloured mosquito nets on wonky bamboo frames. They cost tenpence a night. Nearby, a minute sitting-room was stacked with green bananas. On its mud-brick walls hung two coy pin-ups for the exclusively male clientele, and in the dial of the wall-clock a Longevity God mounted guard against Time.

There was nothing to do. The window in front of us gave on to our local latrine: a row of holes mounded with excrement. The window behind overlooked the station yard where a burnt-out bus was being broken up in a thunder of explosions and hammerings. Momentarily I was tempted to go out and explore the drabness of Wuhu, but instead I lay on my bed in torpor and listened to Jianming chattering about money in his clipped Fujian accent. The hotel had excited the worst in him. He did not so much spit as let the spittle dribble from his mouth on to the floor – the last refinement, I supposed, before giving up altogether. He stopped smoking only to dunk his dried carrots in boiling tea, chomp them like a horse and spew them genially out. He became obsessed by security. Even his bag was closed by a miniature padlock, and every time he went out he alerted me to watch our paltry possessions.

I lapsed in and out of sleep. The stench of the latrines rose sickeningly in the still dusk. Once I woke to see two monkey-masks waving at me beyond the window-bars. Children's voices fluted excitedly. Next moment the masks were shoved back in astonishment from faces so monkey-like that they need scarcely have disguised themselves. They slipped giggling away.

We ate a supper of rice and beans with the woman's family – gnarled ex-peasants, who spoke in thick, shy monosyllables (the l's and sh's in this region almost disappear) and settled down at dark to television. All over our quarter of town the night was filled by white-lit squares of window where every family sat cloistered at its flickering loophole on the outer world.

Jianming grew bored. Doggedly he had returned to the idea of accompanying me to Jiuhuashan and all over eastern China. I was now his great friend, he said, we were so happy together, weren't we. Would I come to Fujian? His flat would be mine. His wife and baby would love me. As he sat grinning on his bed, his ugly face lit with an odd, bright sweetness, I felt the traveller's guilt at collecting incompatible friends, companions of circumstance. Remorsefully I sought for ways of giving him money, but he refused almost in horror. 'I'll be anxious you won't have enough to get you back to England,' he said. He was unsure where England was.

He had grown concerned over my sad and solitary disposition. Every time I started to do anything he would leap up shouting 'Don't worry!' and forestall me. Why was I so solitary, he asked, there must be a reason? Were things sad back in England, in my home?

My silence – the humidity had stifled me – seemed to confirm this insight. 'Is it your wife?' His Neanderthal face was crossed by a sudden, troubled gentleness. He breathed out: 'Your wife has left you. . . .'

Shamelessly I allowed this fantasy to develop, until my will for solitude had attained a bogus dignity. As his commiserations proliferated, I even began to believe in my faithless wife a little, and became quite depressed over her.

By the time I crawled into bed the spectre of his dogging me round China had faded. His voice drifted into silence. The light beyond the barred window shed its black grid across the room, and for a long time I lay guiltily relieved in a bright cage of mosquito-netting. Hours later I woke to find Jianming pulling the net's folds more tightly round me. 'The gnats have got bad,' he said. 'Go back to sleep.'

Even next morning, until the minute before our buses left, he was hoping to accompany me. 'I'm afraid for you,' he said, climbing into my bus after me. 'You eat so little. . . . If you don't eat, your spirit will go down. And there are many thieves in China.' His glance fidgeted round the packed bus. 'You must watch your rucksack . . . I want to come to Jiuhuashan with you. . . . After you and your wife have been separated a while, she'll miss you . . . you'll see.' He was beaming at me with his odd, ugly sweetness. I felt wretched. 'You'll come together again. I'm sure.'

The next moment the bus had started, Jianming was gone, and I was left with the vision of my wife, ghost of a ghost, and the long road to the mountains.

We went through light rain along the flood valley of the Yangtze. Its waters stretched in a mud-brown prairie beside us, as passive as the mud-coloured sky. Along its banks a few cormorant fishermen had hoisted tarpaulins and were sheltering companionably with their birds. Troops of farmers were trudging across the landscape under black umbrellas, and here and there a buffalo-team was tearing the inundated paddy-fields with invisible furrows, men and beasts together floundering knee-deep in silt.

My bus was packed by a drab, vociferous peasantry. In the villages the only colours belonged to family-planning advertisements. A solitary girl was held aloft by garishly painted parents, circled in doves and blazoned: 'A single lovely child in good health.' The peasants' commercial acumen was canvassed by 'One is better quality', and an only boy hurled a toy aeroplane into the future, 'That the Motherland may be strong and flourish.'

'Those advertisements?' The bus-driver guffawed. 'Nobody takes much notice of them out here. It pays to have children now, even if you're fined. Me, I've got eight!' He lifted splayed fingers from the steering-wheel. 'Eight! That's the new agricultural system for you! It's everybody for himself now. I'm a real criminal!'

Every few miles a ghastly collage of crashed trucks littered the roadside, abandoned as they had ended, in eerie still life. Lorries had overturned inexplicably on flat, dead-straight tarmac; buses were tilted vertiginously down banks or had plunged into rice-fields and sunk to their windows.

On the outskirts of one village a silent crowd was gathered. Strings of firecrackers stammered over the road as we approached, and a procession started. In front tramped a double file of women carrying horizontal poles fluttering with prayer-flags, followed by a throng of others in the white caps of mourning. A little band of horns and gongs marched cacophanously after them, and finally, lugged by a gang of peasants in a truss of bamboo poles, a red-painted coffin – an assemblage of planks lashed with ropes – came swaying and creaking along the road. Harnessed to it in front, his frail chest straining at the thongs as if he were pulling it alone, went the tiny widower. He advanced in a terrible, speechless tension. His eyes were screwed into supplicating dots, while his hands held out the tablet of the dead before him in a harrowed plea that its name be seen and read.

The majority of the villagers stayed sombrely behind, and let the procession go. None of them spoke. Nobody in the cortège gave us a glance – only stared at the road in front of them. But in our bus the people stood up grinning and laughing, craning forward, pointing. Even when we entered the silenced village, their mirth and chatter went on. The corpse, after all, was not one of their own; and grief was an event.

Soon afterwards we were climbing into hills, and the tarmac road petered to mud. One by one the passengers clambered off the bus with their carrying-poles and white ducks complaining in panniers. We pushed into mountains where the bamboo forests rolled in silken floods from the valley-clefts, and streams and miniature waterfalls shone out of their ferns. Soon we were turning on ourselves in a blinding whiteness of cloud. Everything was lopped or faded. The landscape had taken on the fragility of a scroll-painting. Stone-paved stairways climbed like Jacob's ladder into empty sky. Bridges spanning gulleys never reached the other side, but looped into nothing as if the artist had forgotten them.

At last we reached a dead-end. I climbed out into thin, cool air. I was among the peaks of Jiuhuashan, one of the four holy mountains of

Buddhism, but I could scarcely glimpse twenty yards in front of me. I passed under a ceremonial gate and followed a stream along a track. Once or twice I heard voices close by, but could see nobody. I fumbled down an alley of booths rigged up with straw matting and bamboo. They were selling pilgrim souvenirs: incense-burners, feather fans, figurines of the Goddess of Mercy. But most were empty, and the pilgrims had become faint noises in the whiteness: coughing, retching, sloshing feet.

At the last moment I stumbled on an enormous monastery. Its roofs reared into cloud and its whitewashed walls, pierced by fortress windows, were obscured by mist at either end. The moment I entered it I realised that the Red Guards had reached even here. In its first hall, where the future Buddha lolled like a bumptious gold baby, the monks were painfully reduplicating their smashed altar panels and images at carpenters' benches.

This tottering giant of a sanctuary, built for hundreds, now housed only fifty. Inside its armour of brick and stone, the wooden innards were rotting and collapsing on one another in a greyed confusion of stairs and passageways. A medieval sombreness pervaded it. Across its central hall, half open to the sky, rain-clouds and incense swirled together. The consoles of its galleries leered with painted heroines and monkey-kings, and great iron cauldrons simmered with the ash of joss-sticks. The monks who inhabited this court went dourly in grey smocks and knee-length leggings. But above it, three stairways climbed to the inner hall, and here they could be glimpsed kneeling in carmine silks to the sound of bells and gongs, or drifting like goldfish exotically through the incense.

But when I slipped inside, the illusion disintegrated. Wooden pillars reared through the dusk to a roof which fired down a salvo of gaudy lanterns. Old chairs and cushions were stacked against fissured walls. Electric bulbs and candle-flame mingled, and the lotus-flower throne of the Buddha winked with fairy lights.

But the tutelary spirit of Jiuhuashan is not the Buddha. The mountain is dedicated instead to Titsang, the saviour-king of Hell, who can spring apart the infernal gates with a touch of his wand; and pilgrims still come in autumn to hear masses for the souls of their dead. A mass would be sung in two nights' time, said the monk who showed me to my cell; it had been ordered by a father for his dead son. He brought me an enamel basin, and a plastic tub for bathing in. The son's soul was trapped in the underworld, he said.

I lay awake in the night, incarcerated by empty ranges of cells. Across the rafters and beneath the floorboards invisible freeways pattered with rats. Once or twice, in the dead of night, there sounded an inexplicable crash, as if they had gnawed through the last retaining joist of some stair or distant chamber. Then silence. Long before dawn I woke to the faint chanting of the monks, muffled by layers of rooms between, and wandered out into the dampness of the refectory garden. Somewhere across the tree-darkened slopes, the air was touched by an irregular chiming and throbbing, as the whole mountain woke to worship with bells and drums. Along the edge of the garden, through the dripping silence of the trees, a firefly hovered.

I ate breakfast at dawn with a young monk in a half-disused hall. He had been assigned to look after me, but appeared almost a child. He stood no more than four and a half feet tall, and his shaven scalp was mottled with ringworm scars.

'Where is your home?' I asked.

'I don't have a home now.' He spoke with childish pedantry. 'My home is here.'

'But your parents, I mean?'

'They lived a long way away. In this province, but a long way away. I never see them.' He was perfectly composed, yet shy, girlish. The loudest noise he made was the sharp, sucking intake of rice from the bowl held at his lips. 'I changed my name when I became a monk. My teacher gave me another name. My parents never even knew it.'

'Were your parents believers?' I, too, was now talking of them in the past. 'Is that why you are here?'

'Yes. I'd wanted to be a monk since I was a boy.'

I asked hesitantly: 'Why?' (He seemed no more than a boy now.)

He looked bemused by the question, and lowered his gaze to the table. It was as if nobody, including himself, had ever asked this before. Then he answered with self-wonder: 'I don't know. I had five elder brothers and none of them wanted to be monks.' He started to smile – either at the foreigner's strange questions or at some undisclosable memory. His family, I guessed, were peasants, and sometimes his slurred Anhui accent was impenetrable to me. 'I was different from the rest.'

'Do you miss them?'

'No.' His voice was almost inaudible now, his gaze still on the table. I had the feeling of somebody trying to talk underwater. 'It's not lonely here. There are eight young monks, and more will come, I'm sure.

More will come.' One day he might be transferred to another monastery, he said, but he did not think so. He expected to stay here all his life. It was not a hard regimen. He rose for an hour and a half of prayer at four o'clock in the morning, then settled to study alone and to prepare for the death-mass, perhaps. Then there would be meditation, which he enjoyed most of all. Simply the stillness of it, he said, the self-emptying. He could not quite explain.

'And you'll never want to marry?'

'No, no!' He cut the air back and forth with his childish hands. 'That won't do! You can't! When we walk, you know, we go with our eyes down,' – he tilted his fingers over his eyelids – 'no looking left or right. Even when we're standing, we must hold our eyes down. That way we avoid seeing things.'

His face relapsed into peace. I tried to picture him on these mountain tracks, staring at his own feet, the path, year after year. I was still forming other questions when he stood up and said formally: 'I'm sorry if you didn't eat well. We're poor here. Just poor monks.'

I had given an impression of privilege, I supposed, with my talk of marriage and moving from place to place – everything he wouldn't know. And now he was looking at my bowl of rice porridge, still untouched beside a mangled steamed bun. He took them away.

Outside, in the dawn, the clouds had momentarily lifted and the peaks emerged in a tree-softened audience above me, scattered with shrines. I wandered them all day, climbing through the rustle of rain by stone stairs which wended among exotic undergrowth. They were trodden only by groups of pilgrims and a few staid-looking holidaymakers with sticks.

Much of the time I walked in blinding rain-cloud, with my eyes fixed monkishly on the track under my feet. Delicate pink mushrooms bloomed between the steps. Ferns and blue vetch appeared. Above them, the bamboo groves which had so haunted Chinese artists lurched in and out of whiteness: a painterly antithesis of segmented trunks and hazy foliage.

The mountain shrines reeked of Hell and salvation. Frescoes of the afterlife multiplied, and figures of the chthonian saviour Titsang riding his tiger. In one monastery where his eighth-century reincarnation lay entombed, seven thousand pilgrims had worshipped every day as recently as the 1930s. The numbers have shrivelled now – it is impossible to estimate the population of believers in China – but they were trickling piously through, and a jolly monk was swinging a chained log against a huge bell to celebrate their prayers. *Bong!* went the bell for a dedicatory candle, *Bong!* for some mandarin oranges offered to Titsang, *Bong!* for a coin from the foreigner: and as the little notes of money piled up and the joss-sticks became a copse, then a forest – *Bong! Bong! Bong!*

In the innermost shrine a monk was guarding a seated statue in semi-darkness. It squatted in a glass box and appeared cast in reddish bronze, but its arms curled disturbingly in front of it and its pigeon chest was a heaped deformity. The monk thrust a torch into my hands. 'There! Take a good look! Go round the back!' The weak light travelled over a hunch back, a skull whose eyes were closed. It was as if all the bones had collapsed inward, suffocating the chest. I realised that it was not a statue at all. It was a mummified and lacquered body: a Ming dynasty centenarian who had died in the lotus position, said the monk. I asked: 'What happened to him in the Cultural Revolution?'

'Oh, *he* was all right.' The monk sounded almost resentful. '*He* was the only one who stayed! The rest of us had to go away and work in the fields.'

Worship on the mountain is tinged with sadness and urgency. It is the lodestar of the bereaved. Its frescoes of Hell show tortures more refined than those of Hinduism (from which they spring), a terror more absolute. In these Chinese Hells, all is bureaucratic. Its countless zones and departments – its eighteen fire-encircled cities, its 180 purgatories and maze of minor dungeons – are staffed by a bewildering civil service of judges, hangmen, administrative drudges and junior demons. The untutored peasant, unsure where his loved one is being arraigned or tortured, must seek out priestly guidance as to which of the shadowy personnel he should bribe with prayers and offerings.

In many a detailed painting these nightmare mandarins sit behind desks heaped with scrolls and fatal registers. As in frescoes of the Christian afterlife, the souls of the redeemed look rather bored; they bathe sedately in the pools of the Goddess of Mercy. But below them, a frenzy of activity is going on, as the damned depart into a region of efficiently administered horror. An echelon of green-faced devils, bald but for random tufts of flame-red hair, turns them in boiling vats, drags out their tongues with red-hot tongs or saws them meticulously in two. Droves of other departed souls, the pathetic *er-kuei* – 'hungry spirits' – rove about unblessed in danger of becoming professional demons themselves. And in the deepest Hell of all, criminals are converted into animals. Fur or scales spread irreparably over terrified limbs, while heads and torsos vanish wholesale into wandering herds of cattle.

When I mentioned all this retribution to the young monk at supper, he looked unmoved. He simply said: 'Yes, that is what happens.'

He was armoured by piety. Before each meal he would join his fingertips delicately in prayer, then tuck in. He would finish four bowls of rice in a ravenous twirl of chopsticks, together with bamboo-shoots, beancurd or cabbage. He had grown used to me by now. Sometimes he would halt his headlong feast and ply me with questions. How long did my government let me travel for? How often did the factory workers eat in Britain? And once, when I asked about the Cultural Revolution, he got up and ran his finger for yards along the carved and latticed wall of our refectory, where I saw that all the miniature gods and bodhisattvas had been diligently decapitated.

'Do you have these gods in England? No?' This left him unperturbed. 'Well, they came to us from India, so perhaps they aren't in the West.' Then he added: 'Do you hold feasts for the lost dead? Do you have a hell?'

In fact, as early as the eighth century, the Buddhist mass for the dead absorbed many features from an eastward-drifting Christianity; and Titsang descended Christ-like into Hell for the redemption of the damned.

At sunset, on my last night in the monastery, the death-mass began in an aura of magic. More than thirty monks knelt on high cushions in the meditation hall. Above their black robes and capes of crimson silk, the bowed and shaven heads lifted from time to time with closed eyes to show timeless, tired faces. An elder monk intoned in a weak, faraway voice. There came a thud and tap of drums, the clink of chimes and miniature cymbals. Then a muttered, conversational chant arose, like the murmuring of bees in a sleepy hive: monks gossiping with the Eternal.

I settled in the shadow of a pillar, and tried to glimpse the man who had ordered this strangeness for his dead son. But at first I could see only a cluster of pilgrims and nuns – peasant girls with cropped hair, in coarse boots. Above the central altar, through parted curtains, the eyelids of the Sakyamuni Buddha opened only in livid slits. A neon striplight cut across his chest.

Slowly the chanting filled and strengthened. The percussive clack and chime of semantra and gongs pervaded it less with music than with mystical punctuation-marks, reshaping time. Drums and cymbals were joined by the reverberation of an iron bowl, and by the plunk of drumsticks on a block of resonant wood, which showed raw from this endless abrasion.

After a while the monks reassembled in a barn-like hall. All along one wall a trellis of inscribed names was plastered – ancestral tablets reproduced over nine generations. Beneath it, the narrow altar was lined with a sacrificial banquet. Piles of chopsticks alternated with bowls of rice and fried vegetables, dishes of fatty noodles and once – for some bibulous ancestor – a glass of liqueur.

The monks' chanting rose again. Their serried pates and spectacles shifted and gleamed like owls' heads in the candle-light. Now I noticed that the father of the dead was standing amongst them – a bewildered old man in a peasant jacket. Over his skull the skin looked stretched to splitting, and the flesh of his face had gathered unnaturally at the mouth, which was crunched forward in an expression of battered enduring. Beside him stood a dark, intense factory worker, the dead man's brother, and a small orphan son in a green tracksuit, whose eyes were shining with tears. From time to time they were ushered forward to prostrate themselves, their heads hammering the ground again and again. None of them lifted his eyes. In that flickering owl-light the massed presence of their ancestors was too formidable – all the past banked up and staring from the wall, each generation more ancient and prestigious than the last.

Back in the meditation hall, five tables had been laid lengthwise to the altar. Here the monks ensconced themselves among lanterns, prayer-flags, bowls, urns – all the furniture of redemption – mingled with teacups and plastic thermoses. High at the end of each table, a senior monk was enthroned cross-legged like a living Buddha. On his head an acolyte had placed a crown – a fantastical burst of jewels and bobbles, dripping white ribbons.

The abbot sang alone in their centre. His words emanated from a face quite empty; its features might have been smudged into plaster by thumb. Soon the incantations were whining back and forth among the five elders, each phrase ending in a haunted grace-note. Under the knocking of semantra, a cloud of gongs and cymbals stirred. The mourners' faces became gaunt with a heartbreaking apprehension. The lament for lost souls was filling the air around them. In grief or bewilderment, the small boy's tears were rolling down his cheeks. From where they sat, the altar curtains amputated the Buddha to a pair of cupped and empty hands.

But the monks seemed casually at home with salvation, as if their chant possessed a sorcery divorced from them. Between the sutras they picked their teeth and yawned, and from time to time an acolyte would go the rounds with a replenishing teapot. The five living Buddhas drank with discreet ceremonial, curling their sleeved left arms around their cups in token of invisibility (or to keep the tea warm). Others would break off their singing and snap out 'More, more!' or 'Fill it up! Right up!' until this ritual seemed inseparable from the redemption of the dead.

To the mourners, perhaps, the monks' burping and drinking confirmed their occult status. The three were strained forward pitifully on their bench. The candle-light cut their faces with identical streaks. Where was their son, their father, now? Into which of the flame-walled cities had he gone? Was he already *er-kuei*, one of the hungry ghosts? They did not know. Perhaps nobody knew.

But now something had stirred the sleepy hive. The chorus was quickening and rising. The gongs and bells agitated under the tap of clappers. The nuns flung themselves forward on their faces, and the chanting elders lifted their stave-heads against their mouths like microphones. Suddenly everybody rose to his feet in a burst of music and a shout of triumph went up.

Then silence. Then the tap of a drum: dry, expectant. Once only the abbot struck the table with a sharp report of wood on wood. And the gates of Hell opened.

A faint smile had crept over the old father's face. The monks had mystically entered the infernal regions, and the worst was over. The abbot touched together little bells – one in either hand – and the rest followed him, scraping and clinking between silences, as if calling to the dead. Now they were preparing to succour the spirits below, 'to help all creation across the sea of pain'. The old man creaked to his feet and left little piles of money at the foot of each table. The boy started swinging his legs, bored. Only the dark brother seemed unchanged, and went on focusing his praying hands which were thrust forward tensely, high up from his chest.

For two more hours the monks sang and sipped tea and hastened the passage of souls over the ocean of fire. In intricate mime the elders' fingers recreated the tortures of the damned, but did so in graceful distortions, like the *mudra*s of Indian dance, so that all pain seemed cauterised. By the flick of three fingers, in an absent-minded blessing, they sprinkled the waters of compassion from the urns of the goddess

Guanyin, the Madonna of the East, and fed the hungry mouths out of the Buddha's bowl by stroking and arranging rice-grains on a paten. It was a long, pictorial act of mercy, ending in stillness, the abbot fingering away a circlet of green beads, with his eyes closed.

Only as the monks tramped out into the night, grinning and spitting, did they seem to revert to what they had always been – a flock of gap-toothed peasants. The ancestral charts were torn from the walls without ceremony and carried into an outer court where the old man was setting off celebratory firecrackers. There they were set ablaze with heaps of blank scrolls – symbolic money for the dead. They flared and faded with the monks' chanting, died away to whitened heaps.

Slowly everyone dispersed, and the courtyard's giant drum and bell put the monastery to sleep with a lonely requiem. As he swung his log against the bell, the solitary monk interspersed its deep, tremendous chimes with a sung counterpoint of plangent sadness, over and over. Out in the courtyard the ancestral names had shrunk to a layer of ashes, and were starting to blow away in the wind.

*   *   *

All afternoon the train dragged eastward along the Yangtze, passing through Nanjing and into a marshy littoral where the imperial Grand Canal moved between ancient towns and shallow lakes. This land is among the richest in China, yielding a threefold crop of rice and wheat, and the houses of the richer peasants were growing up piecemeal as money allowed, awaiting a second storey here, an extension there, in courtyards idle with goats.

My carriage was flooded by factory workers. They were heading, as I was, for the canal-cities of Wuxi and Suzhou, which had mushroomed with modern industry. They shouted their news at one another in slurred accents and plied me with tea and cigarettes. At dusk they fell snoringly asleep with their jackets torn open and their lips curled back from tobacco-stained gums.

A fat sound-recordist from Anhui television squeezed bumptiously into the seat opposite me. He wanted to know all about England, he said, and this meant prices. How much did I earn? How much were televisions? How much was a car? Did I have one? His hands fidgeted plumply with his digital watch, then reached out to finger my shirt. 'Nylon?'

'Yes.'

'Not expensive.'

'No.'

He was trying to place me. What had I paid for my hotel rooms here? How much had the monks asked for food? How much did my wife earn? When I told him that a London hotel could cost £300 a night, I watched the figure spiralling behind his eyes in mute torture. He wanted that room. What did the peasants earn in England? We passed a pig. How much were British pigs?

Whenever I said 'I can't remember', his eyes screwed up in disbelief. What was I concealing? How could I have forgotten the cost of my second-hand refrigerator? He was recreating England from this collage of data, and I saw it reassembling in his head in a surrealist forest of high-rental *hutong* cottages and car-driving peasants, inter-mingled by rather cheap pigs.

He asked: 'Do you like discos?'

'Not much.'

'*No? I love* them.'

I was confusing him. Why, if I came from the rich, disco-ridden West, was I wandering about China in an old nylon shirt?

My head kept dropping tiredly onto my chest, but he continued relentlessly, occasionally hitting my knee to regain attention. I fell asleep, still hearing: 'How much. . . ? And how much. . . ?'

Hours later I woke up to find him gone. Outside, in the glare of platform lights, a man was dangling between the shoulders of two others. His bandaged head and chest were covered in blood, and his face held a confused, animal fear. An industrial accident, thought the men beside me: accidents seep into the press only selectively, or not at all. The next moment the train was driving away from him into the night.

I drew back my bedroom curtain from an artist's distilment of China. Before me the island-scattered Lake Tai receded into paling tints of mist. It was absolutely still. There was no horizon. I might have been standing on the edge of one of those Song ink-sketches which relinquish three-quarters of their landscape to the silken texture of the scroll. A world of haze. A garden extended to the shore in pools and pavilions, whose roofs lifted out of trees. The covered walks, and the hump-back bridges between them, were empty. Even overhead, the blue was overcast with a continuous stain of formless cloud, like the graded wash which fills the painter's sky with vapour. A few sampans slept suspended in nothingness, where the wrinkles on the lake's surface had blurred away.

I opened my window, and heard the stutter of the sampans. They were motorised. Joggers appeared on the concrete car-park in front of the hotel, one of them smoking as he ran. A bus hooted. And the morning broke in.

But all day these mirages recurred. Off a further shore a fleet of more than a hundred junks was following shoals of the translucent ice-fish. Against the mountains the bamboo-framed sails glided in a decorative swarm: they might have rocked into three dimensions off a willow pattern plate. Even the Grand Canal, coiled among the suburbs of Wuxi, unfurled into painterly avenues of jade-green water, plied by barges stacked with amphorae.

The canal is one of China's stultifying prodigies, hacked out by five and a half million men and women – and exacting two million casualties – in the early seventh century. It formed the chief artery between north and south, travelling for over one thousand miles between Beijing and the old capital of Hangzhou, and although the silt and floods of the Yellow River severed it in the end, it remains a vital highway for thousands of miles.

Along the canals of Wuxi the houses droop and peel like the lanes of some proletarian Venice. Their patchwork walls and verandas are wrung dry of colour. Around my passenger barge they drifted in watery veins of grey, their tiled roofs crumpled and dimmed like the scales of old fish. Jasmin and roses cluttered their eaves. Sometimes the surface would darken from khaki to indigo along quays oily with derricks or a lemming-rush of hovels into the water. Then the way would quieten beneath little bridges of jointed stone, or a flotilla of barges would congest the route – barges of clay compacted around wire frames, with a diesel engine retching behind. Three-quarters of the city's goods – fertiliser, grinding-stones, jars of pickles and soy sauce – travelled on leftover junks or on these barges, whose sides rose scarcely a foot above the water.

'Disgusting,' said the man beside me. We were chugging through a flotsam of cabbage-leaves and bamboo. Just here the canal had entered one of its fetid stretches, choked with dredgers.

I turned to look at him. His head was hooded in spiky hair, and his face looked shriven. It was a face I was to see often in Hunan and in the inland provinces of the south: naïve, slightly wild. We enquired conventionally about one another above the stammer of the engine:

homes, wives, jobs. But when I came to ask about children, he looked at me with that terrible, tense brightness which is the Chinese for sorrow. 'I haven't any.' His expression turned doubting, hopeful; he seemed to be debating pathetically whether or not to trust me. 'I've been married eight years. But no. . . .'

I had opened up a pit.

I said: 'In England couples sometimes don't want children at all. They decide not to have them.'

'Is that so?' The laughter crackling out of him seemed part relieved, part disbelieving. 'Is that really so? You mean they *decide* that? For ever? You mean for *ever*?'

'Yes. You find that strange.'

His voice clouded into wonder. 'Yes. So strange.'

We were cruising down a water-lane of two-storeyed houses now, whose back rooms disclosed fleeting privacies – an old woman feeding her oriole, a girl in hair-curlers wondering about herself in a mirror – but nothing so intimate as the trouble I was hearing. I had the feeling, as once or twice before, that my foreignness had become a subtle privilege, and that a man could talk to me more freely than to one of his own.

'My grandparents and parents never mention it,' he said, 'but I can sense them thinking all the time: *You have no children, no heirs*.' He jabbed his finger at the air as if accusing himself in their eyes; he was sharing their disgust. 'With us the greatest crime is to leave no children behind you. Confucius. . . .' He stopped. 'Of course they don't say: *Confucius said*. People don't say that any more. But that's what they're thinking. Because Confucius still *sits in our minds*.'

It was futile to tell him that the government would applaud him. He was being arraigned by a faith far older than Communism, and perhaps more durable.

'You mean in England. . . .' he repeated. '*For ever*?'

'Yes.'

Almost within touch, the rooms gliding past us dangled cupboards, baskets, scrolls. Old men bowed from their verandas, and a coal barge went by with an ancient couple bent over its oars, wasted and tiny-eyed in their unison, survivors from the age of emperors.

I asked the man: 'Have you seen doctors?'

But he raised one hand and levelled off the air high above his head. 'There are doctors who might help, but . . . they're very grand. It's hard for ordinary people.' He fixed his hand with a look of hopeless alienation. 'We just go on hoping.'

Then he fell silent. For another hour, drifting down the canal, we went on peering into other people's lives in their kitchens: lives which seemed at once more humdrum and more mysterious than my own, and which perhaps appeared happy to him.

It was midnight when my train eased into Suzhou, the city of gardens. For two hours I tramped down unlit streets and banged fruitlessly on hotel doors. Then I found the back wall of a saw-mill tousled by shrubs. I pulled out my sleeping-bag, covered myself in insect-repellent and sank gratefully into the darkness. The sky was overcast, but without rain. Glow-worms sprinkled the undergrowth. I lay sticky and embalmed in the humid night, and fell into a light sleep.

Morning revealed an old and exquisite city. Its bones were avenues of plane trees, its arteries stone-banked canals overarched by bridges – waterways which astonished even Marco Polo, a Venetian. White-washed houses sealed the main streets in a skin of carved lintels and lattices, and along the canals the lanes became footpaths of mellow paving. Clay barges glided on the wind-stirred current, parting a drift of leaves and feathers, while above them verandas and fish-scale roofs glissaded and petered out in creepers. And flowers bloomed every-where. Oleanders, yuccas, hollyhocks, canna lilies – they jostled the water-lanes and blazed in the courtyards. They grew not only by municipal decision but by private love, and had seeded themselves in the clefts of walls or under the weeping willows. It was a city of sweet, slumbering intimacy. It had retired.

I realised how much I had missed this man-made beauty of an older China. It was part of the dream-luggage I had unconsciously carried into the country with me, and here, suddenly, it had materialised. For more than eight hundred years Suzhou was a lodestar for scholars – a city producing silks and the finest artist's brushes and paper. In Ming times, civil servants would retire here (as early as possible) to a reclusive contentment in walled gardens, plunged in self-cultivation, conversing on aesthetics, practising calligraphy, penning commentar-ies on the Classics. Far into the eighteenth century Suzhou was China's arbiter of dress and speech, and even today its lilting dialect is much admired, and its small-boned women considered the loveliest in the nation.

When I peered through doorways, half expecting to see the sordid jumble of other cities' courtyards, I glimpsed stone-flagged paths which bent out of sight, leaving behind a trellis of saffron roses perhaps, or an autumn tree. I found myself beaming at everybody. I persuaded myself of the women's beauty, and imagined I saw more sensitive faces (foreheads and cheekbones lifted a little, didn't they?) and heard a softer tongue.

I had read that the city escaped the Cultural Revolution unscathed, but as I ambled along one of the inner canals I fell into conversation with a man whose family had been persecuted. 'The Red Guards came here all right,' he said. 'Some even came *from* here. My family was branded Capitalist because we owned four shops in the silk business. They killed my grandfather and elder brother. Things were smashed all over the city – temple statues, private art collections. . . .'

He was young, but he spoke as if it had just happened.

'What do people feel now?'

'About Mao? I can't speak for everybody.' His lips compressed bitterly. 'But *I hate him*.' It was the first time anybody had said this to me – no cult slogan about 'mistakes' or 'he was seventy per cent good, thirty per cent bad' – just pure hatred for what he had committed. 'Many people hate him. In private people criticise him all the time – we call him The Old Man – and everybody admits that the Cultural Revolution was his fault. Who else had the power to implement it? He was just a peasant at heart.' The man drew his bunched fingers outward from between his eyes. 'He only saw his own way. I suppose he got old, decrepit . . . but still I hate him.'

By evening the restaurant quarter had eased into gossip, and people crowded to the cinemas. After everything they had suffered, after all the disorientation and self-torture, they were released now into an innocent variety of enjoyment. In the booths which lent out comic books, ranks of workers relaxed onto benches to thumb through the feats of Tang warriors or the evil doings of the Guomindang. The pavement amusements featured conjurors, improvised shooting-galleries, a man dancing on his knuckles – and passers-by could now tentatively hold hands without censure, and know that the infant in their arms was not the child of unending Revolution, but their own.

I had been given the address of a college schoolteacher in a suburb outside the city walls, and knocked uninvited on his door. It was opened by a small girl sporting ebullient pigtails. She announced that her parents were out, that her name was Rainbow-Sky, that this name was suitable since she was so bright, and that I should come in and wait. I found myself in a three-room flat furnished with iron beds which doubled as sofas. The only ornaments were a few posters, some peacock feathers in a vase, and one of those pitted stones standing in a plastic tray of water, which the Chinese love. The girl served me tea and sweets, then laid the family photograph album on my lap and went off to her homework.

I eased open the album on the endlessly repeated statements of identity, the same faces set in the same expressions: Zhou and his wife at the Summer Palace, in Tiananmen Square, by the lake at Hangzhou, on the Shanghai waterfront. Zhou looked reticently charming. He wore one of those hardy, amused Chinese expressions, which suggest a perennial awareness of the ridiculous. And when he arrived with his wife and son he duplicated his photographs so exactly that I half expected him to freeze into still-life.

Instead the family became engulfed in hospitality. This meant food. Zhou cleared his desk, and an assembly-line for dumpling-making convened. At one end Rainbow-Sky pounded the dough, in the middle the seventeen-year-old son rolled and cut it into circles, while beside him Zhou inserted the filling and laid out the dumplings – more than a hundred – on to trays for his wife to boil.

I watched them in wonderment. The Chinese relationship to food is as passionate as that of the Russians to drink. It is the national panacea and obsession – a concern which far outstrips that of other famine-stricken nations. It permeates political metaphor, dictates the very unit of population (in *kou*, 'mouths') – even to the 'hungry mouths' in Hell – and the most common greeting is not 'How are you?' but 'Have you eaten?'

Meanwhile all heads were swivelling back and forth at the television. There were three channels, and none showed a breath of politics. The programmes rushed by in chaotic vignettes, and were interlaced by advertisements for watches, cosmetics and stereophonic equipment, all garnished with pseudo-Western brand-names. Sports highlights insisted on a sequence of motorcycle crashes (at every crash the boy mangled another dumpling), a medical programme promoted child-care and breast-feeding, and a 'Teacher's Day' spectacle showed synthetic miming under the slogan 'A Teacher is like a gardener, tending flowers' – which was greeted with derisive boredom.

'Nobody likes those things,' said Zhou. 'The peasants prefer dramas and cross-talk humour.'

I thought of the revolution which these shows must be bringing to the village. Most peasants had travelled no further than the local market town – and suddenly this riot of thought and difference was

[133]

crashing in. After the austere fare of previous years – a handful of dogmatic plays and operas – the impact on the remoter regions was incalculable. Every day some three hundred million Chinese watched the Beijing Central News. It was soporific with success stories, but included straight reporting of foreign affairs and – today – a piece on British military exercises against the Soviet Union (greeted with approval) and a film on Tito. There was a historical tragedy by Lao She, an author liquidated during the Cultural Revolution, and a choice of sentimental melodramas on other channels. There were English language courses, nature films, snippets of advice on sanitation, obscure cultural items. (What, I wondered, were the peasants of Anhui making of the programme on the graduation ceremony from the Juilliard music school in New York?) Later I was to see country families packed ten deep in front of televisions in railway station waiting-rooms, and in distant villages the whole community would assemble on benches out of doors before their one television.

'After this,' said Zhou, 'things can never be as before.'

I spent two days wandering the gardens of Suzhou. My tourist brochure said that they 'crystallised the collective wisdom of the working people of our country', but in fact they were esoteric and profoundly exclusive. The retired officials and merchants, painters and poets who created and inhabited them were steeped in a refined conservatism. Their gardens lay secluded down lanes behind high walls through inconspicuous gates. They were places for *wu wei*, for stillness after the stress and pomp of a government career, for retreat into a precinct which did not dominate nature, but expressed and sanctified it.

In these little spaces, a great resonance of meaning and symbol was contained. Each garden was conceived as a microcosm of the universe. Its prime elements were rock, the earth's skeleton, and water, its veins, over which the seasons swept in a flux of plants and trees steeped in symbolism: the lotus, the pine, the bamboo, the chrysanthemum.

Rocks were crucial. Their shapes and textures became the subject of intense connoisseurship. The most prized specimens had been immersed for decades in the waters of Lake Tai, whose waves hammered them into a phantasmagoria of fissures and perforations. The frozen turmoil of these stones, it was felt, concentrated the wild energy of nature. They were petrified Time. They embodied *Yang*, the masculine, and when placed beside the *Yin* of a lake – the female waters of benevolence – they were of all sights the most right and harmonious. Water was stone's antithesis. It was the blood of the earth, drunk by the kings of old legend in search of immortality. It was the stillness of sleep.

To walk in these gardens is to tread through a consecrated wilderness. Once the Confucian formality of its ante-room and lakeside pavilions has been left behind, the path enters a contrived naturalness and secrecy. Straight lines vanish or crinkle up. The lakes and waterways wind out of sight. Streams dive under miniature cliffs, re-emerge as if from unseen hills. The meander of paths is extended by zigzag bridges.

All this induces a mendicant peace. It echoes the succession of incidents in a scroll-painting, and this is no accident. Painters and gardeners consciously imitated one another. The galleries which thread these landscapes not only unify them but enshrine them in a series of latticed windows, like fragmented pictures, and the white walls – sometimes waxed glossy to change with the changing sunlight – become the blank parchment for a three-dimensional composition: a flurry of rocks, a drift of bamboo.

But when I entered these gardens I found them drowned under sightseers. Conceived for solitude, conjuring with perspectives and clothed in the muted greens and greys of early landscape painting, their magic was trampled into oblivion. Pavilions had been turned into shops, restaurants and bad art galleries. Professional photographers commandeered the delicately planned vantage-points. A glaze of cigarette stubs dimmed the lakes.

I plunged gloomily into the remoter corners, where each small vista was different, but each one spoilt. Here a window gave on to a sunlit slant of plum tree – and at its foot a spittoon. There a bridge spanned a glade where two women were yelling. Nearby, on a pool dark with hanging trees, floated a beer-can. A moon-gate led to a lavatory. In the Humble Administrator's Garden – rigged out for a festival – illuminated elephants clapped their ears, clockwork singsong girls rowed on paper barges and a thirty-foot gold dragon wobbled its head. Everybody was delighted.

Only the churlish foreign devil became filled with a revulsion against tourists, as if he wasn't one. Sooner or later, as one wrecked garden succeeded another, I would charge boorishly away. My outraged head must have appeared in the corners of countless otherwise satisfactory photographs of relatives posing in front of bamboos.

In the Garden of the Lion Forest, where a hillock of artificial rocks rushed violently into the lake, an army of sightseers was photographing itself all over the slope. Beside me a blind man stood with a young woman. 'What is it like?' he asked.

'At the foot of the range,' she replied, 'a dragon is trying to writhe out of the waters, but on its back you can see the faces and manes and shoulders of three lions. They are beautiful. Under the creepers on another side a lion's face is visible. It is roaring over the lake. Its eyes are terrifying. . . .'

The man stood unspeaking, his scarred face lifted to the gouged rocks. He smiled.

'There is a stone forest too,' the woman went on, 'and lions are everywhere in it. Their mouths are roaring out of the thickets. . . .'

A few minutes later they had gone, and I was left gazing at the tourist-littered hillock, wishing for the man's dark or the woman's sight.

But at sunrise next morning, before any crowd could assemble, I slipped into the 800-year-old Garden of the Master of the Fishing Nets, and here, in the compass of an acre, momentarily lost footing in Time. In the outer court stand quiescent rocks. They are a stilling, an announcement. A gallery opens on a little glade of trees. The way bifurcates. And thereafter the eye is bemused by possibility and contrast everywhere. Within a few paces the view is concentrated in gateways, splintered by lattices, unfolded from a terrace. Beyond black eaves a camphor tree shines in isolated brilliance. A moon-gate circumscribes a boulder. In the villa's chambers the windows hang close against whitewashed walls outside: the framed rocks and leaves shine in the rooms' darkness. Here the retired mandarins swim pleasurably into the imagination – cultivating equanimity, exchanging ink-sketches or fondling some rare edition with woodblock colours. Into their hobnobbing, perhaps, a poet drops some choice *vers d'occasion* – and these poems, inscribed on polished black stone, have been set into nearby walls until the whole garden becomes a paper-chase of literary allusions.

> Silvered earth without dust, and the golden chrysanthemums
>   in bloom
> Purple pears and red dates falling on the lichen moss;
> A shaft of Autumn water, and a round moon –
> On such a night, my old friend, are you not coming?

[136]

On such a night the kiosk windows, lit from inside, would glow in traceries of rice-paper or translucent mother-of-pearl, while old companions settled by the lake to contemplate the moon as it 'washed its soul' in the waters, soft with plucked lute-strings and the gurgle of yellow wine. If a man would be happy for a week, ran a saying, he could take a wife; if he planned happiness for a month, he must kill a pig; but if he desired happiness for ever, he should plant a garden.

5. Shanghai

It was a brutal city, and its past did nothing to mellow it. Shallow-rooted in the greed of Europe and of itself, its traditions were ruthlessly mercantile. It was still the hub of industrial China, and the largest city in the land. It offered the highest wages and inflicted the dearest cost of living. While Beijing was dominated and quartered by sterile avenues, Shanghai lay drowned in the ocean of its populace. Through its humid evening, they resembled a whole landscape on the move. They marched eight abreast along the pavements. They broke over every street and square, flooded the shops, poured along the waterfronts, swarmed in the lanes. Cars could only hoot and creep their way through this fog of human flesh, which closed in instantly after them. No city on earth, not Calcutta or Cairo, gave such a sense of overwhelming life. The lower stretch of the Nanjing Road alone was tramped by a million people a day. This, I thought, is what is meant by 'the masses' – something not plural at all, but monolithic. It goes in a white shirt and black trousers. It looks alike. It owns one character and one will.

Shanghai was once the 'lodestar of the Orient' – squalid, glamorous, rootless – and it seemed still to be living on the genes of ambitious peasants migrated here during the British and French rule. It was pulsing not only with its own twelve million inhabitants but with workers from distant satellites, with the unemployed returned illegally from exile, with rough, sturdy men swarmed in from the villages to market, with bewildered crocodiles of tourists.

Yet the crowds sauntered and lingered. While the northern Chinese had stared at me in bovine wonder, the Shanghainese's eyes glittered with opportunism, flickering down my clothes to take in shirt texture, wrist-watch (digital? Swiss? Japanese?), belt, shoes, in a lightning assessment. I had crossed the divide into the south: the people darker, slighter, more animated. They spoke their own quick, sibilant language. The streets were their drawing-room.

[138]

But this habitat changed from district to district. The suburbs were scattered with gabled mansions and walled gardens from the European ascendancy. Mock Tudor and dormer windows overlooked a rumpus of corrugated *hutong* roofs or faded into the streets of a lost colonialism where wrought-iron balconies bloomed into jungles of washing and strings of dried herrings. Then the alleys would open onto a boulevard of dilapidated grandeur. Through half-closed eyes I could dream myself in an American metropolis between the wars, complete with adolescent skyscrapers. But the next moment, down the turn of a lane, the city would become close and vivid again, clogged with trucks and pedicabs, or plunged in a clamour of workshops. Doors stood ajar on Dickensian ateliers where women clattered at sewing-machines all day for a pittance. Then these alleys bifurcated into passages too shrunk for traffic. The sound thinned to a clack of abacus and tingle of bicycle bells. And here at last the inhabitants separated into isolated vignettes – men playing classical chess in the dust with inscribed counters; a pair of old women heaving a cartload of rotted tarpaulin somewhere, and crying to one another in tiny, distraught voices.

Near the waterfront the city had reverted to its mercantile past as if the last forty years had never been. Window-dressing appeared. The streets were filled with photographers' studios and hair stylists. Advertisement hoardings – once strident with the Thoughts of Chairman Mao – were launching White Cat Soapless Detergent, Golden Lotus Shoe Polish and Pearl Cream ('most effective in tenderising skin'). The commercial blonde fondling Ginseng Coca-Cola or tenderising her fashionably white complexion conferred on the product the imprimatur of Western modernity. Dusky, long-haired men were manning impromptu stalls of clothes and gaudy ornaments, or paraded the streets in jeans, their fingers dangling unlit cigarettes. At intervals their faces arrived alongside mine murmuring about illicit exchange of foreign money, then vanished.

An unshaven salesman, no longer quite young, squatted under a lamppost while his partner stood shouting for custom on a trolley of shirts. The man's jacket was slashed open to the waist and the swarthy fierceness of his face confirmed that we were both outsiders, I by race and he by misfortune. 'I'm thirty-seven,' he said. 'I was ten years in the fields in the Cultural Revolution, lost my education, lost everything. I shouldn't be here at all.'

'But you're making money?'

'Yes. Look at these people – we're making over 9,000 yuan a month.' That was £2,000.

'How do you get the stuff?'

'We lift it from wholesalers. That's no problem. Everybody knows somebody. . . .'

They both looked desperately poor. Yet their barrow was crowded and they were raking in money. 'You have to choose your wares,' he said. 'Fashion's important. Fashion's good money.' But he looked bitter.

Fashion: it had rarely occurred to me. Even in this city, which is the modern arbiter of style, clothes seemed to spring only from convention and convenience. The women who had jettisoned their dour jackets and trousers for frilly dresses and socks merely looked as if they had undergone a pleasant change of uniform. But that was the illusion of a Westerner. Broad-checked shirts were in this year, said the man. There was a trend for showing high-necked vests behind open collars, and had I noticed the black stockings peeping through women's sandals?

Further up the street, outside the Huaan Beauty Salon, a girl was shedding furious tears before a little crowd. She tugged at her hair as if trying to uproot it. 'I just wanted it thinned and permed . . . and look!' It shook round her face in a palsy of frizzles. 'I look like . . . like . . . one of those. . . .' She yanked the locks desperately in different directions. From time to time a hairdresser would appear in the salon doorway to defend himself; but the people took her side. The girl beside me translated into giggling Mandarin. Soon the crowd had swelled to over a hundred. Young men accused the salon in a salvo of invective, backed by threatening claques of outraged women. At last the manager emerged.

'Look what you've done!' a man shouted. 'People aren't meant to look like this. You must put it right. . . .'

The tragedienne dashed a flannel over her streaming eyes.

'What do you know?' bawled the manager. 'Do you know anything about hairdressing?'

But the crowd insisted. Its voice rose to a furious babble.

'Just wait a day or two and it'll straighten out!' yelled the manager. 'It's meant to be like this to start with.'

The girl sobbed: 'I don't *want* to start with it like this. . . .'

At last, still weeping and plucking at her straggles, she was swept through the door by the crowd, the management succumbed, and the people continued to glower through the windows for ten minutes until she had been safely ensconced under a hair-dryer.

I wandered away to the only hotel which would accept me – a run-down Victorian leviathan on the waterfront. It was living on its past. The dimmed illustriousness of the state rooms still catered to middle-class weddings, and periodically the doors would disgorge a bridal party in a shock of pink veils and sequinned gloves. But upstairs it reminded me of boarding-school. The brown-painted wainscots along the corridors were scuffed and gouged. I kept expecting the sixth-form bully to come lumbering round a corner, and I opened my locker on an imaginary cascade of football-boots. But in fact the dormitories were full of Western backpackers and overseas Chinese homesick for Hong Kong of Singapore. Tempers were worn. The hardships of travel had turned the backpackers belligerent. Their few phrases of Mandarin had arisen from the demands of getting and spending. China disgusted them.

That night I was kept awake by rats rustling under the beds. When I groped into the bathroom, its improvised washing-line of T-shirts and Y-fronts was being noiselessly crossed by an enormous creature which panicked, fell onto my feet and vanished where the door-frame crumbled into the wall. From outside came the sounds of canned music. I pulled aside the gauze curtains and found myself looking into the courtyard of the local cultural club. It was lit by fairy lights. In its centre a hesitant formation of youths and girls was square-dancing to the strains of 'How Much is that Doggie in the Window?' The weirdness of this scene was heightened by the saccharine lilt of the female singer (the child-like warble cultivated for public utterance) and by the way the faltering lines of dancers held each other's hands without looking at one another. They seemed less to be dancing than engaged in a demure magic.

The voice chirruped to its end. Given the ingredients of some Chinese cuisine, the enquiry as to the doggie's price took on a sad, gastronomic ring. I closed the window and went back to bed.

Morning brought a nostalgic astonishment – imperial Britain's sea-gate to the Far East. Rising from the esplanade where the Huangpo river turns north to the China Sea, the great banks and trading-houses of the Bund still resounded with twenties or thirties assuredness – clocked and flagpoled palaces in Doric or Corinthian fancy-dress. Uncleaned for two generations, their stone loomed iron-grey, dead. They were slightly dissolute now. Here and there an Edwardian dinosaur intruded in lavatorial brick, or thick skyscrapers erupted – once the tallest outside America.

As I walked along their boulevard of plane and camphor trees, I felt a pang of ancestral guilt. Here, at the end of the first Opium War in 1842, the British had implemented their forced concessions to trade and settle, and were followed a year later by the Americans and French. In time a huge International Settlement arose – a cosmopolis immune from Chinese law – and Shanghai became 'the Whore of Asia': a place of half-starved coolies, millionaires, prostitutes and criminals, where hundreds became suddenly rich and thousands died of exposure in the winter streets. The port bloomed into a corrupt sophistication, fattened on overseas investment, cheap labour, opium and extortion. It was a heady concentrate of life verging on the burlesque, like the Hollywood movies it loved and illustrated. At one extreme its Chinese multi-millionaires drove in a cavalcade of Oldsmobiles among bodyguards lumpy with automatics: gangland lords in silk. On the other the factories overflowed with slave children; the streets were parcelled among syndicates of deformed beggars; and every day the tidal river washed back corpses from the sea-funerals which were all that the poor could afford. Meanwhile the exalted foreigner moved between racecourse, club, brothel and church, largely isolated from this sub-world he had spawned.

It is no paradox that the city was a festering-ground of Communism. It combined the inflammatory ingredients of a half-Westernised intelligentsia and a swarming, poverty-scarred proletariat. The Party held its first congress here in 1921, in a house now aseptically restored – stools and teacups set out as if the thirteen delegates might at any moment return. Later the city was both the tinder and the last bastion for the Cultural Revolution, where a predicted uprising to thwart the arrest of the Gang of Four inexplicably never took place.

I wandered penitently along the Bund. Wise after the event, I thought I detected in these dowdy imperial monsters a note of decline. They had not the architectural augustness of British Bombay or Rangoon, but suggested rather the last gasp of the neo-classical, tricked out in Egyptian capitals, *fasces* (always a bad sign) and stumpy colonettes. Inside, their entrails were now mortally diseased. The marble floors and coffered ceilings were cracked and discoloured, and the magisterial stairs unkempt.

None, of course, remains what it was. I found the Jardine, Matheson building turned into a state textile corporation; and outside the old Hong Kong and Shanghai Bank the British lions had been usurped by sentries in plimsolls: it was the Communist Party headquarters. The Westminster chimes of the Customs House were playing 'The East is Red', and in the exclusive Shanghai Club the 110-foot bar, once the longest in the world, was serving drinks to a guzzling proletariat on aluminium chairs. But in the Cathay Hotel (where Noël Coward started *Private Lives*) the stained-glass ceilings still shed their glamour on a foyer rife with art-deco lampstands and balustrades. Brass panels engraved with 'Gibbons of London and Wolverhampton' survived on fittings still stubbornly working. The vintage Otis elevators juddered and jammed, and in musty corners the original crimson carpets remained. At evening in its night-club, a jazz band played Glenn Miller's 'In the Mood', while men in black suits and girls with pudding-bowl hairstyles sipped Qingdao beer and waltzed gravely to 'I Wonder Who's Kissing Her Now'. Twenty-three storeys below, the shriven Whore of Asia lay scattered in dim constellations, saving on electricity.

Next morning, as I strolled along the Huangpo waterfront, I had the illusion of gazing into jumbled centuries, or at a national schizophrenia. Over the surface whole sea-caravans of barges, slung with tyres and crowned astern by grimy canopies, stuttered and coughed under pyramids of bamboo matting or cabbages. Sometimes they would turn under the old cantilever Garden Bridge and into Suzhou Creek which percolates through the northern suburbs. More often they weaved along the open river among tugs and five-decked passenger-boats like Mississippi steamers. Here and there thirty thousand tons of ocean-going liner went gliding to its deepwater berth, while left-over junks rocked harmlessly between, as if on another current of time.

I paid one cent to enter the infamous riverside park, from which Chinese and dogs had once been excluded. An old gardener asked my nationality. When I said British, he grinned then said 'Welcome' – which was more than we had said to him. Another elderly man was copying down a piece of slightly inaccurate history from the park notice-board in a meticulous hand. It read: 'Before Liberation the Park bore silent witness to the Imperialists' aggression against China and their wanton trampling on her sovereignty. . . . To add insult to injury the Imperialists in 1885 put up at the gate a board with the words: No Admittance to Dogs and Chinese.'

The man turned, saw me and was gripped by long, shrilling peals of embarrassment. He tried to speak but couldn't. He simply whinnied in uncontrollable spasms. He dropped his pencil. Laughter (some anthropologists hold) is in reality a nervous response to the unexpected, and the man's nerves were now shaking his whole body, trembled through his lips – which were trying, I think, to say good-morning – and finally sent him neighing and half running into the gardens.

*   *   *

I sometimes imagine that people are born a certain age; and Professor Wu, I felt, had always been sixty-five. He was old and plump, with sad, sympathetic eyes in a blotched face. His hair powdered his head in a dust which seemed independent of the sunburnt scalp below, and it is this head, bowed in thought or sadness, which I most remember.

His life had seen hard changes. He had been studying surgery in Hong Kong when the Japanese attacked the city. It was the day of Pearl Harbor. 'I looked out of my window to see planes dropping a shower of bombs. I remember thinking they were like rat's pellets. At first I thought it was the British on manoeuvres. But then I saw the fires. So my parents told my brother and me to escape in different directions – they thought if one of us was killed, they'd at least have the other left. So my brother went inland to Chongqing, our wartime capital, while I got to Shanghai.'

His hands and knees had converged primly on the chair in my hotel. He looked too rounded, too gnomish, for war.

'At the end of our civil war in 1949,' he said, 'I left with my wife for America.' His voice still tightened at the word 'America' although he spoke it with a New York accent. 'But even after ten years I couldn't agree with the way of life there. I suppose I was brought up too traditionally. In the hospitals the treatment of the poor was unbearable. The New York police would kick out the bums right under our noses. I couldn't bear it. We never did that in China, not in my experience. And the crime . . . and just the way young people behaved. . . .' He did not want to expand on this: he was old. 'And so my wife and I felt we couldn't live there any longer, and we wondered where to go. And we thought: we're Chinese, we'll go back to China and serve the people.' The slogan fell automatically from him, but with a Manhattan twang. Such catch-phrases were part of his generation. They had eaten inwards, like acid or good manners. 'Once we'd made the decision, everything became very simple. I think I'd always planned to return one day. In the China I had left, there were virtually no medicines at all, so I'd chosen to study surgery. You don't need medicines for that . . . just a knife and your own skill.'

Then his face shadowed over, and his voice softened with the mysteriousness of things. 'But the strangeness is that America has followed me here.' He shook his head. 'It's growing in our young. These city young . . . I believe they are the real victims of the Cultural Revolution, although they never experienced it. They live in its aftermath, you see. They have no ideals.' By now his head had sunk halfway to the table between us. 'They only want things for themselves. They don't *produce* anything. They just go into business on their own, selling something or other. That way they make more money than a man on a salary. So they see no point in being educated – being educated is no help in commerce.' It was an old lament: Confucius had placed merchants lowest on the social scale. 'Yes, America is coming here. I can feel the same things in the air. . . .' He looked up, wan and suddenly lost, with his soft, melancholy eyes. 'Have you noticed our young people in the evenings? This year some are going about with *their arms round each other's necks.*' He spoke with bitter incredulity. 'It's repellent. No decent family would let its children do that. That's something they wouldn't even do in the States. . . .'

Strange, I thought, how he had edited parts of the West out of his memory, despite (or because of) his disgust. 'I don't know what we're coming to,' he said. 'How do we stop this . . . this . . . rotting? Somehow we must adapt to Western technology but refuse Western culture.'

'How is that possible?' You could not paddle in those waters, I thought. You swam or drowned.

'It must be a matter of education,' Wu said.

I felt a sudden, sad affection for him. His bent head all at once looked frail as porcelain, frail as this Confucian ghost of education he had summoned.

He guessed my dissent without lifting his eyes. 'Perhaps it's like medicine,' he said. 'If people are sufficiently exposed to Western evils, they'll be immunised.'

'Or totally diseased.' But I laughed my words into harmlessness, because I did not want to see the expression on his bowed face.

Inside the Youth Palace – a quadrangle of tiered galleries – nobody seemed engaged in anything more harmful than sipping Coca-Cola and gobbling cake. The only poster announced 'Participation, Development, Peace'. Along the pinball alley a few youths were playing 'Defenders' and 'Sea Devil' on Japanese computers, and a shop was selling T-shirts inscribed 'Andy's Pub' or 'Personalised Carefree Transportation Honda'. Another read: 'Caution: this shirt is designed for young adventurers to create their new image. All designs copyright Europe New Fashion'. In the basement a rink whined with bumping cars. None of their drivers, I realised, could ever have owned a real car – there are fewer than a hundred private cars in China – and they drove like children, dreaming.

Compared to the past, this palace was drably innocent. Its predecessor in the 1930s – 'The Great World' – had risen in a six-storeyed mountain of vulgarity, jollity and sex. From gambling on the ground floor it ascended like the strata of a tasteless heaven through massage benches, earwax-extractors, ice-cream parlours, jugglers, a stuffed whale, acupuncturists, peep-shows, 'rubber goods' and marriage brokers, to a top floor criss-crossed by tightrope walkers in a storm of firecrackers. As for the singsong girls, the prurient chastity of their high-collared *cheongsam*s grew more outrageous as the storeys ascended. The thigh-high slits which undermined them on the ground floor crept insidiously up the waist and body-cage storey by storey, until, on the ultimate elysium of the roof-terrace they reached the armpit.

I had difficulty finding The Great World now. It stood on the edge of a building-site, and looked abandoned. I sneaked in past a dozing guardian, and found myself wandering along galleries dim with scaffolding. Vistas of sweeping stairs and pillars ended in vertiginous drops, and when I reached the roof I found it heaped with debris. The place was a shell. My footprints meandered so thick in dust over the mosaic floors that I retraced them easily to the entrance, and asked the guardian what had happened.

'It is being remade,' she said. 'For you.'

'For me?' The thought was vaguely sickening.

'For tourists. A luxury hotel.'

I was growing used to these transformations by now. Later I found the old racecourse club turned into a public library, whose desks were packed with youths trying to supplement their qualifications. The Jewish Club had become the city's music conservatory, its rooms still mellow with panelling and burnished leather chairs. Even the face of the academy's vice-president seemed to have taken on a refining polish.

'Our first music teachers were White Russians and Jews,' he said.

'They'd all left by the mid-1950s, but their legacy is still here. We're one of the two leading conservatories in the country. Western music in Shanghai has a long tradition.'

But into this continuum the Cultural Revolution had crashed like a guillotine. For ten years, music stopped. 'I'm a pianist, but I wasn't allowed to teach. The piano was pronounced bourgeois and Capitalist.' He had a disconcerting habit of staring at me after each sentence, as if anticipating some response which I could not guess. I could only stare back. 'The older generation of teachers was vilely treated. They were isolated in their rooms or locked into closets. The heads of most of the departments died in those ten years, many by suicide. It was the torture of the mind they couldn't bear. . . .' The level calm of the words, and his invulnerable face, made this hard to grasp.

'What about the pupils?'

'Children of musical families sometimes went on practising in secret. But if neighbours heard them, it could be fatal. Our vocal students only sang a handful of Revolutionary Beijing operas, and even these they were forced to read in numbered musical notation instead of the "Western" stave. The Beijing opera technique is quite different from *bel canto* too. It played havoc with the voice.' Again, the strange, expressionless stare.

'So you've lost a generation of musicians.'

'Yes.'

We walked out to the conservatory garden. In the sunlight his unnerving immaculacy struck me as a mask. His hair was receding and flecked with grey. 'Our junior students are good,' he said, 'but the seniors were hopelessly handicapped by the Cultural Revolution, and it's too late for most of them. We're begining to get results in the international competitions again, but it will take more than ten years to recover. . . .'

We walked between ornamental rocks, past the bespectacled bust of the conservatory's founder, and my old unease about the Cultural Revolution erupted again. Music, surely, would be the least politicised of arts. Who had the Red Guards been here?

'Just our students,' he said. 'Ordinary students.'

'Were they cruel or just . . . frightened?'

He took a long time to answer. I felt, as sometimes before, that I was posing irrelevant questions. Then he said: 'Some refrained out of pity or disagreement. But most went along with the worst group, who were perhaps politically ambitious.'

'How many took part?'

'Well. . . .' I think his stare was asking me not to press him.

'Fifty per cent?'

He looked pained. 'I'm afraid more than that. Perhaps eighty . . . ninety per cent.' Along the paths callow-faced girls were walking together, and young men sweaty from netball. They saluted him respectfully. We seemed to be talking about a time aeons ago. 'We hope it will never happen again.' He was looking fastidious, distressed. 'Never.'

Walking one day along a suburban street, I glimpsed behind high walls the chancel of a church, and snooped into a close where a mullioned vicarage stood green with ivy. Even the flowers looked English. Down the nave the dark-wooded pews and the clouded glass spread a liturgical sombreness, so that I did not notice the sacristan until he had flitted up beside me – a wraith of a man with delicately boned features.

'I wasn't sure if I was meant to be here,' I said edgily. 'It's empty.'

'You should see Sunday mornings!' he piped. 'We have a congregation of twelve hundred. They overflow the church, out into a chapel and even into an office!' He waved his arm about the nave. 'The harmonium is relayed by microphones, since our organ was smashed in the sixties.'

The Cultural Revolution: its rupture lay across every past. Even in the present people lived with its detritus – split families, brutalised psyches, a whole skein of invisible divides. The old man sat down in the pew beside me: his height seemed to remain the same. 'The organ was a gift from America, but it was so old they had no spare parts for it.' He spoke of it with tenderness. 'And do you know who broke it? Red Guard students from the *Shanghai Music Conservatory*. Can you understand that?' He put on his glasses as if this might help. 'I can't. Nor how they could break our violin.' He said 'violin' in English. The word's poetry seemed suddenly tragic. 'How could anyone break a violin?'

I wondered what had happened to him at that time. His eyes looked bright and vulnerable behind their wire-rimmed glasses. I found myself smiling at him, drawn to his Christian gentleness, I think, although I wished it were to something Chinese in him. I touched his shoulder as if it might break. He seemed such a fragile repository for civilisation.

'The church was closed down,' he said, 'and we were all sent away.

The Red Guards just told us to keep quiet. That was easy. It's easy to do nothing. I was put into a factory making buses, and spent three years hitting at nails with a little hammer. On and on.' He struck frailly at the air with a blue-veined fist. 'On and on. But I never got any better at it. The workers around me were kind enough, but I never did learn. As for this place, it was used as a rehearsal studio for those Revolutionary operas.'

We sat in momentary silence, facing the altar where the makeshift stage had once usurped the sacraments under the voiceless organ. 'What I don't understand,' he said, 'is that nothing *inside* those young people told them they were doing wrong. . . .'

He might have been myself speaking. So, curiously, I became somebody else. 'I suppose it was crowd psychology,' I heard myself saying, 'and they were so inured to obeying authority . . . parents, teachers . . . and the situation was a gift to the more brutal ones.'

'Yes,' he said uncertainly. 'I suppose so.'

But I loved him for his inability to understand. I think I didn't understand either.

'After the Cultural Revolution was over,' he said, 'some workers from my bus factory came to the church out of curiosity. At first they thought it a strange place, but later they became intrigued. They started joining in the hymns. And last year three of them were baptised at our font – two parents and a little boy.'

'I hope they don't have to suffer as you did.'

His hands came up in a flurry of denial. 'No, those times have gone for ever. I'm sure of it. You've seen our young here, how different they are? You've sensed it?'

Yes, I said: *with their arms round each other's necks.*

'You know what a traditional people we are,' he went on, 'but even in the family that is changing. Young people are starting to think for themselves now. And it's a good thing. . . . *A good thing.* I can remember my grandfather all those years ago. When I was in his presence I was too terrified to look at him.' With a downward stroke of his hand he conjured a bearded mandarin – huge at least in his memory. 'And my father too, when he told me to study I'd physically quake.' He shook a paternal finger. 'And now what's happened? When my grandchildren come to see me, what do they do? Do they tremble?' A soft laughter overtook him. 'No! They reach up and pat my head and say "You've got no hair left, grandad! You'll turn into an egg!" ' His delight spun itself out in chuckles. 'I love them.'

We ambled back down the nave. He repeated, as if talking to himself: 'So that time can't return.' Dusk was falling headlong on the English flowers and vicarage windows. He let me out through the churchyard gate. Then he said suddenly: 'Pray for us.'

*　　*　　*

Inside the Arts and Crafts Institute the native genius for intricacy was pouring into jade and ivory carving, silk embroidery, inkstone and paper cutting, sandalwood fan-making, lacquerwork, modelling in dough. The intaglio butterflies gouged in slivers of bamboo had each taken two weeks to finish. So had the minute traditional poems engraved invisibly on a chip of ivory. How many days had gone on the needlepoint portrait of Ronald and Nancy Reagan, I did not ask. The craftswoman's eyes had grown old with such work, she said, and her spectacles were more powerful than any magnifying-glass.

I peered into a painter's studio. From where, I wondered, had his watercolours of blue-eyed cats emerged, his pandas rolling about sucking bamboo-shoots? Had he painted an actual cat, a cat he knew – with unaccountably blue eyes?

He glanced about the cramped studio – 'I only paint in here' – and handed me a brochure about himself, which said he had 'formed his own artistic style by absorbing the good points of others'. It seemed peculiarly Chinese: a kind of humility. He did not claim to be original. The past – the ancestral shadow – lay too long. He smiled a gap-toothed smile. The obsessive Western hunt for originality, for a new language, would have struck him as grotesque.

This, so an expatriate Chinese told me, had been fatally enervating. For the last four hundred years artists had merely copied and synthesised from other artists. Theirs were paintings of paintings, not paintings of life. And when I visited the Academy of Traditional Painting, it was to discover a timeless exhibition by modern artists – the same cloud-perforated mountains, the traditional sparrows flitting inconsequently among bamboo, the familiar cockerels and pines. I roamed disconsolately from room to room. It was as if whole Western academies were to devote themselves to painting in the style of Giotto or Leonardo da Vinci.

A teacher showed me his sketch book. He had drawn sampans moored on a river with some trucks nearby. But in the finished painting the trucks, of course, were gone, and the vigour of the boats had slipped tracelessly into mist. 'This is in the Ming style,' he said.

The academy's principal, a dumpy man in a grey suit and leather shoes, was shambling among his pupils with the self-important gait so hated by Guo. Teachers took a three-day excursion into the country once a year, he said, but this privilege wasn't extended to pupils. 'They stay here. They learn from other pictures.'

I was blundering into territory I did not understand – many subtle reflections of style eluded me – and the only other foreigner at the exhibition, a French technician, was wandering about as dulled as me. He was teaching computer technology in Shanghai. His pupils, he said, mastered detail with mesmerising speed, but the larger, abstract structures fuddled them.

It was a constant Western bemusement. The Chinese have always excelled in the concrete and commonsensical. Metaphysical enquiry seems almost stillborn in their history. Had their brilliance of invention, then, been a matter of trial and error, of practical experiment rather than abstract theory? I had no idea. But it seemed to deliver itself of its creations unattended by the Western passion for explanation. The inventions of printing and paper, of the magnetic compass and gunpowder (concocted mistakenly while searching for an immortal elixir), are only the greatest in a long, civilised roll-call of discoveries which includes porcelain and silk, the mechanical clock, dictionaries and encyclopaedias, map-grids and lock-gates, the use of coal and deep-drilling techniques, the paddle-wheel boat, chain suspension bridges (as early as the seventh century), a seismograph (four hundred years before the Persians), rain and snow gauges, winnowing machines, the humble kite and wheelbarrow. Chinese ships were the first to sail with stern-post rudders and contained water-tight compartments unknown in Europe until a thousand years later. Since before the time of Christ they had built mechanically operated armillary spheres, recorded sunspots and the passage of Halley's Comet, and noted more than eleven thousand stars and planets. In the thirteenth century they invented the equatorial mounting for the telescope, and a century before Copernicus they had guessed that the earth was round.

But who could be sure what precise quality of intellect or imagination all this suggested, or why it had died? Or perhaps it had not died. Perhaps the brilliance at minutiae which the Frenchman had encountered was a resurrection of this supreme practical inventiveness.

'How do you predict development then?' I asked him. 'Are they the Japanese of the future?'

He answered at once: '*Mais oui, certainement.*'

* * *

I was looking at one of those police notice-boards which serve as a warning to the people. It showed photographs of young men at trial, with snapshots of their victims and instruments below. They were mostly thieves and murderers.

'Those sentences haven't been decided yet,' said an old couple beside me. 'Only the last one.'

We gazed at the photographs of a delicate-looking youth standing handcuffed between policemen. He had tried to murder his girlfriend. At the moment of being photographed she had turned her back to the camera, hiding her disfigurement in a shining fall of hair. A razor, with its measurements, was photographed below.

What was going to happen to him, I asked?

The old couple chorused back: 'He's going to be executed,' and lifted their fingers like pistols to the back of their heads. They were smiling.

Criminal sentences seemed to fluctuate arbitrarily. When I visited the municipal jail – a permission secured weeks before – I found many murderers incarcerated there, while rapists and embezzlers were currently being executed.

The prison had been built by the British early in the century, used by the Japanese after them, and by the Nationalists after that. I felt vaguely responsible for it: another relic of colonialism. I half wished I had not come. Four iron gates clanged and rolled back from the walls in succession like the portals to the underworld – and rolled and clanged shut again behind me. Four thousand men and women were incarcerated here. Their sentences ranged from a single year to a two-year stay of execution with life imprisonment. The cell-blocks and workhouses loomed on all sides in palisades of blank concrete and barred windows. Even in September the asphalt valleys between them vibrated with a tense, reflected heat.

I glimpsed blue-clad squads of convicts exercising in the yards, drilled by wardens in sand-yellow uniforms. They looked robotic and all alike, as Chinese are meant to do. Nothing else drew the eye. There was no such thing as distance. The end of all vistas was abrupt and final: a sheer wall topped with spiked glass.

Around the steel-framed cylinder of the central block radiated corridors of work-benches. The walls were plastered with productivity statistics and jolly pictures. Beneath them hundreds of men sat on iron stools among a flotsam of cotton and nylon. The little cones of thread spun and hummed in steel frames. The prisoners were sewing, trimming, ironing. The work looked absurdly dainty. They were making shirts and trousers which would be exported under the giveaway trade-name 'Laodong', 'Labour'. Above them red banners were draped from wall to wall proclaiming 'Celebrate the birthday of the People's Republic of China with excellent attainments'. They earned one pound a month.

I tramped behind the tables with the chief warden, a big, slow-speaking man. I felt like a voyeur. Simply by being here I had somehow lost the righteous separateness of the outside world, but could not touch the penance of the prisoners'. I had merely butterflied over the boundary. They behaved as if I was not there. But the rigidity of their features, the withdrawal of all expression, was their acknowledgement of me, and the moment we left each workroom, a cloud of conversation rose.

In other rooms men were carving ornamental ducks nuzzling at trees and blossom. These were passed to other men who painted them, together with dragons, peacocks and pandas – things they had probably never seen. It was hard to meet their eyes. My gaze pulled down to the tables, the ornaments, their hands. When I glanced at their faces they did not appear brutal or even shifty. A few looked oddly pedantic and scholarly. It was bewildering. I knew they were thugs, thieves, murderers; but they seemed indistinguishable from any crowd in the street. Even their blue cotton uniforms, tagged with four-figure numbers, looked unexceptional.

Did prisoners grow certain expressions, I asked the warden, or anything which marked them out?

'No,' he said. 'Nothing. They look the same to me, the same as anybody else.'

Some workrooms were surrounded by inmates' cells. These were no more than windowless, iron-doored cupboards, eight feet by five, where the prisoners slept in quilts on a bamboo-mat floor, with a bucket for night-soil. In another compound three hundred girls and women were stitching trousers. They bent over old sewing-machines. Their cropped hair unsexed them. A few looked up slyly and exchanged whispers after we had passed, or smiled secretly to themselves. But they seemed unlit, dead in some dream of their own, as if they could bear the outer world only by not existing to it.

I asked the warden why they did no artwork, like the men.

'They have no interest in that sort of thing,' he said.

All along the stairs and in the workrooms slogans proclaimed reform with evangelical certitude. 'Swim to a new bank of the river', 'Confession is the Only Way', 'Don't worry about what you did: worry about the future'. Prison here meant not only punishment, but change. Eight hours' work a day was supplemented by education in four classrooms under the banner 'Study has to be free from ignorance, to promote civilisation and elevate morals'.

'Other slogans are aimed at the staff,' the warden said. 'You see that one? "By hard work you can turn stones into iron, create new people." We believe that. We can make it work. Offenders are changed here.'

He looked as if he knew. I half believed him.

'We have three hundred officers for re-educating inmates,' he said. 'The emphasis is on confession and a return to right thinking.' I thought: the inmates here are probably lucky. Conditions in most prisons and labour camps are atrocious.

We stopped in front of a blackboard chalked with messages from ex-prisoners. The warden translated them. One was from a man sent home on compassionate leave. Looking out of the bus window, he wrote, he saw how China had improved since his internment, and felt guilty for letting down a nation of such superb development. Another message came from a prisoner released three months before. He had served eleven years for murdering his chronically ill wife. But now he was working in a building factory at 80 yuan (some £16) a month. Nobody looked down on him for his past, he said, the factory welfare schemes were wonderful and he felt inspired to work ever harder for the sake of the people.

I listened to these manifestos as if to a clock, something – even if it were true – which sounded mechanical and dead. Who could know, after the relentless psychological bombardment of prison, if these testimonials were genuine? Perhaps their authors no longer knew.

The warden fell silent, as if expecting some response from me. I changed the subject, asked him about escapes.

'No one has escaped. Education reduces the desire to escape.'

What of political prisoners?

'We have a handful of Taiwanese – no more than ten, I think – convicted of espionage. Most political offenders go elsewhere.' To this he added an extraordinary and unverifiable statistic on those prisoners who were recidivists. In the United States, he said, some fifty per cent of prisoners committed crimes again and were caught; in Tokyo, almost seventy per cent. But here, he said, the percentage was a mere three. The system worked. Men were reformed. It was possible.

Yes. In this society it was even probable, I thought, and eerily impressive.

The last corridor in my itinerary led to a makeshift art gallery, hung with the prisoners' paintings. We strolled in front of them, I feeling jaded: even in this humidity the fans were static overhead. But among the predictably academic scroll-paintings and gauche Western hybrids one or two canvases were striking for a conventional but dextrous talent. Who, I wondered, had painted the romantic but stylish picture of Mao Zedong giving up his horse to a young soldier during the Long March? And who was responsible for the portrait of Zhou Enlai – a study of brooding, far-sighted statesmanship, hackneyed yet rather sensitive?

'He's one of our younger prisoners.' The warden looked proud. 'He's only nineteen.'

'What's he in for?'

'For raping little girls. Many of them. He's here for life.'

'May I talk to him?'

The warden looked surprised, but said yes.

Five minutes later Number 2489 stood before us, blinking a little, as if he had emerged from darkness: a sad-faced boy. He was short, narrow-chested. His cheeks and receding chin were still pink with adolescent spots. His eyes flickered between us.

How had he learnt to paint so well, I asked?

'He was taught here,' the warden said.

By now we were surrounded by prison staff and interpreters. The boy answered questions in soft monosyllables. His lips protruded oddly and his front teeth were broken. Yes, he loved painting. Of course he had never seen Zhou Enlai. He had painted him from photographs. Yes, he thought him a suitable subject, noble.

Slowly, through his furtiveness and bewilderment, the faintest flush of pride arose.

I wondered if he had received psychiatric treatment, but the wardens looked bemused by the idea. The political officers taught the prisoners, they said. The prisoners' ideas were corrected that way.

The chief warden said: 'We don't have mentally ill prisoners.'

[155]

So he would stay here for ever?

Yes, for ever.

I looked back at Number 2489 and wondered vaguely why his teeth were broken. His gaze went on fidgeting pathetically between us. He tried to smile.

What did he hope for the future, I asked?

He hoped to paint more, he said. And suddenly, watching him, I received the strong but inexplicable impression – almost a certainty – that he did not want to return to the outside world at all, a world in which a man's crime stained even his most distant relatives, the world of those violated children. Here instead, in this protective shell of walls, he was himself a child again, without responsibility or choice: purged.

*　　　*　　　*

Instead of a dank bell-tent, the acrobats' circus performs in a pillared amphitheatre. As the lights dim, a band strikes up from a balcony dripping with lanterns and tinsel, and ultra-violet lamps pick out the white shirts in the audience and turn it into a vertical chequerboard.

Into the drabness of the everyday world, the performers erupt with a shocking, fairyland glamour. Dancers rotate plates whining on the end of wands. Ventriloquists people the theatre with nightingales. Spring-board artists, clowns, ugly-beautiful contortionists – they all belong to a fluorescent tribe from some other sphere. Their high-rouged cheeks and matinée-idol grins isolate them in a half-sinister artifice. Outside the ring they do not imaginably exist.

But twice the spell is broken. A panda – a poor, beribboned thing – rides a bicycle, slides down a chute and eats dumplings at table, all at the tempo of a crippled human being. It is a spectacle of humiliation. After climbing a rostrum to receive an olympic medal, the bewildered creature covers its eyes against the glare – the crowd thinks this coy, and roars – and flounders forward flat on its face. Once, too, one of the acrobats fails her somersault. For a moment I see only the eloquent pain of her shoulders and bowed head, then she flees in unbearable shame to the curtained door.

But it is another girl, mounting acrobatically on a tier of balanced tables, whom I finally remember. Each table is handed up to her on a long rod, until she has built her way high against the ceiling. And there she hovers now on one hand, now on her head, her torso curved in flawless equilibrium until at last, in spotlit isolation, she bends backwards double, smiling, and plucks from the dark behind her a plastic rose.

*　　*　　*

A mild stomach-ache sent me hunting for a chemist, but the one I found was unexpected. In its window a stuffed deer gazed backward at its tail with dismay, and underneath was the reason why. 'Deer's Tail Extract', read the boxes in English. 'Tonic Oral Liquid. Good for Wind-evil. Good for stimulating mental and physical energy in case of undergrowth, senility, and debility during convalescence, hepatitis, anaemia and peptic ulcer. . . .' Beside it, a figurine of the Longevity God squatted among bottles of snake wine and lizard anti-asthma pills.

I had often noticed these apothecaries' lairs, but had never entered one. Above the counter poked a high forehead, whose owner was mixing herbs. I padded round the shelves. Slivers of deer antler rested on plates like sliced potatoes, and hundreds of lizard skins were bound two by two in purplish sheafs, with their heads still on. A fusty prestige of Latin turned all ingredients and diseases opaque. *Guttae Olei Jecoris Piscis: Pro Infantibus*, I thought, must be the schoolchild's bane of cod-liver oil, but what of 'Indications for Euroliathis, including Nephroliathis, Eurotholiasis, Cystoliathis etc.'? Dried-up ginseng roots writhed in cabinets like an ancient catch of squids. There was powder of pearls (for inducing *Yin* and tranquillising the mind), and enigmatic bottles which read, with a momentary lapse into Latin, 'Suitable for the climacterium of women and men'.

'Can I help you?' The apothecary's brow tilted back above a pale, pedantic face.

I dithered. My stomach-ache seemed suddenly beneath his notice, beneath the sorcerous dignity of his den. I could not even translate it into Latin.

But he scuttled away and returned beaming with a small packet. I read: 'Essence of Frog: good for the intestines.'

'But frogs. . . .'

Had I not tried frog's essence before, he asked? Or was I interested in something else? Perhaps I had a bone-marrow deficiency? Or. . . . He was nervously excited by my potential. His head kept bobbing up behind different sections of the counter. Did he detect a slight cough? Lizard wine was the answer. He spluttered and patted his chest in demonstration, then dropped an imaginary lizard down his throat and closed his eyes with relief. Or what about caterpillar fungus for night-sweating? He scattered a shower of bottles and packets over the counter. I fingered them in desperation. What was safe? Tiger bone? Hypertension longevity paste?

The cure-all seemed to be Ginseng Royal Jelly. According to its specifications it dealt with everything from palpitations to impotence, baldness and anorexia. It dissipated phlegm and boosted blood circulation, expelled wind-evil, dredged the meridian passage and gave the *coup de grâce* to apoplexy. Facial paralysis and hemiplegia dissipated at its touch. Speech impediments unravelled. Tingling and spasm of the limbs ceased.

But there was no mention of stomach-aches.

I picked up a box of oxen penis extract and asked humourlessly: 'What about this?'

'That . . . oh that. . . .' The man's head wobbled quaintly. He started to stammer. 'That is for . . . married men' – he extended a shaky hand to retrieve it – '. . . when they are not feeling strong.'

Covered in embarrassment, he pressed a bottle of snake wine on me. In compensation I bought some frog essence and escaped, planning to donate them to the first resilient-looking person I met.

But I was on my way to a sadder medical establishment. I had bludgeoned Professor Wu into securing me access to the city's mental hospital, founded under American influence nearly thirty years before. Now it admitted nearly five thousand patients every year, and employed fourteen hundred personnel including two hundred psychiatrists. A drop in the Shanghai ocean: but immense.

The Chief of Psychiatry and a young doctor sat with me at a bare table in a bare room. 'You must realise it is very difficult with our people,' the Chief said. 'In the West you are used to speaking out your problems. You'll say "I have this sexual impediment or such-and-such trouble with my family". But that is not our tradition. We internalise all that.' He thrust a finger into his throat as if choking on his own sick. 'We are mostly dealing with people of a very low education. They are not used to self-examination, and they can't express themselves – not such complicated things.'

'And they're ashamed before their families,' the doctor said, 'ashamed before everyone, in fact – work-mates, friends, us. They will swallow back everything.'

'So what can you do?'

The Chief said: 'It's very hard. Free association techniques haven't worked with us at all, and nor has hypnosis. We've virtually given them up. Nor can we practise deep analysis.' I wondered what was left. 'Even in group therapy,' he went on, 'patients just stay silent. The therapist has to select a bright one to voice his troubles, and hope the others may be drawn in. . . .'

So the vital relationship between child and parent was almost always inaccessible to them, too closely guarded by ancient taboos. The Confucian concept of character had taught that men were healed by constraints imposed from outside, not by the expulsion of tensions from within. The whole of their tradition was against them.

We reached the women's wards down bare, clean corridors through dormitories neat and bare too, where the patients' few possessions, sifted for implements of suicide, were closed up in lockers. As we opened the door into the occupational therapy room, some thirty ravaged faces turned to stare, and a regimented clapping broke out. They were expecting us. They wore crumpled mauve jackets and loose pyjama bottoms with the institution's name stitched in red on the left leg. These patients were not mad, like the Chronics, but victims of mental breakdown. They were filling bottles for a cosmetics company, and sewing multi-coloured dolls. The room was bright-lit. The bars in its windows were disguised as long panes. A radio played pretty music. But their faces seemed closed away, their eyes black-rimmed with an inner sleeplessness, or dulled to slits. Only a few turned to me and asked if I was American, and what I did, and a woman with the last traces of a hair-perm kept touching my arm with her fingertips, as if uncertain whether I was there.

We went into a room whose ceiling was slung with tinsel for the Moon Festival. Three chairs had been set out for us. A charge nurse put on a cassette of pop music, and a patient emerged from one corner. She had changed into skirt and blouse, and her hair was tied back from a face of fierce brightness. The doorway filled with women who had wandered off the corridor.

'She's going to dance for you,' the Chief said.

The girl stepped into the clearing of patients. Her arms and palms twisted outward in synthetic coquetry. Then she launched into a solo of weirdly mixed ballet and disco, bold with some choreography in her mind. She danced with a harsh, driven confidence. She twirled and jived. Her legs swept through half-remembered *fouettés* and arabesques, as if from childhood training. She emanated a manic sparkle. She was showing off. This was her scene. Her eyes met ours in flagrant self-delight.

'She's a manic depressive,' the doctor said.

From their doorway the patients watched in a flotsam of drained faces, their skin sallow, their hair a lifeless dust. They seemed to stare at her Western dream across the double divide of their culture and their pain, with a reticent, hopeless longing; while all the time the girl was dancing out her own cliché of America, her movements stereotype but charged with the brittle power of her sickness. When she stopped and I applauded, her gaze on the doctors and on me was flushed and vivid. It said: 'I'm all right. I've recovered, haven't I? I'm going to be all right.' And her audience smiled listlessly in the doorway, and the doctors clapped with me, while she went on standing in the centre of the stark room under its tinselled ceiling, and I seemed to be the only person who found the thing desolate.

After this, in each ward, the patients danced and sang for me. Only in the men's wing did we pass on quicker, as if their humiliation were greater than the women's, or disturbed the doctors more. Most of them sat massed instinctively together at tables, unspeaking, watching the few who played table tennis or assembled packing-boxes.

Their routine resembled that in the West: the same morning and evening drug regimen, the same occupational therapy. Even their categories were similar, with seventy-three per cent schizophrenics and a scattering of organic problems and mental retardation. Only the one per cent of hysterics would have seemed low in Europe, and the epileptic psychotics high. But the differences or similarities, for all I knew, lay more in diagnosis than in fact.

In the last ward we were greeted again by the dutiful clapping. Some sixty women sat at iron tables with orange juice and saucers of dried melon seeds. A saturnine man had arrived from another ward with a violin. He sat awkwardly on the table, facing me. As he started to play, a huge, graceless woman shambled to the room's centre, placed her pyjamaed feet astride, and sang. She sang the Japanese 'Song of the North Land', a ballad of homesickness and exile, while another woman danced this out – blank-faced and mechanical. 'She's a paranoid psychotic,' the Chief said.

Her moon face stared over our heads seeing something of her own, or nothing at all. The violin whined and skirled. Sometimes it stopped altogether, and the only sound was the cracking of the melon seeds in

[160]

the fingers of the watching patients. Then the dancer would freeze, and I would expect her eyes to focus on us or to roam about the room. But instead she wanted to believe in our absence, and continued to gaze beyond us with her terrible vacancy even after all sound and movement had stopped, and I clapped her ritually, and felt wretched.

It was easy to guess how the hospital became a haven. Even if the patients could not stumble out their hurt to an analyst, they lived here in a temporary, stressless vacuum. As in the West, most of them would return to the outside world within three months, where their own families, said the doctor, found their reinstatement hardest. Some returned as out-patients for voluntary occupational therapy. But most vanished back into Shanghai's wilderness for ever.

As the doctor accompanied me to the exit, my questions still rankled. Did the peculiar stresses on these people provoke a different ratio of disorders than in the West? It seemed not. Were those admitted immediately after the Cultural Revolution different? Not really, said the Chief. Did children suffer from their intense parental dominance? Or was the structured family life more secure? Nobody would guess.

Before leaving, I noticed in the angle of one corridor a screen hung with paintings done by male patients. The doctors, to my surprise, dismissed these as simple recreation; but they were violently betraying, more than their artists would ever have been in words. Through the traditional forms a fearful instability was breaking. Their landscapes were lit by lurid colours, or broken up. Their brushstrokes shook.

One picture, in particular, was arresting. It showed in profile a coiffured woman or goddess, half naked. In the palm of her extended hand knelt a tiny man. His head was tufted with sprigs of black hair, and his eyes cast upward to her in prayer. But hers were closed, the face a beautiful mask of indifference. Perhaps she did not even know that she held him.

6. To the South

BY EARLY OCTOBER I was a hundred miles south-west of Shanghai in the city of Hangzhou. An autumn melancholy had settled over its Western Lake – a lake more beautiful than any other in the Chinese imagination. Around it the hills overlap in a dense bloom of trees, scattered with pagodas and temples, and beyond these the sky is hung with ornamental-looking mountains. The whole landscape looks petted and artificial. Pencil-thin causeways travel across the waters. Often, in the brief days I was here, clouds came to rinse the hills clean of substance, and I was wandering in a mist-gentled vacuum of earth, sky and lake. The water became grey air, land elided with sky. As the hills blanched into haze, their delicacy of texture and detail survived in a delicacy of silhouette – the surge and roll of weightless valleys.

Hangzhou itself had declined into a worn-looking maze of *hutong*s and concrete. Even its population – less than a million – was smaller than in the days when the wandering court of the Song, dislodged from the north by nomad invaders in the twelfth century, chose it as their capital almost by default. For the first time the old heartlands on the Yellow River were exchanged for the burgeoning rice, tea and cotton of the Yangtze delta, the sultry waterways and sea-trade of the south. After the vigour of the Tang dynasty, the Song strikes a mellower note, an aesthetic sweetness of decline. Hangzhou, wrote Marco Polo, was 'without doubt the richest and most majestic city in the world' – a metropolis of multi-storeyed mansions and brimming canals, crossed by hundreds of stone bridges, whose thoroughfares were paved in brick and stone. Its people, he wrote, were pale, beautiful and strangely peaceful. In their markets, spices and jewellery had mingled with tinted nail varnish, toilet paper, mosquito repellent. On one side the poorer quarters clambered on each other's shoulders in a mountain of inflammable hovels; on the other the lake lay adrift with island-palaces and silk-awninged barges where the nobles floated with their courtesans over a carpet of lotus-blossoms. It comes as no surprise, in this *fin* *de siècle* metropolis, that its comic entertainers held mock-solemn readings from the Classics and proved in scurrilous word-play that Confucius and the Buddha were women.

Yet human flesh was served as a delicacy in the restaurants.

As I strolled around the lake, it was the muted pallet of the Song painters which came to mind, with its misty areas of empty silk. Already the quiet had purged Shanghai from me. I felt indolent and empty-headed – a figure in a watercolourist's landscape, wandering between willows along a causeway. Although the shores had been ravaged during the Cultural Revolution – monasteries and sculptures demolished *en masse* – the Buddha still sat in his temple at Lingyin: a figure so vast that were he to stand up his head would go crashing through the roof a hundred feet above him. Honeymooners were making wishes here, and an army officer had shed his jacket at the Buddha's feet and was kneeling in prayer.

Opposite, among the steamy ferns and mosses above a stream, a cliffside was carved with almost three hundred figures. They sat high in every niche and cleft, or presided deep in caves, the blessing of their hands blackened by the fondling of passers-by. The rocks dripped with moisture. White tree-roots squirmed about the sculpted feet and faces. Carved under the Mongol dynasty which succeeded the Song, the whole cliff had been turned into a passive hymn of contemplation. The cheeks of its Buddhas were fat as fruit, their lips cusped into ripe pouts. Filigrees of jewels dribbled from their arms and torsos. Pilgrims or sightseers had spattered their laps with joss-sticks, and their stomachs were sooted by candle-flames. In one cave the goddess Guanyin poured out her healing waters, her eyes closed by lichen, her crown a tiara of faded gold. Somebody had piled her feet with sweets.

I borrowed a bicycle and went through hills sown with tea plantations, and into jungled valleys between, glimmering with bamboo thickets and sunk streams. For almost the first time I saw wildlife: bullfrogs, black velvet butterflies and white caterpillars clustered like blossom on their plants. Once a big bronze lizard crossed my path, trailing an azure tail, and once a dawdling stoat.

I noticed that my path was paved with the ruins of some early temple. I was bumping over inscribed stones, and once glimpsed a carved deer under my wheels. I came into a valley where a pair of peasant houses stood, their terraces covered with drying herbs. Inside I glimpsed straw hats and baskets, and an iron-bowled furnace for roasting tea-leaves. An old man was working in an immaculately kept field, squared off by

[163]

bamboo fencing. His son emerged from indoors with a bird-like wife and child. As the little boy saw me he stopped dead with a breathy squeak and rushed against his mother.

'Don't be afraid.' The woman turned the child's face towards me. 'It's only a foreign devil.'

They assembled in front of me, staring, quizzical.

I was just walking about, I said. Were these their fields?

'No, these are rented from the collective, the village. Ours are behind.' The man waved at a straggle of vegetables – not the neatly tilled private plot I had expected.

I asked awkwardly: 'How is your work now?'

'No better, no worse.' He was bright, hardy, smiling. The woman and child were smiling too. The man threw out his hand level with his chest in a gesture of unchangingness. 'Things don't alter.'

I dithered in bemusement, my head filled with China's trumpeted agricultural renaissance. Since the disbanding of Mao's communes, peasant families had been farming their own rented fields, and giving only a fixed quota to the State. In four years, it was said, crop yields had almost doubled, and when I asked in Beijing what would happen if the government were to reverse its policies, somebody had answered bluntly: 'The peasants wouldn't stand for it. They'd rebel.' In this country of land-hunger and overpopulation – one quarter of the world's people farming only seven per cent of its arable land – these policies, I was told, had liberated the peasants from a too-intensive labour on their crops. Now, instead, they were diversifying into poultry-farming, pig-breeding, geese, mink. They were running small factories and hiring out transport. A modest wealth and bustle had broken out.

But the farmer was shaking his head. A new peasant élite was emerging, but he did not belong to it. The government was leasing fields for as long as fifteen years, he said, inviting long-term investment in the land. Some farmers were privately subletting it. Others were hiring labour. But all this had passed him by. He was too remote from things, he said. 'And the changes haven't been good for everybody.' But he was vague about who had suffered.

I had already heard fears about new inequality. The old communal safeguards had dropped away not only from the lazy and the stupid, but from the unprotected old and the merely unfortunate. I had seen signs of a huge surplus labour force hunting for employment in the cities, which were already full of the urban unemployed. The rural welfare system, especially in medicine, was starting to fragment. There were more vagrants about, more beggars. Nobody seemed sure how well the collectively built irrigation works and terracing would be maintained. The peasants were taking out their land from vital (but unprofitable) grain production and turning it over to cash crops. And because children both augmented the family labour-force and safeguarded their parents' old age, the rural birth-rate was spiralling again.

'It pays to have children,' the peasant said, 'even girls.' His son was still staring at me in unblinking reverie. 'In the country you're penalised if you have more than two children, but it's worth it.'

I asked doggedly: 'But you've got richer since the end of the Cultural Revolution?'

Again a look of regret crossed his face – but whether for my ignorance or his poverty, I couldn't tell – and he only repeated that level, changeless stroke of his hand. 'For us Old-Hundred-Names,' he said, 'nothing changes.'

I glanced at the two-storeyed house behind us. 'But this is new.'

'That's my younger brother's. It was built last year. I live in this one.' He gestured to the one-storey house beside it. 'My brother's cost nearly 10,000 yuan to build. It was too much. What we need here is a tractor. We still just work with the hoe.' He paused while his father trudged along the bamboo fence: a stooped and burnished head, smiling. 'We can't afford a tractor now.'

So I had blundered on some rankling family inequality. I rummaged for something to say, but my head was full of clichés about the new policies. The man had given up smiling now. So had his wife. Only their son held out his hand laughing to my bag of oranges, and I gave them to him, grateful to turn my eyes somewhere else. Then I started back towards the track, taking a short cut across an overgrown hill. After a while I was heaving my bicycle past their family graveyard: small mounds set with memorial tablets, like the tombs of tiny emperors.

*　　*　　*

For a night and a day my train cut through mountains eight hundred miles towards the South China Sea and into the province of Fujian, which confronts the Nationalist strongholds of Quemoy and Taiwan across the water. My 'hard berth' carriage was banked with iron bunks. In the one below me an old woman lay motionless on her back all day, her mouth and eyes dimpled in a huge, placid face, and smiled beneficently even when asleep, with her arm curled round her grandson. At night the corridors became dim-lit stacks of exotically sprawled bodies and protruding feet in nylon socks. The floor crunched with discarded melon-seed husks.

Once the train stopped suddenly, waking me by its silence, and I looked out to see empty hills under a moonlit sky. Something gashed and dead was being heaved off the track under our cowcatcher. Then we moved on, with a bleating of whistles, into the night.

At dawn we were ascending the Wuyi mountains. Passengers clambered moaning from their bunks, cradling jars of green tea and packets of 'convenience noodles' which they softened in hot water. I hunted through my rucksack for anything edible, and pulled out a mammoth parcel of biscuits (everything is packaged for groups) with some pears and waxy chocolates.

During the night a second steam-engine had joined us. As we lost our momentum in the mountains, it pushed us from behind while the other pulled – twin giants with burnished red wheels. They hooted forlornly at each other. We followed gulleys along the coils of a river which even here curdled toxic with factory effluent. Lush hills opened and closed on valleys brilliant with rice terraces. Then the river cast up rocks. It made a wild corridor into the mountains. The earth grew juicy with monster ferns and liana-shrouded trees. A tissue of creepers stole over the banks. The jungle flooded in. Sometimes up these slopes the train panted almost to a stop and the overgrown cuttings converged to envelop it, before easing again into a pastoral clearing of black-roofed villages.

We travelled like this until almost midday. Then we crossed a watershed, our rear engine relinquished us, and suddenly we were following a new river – a panic of young, green-white water far below. We were descending.

In the restaurant-car, which was serving bones with indecipherable meat attached, a pair of Hong Kong businessmen hailed me like compatriots. The whole country made him sick, the older man said. If he could, he'd escape Hong Kong before 1997 when China would subsume it. He was fixated by his children's future. He never came here without some sickness in his head. Yes, he felt himself Chinese, but he could not understand the mind of these people at all. 'Look at them.' He glared at the family beside us, a group of farmers ogling our food (we were eating a week's income for them). 'How can I pretend to feel like them? Whenever my friends or I come to Red China, we say we're going to Hell.'

But after he had shambled away, his companion cheered up. 'The old people in Hong Kong are apprehensive. It's harder for them. But we young feel it's going to be OK.' He studied his plate of bones. 'We'll make out.'

Beyond my window, as the afternoon wore on, the mountains unlocked isolated valleys which the falling sun varnished into the illusion of peace. Village roofs dipped and swung above the green stairways of their terraces. Whitewashed walls were bright and unreal in the silence. Momentarily I thought: how beautiful. And I gazed at them with the acquisitive longing of someone hunting a weekend cottage. But they were filled by a rude poverty, I knew: their people were here in the train, bellowing convivially together. So I would greyly discount these idylls, and return to my book. But in the next valley the dream would reassert itself, and the glimpse of a tiled roof under a white wall incite again a childish mirage of Elysium.

But by evening the hills had shrunk. The sun spilt amber over the flattened rice-fields, where peasants were trudging home with their ploughshares over their shoulders. I had time to glimpse a littoral wallowing in banana groves and sugar cane – a China lusher than any I had seen – then night fell, and the lights of Xiamen were spreading over the sea.

I was now deep in Fujian, whose mountains isolated it from the rest of China. With their backs to a steep, poor hinterland, its towns have traditionally turned their energies seaward, and their people – clannish traders and fishermen, who speak their own dialect – had for centuries emigrated across south-east Asia and beyond.

This port of Xiamen – which the Fujianese call Amoy – still seemed touched by an older Europe. Portuguese and Dutch merchants had traded intermittently along all this coast, and the British had prised the city open as a Treaty Port after the Opium Wars. I walked along streets five storeys tall, lifted on whitewashed porticoes garish with neon signs. A Mediterranean ease was in the air. On the pavements sat mendicant letter-writers, and wart-doctors with eerie-coloured bottles and pseudo-scientific charts. Children went in clothes stitched with ducks and cats saying 'Lucky' or 'Happy' in English, sometimes misspelt or upside down or in looking-glass writing by mistake. In the meat market – a spread of dismembered trotters and ears, and intestines ripe with flies – I came across tribal women from inland. They were dressed in psychedelic hues – turquoise trousers, pink and green belts: colours loved, perhaps, for their farness from those of nature. The women clustered together, nervous in the urban sea. They looked like some vivid but downtrodden chorus from a Beijing opera. Beneath their broad straw hats, painted sunflower-yellow and dangling crimson wool behind, their hair fell in tinselled pigtails, and the brilliantly wimpled faces turned to me with stares of disbelief.

The town had been named a Special Economic Zone – a region to entice overseas investors – and its centre of gravity had shifted to a bulldozed area of sprouting factories and hotels. But the older city seemed unabashed. Its markets bloomed with fruit and vegetables unknown in the north, and the fish-stalls slithered with needle-toothed eels, mackerel, squids and blue-clawed crabs still feebly waving.

I found all the hotels full, but an offshore liner, *The Sea Paradise*, had been converted into a hostel and amusement palace. It was the eve of National Day, the anniversary of the People's Republic, and the ship blazed with lights. As my ferry approached it, the Circean strains of 'Jingle Bells' and 'Edelweiss' sounded over the water. Somewhere in the night, ten miles to eastward, lay the Nationalist-held island of Quemoy – a honeycomb of tunnels and batteries. But this evening nothing came out of that darkness but faint, sultry gasps of wind.

The Sea Paradise turned out to be a six-decked Danish liner, the *Prinsesse Margrethe*, sold off to China by a hard-pressed shipping company. Notices in the cabins still said 'Velkommen Ombord' and listed the bus routes to Copenhagen, and the bar was illuminated by tantalising pictures of Danish food no longer available, and signs for 'Smørrebrod'.

A flotilla of boats and ferries was pouring young people on board. A year before, scarcely one live dance-band had existed in the whole country (except in the Great Wall Hotel). Now they were everywhere – two on this ship alone. They exerted the fascination of something still half taboo. In the Scandia Cafetaria couples were dancing self-consciously separate, or holding each other's hands while they waltzed, as if an arm-encircled waist were too intrusive. Bespectacled youths in their twenties looked as callow as Western fifteen-year-olds. They fidgeted at tables round the dance-floor, sipping Coca-Cola or orange squash through straws, and joked in nervy bursts. The girls tittered. Their dresses covered them primly to their wrists, but on the backlit dance-floor the cheap nylon was transparent against their boyish figures and white bras. They danced speechlessly with one another. And the men waltzed together too, their eyes never meeting, the smaller ones taking the female role. It was the function, not the relationship, that mattered. They were concentrating on 'Moon River'. They were being Western.

I was sharing a table with a young man whose wife was waltzing with his sister. 'I can't dance,' he said.

Perhaps this was why his face was sunk in embittered gloom. Its eyelids curved in two seamless crescents – they almost snuffed out his gaze – echoing the droop of his eyebrows above and the droop of a vestigial moustache below. All his features seemed to wilt. 'There weren't places like this before I was married,' he said. 'That made things harder.'

'What things?'

'Just meeting. Getting to know one another. When you're courting, its enough simply that you're a man and she's a girl.' The noise of the band drowned our talk, protected it. 'It's only after marriage that things go wrong. . . .'

It occurred to me that he was slightly drunk. The table was littered with empty beer cans, and his cheeks were flushed.

'In what way wrong?'

But if he had meant sexual disillusion, he did not say so. Under their oblique lids his eyes showed lizardish slits. They seemed only now to register that I was a foreigner. 'There are three reasons for divorce here. First . . .' His hands groped for another beer can. '. . . Men's and women's salaries are often the same now, so the wife doesn't *need* the husband. . . . There's no dependence. So people separate because their wives are too forceful. Secondly,' – these tidy numbers and categories were to haunt my conversations to the end – 'they quarrel over the children. . . . Children. . . .' The idea almost closed his eyes. 'With us, the children are more important than each other. My best friend separated because his wife did nothing but fawn over the baby . . . baby . . . she just poured milk and sugar down its throat. Children are getting spoilt now . . . single children . . . parents and grandparents all adore and coddle them, so they grow up monsters. . . . Really terrible. Especially boys.'

His sagging head jerked up and his eyes strayed to where his wife was trying to fox-trot in his sister's arms. They wore identical expressions: pert and dead. 'And the third problem is mothers-in-law . . . those relationships . . . *poxiguanxi*. My wife and mother do nothing but fight' – he vibrated his thumbs and forefingers in argument. 'My mother is old. All her ideas, so old. When they fight. I nudge my wife. . . .' By now his eyelids had drooped shut, but the effect, far from being tired or pathetic had become one of hard secrecy. 'In the end a son must take his mother's side. You can get rid of a wife, but not . . . your parents.'

When the women returned to sit with us, he didn't say another word. Confused by my presence, they talked only in whispers, or gazed glassily at the unisexual couples circling the floor.

But upstairs, in the Seahorse Club, things were hotting up. Here, on the founding anniversary of Mao Zedong's Red China, a wild-haired youth was gyrating under strobe lights, bawling a hybrid pop song and rocking an electric guitar. The dance-floor filled. Young men in Sanyo T-shirts threw themselves into the mood. A few girls joined them. The men looked louche and rootless. They were the new-style young. But their dancing held none of the dreamy self-immolation of Western adolescents; it was extrovert, unerotic. Only once a swarthy youth and his gypsy-dark girl touched their backs together with a cursory wriggling. Immediately an official in a red arm-band pulled them off the floor and warned them.

And by eleven o'clock the last flotillas of revellers had sailed singing back across the straits.

For a century before the Second World War the island of Gulangyu, just offshore from Xiamen, was a European trading enclave, exempt from Chinese law. It had fallen quiet now – a cluster of sea-girt hills smothered by villas and rich with ginko, cinnamon and cassia trees. All over the island I encountered a lush dilapidation of mansions drenched in Spanish moss and bougainvillaea. They had invented themselves in their own colonial style, lapsing into decorativeness as the ties of the motherland loosened. Balconies and window-frames curved and flowered like those of Portuguese Macao. Here and there a stucco garland survived, a lion-mask or a mutilated angel's head. Everywhere the sheer force of sun had sucked the wood dry and crumbled the stone. Alleys and stairways petered out under shutters bleached wafer-thin. And no vehicles disturbed the streets. Only a three-wheeled hearse, pushed by mourners, carried its coffin to the wharf, where it was embarked on a rowing-boat and rocked over the waves to Xiamen.

Trudging uphill, I pushed through an overgrown cemetery, its memorial stones carved with Chinese characters and Christian crosses. The only dates I could decipher told of short lives. I wondered who had lived them. A woman was lighting incense on one grave, tugging the grass from its half-buried stone. She looked up as I passed, and said: 'My mother.'

Beyond, the hill's summit surged into monstrous boulders, and from here I saw others erupting from all the highest points of the island, smooth as bones, as if the earth's skin had peeled back from them. The sea stretched unshimmering between the mainland and the islands to the east. A liner stood on it, still as a bottled ship, and a pair of Red frigates sailed past, pennants streaming and guns pointed at the sky. Beyond the curve of Xiamen and the empty-looking isles, the Communist bombardment of Quemoy had fallen silent six years before. Behind me a concrete blockhouse stood abandoned, its roof sprouting cacti and its gun-slits stopped with weeds.

Even on this hilltop the temperature must have been 90°F in the shade. For an hour I lay asleep among the rocks, until the silence was broken by a fluting, disembodied music. I looked up to see a flock of tame pigeons fluttering high above me. It was an old Chinese conceit. The flutes wired to their tails were tiny gourds, like blown birds' eggs, so light that if you hold them in your hand you cannot feel them. Now they filled the air with a resonant whining, like the wind in invisible telegraph wires.

At dusk I descended to a beach peppered with ruined blockhouses, and slipped into a warm sea. Then I wandered the restaurants. 'Go to the private eating-houses,' somebody told me. 'They're the ones.' So I sat in a steamy warren full of gorging families. Its counters were lined with mussels, crabs and bass, by ducks whose eyes still shone accusing in their heads, by langoustes, sea cucumber, yellow croaker. Dumplings were boiling over clay furnaces, and the slicing and pounding of bamboo-shoots never stopped. A table of boisterous workmen adopted me. Their questions were familiar by now, even in their broken Mandarin. 'How much do you earn? How much do you get to eat? How much. . .?' They lounged in vests and frayed shirts, their trousers dragged up above their knees, and piled bones and shells on the table in half-masticated heaps. Three stevedores and a beggar sidled in to gawp at me, were moved out by the restaurateur, filtered back. They watched my every mouthful. I avoided the lethal mussels and chicken crushed in its bone-splinters, and opted for dumplings and bass. I told myself that the dirt on my chopsticks was a discolouration of the wood, or so ingrained as to be harmlessly immovable.

After I left, I looked back to see the beggar standing at my place, lifting my empty bowl to his lips.

I roamed the Xiamen wharfs looking for a boat going to Canton. In one harbour a rotting armada of fifty fishing junks lay half sunk in silt, their engines cranking and choking. On the main quay, dotted with overseas Chinese arrived to visit their native villages, a sixty-year-old peasant, who had escaped to Singapore in 1947, was holding court with his country relatives around him. The Western cut of his clothes set him apart. Urbanity exuded from his plump hands, his considering mouth. He was a man of the world. As for his son, a suave Shell executive who had returned for the first time since infancy, he ambled over to talk with me rather than endure his relatives.

'My father's sentimental about China,' he said. 'He has no parents left, so these village brothers and sisters are his family. He revels in being the boss of them all.' His gaze drifted unhappily to them over my shoulder. They looked like dowdy litigants, out of their depth. 'Three years ago he even built a house in the village – it was a symbol of his success. That's typical of these first-generation migrants. Now he's going to give a banquet for the whole place. They think he's rich and important, of course, although in Singapore he's just a cab-driver.'

'And you feel nothing for the village?'

'I?' He dangled a briefcase foppishly from his fingers. 'Well . . . even I . . . I feel a kind of pull.' He appeared a little surprised at this. 'I seem to want to come back. But my wife was born in Singapore and says: "What do you want to visit that lousy country China for? Why not go to Japan?" And my children already feel the same as her.'

The emigrant was talking to his brother now – a grey-haired peasant togged up in his best. The brother's hands were clasped respectfully in front of his crutch, and his whole upper body – inclined slightly forward as he listened – conveyed an extraordinary mixture of pride and obsequiousness.

The young man said: 'These people's whole way is different from ours. They work slower, think slower. You only have to look at how they walk. And the village is desperately poor. They have to farm as well as fish.'

'Winter crops?'

'I don't know. I don't know one crop from another. I didn't ask. But my father's brought them a bicycle and a colour TV. They'd give us a cold shoulder if we didn't do that. They're mercenary, and getting greedier all the time. My uncle will have the only colour TV in the village.'

I said jokingly: 'He can set up a cinema.'

'Yes.' He was serious. 'His family will charge people to come in and look at the popular programmes. They do that in the villages.'

But now the quayside conference had ended, and the Singapore cab-driver came sauntering out. He was moving with a faint mandarin waddle, and his rustic court had fallen into sycophantic step behind him.

I made my way, depressed, to the shipping office, and bought a steerage-class fare to Canton. It was the last ticket left.

That afternoon, as we sailed past the steep profile of Quemoy, policemen cleared the passengers from the starboard decks. I gazed at the island through glass doors with a mob of young Cantonese, who made faces at the back of the policemen's heads. 'I suppose they think we're going to dive in and swim over!'

Someone quipped: 'Why bother when you can tune in to their TV?'

I said: 'I thought that was forbidden.'

'In Xiamen everybody does it.'

We went on gazing until the ethereal-looking island had slid down over the horizon. To the west the headlands loomed tall for several hours where the last Fujian mountains blundered into the sea, then they smoothed to the lowlands of Guangdong province – outcrops of blue rock and empty islands. Then it was night.

At supper I was regaled by workers from a plastics factory. They talked in bursts of boyish jokes which they translated for me into the school-taught Mandarin of the Cantonese south. The swelling sea sent our soup and beer pitching across the table, and once the woman on the chair beside me was tipped on to my lap, complaining all the time. They were in holiday mood, and plied me with questions. Only occasionally – when I told them that in Britain most people received a month's holiday (they received a week) and that we worked five days a week (they worked six) – did they lapse into perplexed or ruminative silences; and when I mentioned that Western governments were full of contending political parties instead of a single authority, the illusion of our togetherness was temporarily shattered, and the girls stared at me with big, uncomprehending eyes, and the men murmured. Finally, when they heard I was travelling alone, I saw that I slid altogether out of their comprehension. All foreigners go everywhere in groups, they said. Always. And they go top class.

But we were already in the ship's seamier suburbs. From its upper deck, status plummeted to family-size cabins, then to the eight-berth cubicles of the fourth class – and finally into the hold where double tiers of bunks massed together in fetid lines. At night we lay banked like galley-slaves cheek-by-jowl. The bunk-ends sprouted hundreds of hanging flannels and the sills of all the portholes were blocked with food. Beside me an old man stretched like a tomb-effigy with a fan across his chest. Above, a Hunanese peasant kept retching down into the spittoon near my feet. I felt mercifully tired. Inquisitive heads inspected me over the bunk-sides, but I feigned sleep and gradually lost my attraction. Little by little the hold fell quiet. The swell of the sea deepened, like a heavy but irregular breathing. The lights dimmed.

But just as I was dozing off, I was rediscovered. A bespectacled face reared from a bunk beyond my feet, and grinned with a mouthful of teeth so disordered that I had the illusion he could rearrange them at will. I was feeling faintly seasick.

'Do you like music?' he asked. 'I've got the latest. Absolutely the *latest*.' His face bobbed up again beside mine, with a cassette-player.

I lied sleepily: 'I don't like singing. . . .'

But he only said: 'Of *course* you do,' and circled the earphones tenderly round my head. I found myself plugged in to Wham! I was instantly deafened. Beside me the man's mouth was going up and down, saying things. But I could only hear '*Wake me up, before you go-go* . . .'

After a minute I eased off the earphones. 'It's terrific. Thanks.' In the airless dark people were starting to be sick.

'But you haven't heard the best bits! You've *got* to hear "Careless Whispers". You haven't heard it in England? Never?' He gazed at me horrified. 'What do you do? What is your name?'

'Thubron.'

'Tampon, ' he repeated. 'I'm Li Yun.' He shook one of my inert hands. The air was stifling. I closed my eyes, but his questions came remorselessly. 'Why are you here , Mr Tampon? I mean, why in fifth class? Why aren't you travelling special class? You're too tall. These beds were designed for us people. We're small because we don't eat enough.' He lifted the earphones again, threatening 'Careless Whispers'. 'What do you do?'

'An engineer,' I said, trying to sound boring. Half the Chinese I'd met said they were engineers. My head was filled with seasickness as I found myself telling him a dribble of shameless lies. My home life was dull, I said. My salary was average. I was married with one daughter. My job was tedious. I'd never been to a pop concert and I was feeling seasick.

'But you must hear "Careless . . ." '

'I need to clear my head. I'm going on deck.'

'But you'll come and see me in Canton?'

'Yes.'

Clutching his business card, I climbed into the solitude which to most Chinese is loneliness. The sky was bright with a haloed moon, and dusted in clouds. I sat under the bridge in a cool wind, waiting for my nausea to disperse. The sea's swell had abated. Behind, in the moonlight, the ship made a trembling, foam-silver passage over the dark. Once, the fugitive brilliance of another liner passed, and to the west a lighthouse threw an intermittent blade across the horizon.

By the time I returned to the hold it was sunk in snoring paralysis. Its bunks had resolved into a giant, two-tiered chessboard, where bespectacled bishops and pawns huddled, with an occasional fat castle. Li Yun lay fast asleep with his earphones on, and I slid unnoticed into my bunk.

Hours later I was woken by the manicured fingers of two slender female hands twined in my hair. They came from the bed end-on to mine. I peered over to see a young woman with her arms lifted elegantly above her head in sleep, like an Arab dancer. For the rest of the night these hands dangled beside my cheek, but withdrew in confusion at dawn.

When I climbed on deck, I imagined that the sun was rising in the north. Then I realised that we must be rounding the great peak of Hong Kong island – a shadow on the reddening sky – with Macao invisible to starboard. Fleets of junks were scattered like insects among the lesser islands, their sails spread to a brisk wind, and an hour later we were sailing to Canton up the silted estuary of the Pearl River.

7. Canton

IT IS AT once the flashiest and most traditional of the great cities. Whereas Shanghai grew sudden and unnatural from its origins, Canton remains rooted in a long, commercial past. The traffic of the South China Sea has bred it more suave and knowing than the northern towns, and the diaspora of its citizens, who have streamed over south-east Asia to the Americas and Europe, feeds back to it a disruptive flood of wares and longings. It has always been a breeding-ground of revolution. During the 1920s Mao Zedong, Zhou Enlai and Chiang Kai-shek all started their careers here under Sun Yatsen. Its wordly acumen, together with its farness from the capital, have encouraged a dissident sense of superiority.

The city slopes southward in the curve of the Pearl River. Its roads move between high-piered arcades in a disarray of old mansions and intruding concrete. Hanging gardens topple from the balconies and every roof sprouts a copse of television aerials, canted at Hong Kong. The streets are threaded by a Japanese fifth column of Honda and Yamaha motor scooters, Datsun taxis and Toyota minibuses. Through them the river flows gentle and sepia, more like a liquid street, where bossy tugs pull trains of five or six barges sunk to their gunwales under heaps of sand, floating downstream with a ramshackle stateliness into the silted gulf. Under the banyan trees along the waterfront, tousle-haired youths sell bracelets and pocket calculators, and roving money-changers send forward their children as envoys for illicit deals.

The narrower the streets, the more ancient they become. The procession of down-at-heel tenements along the main roads splinters into changeless alleys. The houses converge above needle-thin paths paved with long, shining slabs, where two bicyclists can scarcely ride abreast. Doors are stuck with padlocked letter-boxes which look forever empty. Leaky gutters dribble fountains and pelmets of ferns. Sometimes, glancing through windows, I mistook the cramped living-rooms – banked with vases, thermoses, radios, clocks, bulbs, televisions – for little shops. Their people grinned and called out, but their language was incomprehensible to me – a caress of slurred vowels. Every other sentence ended with the upward lilt of a propitiatory *ah*. The courtyard doors were plastered with paintings of traditional house-guardians in full armour, and in the darkness beyond every other window I glimpsed the red lights of joss-sticks glowing high up – as if people were smoking close under the ceiling – where the Buddha sat enthroned in a niche, or offerings of apples encircled the Goddess of Mercy.

I became restless with feelings of exclusion. The newly exotic habitat (a few miles south of the Tropic of Cancer) and the language I didn't understand, reminded me of what I had begun to forget – that I was in a civilisation still elusive to me.

I sidled into a boarding nursery different from those in the north. In a region where no real winter came, the classrooms were airy, and the walls bright with paintings. The children ignored their teachers' pleas and swarmed after me. Their clothes were a rainbow chaos, their hair jaunty with ribbons. They looked uniformly happy. None of them played alone. The smallest group I saw was a quartet of four-year-old boys, solemn and self-involved, dealing out cards on a bench. Others sang and mimed songs in a disharmony of gestures and squeals while a teacher hit an old harmonium.

Nearby, a Gothic cathedral might have been set down all of a piece from France. On the base of its towers were carved 'Jerusalem' and 'Rome' – but 'Jerusalem', by some quixotic choice, had been defaced. At the time of its consecration, in 1863, the bleak enormousness of the building had been mellowed by French stained glass – but now this was gone. Inside, under the rib vaulting, the stone pendants, the Stations of the Cross, a few old ladies were genuflecting and trickling their rosaries between empurpled fingertips. Other worshippers had left behind hassocks and books among the pews, and two lay workers were carrying away the electric fans to 'where they would do no harm'. The cathedral was at once familiar and disorienting. I sat down with a kind of homesickness. The gaunt nave faintly saddened me, as if I were inhabiting some historical loss. The hassock between my feet was crocheted with Chinese characters which I could not decipher.

But behind me, slowly, a congregation was gathering. It numbered over a hundred, thinly scattered through the pews. The candelabra above the altar flashed on in a thicket of coloured bulbs, and Mass went forward in dumb-show. No word of prayer or chant escaped the celebrant at the altar. But the people knew all the punctuations of the service – the genuflections and self-crossings, the moment to receive the wine-dipped Host. The loudest sound was the twittering of sparrows in the vaults.

Beneath the door of the confessional the white-socked feet of another priest tapped listlessly, while above it his blotched forehead swayed back and forth as he listened to two penitents at once. A woman knelt with her child standing vacantly beside her as she confessed. A young man whispered on the other side. I wondered what shame obsessed them. When the bells crashed out and the priest at last emerged, I saw a face which looked past all memory of sin, emptied by age.

I went into the sunlight with the congregation, and picked my way at random through the alleys. Perhaps because people were smaller than in the north, I noticed the old here – wizened crones with thinned hair, and near-dwarf men. A beggar woman sat on a bridge with a notice in front of her – a tale of abandonment – and a deformed child. Her mouth hung in a dumb oval of distress. The child lay naked, discoloured pink and peeling, with one leg bent double under him, its calf attached – by some atrocious aberration – to its thigh. A crowd circled them, unspeaking. The bowl in front of the child was filled with money, dropped in by women and by the middle-aged. The mass of young men only stared and went away.

I came to where the Pearl River, slow with barges and effluent, forked around Shamian island. Here, where the British and French concessions used to be, hefty Doric banking houses and villas lingered in bastard elegance, and the boulevards were sleepy with gardens. I strolled into the pale colossus of the White Swan Hotel. Such hotels – 'For the Merchant Prince of Today', claim the advertisements – were mushrooming up everywhere with foreign expertise: cities within cities, whose Chinese trappings (tiled gateways, dragon-screens in the foyer) were no more than gutted reminders of the nation outside. In mercantile Canton, their luxury seemed to embody less an anachronism than the topmost rung of an ascendable ladder. In the White Swan lobby a twenty-five-foot waterfall dropped beneath an ornamental temple into pools flickering with goldfish. Its shopping-arcade sold mink coats. An Elizabeth Arden beauty salon was opening. In the Japanese restaurant you could spend the monthly salary of a Chinese clerk and still emerge hungry.

But the Overseas Chinese Hotel was filled with a down-to-earth urgency. In its foyer, Cantonese expatriates received their mainland cousins with fistfuls of coupons for the collection of foreign goods. Elderly emigrants in cardigans and silver-rimmed spectacles held magisterial sway, surrounded by humble grins and the shuffle of plastic sandals. Meanwhile, at a nearby depot, lorries from Hong Kong were disgorging Toshiba refrigerators, Hitachi televisions and Philips cassette-recorders.

Half the families in the city have relatives abroad, and a stream of trains, aeroplanes and a daily Hong Kong ferry are met with greedy expectancy. Exhausted with booty, the expatriates wheel and drag their cases along the ramps, their pockets stuffed with coupons, their spare fingers hooked about plastic bags prestigious with the names of Hong Kong boutiques and Kowloon foodstores. Rouged and permed, their wives trundle after them, pushing their Sonys and Hitachis on trolleys and followed by a languid younger generation in summer suits and Yasaki trainers. The docks are in uproar. Cranes swing the precious goods ashore in nets, while a tannoy relays *Carmen*, and there emerges on to the ship's gangway a sauntering file of the fattened and elect. The relatives drool and shout behind the railings. As their laden visitors emerge, they push their children forward like mascots. Greetings are embarrassed, formal. Babies are ritually cuddled. One by one the goods drop from weary emigrant hands and shoulders, and the relatives snatch them helpfully up. Outside the docks a fleet of red taxis gathers to spirit them all away. The visiting patriarch, swinging an important-looking leather briefcase, takes his rightful seat beside the driver, everybody else piles in behind, and they ease euphorically off to a banquet.

I watched them in selfish gloom. Unconsciously, I suppose, I was demanding that they conform to my puritan concept of Communism, or to some pastoral simplicity. But they robustly refused. They had no intention of feeding my romanticism with their suffering. They wanted those televisions.

I came upon Li Yun's visiting-card in my trouser pocket, and was touched by guilt. His address led me down a squirming alley and up to the ninth floor of a concrete block, where I found his flat closed by an old elevator gate. I knew he was in because the whole building was shaking with '*Wake me up before you go-go*'. As he flung open the door crying 'Mr Tampon!' I was reminded of my married *alter ego*, and hoped not to be asked about engineering.

'You've come!' he kept saying. 'You're here!' Then his tooth-crammed smile faded into frustration. 'You've come – and everybody's out!'

He shared the flat with his brother's family and showed me round their four rooms as a melancholy substitute for meeting them. By Canton standards the apartment was spacious, with its own kitchen and a sitting-room given over to a jumble of magazines and cassettes. Across one wall spread an enormous poster of Rambo.

Li produced cakes left over from the Moon Festival, and we tasted these while he reorganised my tour of inland China. His suggested routes were transparently tailored to include himself. His job in the local tax bureau meant nothing to him. He'd take three or four days off, he said, and we could visit resorts all along the southern coast. But why, he asked, did I want to go inland to Shaoshan?

'Mao Zedong was born there.'

'But it's a dump!' he said. 'Nobody goes to those places any more. Anyway, there aren't any trains. Or rather they don't stop. They just go straight through.' This, I knew, was pure fantasy. He just didn't want to go to Shaoshan. 'I'll show you Canton! Then we'll go to Shantou together! That's a good part, on the sea.'

I looked at him doubtfully. 'You like swimming?'

'*Swim?* I can't *swim*.' He made swimming sound Herculean. 'But that area's full of contraband. You can buy it cheap off the streets. The fishermen exchange silks for videos – in mid-ocean, with ships from Singapore. They make a packet.'

'I'm going inland.'

'But you'll need gifts to take home. Wouldn't Mrs Tampon like a Japanese video?'

'No. . . .'

'Then what about your little girl?'

A faint identity crisis began to brew up. I imagined this daughter a little sadly, and tried to discover her tastes. In the end I decided she wanted a Chinese gift, not a Japanese one. '*Chinese?*' The conviction that foreign goods were superior settled over him in a pucker of disdain. 'But where will you travel inland? There's nothing to see there.' He pulled out his photograph album and pointed unenthusiastically to a series of temples and conical hills. 'There's nothing to buy.' In the foreground of each snapshot stood Li Yun, swanky in jeans. There was Li Yun in the Yellow Mountains, in Beijing, in Guilin, in Hangzhou. His stance of mannered indolence never altered, and he was usually overexposed – a blanched column where dark glasses floated, like the facial discs of an owl. 'That's me,' he kept saying. But the scenery behind him was indistinguishable.

Little by little, as I adhered to a stern procession of landlocked goals, his dream of contraband wilted. A half-hearted plea for Shanghai petered out in sighs, and the photograph album was replaced by his stamp album. He was like a child showing me toys. All his collection was Chinese, but in its brief ten years the old stamps of Revolutionary ballerinas and tractors had been usurped by pandas, scenes from classical novels, lunghur monkeys and the Four Modernisations.

Fastidiously, selectively, he began plucking them out: first a panda, then a lakeside scene, then a monkey. . . .

'What are you doing?'

'I want you to give them to your daughter.'

I felt a pang of shame. 'She doesn't collect stamps.'

'But she'll like these.' He unstuck a last panda. They lay in an accusing pile on his palm. 'Take them.'

I was blushing as I pocketed them. My thanks rambled absurdly about. (Chinese gratitude is tersely expressed: profuse thanks may be interpreted as an attempt to escape obligation.) 'I'll send you some British stamps,' I said, and shifted the conversation away. What about his own life, I asked? What about a girlfriend?

'But I'm too young for a girlfriend!' His mouth flashed its disarray of teeth. 'I'm only twenty-three!'

He was being serious. His world still revolved around the camaraderie of school chums and workmates. Emotionally his age seemed fifteen. I had seen such men often in restaurants, suspended in boisterous adolescence.

'I'll marry at twenty-six,' he said. 'Everybody marries at twenty-six now.'

Mr Tampon's identity crisis continued for several days. This was partly because his respectable married image was confirmed by booking into a rather grand (for him) hotel, and by lounging away his second evening in its thirteenth-floor restaurant. But grandeur in China is usually tarnished, and Mr Tampon's grand hotel was very Chinese. The water appeared to have been tapped straight from the misnamed Pearl River, and the bath had been designed for a dwarf. In the restaurant, by the time I discovered I was not ravenous, it was too late. I had already ordered sweet and sour pork, braised duck in fruit juice, egg fried rice and mushrooms in oyster sauce. Canton is the gastronomic capital of China, but my stomach hadn't accommodated.

I took to the hotel café, where meals were small and informal. My table was joined by three clerks, a swarthy leather tanner and a pretty woman with 'Monday' written across her shirt. They came here often, they said, although they couldn't afford it on their state salaries. They drank a concoction of brandy and orange juice, which they mixed in little glasses, and for the stranger's benefit conversed in Mandarin, a language they affected to despise. 'You should learn Cantonese,' one of the clerks said. 'You'll have more fun! Up north they have no imagination. You can tell by the way they lumber about, staring at their own feet.'

'Or they just gaze a metre in front of them,' said another. He touched his fingers to his temples, then shot them forward like bull's horns. 'They don't actually *see* anything.'

'And Beijing's full of Communists,' said 'Monday'. She spoke as if it were infested with lice. 'Party people, you know.'

The leather worker topped up his inch of orange-juice with a gush of brandy. 'It's not their fault,' he said. 'It's the weather. The weather's terrible up there.'

They might have been Andalusians talking of Madrid. They saw the north as pure deficiency: a wasteland of bureaucratic austerity. 'Canton and Beijing are at opposite poles, you see,' somebody said. 'They're the only two cities to have really changed – and Beijing has changed for the worse. You've seen Beijing?'

Yes, I said, but I wasn't returning. I would be going inland instead, to Shaoshan. . . .

'Hunan province! Home of Chairman Mao!' they chorused. 'Mao Zedong thought!' The orange brandies were tipped back derisively. Then they hushed their voices in mock conspiracy. 'They only think it in Beijing, you know. Down here we think our own thoughts.'

In Canton the national obsession with food ascends to a guzzling crescendo. At night the porticoed pavements become a chiaroscuro of celebrants munching snacks or hunting down eating-places. Above them half the neon signs dangle fused, but a crossfire of pop music blazes from stereo shops, and hilarity engulfs the food stalls.

The restaurants rise in multi-tiered pagodas – bursting palaces of merriment and greed. A trinity of statued gods presides in the reception-halls, where lanterns and gilded pillars glimmer fatly under chandeliers like inverted lotus-blooms. On the lower floors the feasters assemble in parties of ten, twelve or sixteen – often all men. Their tables fill up with dishes which everybody shares – sea-cucumber, silver fungus, water-chestnuts in tomato purée, beancurd, abalone soup, giant prawns, toffeed sweet potato. The expectation is unbearable. Every course drops into a gloating circumference of famished stares and rapt cries. Table manners joyfully endorse the ecstasy of eating. Diners burp and smack their lips in hoggish celebration. Bones are spat out in summary showers. Noodles disappear with a sybaritic slurping, and rice-bowls ascend to ravenously distended lips until their contents have been shovelled in with a lightning twirl of chopsticks. The host heaps up the bowls of the guests on either side. Somebody else rotates the laden turntable in the centre, while the banqueteers reach out and lever up a sugared walnut here, a lotus root there.

Yet while the faces above the table show a genial miasma of grins, beneath it half the legs are trembling in a nervous fever which lasts all through the banquet. Calves jig up and down, toes tap the floor to a relentless inner excitation, knees agitate sideways – undermining the jollity above with a quivering and mysterious tension.

From the lowest floor the storeys ascend to suites where more exclusive gorging goes on. Avenues of crimson lanterns lead to caves aglow with golden wallpaper and red lacquered bamboo. Ivory chopsticks clack behind the lattice partitions, dismembering a steamed tortoise or the symbol for 'double happiness' in plum purée. Here and there a couple sits in self-conscious courtship. Isolated from the raucous groups, they look lost. The girl fidgets with her necklace of false pearls. She confronts the man with a flaccid moon-face and vaguely parted lips, unsure of her role, while he holds forth. Sex torments the air between them.

But nearby, wedding parties go forward in a clamour of toasts and speeches. The words are shouted above the din. A storm of flashbulbs captures it all for the family album: the bride in shocking pink, the male relatives sporting rosettes like champions from a dog show. As the feast disintegrates in a litter of discarded bones and bottles, and lipsticked waitresses wheel away the detritus in trolleys, the revellers start to relax. They drink only a little peach wine and *maotai* spirit. They have grown drunk instead on food and chatter. Shoulders are squeezed, forearms patted. Cigarettes are passed from hand to hand in a voluble ritual of offering, disclaiming, submitting. The men slap their knees with delight at every joke. The women pinch each other's cheeks or leave an affectionate arm curled round a friend's waist. Nobody touches the opposite sex.

One of these multi-tiered restaurants specialises in snakes. I found them heaped up live in its windows while a gourmet selected his supper, greedily pointing out a yellow-green water-snake. From the rustling tangle of coils, its tiny head stared back at him indifferently. Other snakes dangled from the warm striplights like tattered electrical fittings.

Inside, the menu listed snake stuffed with shrimps, cobra biscuits, snake and cat soup. The party beside me had ordered serpent-gall liqueur. A posse of waiters arrived with a circular basket from which they pulled out several three-foot snakes. An expert foot was placed on the head and tail of each, and their gall-bladders slit open. From each incision a hard black pellet of bile was plucked out, then the snakes thrown back live into the basket to grow new gall. At the table, meanwhile, the party chatted amiably together. Then the bitter nuggets were dissolved in phials of distilled rice wine, eager hands grasped them, and they were downed in a riot of toasting.

In Cantonese cooking, nothing edible is sacred. It reflects an old Chinese mercilessness towards their surroundings. Every part of every animal – pig stomach, lynx breast, whole bamboo rats and salamanders – is consumed. No Hindu cows or Muslim pigs escape into immunity by taboo. It is the cuisine of the very poor, driven to tortuous invention. Most Chinese still eat only fourteen pounds of meat a year, and many survive at little above subsistence level.

In the rowdy, proletarian Wild Game Restaurant, I interrogated the waitress for anything I could bear to eat. But she incanted remorselessly from the menu: Steamed Cat, Braised Guinea Pig (whole) with Mashed Shrimps, Grainy Dog Meat with Chilli and Scallion in Soya Sauce, Shredded Cat Thick Soup, Fried Grainy Mud-puppy ('It's a fish,' she said) with Olive Kernels, Braised Python with Mushrooms. . . .

If I wanted the Steamed Mountain Turtle, she said, I'd have to wait an hour. And Bear's Paws, she regretted, were off.

I vacillated. I had turned suddenly vegetarian. I played for time by ordering python broth, then glanced furtively round at the main courses on nearby tables, hoping for escape; but their occupants were bent over opaque stews where dappled fragments floated anonymously.

Around us the windows were glazed with pretty pictures of the animals concerned: deer and cats wearing necklaces.

The waitress tried to be helpful. 'What about Dog Meat Ready to be Cooked Earthen Pot over Charcoal Stove on Table?'

I guessed in desperation: 'It's too expensive.'

'Then I recommend Braised Wildcat.'

'Well. . . .' I glanced at a domestic tabby squatting on the veranda beside me.

The waitress followed my gaze. 'It's not *that*.'

She tried to explain it. It had nothing to do with real cats, she said. She wrote down the Chinese character for it, which I couldn't read. In the end, hoping that it was a fancy name for something innocuous, I heard myself say: 'One braised wildcat, please.'

But the soup was a meal in itself. It came in a python-sized bowl, and beneath its brown liquid lurked a sediment of what appeared to be muscular white chicken meat. It tasted fishy. The darker flecks might have been skin. I excused myself by reflecting that pythons (although I had never known one) were less endearing than lambs, which I had eaten often.

The tabby had squirmed under my table. It looked scrawny but dangerously edible. In fact I had the impression that almost everything here was in peril. When somebody brought a warm flannel for my hands, I was half prepared to munch it. What else was nutritional, I wondered? The mosquitoes? The curtains? It occurred to me that should I fall from the fourth-floor stair-well. . . .

The cat was still under my table when its braised compatriot arrived. I lifted the lid to reveal a mahogany-coloured flotsam of mushrooms and indistinguishable flesh. A pair of fragile ribs floated accusingly on the surface. I ate the mushrooms first, with relief, but even they were suffused by the dark, gamey tang of whatever-it-was. The meat was full of delicate, friable bones. I did not know if my faint nausea arose from the thing's richness or from my mind. Several times my chopsticks hit rounded, meat-encircled fragments, like miniature rolling-pins, which resembled legs. I smuggled them to the cat under the table, as a melancholy atonement.

'You don't like your wildcat?' The waitress was peering into the bowl, disappointed.

'I'm rather full.' I smiled feebly, picking the python out of my teeth. But she seemed to understand my diffidence, and stooped down to sketch me an exonerating picture of the whatever-it-was. She drew what looked like the illustration of an Edward Lear limerick: a lugubrious, four-legged ellipse, with a face either cross or upset. But it was too late: I had already eaten it. And when later I showed an English-speaking Cantonese the word which she had written, he translated it 'elephant-cat' or 'cat-fox', and shook his head, non-plussed.

Under my table, the tabby's country cousin had been reduced to a puddle of broth.

*   *   *

'Suffering? All that suffering?' The publisher glanced at the books in his lap with distaste. 'No, nothing much came out of the Cultural Revolution. No great novels, no genius.' The admission caused him some distress. He placed the books beside me. 'Just mediocre talent. That's all.'

'But there must have been *something*?' I was foolishly surprised. After the crushed idealism, the forced exile among the peasants, the broken careers and ambitions – hadn't that generation made any real testimony at all? 'If this had happened in Europe. . . .'

'This isn't Europe,' the man said. 'The educational standard of our youth simply isn't high enough.'

'But it can't be just that. . . . There were millions of them!'

'No, it's not just that.'

He himself was trying to understand. But he looked old and spent. A frost of grey hair sprang far back above his shriven face, and when he walked between kitchen and sitting-room his feet seemed to rattle in their outsize shoes, as if they had shrunk. He lived in near-squalor. Over the black-varnished shelves and table in the sitting-room, his possessions were so few that while he was in the kitchen I noted them all down: two chipped teapots, a modern scroll-painting, an old transistor radio, books, three ceramic plates, a clock.

As for his pessimism about Chinese novels, I thought he was just an old man, ill at ease with the new. But when later I came to read them in translation, I understood him. They were bland and one-dimensional; emotional life was evaded or sentimentalised; their insistent moral tone dulled them.

'You see, in our country there are so many taboos,' he said. 'We're not used to analytic thinking in your Western way. We don't dissect ourselves and our relationships. . . .' He picked up his current reading,

[186]

Graham Greene's *Ways of Escape*, and weighed it on his fingertips. His hands, I noticed, were slender and clear-skinned, like a woman's. 'With us, you see, novels are still instruments of education. Everything – politically and ethically – is *settled*. We don't debate.'

'But something different is beginning, isn't it?' Recently I'd read a newspaper warning that the younger novelists were becoming so Westernised and introverted as to be almost a lost generation. Their gods, apparently, were James Joyce, Heinrich Böll, Virginia Woolf.

'Yes, something's happened,' he said. 'That younger generation has been through everything. They try to examine themselves more deeply, yet. . . . Something doesn't work.'

Later, as I wandered round one of the large bookstores, I found it filled with young people browsing fiercely in a forest of colourless paperbacks. In the section for translated foreign literature and Chinese fiction they stood shoulder to shoulder, turned in dense ranks against the shelves, their books held close against their faces. On the single stand of works in English *War and Peace, Dracula* and *Greenmantle* nudged each other uneasily. Only the political counter was deserted, where the tomes of Marx, Lenin and Mao spread in dry sierras – and the assistant was reading a sports magazine.

I loitered here, hoping to encounter some inquisitive student. Instead it was a young woman who sidled up to me, cradling a copy of *Anna Karenina*. She spoke in the sugary coloratura of Chinese newscasters. She loved Western novels, she said, the modern ones like Somerset Maugham's. 'And we consider Dickens a socially aware writer. And Hemingway. And Orwell's *Nineteen Eighty-Four* has been translated.'

'*What?*'

She giggled. 'You see, our leaders think it's about the Soviet Union.'

'Ah.'

She asked shyly: 'What do you do?'

'I'm a writer.' I had decided not to admit this, but the innocence of her question created its own reply.

'Oh!' Her eyes widened in instant worship. 'I've always wanted to be a writer! When I was at college it seemed so exciting!' She gazed up at me, girlish, awkward. But she only worked in a municipal office, she said.

'A secretary?' She looked very young.

'No. I've heard about your secretaries in the West. But we scarcely have them. You can't type Chinese characters.'

Of course. The whole class of secretaries simply wasn't here. The thousand-character Chinese typewriters were specialist machines.

Most officials used assistants, who wrote in longhand. 'That sort of assistant isn't like your secretaries at all,' the girl said. 'Most of them take over the boss's job eventually. They're usually men.'

'Are men preferred then?'

Very quietly: 'Yes.'

I waited.

She said: 'To get into any institute girls need at least five per cent better marks than men.' A spark of resentment flared. 'Men and women may get equal pay, but the men get the higher jobs.'

Even among the gangs I had seen working on construction sites or spading coal at railroad junctions, it was the women who laboured and the men who drove the trucks.

'It's very old with us that the man is more important,' she said. 'Some husbands still beat their wives.' She fingered the pages of *Anna Karenina* in embarrassment. 'Perhaps women don't end up well anywhere.'

＊　　　＊　　　＊

An old man wheels his wife through the Cultural Park at dusk, and installs her beneath a copse. They share the same cropped grey hair and pain-sunken cheeks. Gently, with infinite patience, he helps her from the wheelchair, and for five minutes she remains with her hands clenched against a stone wall, staring up at a persimmon tree. Also on the wall sit a few boys and a foreign devil. Then, again very gently, the old man pushes the chair towards her, and she settles back in it with something between a sigh and an exclamation. Their faces have taken on an identical expression of concentration on something a long way off. He wheels her, very slowly, away.

Near the park gate I watched two girls debouch from a taxi, vivid with rouge and lipstick. One was dressed in a crimson jacket and jeans, the other in a pink *cheongsam* slit halfway up the thigh. In these drab crowds they blazed like a garish beacon. I had read that 'roadside chickens' were surfacing again in Canton, but had not imagined them as flagrant as this. Even in the centre of a fracas – their taxi was hemmed in by an angry mob – they were brazenly confident. A gang of six or seven men followed them threateningly. One wrenched at the taller prostitute's nose. But the girls took no notice. They pushed through the crowd and postured in a cinema entrance, where other men drifted around them. After a few minutes the girl in jeans walked away with a customer, and her partner was left lounging alone in her pink *cheongsam*.

I wandered into the park and came upon a professional storyteller. It was as if the old and the rustic had discovered him by instinct in a dark corner, for all the benches in front of him were lined by copper-skinned peasants. They were dressed in sun-faded blue and grey – not a speck of other colour in all two hundred. Their blackened toes gripped the benches in front of them. Their skulls were like hardwood buttons. Age and hardship had dented their faces wherever the stubborn bones did not press out, and the men's cheeks and necks were frosted with permanent stubble, from which the beards fell in impoverished shreds.

Behind a bare table under a bare bulb, the storyteller might have belonged to another race. Dressed in a suit and tie, he was dapper and seedy. For two hours he narrated his drama without pause or script. He had the epicene polish of an old-time music-hall comedian. His hair was slicked back. Yet in his mouth the multi-toned Cantonese held a jagged violence. It seemed unable to flow. It moved from one glottal tension to another in menacing swoops and lifts. Only his gestures were fluid.

In that dim light his audience watched him in a conflation of flinty eyes and beetling brows. Occasionally they would turn laughing to one another. But at peaks of tension they froze; their shoulders hunched in their frayed cotton jackets and their faces tautened under a cross-hatch of frowns and wrinkles. Their applause lay not in cheering but in this rapt suspension of all noise and action, for at the end they rose as one man and dispersed without a word into the night; while the storyteller lit a cigarette and walked away.

I caught up with him. He could scarcely speak a word of Mandarin and I no syllable of Cantonese, but his gestures were so eloquent that I understood him. He had started life as a player on the classical Chinese flute, and in middle age had taken up the telling of these traditional tales. The Cultural Revolution had forbidden them, of course, but his memory had sealed them and he had returned from rural exile with his archive intact. I had thought him about fifty-five – his skin smooth, his hair black. But he was seventy, he said. Only when I gripped his hand in parting, did I feel how frail it was – delicate and cold in mine, like a handful of bones.

From a stage nearby, a competing opera had been clashing and shrilling for nearly three hours. Under the warm sky its audience of farmers and factory workers craned from their disordered seats in working vests, mingled with nut-faced women in black trousers, black socks, black slippers. From time to time great blooms of laughter went up. Not an earring, not a necktie, brooch or necklace decorated them. When the drama heightened, a hum of tension enveloped them; when it relaxed they chatted and picked their teeth.

But on stage the world glittered with all the brilliance denied it in life. Actresses nodded under mountainous jewelled coiffures, their lips crimson in whitened faces. The actors marched in dragon-sprawling satins, and were helmeted fantastically in plumes of fox-brush and pheasant-tail. Sometimes, immobilised by four-inch blocked sandals, they became no more than tottering coruscations. New heights of majesty could only be scaled by more outrageous satins, by yet another cascade of pendants or tier of pearls.

Tonight the drama was dominated by a *daoma dan*, one of those Amazons who seem to haunt the Chinese imagination. All was ritualised, absolute. A character's robes and headdress instantly registered rank and personality. A red mask signalled courage, a blue one arrogance or savagery. The grace or agitation of a hand-enveloping sleeve, the tilt of moustaches and bifurcation of beards, the twenty grades of laughter and smile, all established type in an unbreakable code. The audience was not sustained by total illusion, but by something older, half talismanic. A flag-bearing warrior conjured an army. The waving of blue scarves signified the sea. The orchestra perched openly in the wings in a hubbub of violins, lutes, dulcimers and gongs, and characters who were meant to be dead or absent sat flagrantly in view.

For centuries such operas were the channel for popular wisdom. They were performed in temple-courts and market-places, under the glimmer of oil-lamps where the heightened costumes looked natural; and common speech is still littered with saws from their libretti – part of the huge groundswell from the past which underpins all the present. Sitting in that theatre under the fitful stars – beside an old lady shelling monkey-nuts into my lap – I persuaded myself for one hour that nothing had changed at all.

*   *   *

I walked into the food market with a squeamish certainty of what was coming. Under its covered way the first stalls were pungent with roots and powdered spices. Sacks of medicinal tree-bark lay heaped up like firewood, and the air was drowsy with musk. But when I peered closer I saw that several of these piles were desiccated snakes – coiled skeletons and clouded skins – or smaller snakes dried rigid like sticks. I came upon a monkey skeleton, and four bears' paws. There were cellophane bags brimming with dried seahorses, and python skins folded up like linen.

In shallow bins among the fish-stalls, yellow-headed tortoises scrambled over one another's backs – many already overturned and dead – and strings of frogs dangled for sale in pendants of pulsing gullets and legs. The vendors described their wares as 'fresh', not 'alive'. They weighed and dismembered them as if they were vegetables. Throats were cut and limbs amputated at a casual stroke, turtles tossed about like small change.

Then I entered an arena resembling other countries' pet shops – but here it was a butcher's. From its banked cages rose the piping wails of hundreds of cats and kittens – mere scaffolds of fur-covered bones – which were huddled together in a congeries of ginger and white, or were tied to the cage-tops with gaily coloured string. Customers bought several at a time, the meat on them was so scant. They were weighed in mewing sacks and lugged away.

My revulsion, I knew, was hypocritical. When I passed the huddled quails and pheasants I felt nearly nothing, but the thrushes seemed pitiful and the tiered death-cells of the dulled and hopeless mammals angered me. The only dogs I saw had already been killed and skinned, but six or seven racoons lay with their heads buried in their legs, one still hopelessly suckling its young. In another cage sat a monkey – monkey brains are a delicacy – picking at its bars; in another was a porcupine, most of whose quills had already been pulled out. And once I came across a deer lying on a crate, its head tied up with newspapers from which the nostrils still palpitated.

Then I arrived at the owls. They were chained to their cages in a bedraggled row: two handsome eagle-owls, a group of Scops owls and some tufted grey predators which I did not know. Finally, on a cage beside a brute-faced entrepreneur, perched a barn-owl. With its white culottes and heart-shaped facial disks, it was identical to the north European species. Its head and cream-coloured breast, dusted with black specks, were so soft that I might have been stroking air. In its quaint face the eyes gleamed defiantly. It was beautiful.

The man perhaps knew that foreigners did not buy in the market, and he greeted my questions with boredom. He would have no trouble selling it, he said. (Some peasants believed that to devour a whole owl – feathers and all – was a cure for epilepsy.) Then he saw that I was fingering money. So he tugged out one of the bird's wings, pinched its chest and shoved his fingers into his mouth. 'That's the best part.'

For its beauty and its fierceness – and perhaps as a penance for eating wildcat – I paid over the equivalent of £4. Briefly I wondered whether I should have chosen a kitten or a racoon instead, but they would only have been recaptured and eaten. Whereas the owl was a predator, and would survive. The man tied its feet, and I took it away in a carrier-bag. I decided to keep it until I had reached the countryside, and fed it meat on the top of my hotel wardrobe, where it shuffled and snored all night.

8. Mao Slept Here

THE TRAIN CREPT out of the river delta. For the first time I was leaving the Pacific littoral and entering the mountains and plateaux of the centre, which never stop until they fall into the Gobi fifteen hundred miles to the north, or merge with the Himalaya in the west. In my luxury carriage the four berths were each furnished with a pair of black slippers and a muslin-covered pillow patterned in dainty flowers. I shared it with three plump officials. After lunch they stretched out to nap under orange blankets, like crystallised fruit, and fell importantly asleep. In the neighbouring compartments sat a few Hong Kong Chinese with their look of irritably enduring China, and a group of retired army officers on their way to holiday camp.

As darkness fell I hoped the cadres would retire early to bed. I was waiting for an opportunity to release the owl. It crouched unseen in my carrier-bag, but had defecated nervously in the bottom, and the stench was pervading the carriage. The monkey-faced official beside me was reading *Megatrends: Ten New Directions Transforming Our Country*, but from time to time his nose would wrinkle and he would glance around him nonplussed.

I started conversation with the men opposite, trying to deflect attention from the smell. They turned out to be professional painters and administrators in an art museum, but when I asked one about his feelings for landscape, I realised that I'd gone too far. His gaze detached itself, his smile expanded, and he said nothing. But the official beside him looked appalled, and whispered across to me: 'Mr Kung is now Deputy Director of our museum. You cannot ask such personal things,' while Mr Kung went on smiling smugly in front of him through a mouthful of stained teeth.

This indiscretion drove them both to bed. I climbed into my berth and smuggled meat into the owl's beak. It was growing restless with the night. But the *Megatrends* official was still awake, reposing on his bunk with his head supported on his hand, like the Buddha entering paradise. I killed time by inspecting some pamphlets which the railway attendant had handed me. They were like parodies from fifteen years before. I started 'Raptures of Devotion' – the success-story of a citric acid work team at Nantong Distillery. I began to doze. After a while the loudspeaker in the ceiling emitted 'The Last Rose of Summer' in Mandarin, then went silent and the lights dimmed.

Much later I woke to find the train slowing down and whistling feebly. We were among steep, empty hills. The officials in their blankets lay still as tomb effigies. While the train laboured on a forested incline, I dropped from my bunk and eased open the window. The air came soft and warm. Gingerly I tipped the owl on to the sill. For a second, while its courtier's legs dallied along the ledge, I thought it would not fly. It averted its head from the slipstream. Then, like a giant white moth, it opened its wings and vanished into the night.

I closed the window with relief and turned round. Mr Kung's eyes were open and he was looking at me aghast. I had already disgraced myself with him, and now I had emptied this expensive meal into the dark. He buried his face in his blanket.

Just before dawn we reached Changsha, the capital of Hunan province – a bleak industrial city where I changed trains. In 1968 a railway had been built from here to Shaoshan, the birthplace of Mao, and every year for a decade three million pilgrims had descended on the village. But now I sat in a half-empty carriage while for over four hours the train toiled sixty miles south-west. Sometimes it slowed almost to a standstill, lumbering between hills islanded in a gold-green ocean of paddy. Opposite me sat two retired factory workers whose faces were withered contour-maps. Across one the wrinkles fanned comically in light arcs from eyes and mouth; whereas the other's lines plunged down fiercely indented cheeks in a bitter cascade. Set loose by a freer economy and the easing of travel restrictions, they were selling fruit between one province and another.

'I worked in factories for forty years,' said the comic-faced man, 'but now we buy oranges and sell them in the north. We're in business!' The lining of his cap trailed tatters around his ears, and his fly buttons gaped on a layer of worn cotton.

I said: 'Is that a better life?'

'Better, much better! Oranges are the thing. The peasants are doing best now. It's no good being in a factory, on a salary. You need to be a peasant.'

The sad-faced man touched my knee. 'And you? What about you?' He looked perplexed. 'Are you Chinese?' He must have been imagining that I came from the Muslim peoples in the far north-west: one of the thin-featured Uighurs or Kazakhs.

'I'm from England,' I said.

They looked blank. Where was that, the sad-faced man asked? Was it the same as America? And did they all speak Mandarin over there? He hunted for Britain on my map of eastern Asia, his finger trailing fruitlessly round the Sino-Soviet border.

'It's not on this map,' I said. 'It's to the west. An island.'

His finger alighted on Japan. 'There!'

I discovered a streak of patriotism. '*No.*'

'Not on the map. . . .' He looked doubtful of Britain's existence. 'Do you grow rice there?'

'We have cows. . . .'

The comic-faced man said cannily: 'Cows and sheep. That's why he looks like that. So big.' He puffed out his arms and cheeks. 'They drink milk over there.'

But we were interrupted by a trendy youth who bounced down beside me, hoping I had something to sell. Over his cheeks and chin curled isolated scraps of hair, like pigs' tails. He ignored the factory workers, who went dumb, cowed by his pressed shirt and jeans.

'Are you going to Shaoshan?' he asked. 'You must be. Only foreigners go there now.'

I said irritably: 'I wonder what Mao would have thought of that.'

The youth laughed cynically. 'I'll ask him when I go up to heaven, and send you a telex.'

I grunted. His concept of heaven, and the likelihood of Mao (or him) being eligible, were shadowy to me. And I wanted to talk to the old factory workers.

He fingered my shirt. 'Is that nylon?'

'Yes.'

After a while he went away.

The sad-faced man asked: 'What nationality was he?'

'Chinese.'

He frowned. 'We thought he was from overseas. From somewhere like Hong Kong.'

The youth, I realised, had seemed ultramundane to them, although he was only a clerk in a Changsha hotel.

'I think his father's a nob,' the other man said. His voice had soured.

He lifted his hand to some unscalable but disapproved height. 'One of those top cadres.' At the next town they gathered their bags and disembarked.

Shaoshan, when I reached it, was a ghost village. At its railhead the long, canopied arcades of the platforms sheltered nothing. Instead of the triumphal 'The East is Red' and the swarming of devotees, a tinny pop song sounded over the tannoy as a dozen peasants and I trudged into the station forecourt, where the slogans were flaking from the walls. From the park beyond, a colossal white statue of the Great Helmsman, dressed in the flowing robes of his youth, still lifted a hand to conjure the future. But in the nearby street a free market had broken out, and rock music blasted from a shop selling cheap televisions.

I peered inside the post office. It was still dominated by a group portrait of Mao, Zhou Enlai, Zhu De and Liu Shaoqi (who had been airbrushed out during his disgrace, but was now back). The assistant identified them for me hesitantly. 'You are interested in Chinese history?' she asked, then returned to reading her novel.

History, she had said. She was, perhaps, eighteen. She would have been a small child when Mao, Zhou Enlai and Zhu De all died in 1976. Suddenly they seemed to have been gone a century.

Several miles beyond the station, the old hamlet of Shaoshan spread pretty in its cup of hills. The wealth which it attracted during the Cultural Revolution had left its public buildings clean-faced, its houses tall and white among their trees. Now it had fallen quiet. The village square was so empty that a farmer had spread rice over its tarmac to dry, and somebody had set up a billiard-table under the willows.

I booked in to a near-empty guesthouse. It had been built in 1959, said the desk clerk – to accommodate Mao, his wife, and Liu Shaoqi when they visited the village. Her voice held the hurt pride with which the Shaoshan people speak of their dethroned hero.

Might I see his rooms, I asked?

She took me up a path to a separate building, where two suites had accommodated Mao and his wife. In his big, single bedroom stood a scarred desk and a four-poster bed clouded in mosquito netting. Tenderly the woman pulled back its quilt to show the bare boards beneath. 'He didn't like bedclothes. He slept on that.'

'Do people still use this room?'

'It's given to visitors sometimes,' she said. 'Do you want to take it?'

'Mao Zedong's bed?' My voice sounded thin, alarmed. I was touched by a schizophrenic pang of unworthiness and revulsion. I stared around. Were the mosquitoes which whined about the walls, I wondered, the offspring of those which had bitten the Great Helmsman? Then I said that perhaps, if no important officials were spending the night here, then yes. . . .

A minute later I was left alone in His room.

I padded noiselessly across the heavy blue carpet, as if Mao were in residence and I a ghost. When I looked at myself in the wardrobe mirror, I half expected to see Him instead. I felt a tremor of the pilgrim's excitement: He touched this, He sat on that. The room was heady with mana. Had He, I wondered, sat in that great creased armchair pondering the crash of the Great Leap Forward? Did He compose his poem on Shaoshan at the desk where I was scribbling my notes?

I crossed the sitting-room to Jiang Qing's suite. It was almost identical. I returned and peered into Mao's (and my) bathroom. It contained a bidet and the biggest bath I had seen in China – a huge, Mao-shaped oblong set in a white-tiled surround and reached by tiled steps. Above it hung a bar by which the Chairman could haul up his ageing body, and near the tap was a red button for emergencies.

For two days I wandered the Maoist shrines of Shaoshan. The troops of votaries who had thronged here in the 1960s and 70s under their streaming banners in reverent silence had left an echoing void. Several sites were all but abandoned. Here was the duck-pond where the Great Teacher swam, the field which he ploughed, the school where he studied (with an apocryphal picture of Mao astounding his teachers). And at the far end of the village I came to the house where he was born.

It had been built by Mao's father, a tight-fisted peasant who prospered as a grain dealer and money-lender. Nestled beside a valley-mouth where rice-fields surged from the hills, it was at once mellow and mean – a long bungalow of golden brick, its windows barred with wood. Inside, I tramped over stone floors through claustrophobic rooms. They had been pampered and scrubbed into a clinical version of themselves. Yet even in this holy of holies I was almost alone. Only once, a party of young men hurried through as if searching for something else.

But the doors still swung in their wooden pivots, and the outhouses were full of pestles and grinding-stones. In the washroom the carrying-poles and iron-basined furnace were still in place, with stone storage jars in the kitchen and a hook for smoking pig above the clay oven. Photographs of Mao's parents hung beside the narrow bed which had thrust them together at night: the hard-faced man and oppressed-looking woman. They reminded me uncannily of portraits somewhere else, but for a minute I could not recall where or whose. Then I remembered: photographs of Stalin's parents, hanging in his cottage-museum at Gori.

Mao learnt to hate his father and perhaps to hate authority through him. After a local rebellion of starving townsmen, it was the executed rebels with whom he sympathised. Already he was besotted with the renegade heroes of Chinese folklore, reading *The Romance of the Three Kingdoms* and *Outlaws of the Marsh* as if they were history. By the time he left home as a raw-faced bumpkin to attend middle school in Changsha, the prophet of unending revolution was already stirring.

Outside the house, a few stalls were selling handkerchiefs printed with blondes and rabbits. I wandered back to the village square, where a cottage-style museum spread round garden courtyards. It was a museum in the Soviet mould: a didactic history lesson. I walked through room after room filled with little but photographs, texts, idealised pictures and plaster statues. I hunted for somebody to elucidate the captions, but in most rooms I found only a gallery from which the faces gazed out unfathomably: Mao's disciples, Mao's brothers, Mao's generals, Mao.

The museum recorded events up to February 1952, then staggered into silence. The walls turned ghostly from the outlines of vanished exhibits, and the last galleries had been closed for years – because of 'mistakes', said the staff. The windows were papered over.

Their reconstruction would be a nightmare. Who could rewrite that history? How to record Mao's 1958 Great Leap Forward which had left the country prostrate? Or his conjuring of the Cultural Revolution? Or the Chairman's choice of the long-disgraced Hua Guofeng as his successor? And how to treat his fourth wife, the witch Jiang Qing? The Communist achievement – the enormous, uneven strides in welfare, education and industry out of the sordid and confused past – had somehow to be harmonised with the gaping flaws in its progenitor. The past must be redefined – as often before – to serve the needs of the present. But when?

It was safer to leave it alone, I supposed – and nothing was apparently being done. When I peered through the gaps in the windows I glimpsed a wreckage of broken plaster busts, pictures, smashed slogans: a limbo of defunct mythology. I was caught spying by one of the museum attendants, but he only said sheepishly: 'We don't know how to label them,' and went away.

Labelling: the old necessity. Things should be correctly named, said Confucius, 'so the human spirit is not beset by misunderstanding'. The imperial Chinese categorised and numbered everything from the Five Colours and Five Tastes to the five varieties of creature (scaly, feathered, naked, hairy, crustacean). Under Communism the prefabricated class labels – Rightist, Leftist, Bad Element (twelve categories), Capitalist Roader, Revisionist – have become cruel substitutes for thought; and the power of the Chinese concepts is perhaps heightened by their embodiment not in a fluid alphabet but in immutable ideograms. Political life is riddled by such definitions and figurework. It is hard for anyone to keep abreast. As early as 1951 the Three Antis campaign (anti-corruption, anti-waste, anti-bureaucracy) melted into a Five Antis onslaught on bourgeois businessmen, to be echoed long after by an Eight Antis crusade against intellectuals. Then there were the Four Pests – rats, flies, mosquitoes, sparrows (later elevated to five by the addition of Rightists) – the Three Loyalties and the Four Infinities, the shining Four Bigs, the pernicious Four Olds, the Three Prominences and the struggle to erase the Three Differences. Schoolchildren embraced the Five Loves and liberals welcomed the Four Great Freedoms until they were expunged from the Constitution in 1980. Others had to cope with 'one-struggle two-criticism three-reform' or the 'one point two plans tactic'. Recently newspapers had advocated the Four Beauties and the Five Stresses – a campaign for hygiene and morality – and everybody was now concentrating on the Four Modernisations.

The typically Confucian purpose, of course, was not to discover truth, but to educate behaviour. Thus complex assessments withered into percentages. Until Mao's death the Cultural Revolution was proclaimed 95 per cent good and 5 per cent bad, and it was now commonplace to judge Mao 70 per cent good, 30 per cent bad. Was this habit of quantifying contagious, I wondered, as I wandered the museum? Was the museum 80 per cent good and 20 per cent bad? And what about people? I looked bleakly at the attendants. Were they an unknown quantity, or a herd of vulgar fractions?

From these melancholy conundrums it was a release to walk into the hills above Shaoshan. The corn lapped about my feet and I set the cottage dogs barking from one valley end to another. Towards late afternoon I came to a pond in a bowl of pine-covered hills. Its banks were glazed with pink flowers. A solitary peasant was sinking netted basins in its shallows, and marking them with wooden floats. He noticed me with a little cry.

'This lake's too small,' he said. 'There's a bigger one on the other side, with big fish.' He spread his hands in the fisherman's universal boast. After a while he hoisted his wooden bucket, which held a few shrimps and minnows, and took me back to his home. It was a big farmer's house, as Mao Zedong's had been, with the same stone floors and wood-barred windows, and peppers for the hot Hunan cuisine dangling in the sun. Straw hats and baskets hung on the doors, and the ceilings were matted with reeds or old cardboard boxes stitched together. A black dog called 'Big Voice' wandered in and out. In the main room, padlocked chests and canopied beds painted with tigers and flowers had been raised on stones against the damp. A hole in the floor received briquettes of compressed coal-dust, which burned noxiously all winter. One bamboo table supported a small, blurred television, and from all along the walls posters of Shanghai film-stars shed an outlandish glamour.

The man and his elder son went barefoot, and his wife's only ornament was a steel headband. She served me *maotai* and green tea, with a dish of pungent roots. But their daughter was a waitress in the Shaoshan guesthouse, and the posters were hers. Sulky in tights and a scarlet blouse, she was too embarrassed to speak with me. She took off her new shoes and dangled her feet moodily from her bed. The old man was delighted with her. 'Very modern,' he said. 'Very clever.'

As for his farming, it was doing well. Their paddy-fields were prolific, and they were planting their own vegetables higher up the hill, and breeding chickens, he said. 'Some of our income goes to the government, but mostly it's ours.' He gurgled pleasantly on an ancient silver water-pipe. 'In the old, collective days people didn't care. Nobody worked. Now even the lazy ones work their own land, and the incapable ones' – he added disdainfully – 'have gone into business. They trade between town and country – clothes, food, anything. They're no good for anything else.'

'You've never been tempted to do that?'

'Me? Why should I? I've gone into pigs!' He pointed at the rear wall. Beyond it, in the silence, I heard a noise like a heavy sea slopping against the bricks: a communal grunting. 'In the Cultural Revolution we were allowed one pig and two chickens. If you kept more, you were a

Capitalist. But now it's different. And pigs fetch 2 yuan a kilo. Every pig's worth 200 yuan!' He beamed at this porcine windfall. His mouth was filled with expensive gold teeth. 'You can make 1,000 yuan a year out of pigs!'

Back in the guesthouse, the suite which I was occupying was suddenly less amusing. The year 1959, when Mao had slept here, had sealed the fate of millions as his simple and benighted vision of the Great Leap Forward exacted its toll. The next three years would see sixteen million dead of famine. On the Great Leap's inception, farming had been totally collectivised, and steel furnaces improvised in a crash programme of industrialisation. 'Overtake Britain in fifteen years!' the slogans had yelled. The results were disastrous: agricultural chaos and a mountain of scrap iron. By the end of 1958 there had been peasant insurrections, and Mao had stood down as head of state (but not as Party chairman) in favour of the more pragmatic Liu Shaoqi.

By 1959 he must have seemed irreversibly in decline. He had failed in the first and oldest task of emperors: to feed his people. And by Heaven's punishment, it seemed, he had no posterity. His four marriages had yielded only two sons. One had been killed in the Korean War, and the second was mad. Any other man would have been broken. Yet already Mao was brooding on schemes for reasserting his tragic dominance, and I kept wondering what he had been planning here. The room became unnerving. I was trapped, half unwillingly, on holy ground – by the sorcery of filling the same space, brushing the same surfaces. Every time I dangled one of my dirty garments from a coat-hanger, or turned a tap to wash my hands, I was conscious of whose coat and hands had preceded mine. As I lay in the Chairman's bath, I wondered: if I should press that red button, would Liu Shaoqi appear?

But no. Remorselessly Mao had engineered his downfall, and he had died in an obscure prison in 1969.

I climbed delicately into the bed. In the darkness I could see only a disembodied window faintly shaped by light beyond. The mosquito netting hung about me like a shroud. My presence here seemed an obscure sacrilege. After a while I drifted into sleep. But it was broken by a bourgeois nightmare in which the people I most loved – a woman, my parents – were engulfed by an immense crowd. I woke up shaken, wondering where I was. Then I noticed the stars tangled among the trees in the window, and by their glimmer saw Mao's great bed white above my head. It was as if I were lying in the bottom of a sarcophagus too big for me.

*　　*　　*

'My father used to practise calligraphy with a feather pen,' said Weidong. 'Quite harmless, you would think. "Up with Mao Zedong, up with Jiang Qing, down with Mao Zedong, down with . . ." and so on, just practising. But one day in the Cultural Revolution he threw away his used paper and somebody denounced him for writing "Down with Mao Zedong". He was tortured as a reactionary and imprisoned. My brother and I were beaten up by our schoolmates because of it. I'll never forget.'

From the topmost berths of the carriage, he and I stared across at one another. We lay on torn straw matting. He looked at me with a moon-face circled by floppy spikes of hair. He was twenty-two.

'After that, before every meal, our family sang "The East is Red" in front of a picture of Mao, and I'd say "Thank you for my meal, Communist Party, thank you for my meal, Chairman Mao" when I should have cursed the old man and thanked my father and mother instead. But of course I was only thinking of my breakfast. And it was just a song.'

He spoke with an oiled secrecy. But the men in the bunks below us lay asleep, and our voices were lost in the whirring of the fan on the wall and the drumming of the train-wheels.

'Before I became a teacher I had to work in a water-pump factory in Sichuan,' he said. 'We had two hours' political indoctrination a day. We were bored stiff. We just agreed with whatever was said, and thought about something else. And now those words – Communism, Socialism – if you say them, people don't know what you mean any more. They just think you're odd, political. Those names are finished.'

I handed him a biscuit across the aisle, as if to compensate. He threw me back an apple. The fan between us turned from side to side like a blank face, lifting and lowering his hair in a tidal halo of spikes.

'Communism.' He seemed to be testing the word. Then his voice turned smooth, prurient. 'Nowadays the Party cadres abuse their rights. Leaders in the local commissions are notorious for raping. If the girl wants a job, the official can take advantage of her.'

I said: 'That's not rape.'

'No, but the cadre's sons will literally kidnap a girl. Or they promise her a favour if she'll come to their office, then shut the door on her. . . .'

'You read this in newspapers?'

'Not newspapers, no. I hear from my friends – on the grapevine.' He let out a lilting laugh. 'It's not surprising. Our novels and magazines are full of these things now – intercourse, three-cornered relationships. The government's labelled those journals Spiritual Pollution, but you'll still find them in the small markets. . . .'

He spoke with oddly mixed naïvety and scepticism. His name, Weidong, meant 'Defend the East' – babies in the 1960s were often saddled with such names – but he was born too late for illusions. He had been brought up in a time of political exhaustion, in meaningless-ness. Among his peers he was thought very clever, he said – his voice turned silky with self-esteem – and he was deeply ambitious.

'I want to do something to make me recognised,' he said (he didn't seem to care what the something was). 'That's why I should join the Party. I'll say "I believe in Communism", whatever. But the truth is I believe in the present policies. They're the only ones that are practicable. Even people who shout *Communism, Communism* don't believe the real thing can ever be reached. It's always over the horizon. It's impossible.' He added boyishly: 'Do you think I'm clever?'

'Then are Party members just ambitious, like you?'

'Yes.'

The train came to a stop in the dark. The lights went out, the fan stilled and I realised that the carriage was full of snoring: tenors, altos, basses. There were pig-like snorts and musical tremolos, asthmatic downdraughts and stertorous roars. Weidong's voice dwindled to a whisper. 'I think people who dislike the Party have an incorrect outlook,' he said, lapsing into jargon. 'If you want to be formally recognised, you must join it.' He could no longer hold back his self-applause. 'Do you think I'm clever? Am I intelligent?'

'But you don't believe in it.'

His face had become an opaque circle in the dark. 'Well, China can't change policies too quickly. But I think that in five or ten years everything will be clear. Perhaps then we'll call it Chinese Socialism – something quite different. Do you think I'm clever?'

I closed my eyes, pretending sleep, and only heard a last 'Do you think. . . ?' before the pretence became reality.

The sun rose on a land subtly different from the one we had left. The paddy-fields still swirled round the villages, but mesas of waterless red soil had appeared, and lonely hills stuck with pines. We were approaching Guilin – a scenery distilled by painters and poets into the quintessence of Chinese mountains. Yet nothing gave me to expect the crags which suddenly muscled into the sky. They circled the concrete blocks and smokestacks of the town in an aureole of shooting peaks and cones. They were not a mountain massif but a fantastical hubbub of separated hills, rising sheer in their thousands from the valley floor. I ached to walk among them.

But first I had to confront the town of Guilin. A long-time Nationalist stronghold, it had been blitzed by Japanese aircraft in 1944 and had survived as one of the ugliest towns in China. Now tourism was shoddily recreating it. There were poor Western-style restaurants, some dirty coffee-shops, discount tour-operators, money-changers and a pervasive black market. A jeans bazaar was in progress. On the main street stood an advertisement for breast-enlarging apparatus. Soon, I thought, foreigners would be looking back with nostalgia to the days of native reticence and boorish curiosity. As for myself, as soon as a place adapts to me, I lose interest in it: it has obliterated itself.

I found a room in a hotel typical of inland towns – barracks reared in the 1950s during the years of Soviet amity. The façades of these hotels are always soullessly imposing. You imagine they may be too expensive. But as you enter the split-level lobby, with its shoal of bored receptionists, your suspicions rise. A debased grandeur rules. The resonant corridors and stairs shrivel to penitential bedrooms, and the bathrooms are a series of humourless water-jokes. In mine the floor was impregnated with cigarette-ash and old toe-nails, and the elaborate patterns on the curtains turned out to be whorls of grime.

It was the pretension which jarred, not the dirt. On the pavement outside, a band of blind beggars played in a cacophony of clappers and two-stringed viols, and set up an ageless, heartrending plainsong. One of the women struck a plate with a stick; another had attached two bells to her toes, and jingled desolately. Their eyes were closed on bloodshot slits and their heads bowed in shame.

I bicycled hopelessly about. The place seemed to be cursed. In front of me a cyclist bowled over a woman, and turned only to spit before pedalling on. After that I kept noticing petty brutalities and sordidness. I drew alongside two local peasants who were visiting the town for the first time. 'We just want to get back,' they said. 'It's the air here. It soaks into you. In the country it's pure.' They felt as lost as I did. 'We're going home.'

That afternoon I discovered that the same erosion which had

contorted the ground above seemed to have rotted it below. In a labyrinth of floridly lit caves the guides alighted on formations resembling cauliflowers, dragons, shipwrecks, pagodas, mandarins and baby elephants. I could scarcely ever make them out. But above us the ceilings flowered into a witching stone vegetation. It was as if the dizzy scenery on the earth's surface had been fancifully inverted, and was plunging out of a stone sky.

Next morning I made for the mountains up the Li river – sailing on a tourist boat with a fleet of others nose to tail for thirty miles, loudspeakers prattling. But as the Li unfolded, everything else was forgotten. It made a green corridor between the hills. Every bend disclosed a new assemblage of pinnacles, some plunging sheer three hundred feet, others erupting into saddles and ziggurats. The detritus from a primordial scabed, they had been smoothed and gentled by wind and scrub to these soft sugarloafs and blunted needles. As they receded into the distance they filled half the sky with an insane, Gothic beauty. In places they all leant one way as if blown by a prehistoric wind, until far beyond, with the simplicity of a pencil-stroke, a curtain of other mountains was drawn seamlessly across the sky to confine them.

After the first snapshots of one another, the sightseers went quiet, aligned in chairs on the upper deck. Here and there beneath us the banks shelved to green peninsulas, and I saw that paradise was inhabited: skinny children splashing with water buffalo in and out of the shallows. Cormorant fishermen floated by on rafts of bamboo trunks, or lay asleep by their sampans with their birds standing in line beside them.

Then the banks would converge again. Sometimes cliffs loomed across our way four, five, six hundred feet high, slashed by fissures and scrawled with a hieroglyph of shrubs. We crept like mice under their lea. Our klaxon moaned against the rock. Once I noticed a boulder detach itself from a summit so distant that it floated down like a bundle of dark straw and landed without a sound.

The girl sitting beside me had noticed it too. We exchanged glances, as if we had sighted a ghost. 'I've never seen anything like this,' she said. 'Is there anything else like this?' Her wide-set eyes blinked behind steel-rimmed glasses. She had a plain, cloudless face. 'But we're going too fast. I want to stop.'

'You could try walking later.'

'I'd just like time to look. Back home I sit and look at trees for hours.'

But home was far away, in Beijing. She had been posted south to a medical college in neighbouring Guizhou, one of the poorest provinces. She was missing her husband. 'When I first arrived here it was months before I told people I came from Beijing. They think anyone from the capital must be stuck-up. But now they've discovered I'm homesick, and they're rather kind.' She shook her hair loose from a confusion of grips and elastic bands. 'But I want to get back home. Too many young people are separated. That's how you get divorced.' She suddenly frowned at me. 'You in the West – I've heard you do what you like, that the government doesn't separate you. So tell me: why do you divorce so much?'

The question invited some simple, irreducible reply. Under her girlish gaze I tried, but failed, to supply one.

In the end she said: 'I don't understand divorce. My parents have been together thirty-one years.'

'Happily?'

'Yes.' She beamed at the hills, the river, as if happiness were the norm. 'My father's a slippers-man, as we say – placid, like me. He runs about the house after my mother, who gets in tempers with him. When she goes off to her room, my father tells us all to move about on tiptoe because mother's in one of her rages, and he sends her tea and I make her bed and after a bit everything's peaceful again.' She gazed down on a drift of butterflies. 'It's tough being a mother.'

'You've got children?'

'No.' She said stoutly: 'And I don't want any. Friends in my husband's factory, who all have children, ask him: "Where is your child?" So he wants one.'

'A son?'

'No. He thinks girls are neater and better behaved.' She chuckled. 'Perhaps we'll have one when I return to Beijing. I don't want one in Guizhou. For days I can feel the people there are all right, and that I understand them. Then something separates me. . . .'

'What sort of thing?'

'Something in their minds. Something . . . well, primitive. Books, for instance. They enjoy the kind of old-fashioned books I hate. Books which tell you what to think, which decide for you. I want to make up my own mind what I think.' She said it with a trace of defiance, as if at some time she had suffered for it. 'Those books even talk about "the enemy", but really I don't understand this word.'

Enmity, divorce: I envied her the things she didn't understand. She added rhetorically: 'Who is the enemy?', then caught my eye and laughed in sudden embarrassment. It was evident to both of us who the enemy was meant to be. She said: 'We were always taught that you Westerners were demons, you know, real foreign devils. Our films and comics used to portray you as monsters . . . physically. . . .'

I pulled a ferocious face.

'That's right!' she said. 'And how did you picture us?'

'As too small, and too many.'

'But that's quite right,' she said solemnly. 'There are many too many.'

Our voyage had reached its end at the fishing village of Yangshuo. But the place was drowned in tourists, and the lure of the peaks, thronging on all sides, was too much for me. With a lightened rucksack I pushed along a tributary of the Li and into the blue.

The silence was utter. The rice-fields flooded between the hills in quilts of amber and brilliant green. Split by their peasants into a collage of crops and harvests, with herbs and vegetables between, they spread through the valley without an electricity-pole or even a cart-track to scar them. They could have belonged to any time. Their tiny villages were folded agelessly into the fields. Here and there, river-water slopped into a fish-pond through bamboo pipes, or a stone bridge hunched over an irrigation channel. Once some buffalo passed me in a file of bulls and croaking calves glistening with mud, and nobody driving them. Once I crossed the river by a rope-ferry, paying the man a farthing.

Out of this calm, the peaks rose like some profound geological mistake. Whenever I mounted a pass I would see them bumping against one another in six or eight concentric waves. In that clear, foreshortening air the closer ones appeared near enough to touch. The vertical incrustations of their stone shone intricate like tree-bark. If I stretched out a hand, I thought, I might pluck off the maples which burnished them.

For two days I rambled indolently among their shadows. Between valleys I took the stone stairways laid down by villages, and would glimpse the farmers toiling up below me in crocodiles of decorated straw hats, or waiting in curiosity above. They watched me without territorialism or hospitality, simply extended a mystified, communal greeting. 'Where did you sleep? Aren't you afraid?'

'What of?'

But they didn't know. They were voicing only the immemorial fear of the farmer for the void, where the sown and the wilderness were so abruptly divided.

I asked: 'Are there dangerous animals?'

'No. Snakes, perhaps.'

'And people?'

'No.'

Sometimes the paths dropped into pine-scented glades, where beetles droned and thumped into me by the score, and bees drowsed in the undergrowth. After Canton, the survival of even these creatures warmed me. I idled near lizards and russet caterpillars. I tried to identify birds. In the flailing noon sun I would doze under a rock-shelf, my hair stuck with sweat, while troops of unidentifiable insects countermarched among my biscuits.

But always my eye was tugged back to those differentiated hills. I was nagged by the fancy that they were man-made but now so weather-blasted that they had reverted to cliffs – donjons and follies half formed, or formed too long ago. It was this illusion of unproclaimed life, perhaps, which the classical painters had loved – a land which had been subtly domesticated. Round the next valley-corner, I felt, a full-blown palace might flood out on its plateau, or one of those cones shake off its disguise of shrubs and burgeon into turrets.

For these, sure enough, were the fantasy mountains of the scroll-paintings, bodied out in living rock. They rose all of a piece, like models. Bushes and ferns tumbled from their crevices in an artist's heaven of angles and textures. Their scarps were outlined in nervous, broken strokes. An occasional cloud wreathed them with spatial depth. Motionless, they awaited only the artist's cypher of coral inkstone to be stamped in the sky alongside.

As I wandered between hills and river, I seemed to be travelling through one of those Ming handscroll paintings, in which the scenes pass in ethereal comic-strip. As the handscroll unwound, the view shifted. A foreground of rocks, tinted in rattan yellow, opened on a wriggle of blue water (with a peasant sketched in, for perspective). Beyond them, a light ink-wash blurred the horizon in mist. It was almost dusk, and I looked for somewhere to camp. Another tug at the scroll and a new mountain appeared, bandaged in green with a stippling of snail blue in the crevices. I scrambled up its lower slope and found a level strip of earth, where I spread my sleeping-bag and awaited night.

As the sun set, the cliffs stirred into life. The cries of strange birds arose and reverberated in the rocks. They sounded musical and mysterious in their isolation. Things whistled and scampered. By nightfall the whole land was clicking and chirruping, and there was a flurry of wild wings. Two owls saluted each other from different valley-sides in abrupt, single hoots.

The peaks leaned jet black above me, and corralled the sky into a depthless blaze of stars. It was hard to sleep under them, and sultry. They curved in a brilliant mass from crag to crag – great blisters and outspread pelts of light. I watched their procession for hours from horizon to confined horizon. The endless shrilling of the cicadas became the sound of the stars turning across the sky.

Later something rustled over the leaves beside me, and carried away my packet of preserved dates, but I never discovered what it was. And once I saw a firefly trailing high above the valley, before it extinguished itself. I don't remember sleeping at all.

A slow dawn separated the mountains, and leaked a buttery light over the fields. I packed my rucksack and descended through a dust of crimson leaves and berries. The ground was sodden with dew. Then, in one of those unplanned moments which meet the vagabond walker, I reached the edge of an enclosed valley. Encircling mountains seemed to seal it off from men, or anything at all. Embalmed in the young sun, its rice-fields and fish-ponds had turned to mist and silver. Nothing moved. I had the momentary impression that I was looking into a country still unborn, whose quality of peace – an artist's pigment, perhaps – was missing from elsewhere.

Then a dog barked. A wind butted the trees. The cry of a farmer arose, nagging his buffalo – and the day began.

9. The Land of Peacocks

THE TRAIN TO Kunming in the far south-west meandered for over thirty hours across northern Guangxi and the impoverished province of Guizhou. After nine hours I looked out in the dawn to see the peaks still rising – but half-heartedly now, and from a paler soil. All that day we levered ourselves painfully into rolling uplands. The rice had already been harvested from a cracked soil, where winter vegetables were sprouting. The hills steepened around rock-cluttered streams, and the villages grew poorer, more contained. Some spread smaller than their own cemeteries. A few waterwheels turned in the fields.

My compartment was commandeered by a family of Hong Kong Chinese. They spoke no Mandarin, but we passed apples and goodwill between us, and the time slipped by. They were dowdy and poor: the men stocky escaped peasants, who went to bed in designer-style underpants; the women disgruntled, forever tucking herbal pills into their cheeks. But when they disembarked at Guiyang, the derelict-looking provincial capital, a feeble cheer went up from a platform of circling relatives. Then I realised how glamorous these expatriates must seem – the matriarch crowned by henna-tinted hair and wearing a pea-green cardigan, the men with their two-tone shirts and the indefinable halo of a wider world.

They were replaced in my carriage by a different phenomenon: the girl too poor to marry (or so she said). She was thirty, perhaps, and hard-faced. She taught at a science college in Kunming, and with a salary equivalent to £4 a week she could scarcely afford her books. Already she walked with the invalid gait of middle-aged women. She spoke of her college with bitterness. People were all the same, she said, as if they were aligned against her. Her students were all the same, just interested in themselves. Her colleagues, she said scathingly, were typical of those everywhere (men were all alike). Her future she did not know. Only when she spoke of children did her expression dismantle into a kind of grief-stricken charm. She would probably never have them now.

Outside, the plateaux rolled treeless to the sky. The thin integument of earth was half washed from the rocks. They beat up naked beneath it. Before nightfall came signs that we were approaching Yunnan province – a dark, tribal people hacking at the earth with spatular hoes, their women vivid in aquamarine dresses.

Tucked in the cleft of Burma, Laos and Vietnam, Yunnan is peopled by more than twenty such races. Within a week I planned to be walking in the jungled borderlands where the warrior Hani and Yi tribes live, and the beautiful Dai.

'They're all the same,' the teacher said. 'Their cultural level is very low. Did you know that the Dai only used to wash their hair three times in their lives – at birth, marriage and death?' She added humourlessly: 'But since the 1949 Liberation they wash it at least once a year.'

I felt a twinge of fraternity. My own hair had not been washed for weeks.

Kunming, the capital of Yunnan, lies between sub-tropical jungle and the northern tablelands descending from Tibet. Built on a plateau of lakes and gentle mountains, it is the terminus of the Burma Road which was once China's lifeline to the West, dug with the bare hands of 160,000 coolies.

Despite the hovering tribal presence, I found a city seamlessly Chinese. Its morning parks were filled with the ghostly gyrations of *t'ai chi*, while the same old men seemed to be ogling their bird-cages and the same young ones swotting on the benches. Street after street kept pure the two-storeyed wooden houses which had vanished from other towns – a cinematic procession of latticed windows and tiled roofs tangled in grass. Every house could unfold to the street with a parting of bronze-red shutters and collapsible green doors. They were like wonky theatre-sets which extinguished or displayed themselves at will. In one casement an old man might be smoking his water-pipe in the darkness, bathed in a gurgling plenitude of smoke, while his wife cooked in the bright-lit rectangle beside him, and their daughter, unaware of either (or of the foreign devil outside) was combing out her hair in a rectangle above.

The streets were a pandemonium of pavement skills and quackery, swaddled in pollution. Their mimosa and eucalyptus trees were dripping dust, and the sycamores already stricken by autumn, their leaves curled on the ground like brown crusts. Signs of poverty were everywhere: blind men, cripples and many of those tiny victims of malnutrition, wizened before their time. Beyond a group of shifty youths (selling photographs of coy pin-ups) I came upon a line of terrifying pavement dentists, working their drills by treadle. Beside them a 'foot and ear' specialist was dabbing the same white glue on to the face or feet of every customer – boils, moles, verrucae. Four or five barbers had set up their dressers beyond, where they manipulated nothing but archaic tweezers and outsize scissors.

Down one of these streets, in a moment of surrealism, a student wavered up behind me on his bicycle and requested in punctilious English: 'Excuse me, sir, how many children did Charles Dickens have?'

'Four,' I guessed.

'Thank you, sir,' he said, and wobbled off into the crowds.

Across the road a troupe of blind masseuses was pounding clients seated on low stools. A dwarf woman massaged her patient by violent rotations of her knees and forearms, as if she had no hands. Another was attending to a man with a gashed and infected knee. He covered his face in agony as her fingers kneaded the wound, then uncovered it again with a crucified smile when her hands moved away. Later I noticed him keeled over in a municipal flowerbed, exhausted with pain.

It was in a coffee-shop nearby that I met Hua. Her wrinkled, girlish face attracted my attention, and I sat beside her on purpose. She was in her late fifties. Her too-thin hands fidgeted round her coffee-cup. She could not drink fast, she said. Coffee made her tremble. Her readiness to confide was curious, but then nothing about Hua was usual. Soon she was talking about herself with a garish egotism.

She had been born into a high-class Manchurian family, she said, and educated at mission school. In 1945, after the Japanese surrender, she was living in Harbin as a seventeen-year-old student. 'But one morning I looked out of the window and cried out to my parents "There are hundreds of foreign devils here! Ones I've never seen before." It was the Russians in their odd, peaked caps. They stayed in Harbin a year, and some were billeted on us. I used to stitch their clothes and humour their officers, so they wouldn't touch me.' The coffee-cup was shaking at her lips. 'One night they drew lots as to who should sleep with me. The winner was a huge, wild man. They took the bullets out of his revolver before he came to me. But I ran away and lay down between my parents on the *kang*. My mother kept valuables there, and I threw them all at him – cups, opium pipes, teapots. I wanted to kill him. But there were fourteen or fifteen others outside . . . and they . . .' she faltered – 'and they . . . they . . . took him away. . . .'

Her face went hard, disoriented. The lines of her jaw and cheeks suddenly tautened to show a glint of silver-capped teeth. I realised that she had been raped.

'After that my family decided it wasn't safe for me any more, and that I had to go away. So I cropped my hair like a boy and wore a shapeless overcoat. In those days money in China meant nothing – you had to own piles if you wanted to buy anything. So my family contributed their jewellery – gold and diamond rings – and I sewed them into the lining of the overcoat, and made my way to my sister in Beijing.'

I didn't know if it was her coffee or her memory which set her hands trembling. But her sister and she had parted ways. Her sister had joined the Communists, while Hua had fled south to the Nationalists, first to Chongqing, then to Kunming – one of their last strongholds – in a Flying Tiger piloted by American mercenaries. 'Of course I should have made my way to Hong Kong. That would have been freedom. But I couldn't know the future. . . .'

Then the Communists came. She must have been deeply implicated. I could not tell what she had done, or why she had flown south in the plane of a Nationalist general. She had the ambivalent manner of an old renegade – at once defiant and broken. 'The Reds took away everything I had – the rings, everything. I refused to say the things they wanted, I wouldn't conform. How could I declare that I hated the Americans and loved the Russians after what had happened to me? But that was what was required in those days. . . . So I was put into a type of labour camp, where we broke stones for roads' – she added almost casually: 'for twenty-eight years.'

My gaze travelled over her scarred face and neck. Twenty-eight years: the heart of a life. But she had survived with an unreconciled anger. Only in 1981, with new policies, was she freed. Now she lived in one room, on a pension. Almost her only personal possession was a photograph of herself taken forty years before, with a young man. She did not talk of him.

'My neighbours think I'm mad,' she said. 'They say, "There's that insane old woman talking to herself again." But actually I'm talking to my cat. Sometimes I sing to it.' For a moment I thought she might weep. 'They think I'm mad, but I think they're stupid. Almost every Chinese – really stupid. If the government says "This is blue", they repeat "This is blue". If the government says "No, this is red", they repeat "This is red". That's how they are.' She added in an undertone: 'Which is why it's good talking to a foreigner. I have more in common with foreigners.'

'You have relations left?'

'I don't know where my family is. Scattered about Manchuria, perhaps. I don't want to find them again.'

She had become too deeply estranged, too shamed, whatever she had done, whoever she had known. She lifted the cup angrily to her lips. 'The one I cared for was my younger brother, but he was killed in the Korean War. Trainloads of Chinese went south then, and nobody ever came back.'

She must once have been rather handsome, I thought, with her vivid eyes and fine hands. Only a few grey hairs trickled in the black. But she couldn't stand against her whole people and emerge unscathed, and there was something disordered in her, tumultuous, as if their judgement on her had half fulfilled itself.

'In China you must conform,' she said, 'but I can't. That's why they think I'm mad. I challenge everything, you see, and that's madness here. I ask *Why? Why?*' She laughed for the first time, bitterly. '*Why?* is not a Chinese question.'

*　　　*　　　*

Eight miles into the hills above Kunming, in a secluded Buddhist temple, the prayer-hall is lined by fantastical figures. Traditionally the ascetic saints, called *lohan*, are portrayed more personally than the bland Buddhas whom they attend. But I had never seen any like these.

Ranged in double rank along the walls, they surge forward on a mystic ocean, outlandishly modelled in clay and brilliantly coloured. Each is violently original. Child-like or decrepit, their faces powdery white, they arrive in a swirl of cloaks and pantaloons like a posse of celestial clowns. And just as frescoed Christian martyrs cradle the instruments of their mortification, so each of these crazed saints is identifiable by his looks. The eyebrows of one are so long that they spill down into his hands. Another's right arm shoots out like elastic eight feet to the temple's ceiling. Yet another, ludicrously tall and infantile, hitches up his pants as he paddles in the billows. Above him, a buck-toothed ancient is nonchalantly flying in on a stork.

There must be some seventy of them. Sad-eyed *lohan*, worn out by prayer or worry, jostle against obese hedonists with mouths like half-moons. Faces shrivelled with abstinence or scarred by years of battle hobnob with eccentrics whose foreheads are pinched into horns or mounded in bumps. Most of them are bald, or tufted with scant, oily locks, and their fists are closed around snakes and obscure roots, scimitars and begging-bowls.

As they come surfing over the waves, their feet are seen to be balanced on an armada of sea-monsters. Cat-faced crustaceans in rainbow colours leer just below the breakers, with a ghastly squadron of scaled and studded amphibians. The *lohan* ride them with rough abandon. The whole lunatic navy is making for a landfall, and leans forward in readiness. For the sea which carries them is poised to break over the temple floor, where the saints threaten to alight from their mounts and wade into the everyday world.

But how, I wondered, had they arrived here in the first place?

Information was scant. They had been modelled by a noted Sichuan sculptor named Li Guangxiu, I discovered, at the end of the last century. But beside the transcendental Buddhas they had struck too earthy a note. They were considered in bad taste. And the rococo master was never heard of again.

I wandered planlessly along the margins of Lake Dian. To its north, Kunming was stifled in smog, but for miles along the western shore the forested hills sprouted temples. They were a favourite haunt of honeymooners, and as I climbed here I was adopted by the pair strolling ahead of me. I had often seen honeymooners in the towns along the Grand Canal and had wondered about them. Novels and television brimmed with dramas of soulful longing, but I had seen no trace of these – or any other passion – in the consummated couples.

I became sensitive to symptoms of feeling between Feng and Lijun. She was a Shanghainese and he from Canton, so they conversed in the lingua franca of Mandarin. They had known each other three years but had only courted shyly in parks and cinemas before the onset of their four-week honeymoon. Every night their Kunming hotel room was costing them their combined salary for a week.

We followed other tourists up tunnels and stairways gouged in the cliffs. From time to time we emerged onto terraces by rock-cut Taoist shrines high over the lake. All along the western shore the clouds were poised bright and unmoving above the hills. Feng and Lijun tramped a little separate, he in front of her, cameras at the ready. His high-blocked shoes were worn down to their metal heel-rims, one of which was loose so that he clinked like an ill-shod horse. Lijun followed him in high heels. Her jeans were neatly pressed and her blue woollen cardigan spangled with seed-pearls. At each vantage-point – verandas and rocks a thousand feet above the lake – they would assemble for snapshots. Feng would face the lens in a grinning roundel of spectacles and hedgehog hair, Lijun present herself in profile, her pony-tail tresses pulled back from a big-boned face. 'Why don't you put on your dark glasses?' he would ask her each time, although there was no sun – dark glasses were quintessential chic – and she would perch them obediently in her hair.

She was hesitantly tender with him. Sometimes she curled her hand inside his arm or laid it lightly against his back. He took no notice and she appeared to expect this. They were like old neighbours, distantly acknowledging one another. But from time to time she would trip ahead of us and pose demurely in front of a photogenic backdrop. So Feng would come round the corner to find her nonchalantly framed by a wave of mountains, or gazing in well-lit wistfulness over the rocks. Sometimes he would photograph her, sometimes walk on.

These ritual snapshots seemed the heart of their journey. They never stopped to read the ancient poems carved in the cliffs, or to look down at the mottled beauty of the lake. I could not tell whether they admired the scenery at all, or simply cherished the idea of themselves in it. Once or twice I hung behind, thinking they must want to walk together. The cliff-tops were scattered with pavilions where nobody sat, and over the lake surface, quartered by the wind into ruffled lights and calms, a fleet of junks was sailing. But Feng and Lijun never diverged from the crowds.

In one shrine, beneath a rock-hewn Buddha, we placed coins against the incense-bowl for good luck. The coins were meant to stick to the metal, but mine kept falling off, and Lijun frowned. 'You must get it to stick.' She was suddenly serious. Feng's coin and hers had adhered easily to the bowl, but mine refused. Even after I had licked and attached it, she went silent for a while, as if it were an omen.

Among the boulders scattered along the hill-summit stood a photographer with a jaded horse. Clients who mounted it had a choice between sporting the helmet and tin sword of a feudal warrior or putting on a black stetson and pretending to be a cowboy. As we neared the stand, some buried fantasy seized hold of Feng, and he demanded to be immortalised as a cowboy. He clopped over to the photographer, paid one kwai, and addressed an envelope to himself so that the snapshot could be forwarded. But he did not know how to mount. The horse was harnessed in peaceful bells and cushioned with a pink bath-towel. But Feng was little more than five feet tall. He smiled sheepishly. He tried to hook his foot over the horse's rump. His glasses fell off. Lijun burst into a fit of giggles. Finally the photographer and I grasped his ankles and levered him trembling into the saddle.

But once the camera was on him, his fear faded. He behaved precisely like the sightseers photographed at the Ming Tombs, or posing with a loaned car – the last wish-fulfilment – in Beijing. He was engulfed by a yearning to be the Lone Ranger. He flicked the dust from his jeans. He tipped the stetson rakishly over his eyes. He looked a perfect fool. Then he lifted the plastic pistol ('Browning 22, Made in Shanghai'), squinted along its barrel into the glare of imagined badlands, and drew a bead on the horizon. Lijun had stopped giggling by now (in any case, one kwai was expensive), and Feng's jaw had set melodramatically as he picked off half a tribe of Sioux. Then the camera clicked. For an instant he held his pose, then his feet disentangled from the stirrups and he was nursed triumphant to the ground.

After this I settled above the lake alone, and watched Feng and Lijun snaking with the crowds down the hillside below. Once I spotted her blue-cardiganed figure trotting fifty yards in front of him; then, while he was out of sight, she turned and arranged herself against a pavilion balustrade, silhouetted among the boulders.

She made a perfect picture.

*   *   *

Occasionally, through the staid crowds of Kunming, I had glimpsed tribespeople passing in a proud heresy of flaring reds and enamel blues and a trail of tassels and beads. Such long-despised races occupy semi-autonomous regions along all the frontierlands. They number less than seven per cent of China's population, but spread over half the country. In a forest of eroded limestone near Kunming, I had seen Sani women in black surcoats and blue turbans; around Lake Dian, the Bai wore sashed jerkins whose sleeves dripped in harlequin layers. They reeked of jungle and distance. It made me restless looking at them. But the Bai seemed crushed by the enormousness of the city; and the Sani in their stone labyrinth were acting as local guides. Umbrellas hung from their sashes.

But south to the borders of Burma the grip of the ethnic Chinese, the Han, starts to loosen. Ever since this region of Xishuangbanna fell to the Mongols in the thirteenth century, the Chinese have rumoured it an earthly paradise: 'the Land of Peacocks'. Its jungled mountains remain half inaccessible, and the Buddhist Dai peoples, whose kingdom this once was, still farm the peaceful valleys beneath.

I had already received police permission to travel here, but I did not know how far I could penetrate. At Kunming airport the only planes were a squadron of MIGs and a dumpy twin-engined Antonov, which I boarded. The sky was warm and clear as we took off. Beneath us, the plateaux descended among forested hills and rivers crimson with silt. I saw scarcely a village. This mountain earth, the colour of muddy rose, was too leached and eroded for easy farming; it tinted the whole land in a whorl of fiery fields and a bloody trickle of streams. To the west, huge unruly rivers – the Mekong, the Salween, the eastern tributaries of the Irrawaddy – surge in parallel through the mountain corridors which sever China from Burma. It was in these malarial abysses that Kublai Khan, attacking west, left half his army dead.

We were flying into the hub of south-east Asia. The Yunnan tablelands had foundered exhausted into jungled valleys, where the curves of rivers still left shining terraces. Soon we passed over the grotesque blood-vessel of the Red River, flowing south-east toward Hanoi before spilling into the Gulf of Tonkin. The frontiers of Burma, Laos and Vietnam were converging ahead of us.

We landed near the town of Simao, ringed by forest. The townsmen mingled with soldiers. We were less than eighty miles from the Vietnamese border. I took a cell-like room in a run-down hotel whose washrooms were open latrines piled with turds. A plain-clothes policeman traced me here, leafed through my papers in silence, and went away.

Next morning I found a bus going south to the Mekong, and for six hours plunged down through rain forest. It was mid-October, the end of the monsoon season. The bus was crammed with Han farmers and townsmen, but I felt I was scarcely in China at all. Outside, the world had subsided into a sodden slumber. Blowzy insects whirred and bumped among the creepers. The valleys poured out trees and plants, while luminous clouds rolled from their clefts or hung in thin dusts on the heights. Then we entered the vale of Jinghong, the region's toy capital, and were released into paddy and sugar-fields where the Mekong river wound.

I settled here for four days, and lapsed into torpor. Active life – even the desultory, slow-motion life of other provinces – had been stilled to the peace of a cul-de-sac. The earth steamed with a surfeit of rain and sun. In the markets three or four different peoples – Bulang, Hani, Dai – mingled in a patter of indecipherable languages. The Dai were a delicate, slim-hipped race, like the Thais (to whom they are related), and their faces were touched by the same softness, and by the convexity of petite brows which seemed to retract their eyes. Their ancestors had arrived here while hunting a golden deer, they say, named the region 'wondrous land', and settled down. Now they filled the markets with a Polynesian innocence of colour. Beneath the women's bodices and filigreed belts, their sarongs shone yellow and royal blue, and were decorated with peacock-feather patterns. They moved among the Han Chinese with a violent, tribal glamour, their chignons bound in pink scarves, their ears dripping gold pendants.

And there were other, surlier groups, come down from the hills. The bellicose Hani trooped all in black: black culottes and leg-bands, black headdresses circled by silver coins, babies slung from their shoulders. The Bulang women went in peaked white bonnets. Since infancy their earlobes had been pierced and distended by plugs of cork, and now gaped empty or were hung with silver rings. The older women's lobes dragged down to double their natural length. Their teeth were blackened from chewing the sap of the lacquer tree. But in the markets these remote people made little noise and when the Dai bargained with the Han middlemen over their onions or brushes, the women employed a subservient pathos.

'They've no education,' said the Han contractor in my guesthouse. 'It'll take years before they're really civilised.'

He had just travelled down from Kunming to buy tree-fungus for his government firm, only to find that it had all been bought by another government firm. Why hadn't he telephoned, I asked? There was a telephone line to Jinghong now. But he only groaned. The whites of his eyes were deep yellow, as if he suffered from chronic hepatitis. He mumbled: 'These Dai . . . if they were clever, they wouldn't live like they do. They'd either make business, or go into something different. But you've seen how they live. . . .'

I wondered aloud: 'Perhaps they're not interested in business.'

But he could not conceive this. 'They're just too primitive,' he said. 'During the Cultural Revolution their monks were put to work in the fields instead of jibbering to God. But even that didn't change them.' He lifted his hands and diseased eyes in a parody of prayer. 'They're all pretty thick, if you ask me.'

For a man who had just spent eight working days in a useless business trip, he was on delicate ground.

'They must resent you Han people,' I said brusquely. 'Where did the Red Guards come from? Not from the Dai.'

'No. Not even from Jinghong. They came from Kunming.'

I imagined those busloads of zealots pouring over the valleys and uncomprehending farms. 'The Dai can't like you very much.'

'No, I don't think they do. And they speak another language – something like Thai – so we can't understand what they're saying.' For the first time he looked discomforted. 'They might be saying anything.'

I borrowed a bicycle and took to roaming the valleys. Above their lower slopes, dense with rubber and banana trees, the jungle shimmered with sunlight and warm rain. In the fields beneath, where rice interspersed with winter corn, the peacock beauty of the women sustained the legend of paradise. They called to one another in a tongue gentler than Mandarin; their hair was stuck with flowers or released glistening to their waists.

I rode past villages of communal houses hoisted off the ground on stilts. Their wooden walls were not sealed against the cold – which never comes – but laced together windowless in slats, and opened on verandas hung with sweetcorn. Cattle and water-buffalo were stabled underneath, with chickens and inedible dogs. Above, the roofs reared precipitously in thatch or tiles while cactus and bamboo fences enclosed a sordid jumble of gardens, burgeoning with papaya trees and fetid ponds. In this rotting paradise everything was over-ripe, going to seed, yet flowering again voluptuously out of its own decay. Each leaf of the banana trees grew taller than a man. Black sows dragged their uddered bellies through the foliage beneath. The tracks had become waterways clogged with buffalo dung.

Even the sacked monasteries were rebuilding. I found gangs of young men reinforcing them with bamboo poles, and old ones repainting the beams in vermilion and gold. The Buddhist sutras were whining again from their halls. Often I found the acolytes disposed indolently about their verandas in robes of saffron and cerise; and once, rounding a corner in a village, I almost crashed into a billiard-table where two monks were challenging the locals to a game of pool.

Compared to these stilt-villages, the cottages of Han farmers were grounded in paddy and business. Many had been built in the 1960s by immigrants resettled here from northern cities, and it was near one of these that I wandered into a rubber plantation to escape the noon sun. All down its pale-trunked aisles, diagonal scars in the bark were bleeding into cups tilted askew beneath them. I leant my bicycle against a tree, and sat down to a forbidding picnic of cold rice and peppers.

'Are you from America?'

He had materialised like a goblin out of the shadows: a peasant in patched shorts and mud-spattered shirt.

'No, England. Are you from here?'

'I'm from Wuhan, on the Yangtze.' He hovered in front of me on spindly bow-legs. 'When my parents died, the government moved me down here. Up there my work paid too little.'

'And how are things now?'

'Very poor. A little better than before, but very poor.' He gestured at the cups sagging against the tree-trunks, and revolved his tired hands in a ghostly extraction of rubber. 'There just aren't enough of them.'

I asked: 'Can't you do anything extra?'

He fingered his torn shirt self-consciously. I could not decide his age. He seemed to waver between boyishness and senility.

'What extra?' he said. 'I work the plantation with my daughter. I just have a daughter.'

I asked incongrously: 'Why not try and buy a pig?' There seemed to be money in pigs.

Yes, he said, he'd heard. But he couldn't afford one; the market prices in Jinghong were too steep. He spoke as if a pig were a palace. And all the time he was gazing at me with unconcealed wonder. His expression was quizzical, oddly sweet. 'England? England. . . . That's a good place.'

'You know of it?'

'No, but it must be good. Look at your arms, your chest.' He lightly touched my forearm. 'How old are you?'

'Forty-six.'

'Well, I'm only fifty-four, but look at me.' He raised his arms: they were pared to the bone. 'So I know England must be a good place, if you can eat like that. . . .' His eyes strayed to my bicycle. 'And that . . . is that English too?'

'No, Chinese.'

He tapped it wistfully. He could not afford a bicycle he said, not like the rice-farmers. 'Even the Dai are wealthy now. They wear wrist-watches.' His own wrist was bare, and thin as rope. 'And they've all got bicycles. Well, not all, but most. You've seen them?'

'Yes.' I had often passed them with their wives perched side-saddle behind in wide-brimmed hats. Occasionally I had even seen young Han and Dai bicycling together. 'And what are the Dai like?'

He said simply: 'They're good people.'

I think I was too alien even for his envy. He gazed at me with his peculiar, sad sweetness, as if my presence made him nostalgic for some unreachable well-being. Momentarily I saw myself in his eyes – taller than anyone he had ever met, uncannily pale-haired, and fattened by the mystery called England. Inexplicably I was in his rubber grove.

I badly wanted to give him something, but in the bag on my handlebars there was only a cheap purse (gift of China Airlines) which I proffered him for his daughter. He clasped it against his chest.

As I climbed on to my bicycle and shook his hand, I said: 'I hope you have luck,' but it suddenly sounded empty, irrelevant. Luck was a luxury. From this man's life possibility itself had been worn away.

For a long time, as I bicycled down the track, I glimpsed his thin hand waving.

Early one morning I joined a passenger-boat sailing twenty miles down the Mekong almost to the Burmese frontier. I did not know if I was allowed on board and it seemed wiser not to ask. In the stern lounged a few soldiers and Han farmers cradling baskets of poultry, and some Dai peasants strapped about with knives. The poop was stacked with jars of offal bought by tribespeople in Jinghong. Their women sat amongst them, belted in ten-deep layers of cowrie shells. We were sailing to the end of China.

Out of its shallow sands and rice-flats, where the clouds billowed like a forest fire, the river narrowed into hills and never relaxed again.

Down its banks bamboo and fig trees, hung with lianas, drifted a hundred feet in motionless cascade. The river flowed red with silt, its surface silvered by miniature whirlpools and sudden rapids. Sometimes it seemed to be flowing in two or three directions at once, streaming laterally across its own bed or rippling in inexplicable bores backward over the main current. Occasionally it narrowed to less than a hundred yards across, gushing between grey rocks, and the steersman would stop talking and forget the cigarette burning against his lips as the wheel whirred through his hands.

It was impossible to travel on this river of evil memory without completing its voyage in my mind. Ahead of us it plunged out of the Golden Triangle down the unnavigable gorges of northern Laos and deep into Cambodia. South-eastward from Phnom Penh, the desecrated capital, it flowed over half-drowned freighters sunk by the Khmer Rouge, swelled past the Vietnamese re-education camps and widened at last where the boat people, every dusk, awaited the night tide out to sea.

But now, a few miles from the borders of Burma, the red torrent was littered only with bamboo driftwood. Sometimes my boat halted at jetties under makeshift settlements, and threw out a plank for the peasants to disembark; sometimes it simply rammed a river bank and the tribespeople clambered ashore and vanished into virgin jungle. At last, as the hills before Burma rose streaming and brilliant with cloud, we berthed at the outpost of Ganenbang.

It was a scattered village of Dai and displaced Han. But even here the Red Guards had penetrated. On its outskirts I came upon a half-wrecked monastery. The tiles were glissading from its roof like a pack of discoloured cards, and on its altar the surviving monks had recreated a coarse clay Buddha – eyes, smile and aureole daubed on like magic emblems. The temple reeked of animism. Its ceilings rained down lurid prayer-flags and lanterns, painted snakes, peacocks, forest godlings. The Buddha's feet were cluttered with corn-stooks and food-offerings. A group of saffron-robed boys, monks for a year, were learning to write the rounded Dai script, and two old men were redecorating the altar with slips of coloured glass. They motioned me to eat with them.

But I was heading for the rain-forest. From a distance it heaved in a tissue of impenetrable green. Here and there some white-limbed tree hoisted a parasol of dripping ferns, or hung suffocated in a stark skeleton under the creepers. Often the tracks beneath tapered away.

But sometimes, swarming over those dead white limbs, the lianas had carved out whole aerial caves and corridors. I pushed forward under sunless tunnels, to the cries of birds I never saw. Fallen bark crackled under my feet. I waded through invisible spiders' webs. They brushed my arms like a cloud of alighting insects. Sometimes blackened bamboos arched overhead in a cathedral of dying leaves. But everything was inextricably tangled, so that I could not tell if the bursts of mauve-pink flowers bloomed from plant, tendril or trunk.

Underfoot, the earth festered. Termite-riddled trees had half turned back to soil. Bamboos mouldered to the ground in segments, like old flutes. The ground sent up a damp fetidness. Within hours of falling, every leaf was perforated with insects' bites, and dead birds and snakes had been scoured clean beneath feathers and scales still shining.

I hoped to see animals – gibbons, wild oxen, perhaps even a specimen of the rare golden-haired monkey which had turned its back on me so rudely in Beijing Zoo. But I glimpsed only a fawn tree-rodent which vanished instantly, and butterflies flying up to the sun.

The only creatures that ignored me were the spiders. White-speckled monsters with hooked legs and globular tails, they clambered round their webs in revolting slow motion and crammed their victims wholesale into their maws. At the first patter of rain in the forest, they would bind up their webs in glutinous orange balls, then hang upside down on a few guy-ropes, and sit things out.

Once only, I saw a troop of the dangerous Hani in their black leggings and headdresses. But the men were unarmed and the women plodding under high baskets, their silver-studded jackets open on pendulous breasts – and all of them too old and small and burdened to offer any threat.

Circling back to Ganenbang, I came upon a decayed shrine. Its door had been shredded by termites and it parted like a leaf at my touch. Inside, on the rough altar, sat a statuette of the Goddess of Mercy. The remains of tapers lay in front of her, with dead flowers and some decayed packets of cigarettes. Flanking the entrance, the two door-guardians were grotesquely eaten away. For a moment I thought they were corpses. From their crude bodies the colour was almost gone, and the weapons had dropped from their hands; but their heads were distorted, like animals', with bared teeth and the eyes of demons. For weeks afterwards they recurred in my thoughts, as if they had conveyed something which I did not understand.

I spent that night in a dormitory full of construction workers and gecko lizards. For hours the men pushed their heads genially between my mosquito netting and shouted the familiar questions: food, prices, where was England, why was I alone?

I couldn't sleep. Long after their inquisition had subsided, I slipped outside and strolled in the warm dark. The village had fallen silent, even its dogs. To the south, beyond a profile of hills, the moon was rising over Burma, with a wheeling mass of unfamiliar stars.

10. Through the Gorges

Almost everyone who has travelled for long alone in China becomes prey to an insidious attrition. For several weeks I had noticed this slackening in myself, and wondered why. Some undefined sickness seemed to be coming over me. Whenever I found a hotel mirror I would inspect my eyeballs for the onset of hepatitis, and in the jaundiced light of thirty-watt bulbs became convinced that I was turning yellow.

But the malaise was compounded of other things. Since leaving Canton I had scarcely eaten a nutritious meal. The southern breakfast was a bowl of rice porridge laced with gherkins, an impenetrable steamed bun, a few peanuts and a glass of hot, sweet milk. I had already dropped a stone in weight, but the bun and the gruel remained inedible. I was slowly losing stamina. In the scrimmage for tickets and bedrooms I had become dourly irritable. The buffeting in trains and buses, the mass and proximity of bodies, their bawling and spitting, now induced a creeping tiredness. 'The people is a mountain, the people is a sea', say the Chinese ruefully, and I felt suddenly drowned by them. There seemed to be nothing in the world that wasn't a Chinese. Their remorseless, laboratory staring – the stripping of all privacy – had reversed our roles: I had become their subject. And the hotels offered little escape. Single rooms, in this plural land, were unknown. Even the lavatories were usually a line of communal holes in the ground, where men squatted ceremoniously in the excrement, reading newspapers. I was starting to close myself away. Things which I had previously accepted now preyed on me: the aesthetic drabness and sameness, and that pervasive smell – cooking-oil, urine, stale fish, whatever it was. The people's slowness of thought and movement had irritated me at first. But now I was trudging as lethargically as everybody else: a victim of protein deficiency.

Outside Kunming railway station I was stopped by a frenzied worker. 'They wouldn't dare do it to you because you're a foreigner!' His face craned furiously up to mine, then glared back through the station doors. 'They pretend there are no rail-tickets when there are piles of them! They save tickets for friends so they'll get something back some day. Then the friends sell them on the quiet for more. It's a racket.' He yelled back at the door: 'It's a racket!'

In my fourth-class carriage to the north, I spent a day and a night squashed among Sichuanese tin miners. Their questions were suffused in titters. Opposite me, two girlish army officers kept fingering one another's insignia – yellow stars on collar and lapel, which had just been instituted. I felt fragile and choleric. The miners repeated everything I said with incredulous hilarity at my Mandarin. The legs of the man beside me kept quivering. I wedged my feet against his, to stop them. I thought: my nerves must be at breaking-point.

By nightfall people covered the floor in a jigsaw so dense that there was no place left for them to spit. They squatted two abreast along the aisle, or laid sheets of newspaper and cardboard under the seats, and slept there. I was wedged bolt upright, envying the supple Chinese body. The miners had retractable legs, tucked tidily under them, and the two soldiers curled up intertwined. I tried to create a headrest by standing my rucksack between my feet, but I overflowed the aisle and everybody clambering past me jolted my shoulder-blade. This happened once every five minutes for more than seven hours. Meanwhile the train pulled south through one of the most tortuous rail-routes on earth, traversing valleys, peaks and Yangtze tributaries on a track only completed in 1970, after Herculean effort. Over almost seven hundred miles it entered 427 tunnels and crossed 653 precipitous bridges. Near its end, a hill is covered by the graves of those who died constructing it.

I woke to see the sun drawing a pink blind down the mountains. I groped my way to the restaurant-car, but there was nothing to eat except steamed buns. For hours the train delved in and out of tunnels. One-third of the journey was passed in darkness, so that in between the landscape flickered like a series of disconnected slides. The arid rush of a ravine beneath us would be obliterated in blackness and succeeded by an overshadowing mountain, veined by tracks of scree or hung with a waterfall. I gazed sleepily out on them. The carriage was embalmed in cigarette smoke, which thickened and curdled as the hours wore on. The tin miners talked at me in thick, Sichuanese dialect. I was too tired to understand much.

Then the vet arrived, oozing status. His flashy tie and check shirt seemed less a covering than an exaltation. His balding forehead was veneered in locks scraped across from the far side of his head. One of the miners had left for the lavatory, and the vet pushed into his seat. He beamed with a pitiless *bonhomie* and sureness of welcome. He showed off his few words of English before reverting to Mandarin.

I answered his questions in dulled dissociation, depressed irretrievably by my dislike and my tiredness. Of his face I recollect little but teeth and glasses: aggressive, smiling, merciless. And our conversation has now resolved into half-remembered tatters.

'Do you know where I work?' he asked, as if I were telepathic. 'I work in the animal quarantine office of Sichuan.'

'In the villages?'

He answered with uncontrolled horror: 'No! No! In Chengdu. In the capital!'

He wanted to exhibit his knowledge of Western European culture, which was muddled. The words 'Shakespeare' and 'Hamlet' dribbled smooth and unread from his lips. The tin miners stared at him. I started to like them.

'Shack-es-peer is famous in our country. He wrote fifty plays. . . .'

'No.'

'Fifty plays, and. . . .'

My eyes strayed to a soft-porn romance sticking out of the vet's pocket: a current favourite. I was surprised to find myself angry.

'The Western languages all come from Latin, don't they?'

'No.'

'Certainly they do. . . .'

By now we were hemmed in by an audience of clustering faces. The corridor was blocked and the workers in the compartments to either side were peering over, everybody listening to the brilliant vet and the sick Mr Tampon.

'We're new friends, aren't we?' He leaned smugly towards me. All the surrounding heads leaned forward too. He banged my knee with his fist. 'Aren't we? I am very happy. Are you happy?'

Silence.

'Are *you* happy?' He banged my knee again.

'Oh yes, of course.'

Sometimes when we dived into tunnels, the carriage's lights refused to go up and there were roars of acrimony. During these minutes I hoped to escape conversation. But no. The encircling faces, signalled by their cigarettes, only leered closer, like predatory fireflies, to the dark gap where I sat. The vet's fists continued to locate my knee. 'Western history begins with Jesus. . . .'

[228]

I relieved my fury by making faces at him in the dark.

Then we shot out again into a vertiginous seesaw of mountains. The vet produced a red booklet. 'Now I will teach you some important Mandarin.' He regrouped the locks over his forehead like a badge of office, and incanted in English: 'The Four Modernisations are Policy One of our China.' The fist crunched onto my knee. 'Repeat, in Mandarin.'

My temper was rising. My head jerked to the window. I said: 'Look at the scenery.' Below us a precipitous valley dropped, and a white spate of streams. But nobody's head turned.

'The Four Modernisations are Policy One of our China. Repeat.'

I told myself I was only practising the language. 'The Four Modernisations. . . .'

Remorselessly he went on: 'There are many political parties in China.'

I snapped: 'But only one big one.'

'No, many. Look. This is my party card. Now I will teach you some more.' He held up the red booklet to me, and said in English: 'I am member of Worker's Agricultural Party of People's Republic of China, but my faith is in Communism.' The teeth and glasses bored closer in self-delight. 'Repeat in Mandarin.'

'I'm tired,' I said. Outside the window, gliding level with us but high above the valley, sailed a golden hawk, oblivious of the train, the Four Modernisations and even of the vet's prestige. We were deep in the big upland province of Sichuan, which descends eastward from barren plateaux to the fertile plains of the upper Yangtze.

The vet proclaimed: 'China and the West are friends now. The Russians are evil, they have a KGB. We do not have secret agents in China.'

'You do.'

He looked startled. 'What?'

'*You do.*' For all I knew, he was one. 'Every country has them.'

'Well, perhaps. But now it is different in our China. We can all say what we like. We're not afraid to talk to you. We're free.'

The miners grinned agreement. We plunged into our four hundredth tunnel. The lights faltered, went out, but the fireflies all nodded. 'We're free.'

Momentarily I wanted to ask them if they would dare publicly to reject the Communist Party. But then freedom meant different things. As I looked round at their faces in the next burst of daylight – the effeminate soldiers, the naïve miners, the fat-featured vet – I believed that they felt they were free. Their freedom was not mine, but it was greater than any they had ever known; and by the time the train pulled in to my destination – the little town of Emei – I was dozing companionably on the shoulder of the pit foreman beside me.

It is old in Chinese belief that the natural and the moral orders interknit, and Mount Emei – highest and most remote of the four sacred mountains of Buddhism – was for centuries accounted a god, a mystical influence on men. In its heyday it was studded with over a hundred temples and monasteries, but fire and unrest had depleted them long before the Red Guards raged through. The Baoguo monastery, where I spent the night, was one of the few left. Here, among the foundering halls of a sanctuary many times rebuilt, I slid back into the ambience of pilgrimage. Through the walls of my wood-latticed cell, the night hours were punctuated by gongs and drums.

I was woken by chanting at dawn. Already a few pilgrims were about, and incense rising from the altars. The climb to Emei's summit spiralled for more than six thousand feet and forty miles above me. It would take two days. But the clouds had fallen so low that the mountain was all but obliterated. I walked isolated in whiteness through a forest of rain-dripping trees. Beneath my feet the stone stairway vanished upwards into air, and the land on either side seemed to fade into an abyss. I passed porters carrying atrocious loads of bricks and vegetables. They fell behind in mist, as if I had dreamed them. I could not tell how high the peaks loomed above me. Only occasionally, out of the whiteness where I thought the sun might hang, a ghostly file of pines would emerge, or a shoulder of grey stone.

The sacred way was almost derelict. A motley of booths and shacks lined it with walls of matted straw and tarpaulin roofs. Some still sold food and herbal medicine to passers-by, but most stood deserted. In others, a few pilgrims and hardy sightseers were slumped on rain-streaked benches, mud oozing underfoot, or were eating egg and noodles served from charred stoves, with the clouds swirling in.

After five hours I reached the temple dedicated to the mountain's protector, Puxian, embodiment of universal light. Where almost everything else had been cleaned away by fire, his statue had survived here for a thousand years, and when I saw it I realised why. He rode a sixty-ton life-size elephant in copper and bronze. Its columnar feet were planted foursquare on bronze lotus-pads. In its saddle Puxian was perched close beneath the temple's dome and gazed down from the dimness with an epicene beauty. At every solstice, it is said, the sun shines through a perforation in the cupola and strikes the jewel on the god's forehead. But now only a few monks presided beneath, looking crushed and old in their worn leggings and outsize boots.

Beyond, the way was a stone ladder into clouds. Around it the trees stood colourless and delicate – stencilled in pearl or washed away to tracings on the opaque air. In this invisible forest, I heard birdsong and pilgrims calling to one another. Almost unnoticeably, it began to rain. It fell with a vaporous quietness: I was climbing in its cloud. When I paused, I could hear it dripping unseen in the forest. The only movement was the quiver of the struck bamboo-stems, and the soundless fall of leaves, one by one, on to the earth.

My old ski-jacket turned out to be leaky. The damp infiltrated my pullover, shirt, vest, and flapped in the hood against my ears. All round, the rain-faded sky and trees had become softly unreal; only the stairway was hard, like a causeway across some other, shifting substance.

On the higher slopes the pilgrims grew fewer and hardier. A robust old lady with a staff descended out of clouds above me. A string of prayer-beads swung from her neck at every stride. But as she bustled past, her expression grew motherly. 'Go slowly-slowly,' she mewed. Soon afterwards I was overtaken by a honeymoon couple – she a soldier, he a policeman, in full uniform – holding each other's hands. Then a cluster of Tibetans marched past – a tattered aristocracy in silver bonnets and lambswool coats, dangling ceremonial daggers. The rain intensified, until I could not see fifty yards ahead. A familiar ache was throbbing along my sinuses. I was resting more and more often. Why, I wondered, did people have to undertake these blood-pounding assaults on the sublime? A long time later, I came up behind a woman older than anyone I had seen here. Her face had taken on the pain of her bound and crippled feet – her eyes screwed to dots and her cheeks inflated around a tiny exclamation-mark of a mouth. Step by step, sideways, she was hobbling up the mountain, alone.

At random points along the way, monkeys had set up toll-gates for food. If unrequited they could turn vicious, and it was the custom for pilgrims, after running out of propitiatory peanuts, to show them empty hands. I was tramping upward, my eyes on the stairway, when three hefty apes lumbered out of the bamboo. Their hair was dark and spiky with rain. They settled on the steps in front of me and waited, their bright-red faces aslant. Clinging to the belly of the leader, its body concealed in her fur, was a sad-faced baby. It looked out like a droll mask. I tried to circumvent them. But they came at me with threatening coughs and squeals, and extorted my last biscuits.

It had become very cold. Once the way led through a dying monastery. In the corner of its stone-flagged hall a single monk slept in his quilted overcoat, as if awaiting reincarnation. The clouds seeped through the cracked walls. A candle guttered on the altar, where the offerings had dwindled to an apple.

By now the way had levered itself up through pines and cedars, and was muddling along in shining slabs, frayed by the tread of generations, and old with their memory.

At twilight I reached the temple where the bodhisattva Puxian had flown in on his elephant and washed away mortality in a pool. It was still haunted by water: water in its every incarnation. Drizzle and mist had turned its courtyards to slithery rinks and extinguished their incense-burners. Rain-clouds flurried through the doors, and glistened on the flagstones of the shrines. Nothing was to be heard but slopping, splashing, dripping. A line of sodden monkeys was sheltering along a veranda. In the prayer-hall the straw mats were half rotted away, and the mildewed Buddhas squatted behind glass casements, as if in fish-tanks. Several of the monks had hacking, tubercular coughs. The clatter of rain on the roof drowned out their chanting.

By now I had a streaming cold and my ears were numbed by tingling. A monk led me to the guest-rooms. But damp had penetrated here as surely as a fine desert sand. It glazed the floorboards of the corridors, and streamed down the walls. In my cell a scroll-painting showed a waterfall pouring from wooded peaks. Out of the window was nothing: just a blank of sky, and an empty drop down the mountain.

The monk said weakly: 'You're English? I would like you to teach me some phrases for our foreign visitors.' He took out a notebook. 'I wish to say: "Apology: we make our own electricity here, so there is no light."'

My voice rang inside my ears when I spoke. It seemed not to sound outside my head at all. But he repeated my translation several times, and wrote it slowly down.

'I also wish to say: "Up here we have no well. So we are lucky that it is raining, and we can wash."'

This too was repeated and written down. Then he wandered off along the passages, and I heard his incantation fading away: ' "We have no well . . . there is no light. . . ." '

Just below the monastery I found a bamboo shelter where a man was cooking. I sat on his bench, too tired to care about dirt. I could not distinguish what he had cooked by the flare of the lamp, but I bolted it down as a bulwark against the cold.

In the monastery, when I returned, a family of Tibetan herdsmen was circling the aqueous Buddhas, necklaces glinting through their rags. Bowls of candlewicks lit the statues now; behind their misted glass they showed only a gilded crown or hand. The rooms around mine were loud with retching and coughing. Moisture had crawled into the bed coverlets and grimy pillows. I extinguished my oil-lamp. Long afterwards, I was woken up by the sound of rats gnawing. I had a drowsy fantasy that they were chewing through the last pillar that held the monastery above the abyss. But I drifted back to sleep without caring.

All night and all next day the rain poured down. I struggled towards the summit through a land which seemed to be ageing before my eyes. Vast, half-dead cedars writhed from the undergrowth, their trunks oozing moss and creepers. Once or twice the clouds parted and I glimpsed an ocean of peaks below, rolled in mist, and mountainsides rusty with maples. I was tramping through a Gothic forest of junipers and fern-dripping rocks. The ghosts of birds flitted between the branches.

Higher up sightseers had arrived by a lorry-track on the far side of the mountain. They came chattering down from the crest in mud-spattered slippers and high-heeled shoes, with jolly pink umbrellas.

I reached the crest half an hour later. It was entombed in whiteness. I might have been anywhere. Its temple was as waterlogged as those below. In the sanctuary a dark Buddha sat in saffron gown and sequins. A handsome elephant waited behind. The intricate permanence of their bronze, housed in these flimsy walls, suggested a stupendous, forsaken past. A wizened monk sat by the altar and struck a cauldron whenever a pilgrim kowtowed to them. He thought they must be over five hundred years old, but did not know. He had even forgotten how long he had been here himself. 'I think thirty, forty years. . . . I can't remember. It's so cold up here. You just wait.' He was huddled in thin, damson-coloured robes. He coughed.

'But you go down the mountain sometimes?'

'I go to buy things in the village, three times a year. That's all.' He looked at me with flinty eyes, preparing a question. 'Tell me, are there Buddhists in England? . . . There are!' He banged the cauldron in celebration.

'We have Buddhists from Hong Kong.'

'From Hong Kong!' He banged the cauldron again. 'And are you one?' He lifted the hammer in anticipation, lowered it again, crestfallen.

'English Buddhists never come here,' he said, 'I don't know why, and even our young Chinese . . . they don't seem to care.' The mystery of this furrowed his brow; then he added: 'But as they get older, they start to bow to the Buddha. Then I strike this. . . .'

A short way above the temple, the mountain found its end in a precipice six thousand feet above the plain. In clear weather the plateaux before Tibet, lifting towards the eastern Himalaya, swim into view in a shining palisade. On other days, when afternoon clouds are banked beneath the peak, a phenomenon called the Buddha's Aureole occurs. Then the sunlight, refracted through water-particles in the clouds below, rings the pilgrims' shadows there in a nimbus of rainbows. In past centuries Buddhist devotees, staring on the mirage in wonder, hurled themselves ecstatically into the void.

But I found the summit hung in isolation. The mist packed a luminous brilliance round it – no hint of shape or movement or colour. It was a blinding abstraction. Step into its light, and you would fall for ever.

*   *   *

Chengdu retains something of the grandeur of a lesser Beijing. It is, after all, the capital of a province whose population exceeds that of Britain and France combined. The enormous rectangle of its moat still delineates the walls and battlemented gates hauled down in the 1960s, and its main thoroughfare moves in a quadruple avenue of trees and tulip-shaped street-lamps to where one of the last statues of Mao rears its hand in avuncular greeting – a greeting no longer returned. Behind him the old prefectural palace of the Manchus was blown up in the Cultural Revolution, to be replaced by a Soviet-style exhibition hall.

My bus-ride from Mount Emei to here had been the climax to weeks of attrition. My sinuses had throbbed blindingly and a gamelan orchestra was tuning up inside my ears. For a day after my arrival my jarred body remembered the unsprung bus. Then, slowly, the sun and crisp air revived me. In my hotel, the luxury of carpets and hot water and edible meat became grossly addictive. My headache drained away and the gamelan played pianissimo. My hurt ears evened up.

I had gained my second wind.

I took to wandering the streets. Among the half-timbered houses peculiar to Sichuan, I felt I was roaming an uncensored corner of Tudor England, with its filth still in place. The alleys were boisterous with markets, and the garrulous temper of the Sichuanese overflowed restaurants and tea-houses down half the alleys.

I blundered into a second-hand bicycle market. It swarmed with people too impatient to join the usual lists for new machines. (You might wait two years, a man grumbled.) Among its hulking black roadsters – no gear or drop-handlebar in sight – a subtle snobbery prevailed. They defined their owner's status as vulgarly as cars could in the West. Specimens of the prestigious Shanghai-built *Everlasting* or *Phoenix*, and the up-market *Flying Pigeon*, were muddled in with a humble scrapheap of others. The vendors sat behind their models in lethargic lines. In front, the buyers scrutinised them like horse-dealers in an orgy of chain-tugging, brake-testing, pedal-twiddling, rust-hunting. A good specimen could cost a year's salary. One woman was trying to trade in her fashionable *Feide* for a child's *Cuckoo*, and a Cantonese *Three Rams* was the focus of a hubbub of waving bicycle licences and receipts, as two people tried to buy it at once.

I hired an inglorious *Chengdu*, and went to visit Xigun. An acquaintance in Shanghai had given me his address, but had told me nothing about him, and on telephoning his office in the municipality I had been informed darkly that he was now in hospital. I expected to find him seriously ill.

And perhaps, in his mind, he was. He lay fully clothed on his bed in a privileged ward for two. His right hand rested over his heart in supine hypochondria, and he was staring delicately at the ceiling. 'I heard you were coming,' he said.

I looked down on the face of a sad Mao Zedong, a dust of greying hair swept back from a wide forehead. 'What's wrong with you?'

'I've already been here ten days, and they still don't know.' He spoke in fluent English, with a faint mid-West accent. 'I had slight palpitations. My pulse dropped to forty.' He eased his shoulders against the pillows. 'I've been at my desk too long. Years and years. . . . So I'm having a rest now. This ward is for high officials, for those above grade fifteen.' He was basking. 'I'll probably stay another ten days. . . .'

'How are they treating you?'

He sat up, patting his hair. 'I take herbs three times a day, in a kind of soup. That's all.' He sniffed the air. The smell of disinfectant was drowned in the musty fragrance of a spice market. 'But the food here isn't much good. There's never enough.' He was sitting bolt upright now, buttoning his jacket. He looked me up and down. 'How come you got in here?'

The Americanism fell strangely from him. 'I just asked my way,' I said. 'How do you speak English so well?'

He swung his feet to the floor and glanced at his watch. 'I was adopted by my aunt. My parents gave me away to her.' He left this mystery dangling in the aromatic air. 'Look at the time, it's only seven! There's time to go to a restaurant!'

There was no stopping him. Within half an hour we were ensconced in his favourite eating-house, surrounded by fiery Sichuanese dishes: pork, lamb, dumplings, onions, all steeped in garlic and pepper sauce. They brought a rash of sweat to our faces. He threw off his jacket and cardigan, unbuttoned his shirt and loosened his woollen vest. First my anorak, then my pullover crumpled to the ground.

'This'll put my pulse up!' He felt it joyously. 'It's up already!' A sudden impishness seized him. He fired a fusillade of pork and mushroom into his mouth. I had never seen anyone look healthier. 'Tomorrow my municipality is banqueting a Japanese delegation, but I can't be there. I'm too ill. . . .' This thought trailed away, reassembled. 'Perhaps I could appear, and everybody would say how brave and conscientious I was.'

'Provided you didn't eat much.'

'Yes. . . .'

The idea faded.

More food arrived – aubergines, carp in bean sauce, spiced cabbages. From the hall upstairs came rhythmic music.

'What's that?'

'Dancing,' he said. 'Just for young people out of work, people doing business. They're the only ones who can afford it.' His chopsticks flickered among the carp bones. He added: 'My mother taught me dancing. . . .'

I had been waiting to unravel her – the woman who formed his English. 'The one who adopted you?'

'Yes. She was an American, married to my uncle. My parents gave me to her when I was a baby.' The flush of eating had left him now, and his voice had gone soft. He wore a look of adolescent melancholy. 'It was this woman – I call her my mother – who taught me about fineness of character. She taught me never to be cruel, not even to animals. You know, we Chinese can be very cruel. Crueller than you.'

I had hoped not to hear this: not so simply, so completely. I could not think of anything to answer.

He said: 'After my mother went, it was hard to find that gentleness among us Chinese. Very hard.' He had given up eating. This alien woman had become a homeland which he never found again. He did not mention his wife. 'My mother never realised that I knew I'd been adopted. But I only had to look at my face in the mirror. I wasn't pale. I had no trace of anything but Chinese. Besides, we had relatives, and they told me. But right until the end, she thought I didn't know.'

This boyish reticence seemed deeply Chinese – a sensitive double-bluff which had helped preserve her from the sorrow of her childlessness. I began to like him. 'She was very loving,' he said. 'I've never forgotten her. But it all seems long ago now.'

'She died?'

'No. But when I was just fourteen, she left us. She went back to the States.' He gave a pained little laugh. His expression had regressed to a homesick youth's. If people are expressed by a time of life, I thought, then Xigun's life inhered there: at fourteen years old, the year she abandoned him.

I said: 'She divorced your uncle?'

'No. But she had to go back. You see, it was 1948 and we were being chased south by the Communists. She might have been killed if she'd stayed. She hoped to return. But later I couldn't write to her – not even after 1955 when things got better. If I'd written, it would have made things worse for us.'

He looked jaded now, an invalid. I could not sense why she had really gone, or what he really believed. The reasons he gave were enough. But the desertion remained.

'Some years ago,' he said, 'a man from the World Bank visited our municipality and said he would try to trace my mother for me.' His voice was a maudlin whisper. 'But she had died in Oakland, California, in 1975. If she'd only lived a year longer, we might have met again. Because after 1976, you know – the end of our chaos – it would have been possible to write to her.' He repeated, as if trying to understand it: 'But she died in Oakland, California, in 1975.'

I knew he was hurt, because he was smiling.

*   *   *

I bullied my way on to the fourth-class carriage going east to Chongqing. The crowd which packed the seats was rough and silent. Opposite, an androgynous-looking child in fluorescent pink and green clothes settled down to stare at me. I fell asleep for more than three hours, and awoke to find him unmoved, still staring.

We were pushing through one of the most fertile and densely peopled regions in the world – the red basin of Sichuan. Locked in high mountains and its own seasons, its diverse crops had been elaborately irrigated for over two thousand years. A mild climate dims it in mist – a mist that is almost perpetual. When the sun shines, it is said, the dogs bark. Outside my window, terraces carved and quartered every incline of its hills; the valleys twisted round chessboards of red and green, where winter wheat and vegetables burgeoned – sesame, sweet potatoes, soya, rapeseed.

But the slopes were deforested. The chestnut and cypress trees had been hacked down to fuel the steel furnaces of the Great Leap Forward, cleared for grain fields during the Cultural Revolution, and now felled to make way for cash crops under the Responsibility System. It was a fertile land, but bereft.

At dusk the Yangtze surged in a colourless flood out of the south to meet us, and an hour later we sidled into the railhead at Chongqing. I took a bus to one of those mammoth hotels built in the time of Soviet concord. This one was prodigious: a bastard Ming palace in ochre and sea-green. In the night it seemed to requisition half the sky. Its galleried wings were heaped around a domed hall – a spurious Temple of Heaven tricked out in every whimsy of phoenix and dragon, and turreted in pagodas. Its true ancestry, I suspected, did not belong to the domestic modesty of China at all, but with those wedding-cake Stalinist sanatoria around the Black Sea. And behind its banked colonnades, the suites were familiar. In my room the washing-line doubled as a viaduct for rats. I shared it with three sick Japanese students. We paid a pound each.

Next day I tramped the fortress-city with growing awe. It covered a rock peninsula where the Yangtze and Jialing rivers meet, cooped in a polluted theatre of mountains. Withdrawn from the eastern plains behind the Yangtze gorges, it had been seized on by the Nationalists under Chiang Kai-shek in 1938 as their capital against the invading Japanese, and two million refugees had flooded in. Every May, when the fogs lifted, the Japanese air-raids began. On moonlit nights the bombers would follow the silver corridor of the Yangtze to its confluence with the Jialing, and no black-out could hide the long crab's-claw of the promontory below. There was scarcely an anti-aircraft gun to defend it. 'Sichuan', say the Chinese – 'first to rebel, last to yield.' The people burrowed down into the rock. Corrupt, insanitary, stubborn, the city survived.

Now it had mushroomed into an industrial Gehenna of six million. It spent its summers in furnace, its winters in smog. Any Japanese pilot flying over it would be asphyxiated. Besides my outlandish hotel, there was no colour in the whole place. The Jialing heaved down through mud-flats on one side, the Yangtze from the other, colliding in a churn of docks; and sandwiched on its rock between them, the city had risen again into the fascination of its old ugliness. Alone among Chinese towns, there was not a bicycle to be seen. Tunnels and cableways wobbled and burrowed and swung through its murk. Scarcely a building exceeded forty years old, but they were sooted and grimed until they looked coeval with the rock they rose from. Old shelters and stairways riddled the cliffs. Some were held back from suicide only by thin brick piles or bamboo stilts. Their back windows perched above oblivion. Here and there a stairway dropped into some gulley which had escaped the Japanese – a seam of black-roofed cottages. They stood up only by a chance equipoise of rotted wood and stone.

The people looked ill and drained. They plodded their hill-streets in wan fatigue. For the first time I felt winter had come. A suffocated sun was being rolled across the sky on waves of chimney-smoke. Ash appeared from nowhere out of the air.

I fell in with a rosy-faced man who was roaming about as bewildered as I. He had been evacuated here as a child, and had returned for just a day. 'But I don't recognise anything.' He was gazing about him in confusion. His brass-buttoned jacket and silver-rimmed spectacles suggested status. 'Everything I knew has gone, except the old Hong Kong and Shanghai Bank. Seeing that gave me quite a jump. I was at school in a little village over the river, cut into the rock on bamboo supports. Chongqing was just a desert then, people living in the ground.'

'Did you expect to be defeated?'

'No!' His tone brightened with the quixotic optimism of his people. 'None of us boys believed that. We were absolutely confident.' He straightened his jacket. 'Odd.'

He was fascinated by his own confusion, by the intervening years which all these new buildings signified. 'We used to watch the Japanese bombers flying in,' he said. 'Then a few anti-aircraft guns would open up, and once I saw a plane go down on fire and land in the town. The mess was ghastly. It crashed on the nothern spur' – he gestured vaguely behind him – 'and now I can't even find the spot. Even my school is swamped by suburbs – a little brick place squeezed among flats.' He focused me. 'You're not American, are you? . . . Well then, that's all right. Because there's one place worth seeing here. It's called the US–Chiang Kai-shek Criminal Acts Exhibition Hall. You should see that.'

I took his advice, and crawled by bus along the southern bank of the Jialing. Mile upon mile it was dogged by belching suburbs: steel-mills, collieries, chemical and machine factories. A seedy Manhattan was piled on every cliff-top. The nondescript Criminal Hall had been built near the prison and headquarters where Americans helped train Nationalist secret agents. The Nationalists, of course, had used them against the Communists, and the Hall was a cry of outrage and martyrdom. A few manacles and torture instruments mingled with photographs of concentration camps and of those executed. There was an enigmatic snapshot of an American sergeant biffing a Chinese with a boxing-glove, and a rash of glorifying paintings which detracted from the sombre pathos of the rest. A trickle of young people wandered about these exhibits with detached respect. It was becoming old history now. They were referring to pamphlets. They read out the captions for me, and did not ask my nationality.

In the hills behind, a prison had been preserved. But it resembled a film-set: toy-like, with thatched guard-houses, wooden bars and puny doors. There were gaps in the electric wire which circled its tiled walls. Beside the cell doors hung photographs of those executed – some no more than teenage girls and boys – but already distanced by the spectator's knowledge of their end. Behind the prison a waterfall fell into the valley, grotesquely pretty.

*   *   *

The black rock of Chongqing fell astern. For two or three miles its factories and wharfs littered the shores, then my steamship moved between villages towards a horizon whitewashed by mist. On either side a long echo-chamber of headlands faded away while the Yangtze rolled between in an auburn flood, without glitter or pattern or sheen.

I sat in the prow, alone with the excitement of the river. Already it had descended more than two thousand miles from the glaciers and snowfields north of Tibet, and had poured through the precipitous valleys abutting Burma. Eastward it sliced China definitively in two – the third longest river on earth (after the Amazon and Nile), almost four thousand miles from its source to its end in the China Sea north of Shanghai.

On my rusting, five-decked steamship, *The East is Red No. 24*, the first class had been eliminated as a concession to equality. But the second class, segregated near the prow, enshrined twin-berth cabins and a carpeted lounge. It was occupied by a handful of foreigners, complaining, and by a few high officials afflicted by the 'cadre's waddle'. They pompoused up and down its passages as if the boat were under heavy swell. The third-class cabins, hung with defunct fans and striplights, were inhabited by lesser officials (and me); while the fourth-class sank to galleries lined with twenty-four bunks each. Along the corridors and stairs, a ragtag and bobtail class slept amongst its luggage, or improvised beds from matting in any nook it could find.

For a day we floated towards the gorges by which the Yangtze storms down into the plains. The only agitation, as yet, was the judder of our diesel engines. I commuted statelessly between the different classes. Among the foreign élite a Chinese businesswoman from Singapore was bewailing the native Chinese. 'I've been trying to do business here for a month,' she told everyone disgustedly, 'and what do I get? I wait a week in a hotel room, and then nothing – or just half an hour's fobbing-off. So I'm reduced to bribing everybody. That's what they expect.' She spoke with the unyielding scorn of the escaped compatriot, looking back at her past, her people, without the sentiment of a foreigner. 'These officials don't care a thing for their company or nation. Just for their ego. They earn so pathetically little, you can buy them all, from a provincial governor down.'

On other decks I was surrounded by English language-learners, by two owl-faced psychiatry students studying behaviourism, an old professor of metallurgy and a shoal of delegates from the interminable business meetings, returning to Shanghai or Nanjing in office time. In a sheltered corner, a huddle of youths was grinning and confabulating, engaged in traditional cricket-fighting. They spilled their champion insects out of china pots into a sand-strewn tray. The tiny gladiators hesitated, chirruped, then locked their forelegs in a brittle wrestling-match, while their owners egged them on with toothpicks. The defeated one would scamper out of the arena altogether to a chorus of recrimination, and a few coins pass between the youths, covertly gambling.

Our boat slid to its night anchorage between reefs winking with lamps – green to starboard, red to port. In past centuries, travellers and imperial customs officials would be greeted by the lantern-hung skiffs of courtesans, circling the waters to the lilt of lutes and violins. But now we drifted among unlit barges, and nothing came to meet us but light rain and a flicker of bats over the calm.

From her warm-lit cabin on the service-deck, the radio-operator was singing to herself snugly. When I peered in, she broke off in giggles. 'Are you alone?' she cried. 'Why are you alone?' Newly married, with a baby girl, she gave out a glow of innocent fulfilment. She was stitching an orange overcoat for the baby, lining it with fur. 'This is what I do when I'm not sending messages. What do you do? Aren't you with your work unit?'

'I'm a kind of . . . work unit on my own.'

She began feeling sorry for me. She was boiling noodles on a little stove. 'Why aren't you married?'

I had not the English, let alone the Mandarin, to answer this. I said: 'There must be Chinese men who don't marry, aren't there?' But I realised I'd never met one. 'Aren't there men – for instance – who have fallen too much in love with a married woman? Or who prefer solitude?'

'No. No!' she said blithely. 'There's *nobody* like that in China. I'm sure there isn't. There *can't* be. Without a home, a person can't be happy. And a home is a wife and child.' She stirred the noodles with concern. 'My husband has just told me he's missing me. When he says good-night, he always says he's missing me.'

I glanced round the cabin, as if this eccentric might be sleeping in a cupboard or under the bed. But I saw only her straw-matted bunk, empty, and a wash-basin displaying a bottle of 'Bee and Flower' shampoo. 'Where is he?'

'Oh, he's not here! He's a radio operator on one of the other boats.' Her laughter tinkled secretly. 'Sometimes we chat in Morse code . . . just a little.' She whirled the pan from the stove-ring and ladled the noodles triumphantly into bowls. 'You see! If you'd had a wife, you'd have eaten by now!'

That night, as I lay in my bunk, I wondered what messages were bleeping down the Yangtze in the dark. '*The East is Red No. 9* to *The East is Red No. 24*: At longitude III° fifty minutes west Nanto . . . have you finished Xiaodan's coat? . . . I miss you. . . .'

Next morning we entered the 130-mile gorges which sever Sichuan from the eastern plains. Black cliffs rose sheer a thousand feet and reeled into the distance until I could not tell if their silhouettes were cloud or stone. The wind was channelled to a screaming corridor of air. Thin rain blurred away all colour and texture. At the vanishing-point of each gallery of water, the mountains fell in an unbroken wall or sent a fishtail of rock crashing diagonally from hundreds of feet above. The river twisted into boils and cataracts. At points it ran at almost twenty knots; under its rush lay a graveyard of ships.

Most of the passengers had been driven below deck by the rain, but the professor of metallurgy joined me near the stern and quoted Tang poetry, which he had loved as a boy. During the Tang zenith, in the seventh and eighth centuries, the Yangtze had been nostalgically celebrated. To poets it became a symbol of evanescence, of time passing. Its rush and echo make a noise through all their verse. At its most savage, it filled voyagers with a numinous awe. The unearthly wail of gibbons haunted them from its cliffs. Here the water-demons had shed their ancient scales and appeared as nymphs wrapped in aqueous light. The crags took animal shapes and names, or became petrified goddesses. Their feet were strewn with sacrificial wreckage.

Sometimes we saw trackers' galleries cut across the scarps. Along these, teams of coolies, harnessed to towlines of braided bamboo, used to haul junks and barges upriver, while the ship spread its sails for any supporting wind and the crew let off firecrackers to distract the evil spirits. In a whole day they might advance a third of a mile. When winter spread the galleries with ice, the trackers sometimes lost their footing and men and craft were swept away together. Occasionally ships' crews can still be seen hauling boats round the current's ugliest points, but tugs and winch-barges have almost replaced them, and the tracker's bitter profession is dying out.

Often the river stilled to an aisle of uncanny beauty. Then the slopes eased to lonely farmsteads, and a few sampans took to the water. The cliffs would separate on high valleys, where clouds dangled as if caught on invisible hooks of rock, and flood-courses scarred their floors with silt.

The metallurgy professor had gone below by now, and I was left with an ex-army officer, impervious to rain. Under his outsize cap fell a long, goofy face in thick-lensed glasses. He was eating roasted melon-seeds, whose husks he dropped fastidiously overboard, and was taking covert swigs from an unlabelled bottle in his jacket pocket. He worked in industry now, he said, but he planned to disembark at Nanjing where he had spent two years in artillery school. Those had been the best years of his army life. The other nine he had endured on the Soviet-Mongolian border. If the Chinese conceived of an enemy now, he added, it was not the Americans, but the Russians and Vietnamese. There were still artillery battles with Vietnam every day.

On trains my conversations with soldiers had always floundered into banality. But now, in our isolation – and perhaps in the warmth of his drink – the man relaxed. Periodically he took off his cap and spectacles to clean the water from them, and this produced an unnerving change. His goofy look vanished and there emerged instead a pair of sombre eyes and heavy lips, a Levantine urbanity. He spoke fast, aggressively. And when he turned to look at the river, the confusion between these two personae – the bespectacled goof and the bare-headed entrepreneur – was confounded even further. For then I saw a brutish profile – a receding chin and low forehead which puckered over his eyes in a Neanderthal query.

'I spent eleven years in the army,' he said. 'The worst of it was that the men were all peasants. They'd never even been trained to wash or clean their teeth, so they stank, and their teeth rotted away. Officers kicked and slapped them continually. I did it myself.' He cuffed the air and hacked at an imaginary bottom. 'Sometimes at target practice they'd just fire all over the place and I'd get furious, this terrible anger coming up out of my throat.'

In his goofy cap he looked too foolish for anger – a long, sad nose and chin under myopic eyes. But I remembered his protean changes. 'The men were riddled with superstition too,' he said, 'which often made them careless of life. Some of them believed they'd be reincarnated as bigger men if they were killed, while their enemy would go down to hell. These types of soldier often didn't show fear.'

He tugged off his cap and wiped his spectacles on its lining. The fool was instantly transformed into a sophisticate. 'Superstition . . . soldiers killed themselves for that.' His mouth curled. 'A man in my own unit did. When I heard the shot I ran as fast as I could to him, but he was gasping out blood and by the time we got him to hospital he was dead.

He'd shot himself through the heart, because his parents had refused him marriage to the girl he loved. She'd been born in the Year of the Tiger, you see, and he in the Year of the Dragon – and those signs are incompatible. The dragon and tiger do nothing but struggle against one another, so the four parents forbade the marriage.

'In the next unit, a soldier was persecuted to breaking-point by his officer. The army's full of officers like this. They make it unbearable for the men, so the men crack. This man took a machine-gun and blasted his officer to death. Then he pulled the pin out of a hand-grenade and blew himself to bits. He left a suicide note – that's quite common – saying he was sending his officer to hell and himself to heaven.

'The trouble is these men can't find women. Private soldiers aren't allowed to marry. Even officers can't have their wives with them unless they've been in the army fifteen years. Instead they go home once a year for a month – and that makes trouble with babies. If their wife doesn't conceive that month, they have to wait another year. Quite a few officers were childless. I, too.'

'And what do the private soldiers do?'

He looked away, presenting his brutish profile. His eyebrows made a coarse awning over his gaze. 'That was really disgusting stuff. Some of them used to go with one another, or even with animals. Pigs and horses mostly. We always joked about the men who fed the pigs. But if a soldier was caught, he'd be sent back to his village.'

He shook the raindrops irritably from his spectacles again. Around us the world had become a grey-blue tempest of stone and water. The sky was cooped in a jagged circle of storm overhead, and the scarps decapitated by rain so they looked as if they had been poured from the sky and frozen in mid-air.

He said: 'All that makes you more sympathetic when a soldier gets a woman. In my unit there was a man who sneaked out of camp at night and walked fifteen kilometres to sleep with a peasant girl. He just tapped on her door and got in without her family realising. Fifteen kilometres there and back in a night!'

I said vaguely: 'Perhaps she was pretty.'

'No. I was the man's officer, and after I discovered it I had to interview her. She was hideous. She had a club foot. Fifteen kilometres ... I might have had him arrested, but I just made him confess and sent him back to his post. It seemed to me that a man needs a woman. And in those days, in the 1960s, the soldiers had no television and no radio, nothing. Now every company has a television, and you can see the men staring at it with their eyes sticking out. Most of them have never seen such things before. Especially the Western programmes. They'd always been told that people under Capitalism were poor, and suddenly they see these pictures, and hear the world news, and they start asking themselves questions.' He revolved his fingers at the side of his head, drilling inside. 'Questions, questions, questions. . . .'

Soon afterwards, as if he felt he had said too much, he grinned abruptly and descended the stairs below deck.

The rain abated, but the mist thickened. Then we emerged from the gorges. One moment we were worming down a precipitous lane; the next it had fallen away and we were headed blindly for pure whiteness – for that place feared by early men and loved by children, where the sea tips over the edge of the earth.

But instead we arrived at the massive Gezhouba hydroelectric dam. Its completion the next year would raise the river's level sixty-five feet higher in the gorges, but now it lowered us through its locks on to a river utterly changed. We were still a thousand miles from the sea, but little more than a hundred feet above it, floating through a slovenly sprawl of waterways over the plains, a miasma of lakes and winking evening lights.

11. China's Sorrow

WHEN I LEFT the north at the end of the summer, the cottage doors had stood open to the sun, and women had meandered the parks with their babies thin-clad in bamboo prams. Far into the sultry evenings men had sat out on the pavements playing chess, their trousers hauled above their knees, while at night beneath the bridges the peasants snored half-naked on their carts. But now, in November, as I returned into the Yellow River basin, I found a winter hemisphere reverted to colourlessness. Its pavement life had vanished. In the markets the vegetables had dwindled to cabbage and celery. The cold was dry, penetrating. Sanitary masks lent the people a ghoulish anonymity; their heads were retracted into quilted overcoats, and their hands disappeared down padded khaki sleeves.

I studied my route with unease, tracing it across the map into brown and violet regions of cold. Westward along the Yellow River, it penetrated the early heartlands of Chinese civilisation – Kaifeng, Luoyang, Xian – pushed north to the old Communist stronghold of Yenan and south-west to the bleakness of Qinghai, province of labour-camps; then northward again to where the Great Wall – and my journey – ended in emptiness on the south-west fringes of the Gobi.

Haunting almost all this map, and watering a region twice the size of France, the Yellow River twined for three thousand miles. So intimately was it identified with the land that its peace or turbulence had once mystically reflected the fate of the ancient empire. In myth it flowed down from the night sky as an extension of the Milky Way, and its waters yielded up the plan for the *I Ching* on the back of a giant turtle. But it was so capriciously violent that in early times, every year, a young woman was committed to its depths as an appeasing bride for the river-god.

I took a bus from the provincial capital of Zhengzhou twenty-five miles to the river, and spent the day walking its banks. In summer it heaves with a brimming menace, and even now it flowed less like a river than an unreflecting lake on the march. It was shipless, silent. I could barely see across it in the haze. Far to the west, after splashing out of plateaux north of Tibet, it had slowed to this stately crawl, performing a colossal loop between the Ordos desert to its south and the steppes of Inner Mongolia – a flood navigable by little but skin boats. Then it had plunged five hundred miles through hills compacted of wind-blown sand, tugging down terraces wholesale as it went, and now rolled before me thickened by the highest silt content of any river on earth – thirty-four times heavier than the Nile. With every cubic foot of water went more than two pounds of soil. Its sand was smeared in shining banks across the surface as far as I could see. So dense was it that the river carp are said to leap into the air in search of oxygen; and in parts of the river-mouth the silted plain has invaded the Pacific at the rate of a mile every two years.

These massive deposits have raised the river-bed fatally, and year by year its dykes have been frantically heightened alongside. Often now it flows on an elevated channel twenty-five feet above the fields – a mile-wide flood contained only by frail-looking artificial banks. Its past is atrocious. In recorded history it has burst its confines more than fifteen hundred times. The people call it 'China's Sorrow'. Often it has changed its bed altogether. In 1851 it charged headlong through Jiangsu province, then wandered about for two years before adopting the bed of a minor river. It broke its dykes again in 1877, leaving a million people dead. In 1938 Chiang Kai-shek deliberately breached it to delay the Japanese: nine hundred thousand Chinese were drowned or starved to death, and the river meandered untamed for nine years.

Perhaps because of this, the nearby city of Zhengzhou seemed to lack a past. It had recovered its ancient prosperity only as a railway junction, overblown with thousands of red-brick apartment blocks locked in compounds.

I debouched from my bus into a crowd packed thirty deep before a spectacle I could not at first decipher. I was hemmed in by men jostling, women and old people complaining that they had no view. But when I saw what they were watching, I felt a light sickness. A squad of police motorcycles was aligned across the main square, and fourteen men and a woman had been hauled from the side-cars, with their arms bound behind them. Flanked by armed security officers, they were lined up in abject submission. One youth was slumped double, theatrically despairing, as if he had stomach cramp; and the slight, middle-aged woman looked utterly ruined, so that I thought she would faint. She was saved from falling only by the policewomen's hands on the rope across her breast, and her head swayed adrift in greying hair.

Behind them a tribunal of five officers sat with microphones at a table. In their starched uniforms splashed with scarlet and yellow, and their needless dark glasses, they could have been film-actors in some Latin American drama. They were sipping cups of tea, and passing the thermos between them.

Then the microphones crackled and the prisoners were advanced *en masse*. If their faces lifted, the guards on either side rammed them down again. One by one they were pulled forward for an account of who they were, and again for a description of their crimes. They were mostly small-time thieves and embezzlers. Their eyes shifted beneath their lowered brows. Next the local television team arrived. The guards jerked up the criminals' faces by the hair or ears to face the cameras. 'This is Yi Naixian, robber, embezzler of 1,400 yuan of the people's money from Number Seven Factory. . . .'

I watched the crowd for some reaction. But it displayed no anger, no pity. It merely chatted to itself, and by now its front ranks had settled down comfortably on the tarmac to watch. I could not tell if it empathised with the avenging law or with the broken individual, or with nobody at all. My old obsession with cruelty and conscience had risen again – but muffled, diluted by the past months, as if I myself could no longer be outraged. These people now seemed natural. It was faintly alarming. On the edge of the square an old woman was selling beancurd, and three men lay fast asleep in the back of a truck. A few passengers were walking in and out of the railway station. I was reminded of those peasants who go about their business in the backdrop to old masters' canvases, ploughing or hanging out their washing during the Crucifixion. Here public example was a timeless spectacle. In punishment, even in execution, the individual routinely served the mass.

The porcine officer in the centre of the tribunal was reading out the sentences now. But the loudspeaker system had failed, and his mouth was moving wordlessly up and down. Unaware that he went unheard, he rustled his papers grimly before him. His voice made a faraway yapping. The junta flanking him was too important to move, only stared anonymously through its sunglasses. The prisoners went on looking pathetic. Only one man – a giant with a merciless expression – refused to lower his eyes. Every time the guard pressed his head forward he jerked it defiantly back, and stared sheer through the crowd in front of him. From time to time, between the fate of one prisoner and another, the officer paused judiciously to sip tea. Once or twice the loudspeakers spluttered into life, and we would hear: 'Re-education through labour . . . ten years . . . sentenced to . . . years. . . .'

As far as I could tell, none was for execution. The cold lightness in my stomach abated. Next moment the prisoners were being dragged back into the side-cars, the woman almost lifted from her feet, and their heads thrust down between their knees. Only their bound hands stuck up above their backs as the cavalcade circled away.

*　　*　　*

Fifty miles to the east, the old capital of Kaifeng was sleeping forgotten. The Yellow River had inundated it time and again, sinking its artefacts in silt, and its population had barely risen for a century. It was a city of vestiges. Autumn smeared it in creamy sunlight. At its core the centuries mingled with dilapidated naturalness – streets of worn and much-painted brick. It was variegated, restful. Even the map which it published of itself was out-of-date, and was furnished with rallying-cries which more sophisticated places had dropped: 'The people of Kaifeng are working with stamina and diligence, marching toward the aim of a great modern socialist nation', and so on. In fact the city was full of sleepy officials marching nowhere in particular in old-fashioned jackets, ranks of pens conferring status on their breast pockets. Its clerks emerged from office courtyards where spirit-screens stood – screens inscribed with outworn Party slogans or banked about by potted plants. In my hotel the only other foreigner was a Hong Kong engineer brought in to repair a polyester knitting-machine.

In the eleventh century, when Kaifeng was capital of the Song empire, the population exceeded a million, far greater than now. Its axial streets and wards were laid out with geomantic accuracy, and its palace was so symmetrical that the first emperor is said to have announced to his advisers as he sat enthroned: 'My heart is as straightforward as all this, and as little twisted. Be ye likewise.' The power and brilliance of the Tang dynasty gave way to an epicurean refinement, to avenues lined by peach and apricot blossom, and blue-tiled palaces newly graceful with ascending eaves. Philosophers and painters busied themselves with fresh perspectives, and raised to their lips the sea-green bowls whose beauty has never been excelled.

All this lent a pleasurable mopiness to my wandering. Scarcely anything was left. The walls had been breached by goats and children, and dribbled across wasteland with towers so sunk in silt that they scarcely reached to my shoulder. No temples from that time survive, and those which replaced them never recaptured their virile splendour. All through China the subtle tapering of the Song columns is lost, and over the centuries the lines of temple roofs and eaves have straightened out. A less dynamic shape has appeared, at once more staid, prettier, duller.

I loitered devoutly along the overgrown moats of the music terrace, where the Tang poets had recited. Outside a nearby house, an altar was spread with funerary cakes. Paper wreaths and prayers dangled alongside, inscribed by friends in honour of the dead. An old lady, eyes red with weeping, stooped to the ground at the approach of a younger woman, knocking her head in kowtow on the stones. Her friend lifted her up and comforted her with endless, formal pattings of her hand, then gave her a bag of steamed buns as food for the dead.

I watched them from a copse of bare trees, and was touched by a sad reassurance. The belief that a country might change profoundly at the stroke of a political axe had never seemed more futile. For ten years the Cultural Revolution had railed against Confucian ritual. Yet the dead were still being nourished in Kaifeng.

What the women believed, I could not tell. Mao Zedong had described the peasant as a blank sheet of paper awaiting Revolutionary inscription, but in fact the paper had always been scored with a deep, incoherent language of its own. The old ways continue everywhere under Marxist disguise. Now, as in imperial times, rule is less by law than by a collective morality. Beneath the age-long supervision of one another in clans and street committees, lies the timeless ideal that a person melt harmoniously into the mass rather than visit his individuality upon it.

A small delegation had approached the house of mourning, and its women enfolded the bereaved appeasingly in their arms. She sank her head on their shoulders one by one, wiping her tears with her sleeve. It is the belief of most ordinary people that there is no personal survival. The dead continue as a chain of rememberance. They, like the living, are collective.

This old submersion of the individual, I thought, was perhaps why Communism here saddened me less than in other Marxist countries. It seemed to do less violence to its people. Here history had anticipated it. The constraints it imposed were already internalised. Soviet Marxism had risen from a Christian bedrock: evangelistic, dogmatic, exclusive. But the Chinese faith seemed tinged by something older, more sceptical – an acknowledgement of mutability.

A melancholy pervaded my days in Kaifeng. Everything I searched for seemed lost or incomplete. When I pried down Teaching-the-Scriptures Lane, hunting for some remnant of its Jewish community, I was repulsed by barred windows and high walls.

How this community arrived here, is unknown. Perhaps they were emigrants from India, perhaps merchants along the Silk Road through Central Asia. In 1163 they built a handsome synagogue, and kept wealth and position for several centuries. They numbered over a thousand. But by 1860 the impoverished sect looked utterly Chinese, and had been decimated by floods and by the Taiping Rebellion. A German Jew who visited them found the synagogue in ruins, although an improvised prayer-hall still contained a confession of faith engraved in stone: 'We believe that Adam was the first man. Abraham was the founder of our religion. . . . Those trying to picture the Lord in stone, or in any other ways, are wasting their time. . . .'

A few years later the community had fallen apart. Starving, its people dismantled the synagogue with their own hands, and sold off its timber and stones. A visitor in 1866 found nothing there but a water-hole and an inscribed stele commemorating the synagogue's building; and later travellers reported no more than a few illiterate families, ignorant of Jewish customs and beliefs. They remembered only that their ancestors had been 'Israelite'.

I plodded down paved alleys, secretive and poor. Their doors swung on stone pivots into courtyards deranged with rubbish and chickens. The site of the synagogue was a gutted fountain in a hospital forecourt. A girl was pulling her sick father past it on a cart. A young man told me that three of the Jews' commemorative stelae stood in a local museum, but that it had been closed all year. 'Those people all died out or went away,' he said. 'There's only one family left now. An old lady and her children. At least they claim to be Jews.' He took me into a courtyard cluttered by hovels. Posters of door-guardians were plastered to their jambs. At the end stood the shell of a house: two windows framing emptiness. 'They must have gone away,' he said. 'I'll find out where.'

But nobody knew.

These glancing absences continued. It was in Kaifeng that Liu Shaoqi, once the most powerful man in China after Mao, had been imprisoned secretly and died. But I could find no memorial to him. After 1960, with Mao diminished by the Great Leap Forward, Liu had steered the country into a more pragmatic course. But Mao associated his relaxed policies with feudal misery, and it was partly to suppress them, and to reassert his dominance, that he encouraged the Cultural Revolution. Liu Shaoqi was purged, and by mid-1968, under house arrest, he became chronically sick and never left his bed again. A year later, denied the drugs he needed, he was flown at midnight to Kaifeng, there to die far away from the gossip of the capital. His corpse, labelled 'highly infectious' to deter the curious, remained three days in the vaults of the Golden City Bank, and was then cremated under a false name.

All this only came to light in 1980, when he was posthumously rehabilitated. His disgrace was branded 'the biggest frame-up in the history of our Party', and the accusing finger pointed silently at Mao. For years – as long as a whole generation could remember – Liu had been stigmatised as the embodiment of reactionary evil. Now he was proclaimed a Marxist hero.

Secrecy still surrounds the place where Liu died, although a Western reporter located it in 1983. I followed his steps past the disused Golden City Bank – its windows still meshed in iron – to a compound of municipal offices. Yes, said the guard at the entrance, this was where Liu had been imprisoned. He jerked his thumb at a porticoed enclosure, ablaze with chrysanthemums. 'He died over there. In a big room.'

But when I enquired at the city's foreign affairs office, the deputy director was surprised, even angry that I knew of the site. He said: 'No, there is no memorial. No plaque. Nothing. And we do not allow anybody to see that place. Not anybody. Not on any pretext.'

The Party has never taken the final step of officially laying Liu's death at Mao's door.

*   *   *

Early one morning I boarded a soft-berth carriage for the three-hour journey west to Luoyang. An elderly German accountant was still dozing in one bunk, and had left his artificial leg on the floor beside him. I found two young Chinese staring into this pink tube and whispering together.

They belonged unmistakably to the new *jeunesse dorée*. They dressed

[253]

punctiliously, pulling on crimson long johns and buttoning coffee-coloured shirts. Their ties and cardigans were a discreet uniform. They slipped on high-blocked shoes. Were trousers being worn flared or narrow in the West now, one of them asked? He couldn't make out. He glanced mystified at mine, which hung shapeless, then tugged on a pair of Japanese jeans. 'And what about moustaches? I hear moustaches are *in* now. But we Chinese can't grow them like you do. Is it true that you shave every day? We shave twice a week. . . .'

They became puerilely boisterous. They reminded me of men from my own past and culture. Unclouded, sleek with privilege, they had entered the firms where their fathers were bosses. I was slightly annoyed to like them. They had well-to-do relatives in Hong Kong. Every few months they travelled to a business meeting. But nobody really discussed anything, they said, just listened to lectures (or slept). These events, they confirmed, were field-days for the pompous waddlers.

'But it gives us the chance to travel,' one said. 'We escape the office in Xian. Xian's a dump.' He looked mournfully out of the window. 'So is Kaifeng. So is Zhengzhou.'

'What about Luoyang?'

'That's a dump. I was born in Shanghai, and after that anywhere's a dump. All this part of China. . . .'

We stared out on a pale earth. Sometimes no rain fell for eight months on end. The mud-walled villages looked half worn away among fields of winter wheat and cotton. Lotus plants tapered up from half-dry pools.

Perhaps it was the onset of winter which turned Luoyang so desolate. From the station my motorised rickshaw whined into a red-brick tundra, where the wind cut down half-empty streets. Slippered joggers made a geriatric patter over the tarmac. In my hotel, a Canadian teacher was taking refuge from the local technical college, where the isolation of his twenty-year-old students had dazed him. They were ignorant of their own history before 1949, he said: as for the West, not one of them had heard of the ancient Greeks or the Roman Empire.

Luoyang's history, too, was drowned under modern urgencies. It had been China's premier city during the middle centuries of that elusive Roman Empire (from which the emissaries of Marcus Aurelius reached it in AD 166). But from the days of its long, intermittent importance, scarcely a free-standing building survived. Its monuments, instead, were rock-cut shrines. From the time of the Northern Wei, who moved their capital here in AD 494, to the declining years of the Tang four centuries later, the cliffs above the river were riddled with tier upon tier of cave-temples and a hundred thousand statues.

Where the river tautened between steep banks, I saw cormorant fishermen poling their craft upstream, and above them, dashed with yellow-flowering scrub, hundreds of niches hung gutted of their carvings, or held only decapitated trunks. The marks of saws were still on them. Nineteenth- and early twentieth-century Western antiquarians had shorn off the heads and bodies for transport to Europe, and lifted murals wholesale from the rock to re-erect in American museums.

But other shrines were serenely intact. I studied them in amazement and ignorance. The Wei sculptors had clothed their hard limestone Buddhas with an exactitude of lightly incised robes. But beneath this beautiful carapace the bodies bulked geometric. Their haloes rippled over the walls behind them in massed, concentric rings, enclosing thick necks and the faces of overweight angels.

In one shrine I came upon a young American and a Chinese girl whose fingers rested tentatively on his arm. She was statuesque, with proud Mongolian cheekbones. They had been married the year before, she said – he a teacher, she a Beijing student.

The man clambered to a temple higher up, exclaiming at its beauty. But the girl stayed behind. 'My family were appalled by our marriage,' she said. 'They told me I'd be bought and sold in the market as a prostitute. Literally.' She shook back her head defiantly. 'My father – he's an old official – will never get over it. He senses people saying all the time "That's the man whose daughter went over to the Capitalists".' She showed no residue of shame. 'Because people here are very simple. My grandmother wondered why I wasn't afraid that my husband would kill me in the night. Even my own friends thought he just wanted me as an oriental slave in the house. They all said: he plans to make a profit out of you.'

It was depressingly familiar – not only the xenophobia, but the crushing practicality. She said: 'People have heard about divorces in the West, how free it is. They thought he'd just drop me, get bored with me. They never thought of *me* dropping *him*.' Her laughter tinkled icily. Momentarily I wondered how much personal love, and how much ambition, had compelled her to this marriage.

Her husband was inspecting caves ahead of us, greeting each shrine with 'Fantastic! Look at *this* one!', and soon we were wandering among seventh-century sanctuaries carved at the pinnacle of Buddhism in China. Their figures were sculptured almost free of the living rock. Rivulets of damp had eaten away their colours and scarred their cheeks in unintended tears.

'I don't see anything in them,' the girl said. 'They're a mess.'

The right hand, raised in blessing, was the vulnerable one, separated from the mass of the body. Its fingers were often shorn to leprous stubs, or the whole hand – and blessing – gone. Around the Buddhas their guardians and disciples hovered in half-obliterated throngs, touching their fingers in prayer or clasping chalices. But as they waned in status, a mortal grace and sensuousness began. Infant souls emerged from lotus blooms to reincarnation; celestial musicians drummed and fluted; and once a flock of angels whirled across the cave ceiling in a tempest of fluttering robes.

The girl said stonily: 'My husband likes these things.'

I asked her: 'Did officials try to stop your marriage?'

'Oh yes. They came and talked to me, on and on. Can't you find a husband in all China, they asked? They always came informally, as wise father-figures. But the pressure was on. In the end I threatened to kill myself. I thought: I'm not afraid of death, so what else do I have to be afraid of?' She tossed back an abundance of liberated hair. 'Actually, I've always got my way. I'm used to it.'

I laughed. 'I thought you were.'

'I was independent even as a child. I never asked anybody for help, not even my parents. At parties I was the gang leader. My teachers complained that I was arrogant.' She left this charge unresolved in a cave full of Buddhas. 'You have to be strong, because gossip is a terrible thing here. It can blacken you, your job, your family, everything. That's how people commit suicide. Rumour destroys them. It can reach vast proportions. Even close friends won't say a thing to your face. But behind your back there's this great noise going on.' Her voice involuntarily dropped. The hands of the Buddhas seemed to be silencing scandal. 'The rumours were ghastly in our case. They followed me about, growing bigger all the time. At first my husband was aged forty and had a child already. But that wasn't scandalous enough, so he became fifty with two children. Finally I heard he was about sixty and had daughters older than me. And everyone believed it. If things are repeated often enough, people take them for fact. "Three times makes a tiger", as we say.'

[256]

We wandered through other shrines. Her eyes swept their Buddhas indifferently. The Indian abstractions had drained away from them, and a native earthiness had emerged. They were like corpulent businessmen whose faces, if they had possessed colour, should have shone beef-red. Their lips had thickened into judicious smiles. They seemed about to quote stock market figures. Their hands were so big as to contain a hint of threat. Even the greatest – a 56-foot-high personification of the Vairocana, the principle of creation – resembled less a metaphysical concept than a Tang dynasty marshal, compassion-less, his head circled in flames.

The girl surveyed him impassively. 'That one's a bit better,' she said.

I did not think her husband stood much of a chance.

'This terror of gossip was worst in the Cultural Revolution.' She had waited until nobody was near us. 'It was like medieval times with you – I've read about that. If the Church said someone was a heretic, everybody turned against him. I think our people still live at that primitive level. My husband used to believe we were less selfish than Westerners, but I can tell you the selfishness is just extended to the group. You identify your interests with theirs.'

I wondered uneasily what she had done during that Revolution. But when I asked, she remained unperturbed. 'I had to be a Red Guard, but I always stayed at the back. I couldn't hit anyone. I just couldn't do that.'

I looked at her in rude surprise: 'Why not?'

Her face went subtly blank: the familiar reaction to a question not asked before. 'When somebody was badly beaten up . . .' she began hesitantly, 'I felt . . . too much pity.'

It was a region of deepening harshness. Its brick-and-mud villages stood unfattened by any new building. A few tractors and draught horses were about, but alongside them the peasants laboured beast-like over the pale earth – often teams of women in harness, with a man at the plough behind them.

The verges were grey with frost, and my bus to Shaolin monastery, where kung fu originated, slithered and blundered in and out of pot-holes for sixty miles. We passed a crashed tractor with the body of its driver lying by the road, deserted. Somebody had covered his face with a tarpaulin. The blood was dry beneath him and the tarpaulin glazed with frost. The passengers stood up as one man, breathing 'Ai-ye!' and went on staring until the wreckage was lost to sight.

After two hours the road ascended into hills where cold tarns shone. Then it dropped towards Shaolin. Here, on the central holy mountain of Taoism, the sixth-century Indian prince Bodhidarma – founder of the Zen sect of Buddhism – was said to have settled for nine years' ceaseless meditation, sitting bolt upright in a cave, and it is to him that the formalising of kung fu is attributed. A version of this most ancient of martial arts had been practised as early as the second millennium BC, but it was the monks of Shaolin who developed and codified it by studying the way animals attacked and defended themselves in the forested mountains. It became a violent counterbalance to the stillness of their meditation. In its heyday the monastery boasted two thousand monks, five hundred of them warriors. Their feats passed into legend. They were petitioned for help against bandits, Japanese pirates and even imperial usurpers. In Ming times the masters of all the country's warlike disciplines would ritually assemble in the Shaolin halls and even Japan regarded the monastery as the mother-shrine of its martial arts.

The monks built it by a stream in the holy wildness of this mountain, but now the slopes were stripped to a scattering of autumn trees, and our bus came to rest in the artificial tumult of a pilgrimage site. Two squadrons of schoolchildren were practising kung fu on a tarmac bus park, and the way to the monastery was hugged by souvenir stalls selling kung fu swords, sweatshirts, daggers, trainers, manuals of self-defence and outlandish medical advice.

The place had become a cult, as it always used to be. Since the early 1960s, all over south-east Asia and Europe, kung fu films had been set in studio replicas of Shaolin; but in 1982 the Beijing government at last authorised a Hong Kong company to shoot a film on the real site. The result, *Shaolin Temple*, was based on the legendary rescue of the first Tang emperor by thirteen warrior-monks. It sent a kung fu craze through the whole nation. Martial arts clubs multiplied in every province. Tens of thousands of youths wrote to the monastery – some of them in blood – asking to be enrolled as fighting monks. Children absconded from home to reach it. In a state-orchestrated drive to exploit the enthusiasm, special schools, even kindergartens, were rushed up around the precinct, while dozens of seedy lodging-houses appeared and wily ex-monks offered private tuition.

But in the cold brilliance of that November day the heart of the monastery looked dead. Many of its courtyards were locked up, their porticoes stifled in bamboo, and their trees had burst into melancholy fountains of red and yellow. The fifty-odd monks seemed mostly decrepit or very young, separated by the vacuum of the Cultural Revolution. But when I asked an acolyte if they still practised kung fu, he cried 'Yes, yes!' and tore open his monk's gown to reveal a tracksuit underneath.

The old practice hall was lined by ritual weapons and its brick floor worn with forty-eight indentations where generations of monks had planted their feet in training. The correct standing posture alone took them three years to master. They slept suspended from beams like monkeys. They tempered their fingers to steel by exercising them in pots of beans or sand until it was said they could thrust them into an opponent's body leaving five bloodstained holes when they withdrew, or could tear off his flesh piecemeal. They hardened their fists by pounding a thousand sheets of paper hung on a wall, until over the years the paper was destroyed and the monk was punching the bare stone with all his strength. Their legs were muscled by running with bags of sand bound to their knees, and their heads were inured to pain by years of battering, first with a wooden club, then with a brick. Their hearing had been sensitised by listening to the night wind for its direction, emulating Bodhidarma who eavesdropped on the ants moving in his cave. And all this diverse energy was centred in a body turned nearly invulnerable by an esoteric regimen of breath-control. By the time they were masters, the monks could jump lightly on to city walls (it was rumoured) and could split a dozen piled copper coins with one delicate swordstroke. They knew how to strike the thirty-six secret death-points in the human body, and were initiate in the seventy-two blows which created paralysis.

In one of the monastery's halls were frescoes which the fraternity would study as pictorial manuals. They are now bisected by obliterating streams of damp, and after two and a half centuries their paint is flaking away. But the legend of the thirteen warrior-monks is still discernible as they charge like comic-strip heroes in a scrum of bald pates and jutting beards. They brandish flimsy staffs, or nothing at all. But spears and banners go down like nine-pins before the flurry of their fists, savaged men-at-arms collapse into the stained plaster and riderless mounts gallop out of the picture altogether, kicking unanatomically behind them.

Yet it is the murals of monks training which are most extraordinary. In these the traditional secrets are laid bare, and to experts every movement is instantly recognisable. The monks are exercising in courts ringed by arcades, where their elders gesture in a flutter of weak hands. Pale blues predominate in a halcyon backdrop of gardens and temples. But in the foreground is a rumpus of kicking hermits. They hack and feint and push each other's noses in. They seize wrists and elbows in complex ambushes, their sashes and prayer-beads twirling. Their bald heads and rounded features give them the look of venerable babies, brawling in a playground. Yet their expressions are placid masks. Even when falling, they smile impartially, and their lethal feet are cosily slippered. Only a few old and hirsute monks, generally painted brown, are wrenched into grimaces and bulging eyeballs.

Now the eighteen-hour regimen and gruelling endurance tests belong to the past. The most deadly blows are no longer taught, and for the thousands of aspirants in schools outside the monastery the union of kung fu with meditative Buddhism – the spiritual wholeness – has been severed. In the secular furore surrounding them, only the handful of younger monks, perhaps, may carry on the tradition of their forebears.

These veterans lay buried beneath a forest of miniature pagodas close under the hillside. The yellow-tinted memorials, all different heights, were tilted gently in the unevenness of their earth. Under each one the ashes of an abbot had been interred. They numbered more than two hundred. Their tawny stems lifted to lotus-bud finials, and were lightly carved with gates, as if they might open. Many dated back to Tang times. The glades between them were adrift with fallen leaves, so that the stone, the trees, and the earth above those ancient pugilists all shared the same flaxen softness.

It was mid-afternoon before I left. On the far side of the mountain, I knew, stood a Taoist sanctuary, and I boarded a bus running close by, not knowing how I would return to Luoyang. Within five miles we passed the body of a child, run over on a crossroad. A few rocks had been placed round it, to stop it being mangled again. The feet stuck out from the fragments of a cardboard box assembled above, and the shoes had been placed alongside. On the pavement nearby squatted some old men, watching, as if it might resurrect. I heard anger in the voice – it was mine – asking 'Why do they just leave the child there?' Silence. 'For the police?'

Nobody knew. Perhaps for the police, they said, perhaps just for somebody to collect. They turned their gaze to the front of the bus.

I got off where the sanctuary stood under a bare mass of mountain. The winter light had gone sour. Beyond a fortified gate, a series of deserted courtyards mounted the slope. Their stepping-stones were worn in deep curves. Their junipers looked turned to stone. Perhaps it was my depression which dimmed the place into such melancholy – its interlock of gates and temples decaying, its lion-dogs blurring into moss, the stelae cracked on their silently screaming tortoises. The blue-robed priests were beating gongs to gods and immortals I did not know, to emperors who had honoured the mountain with sacrifice, and to a pantheon of disciples fingering lutes and fans. One and all shone hideous in plaster.

The Taoist priests looked poor and few. Their braided hair was circled by black bands. Their belief was as old as Confucius, but had long ago been tainted by sorcery and myth. Yet traditionally it had sanctioned the poetic and mystical instincts denied by the state religion. While Confucianism attempted to fix all things in a timeless order, Taoism embraced the world's flux. To its strict adherents, it became a solitary flight from social dues and hierarchies, a reinte-gration – a self-stilling – into the universal harmony.

The sanctuary's priests were mostly old. One had graduated in economics, and then had *kan pue hung chen*, as the Chinese say, had 'seen the whole world in its vanity'. But he spoke to me only in smiles and platitudes. The higher and deeper I penetrated the sanctuary, the more desolate it grew. Once a quartet of bronze sentinels rose from the grass, almost twice life-size, their fists closed around vanished spears. Then the stone stairs ascended to terraces rustling in weeds, to blackened arks of shrines whose paint had gone, and culminated at last in the brick temple where the emperors had sacrificed to the mountain. It was gutted now. But beyond it, and beyond the Revolutionary havoc which had slashed its friezes and lintels, surged the inviolate strangeness of the holy peak – a pink enigma in the sky, and the last object of worship.

The fight to board buses or trains – the old women crushed against the doors, the children bruised in their mothers' arms – repeated itself as I caught the last bus back to Shaolin. I settled on the floor, feeling exhausted. After a mile an argument broke out between two old men. One had accused the other of buying the wrong ticket. The next moment they were swinging blows at one another, while their voices rose in falsetto and a roar went up as half the passengers took sides. I ceased to understand what the old men yelled. Their senile punches hit the air in a phantom flurry, and every few seconds brought a salvo of abuse from rival factions. Now was the usual moment for a respected elder to salvage everybody's dignity with some compromise. But no such elder was present. The only elders were scrimmaging. So the bus came to a standstill, and for three-quarters of an hour the feud swelled, abated, exploded again, until the younger patriarch left at last in a downpour of acrimony.

I caught a ramshackle bus going north from Shaolin. I wedged myself into a seat and hoped for a few hours' peace. But no sooner had we picked up speed than we were flagged down and boarded by two policemen. A new fracas broke out as they made to arrest a devious-looking youth in dark glasses.

'Why are you wearing those glasses?' one of the officers demanded.

'I've had an accident.' The youth whipped them off to show a bruised eye, then replaced them. But the officers stopped the bus and pushed him out, the passengers all following.

They must have been hunting him, for within minutes a police van appeared and disgorged five plain-clothes men. As the uniformed officers advanced to meet them, the youth was left isolated among the passengers. Their rustic faces hovered round him, muttering. His long hair and suit evoked a background different from theirs. Nobody touched him. Perhaps he was Somebody's son. He turned away from us, his dark glasses still in place, and stared over the hills. The tightness of his back and shoulders looked mutely desperate. The crowd made a semicircle round him, but it was drawn back five yards. There was nowhere for him to go. When the plain-clothes men came for him, an obscure battle of wills began. It was conducted in fierce, inaudible questions and answers, then they escorted him to the van, and the only touch on him was a single push from behind. He walked amongst them as if either feared or contaminated, and nobody knew, or would disclose, what he had done.

I subsided in the bus beside an elderly peasant cradling a pannier of vegetables which kept spilling on to the floor. The light had drained out of the hills, and in the dark his face was indistinguishable. I asked as softly as I could: 'Do you get so much crime here?'

But he fanned his hand against his lips, and looked away. The darkness, instead of protecting us, seemed to fill the bus with ears.

[262]

Somewhere behind us, the policemen were sitting. But a minute later, as we clattered over pot-holes, he murmured: 'Yes, there's a lot . . . theft, murder . . . rape.'

'What had that man done?'

'I don't know. But he must have been a rotten egg.' Then he asked: 'Are you Japanese?'

'No.' The question only faintly surprised me. 'English.'

'English.' He thought about this, then said: 'I saw some Americans once. With enormous beards. Very curious.' His hands splayed out wonderingly from his cheeks. 'But you're the first foreigner I've ever spoken to.'

I felt a bizarre responsibility. I was suddenly ambassador for the whole outer world. But then the outer world was a shadow here. Even I was beginning to feel it. The country seemed to grow harsher, older, all the time, as if something were closing in.

'This is very poor land, this part of Henan,' the peasant said. 'We have a saying: "East to West means riches to poverty". The rich provinces are all near the ocean, I'm told. Here we're too far inland. We're just wheat farmers, and in winter it's too cold to work at all. Families stay indoors.'

'What do they do?'

'They just try to keep warm.'

'And you?'

'I've got animals to look after.' He lit a cigarette. The match's flare disclosed a pair of tiny, peaceful eyes. 'But things are better now. I own twenty chickens, four pigs and a cow. Not much of a cow, but a cow all the same. We've a good house with a well, and a television. And bicycles. How are bicycles with you? To me they seem a very fine invention.' His cigarette glowed and died like contented breathing. 'I've even bicycled to Zhengzhou. My son works in a bank there. He's an *official*.' He caressed the word. I could sense his pride burning in him gently, continuously, like charcoal. It seemed to explain him. 'My son, a cadre. And I'm just a peasant, a small potato. When you go to Zhengzhou, you'll see it written up. The Agricultural Bank. That's where he works . . . an official.' He recovered some cabbages from the floor. 'In your country, are you an ordinary person or a high-up?'

'Things aren't the same over there.'

He paused in perplexity. 'Then what do you think of things over here?'

[263]

At that moment I did not want to think anything. During the day I had seen a fight, an arrest, and two corpses. I was very tired. 'Your people have been kind to me,' I said, and watched the cigarette flare gratefully in the dark.

* * *

A hundred miles west of Luoyang, where the Yellow River floods down to meet its tributary of the Wei, the province of Shaanxi begins. Its northern regions are corrugated with loess hills, stretching to Inner Mongolia beyond the skeleton of the Great Wall, but in the south it mellows to the fertile Wei valley and the great city of Xian.

Modern Xian was rushed up by the Communists soon after 1949 in a drive to redress the industrial imbalance between the inland regions and the coast. A vast rectangle of Ming ramparts encircled it, bulging with crenellated towers, but enclosed almost no building older than itself, like armour for a body which had gone. The streets gaped wide and straight on their old courses. Their camouflage of trees had thinned into winter, exposing a loose-knit frontage of concrete and tile-brick. Beyond the walls the suburbs were studded with the smokestacks of steel and chemical works, and in their pervasive haze the old avenues tapered to a sepia unreality. Modern vistas were closed by a bell-tower or a moated gate far away, floating like the entrance to some other, more exuberant, more exquisite city, which no longer existed.

Capital of eleven separate dynasties, Xian had been the chosen city of Qin Shihuangdi, the first emperor of a unified China, and for two hundred years was the seat of the brilliant Han dynasty. In these two centuries the people were welded by common laws and language, under a central power whose paternalistic tyrants lie under grassy mounds north of the Wei river.

Then in, AD 618, Xian became capital of the incomparable Tang. For years it must have been the greatest city in the world. Its ramparts ran for a circumference of twenty-two miles, and protected a population of two million. The present walled city occupies a mere seventh of it. It became a cosmopolis of world trade and culture, while around it the empire spread from Korea to Samarkand.

Yet so sudden was the city's decline, and so vulnerable its wooden temples and palaces, that little remains except a pair of pagodas rising huge and stranded in the suburbs. Only in the provincial museum, which houses a library of 2,300 titanic stone tablets dating back two thousand years, does it become possible to imagine the early capital – to envisage the men who filled the agate wine-cups now illumined under glass, the women fumigating their silks with little silver censers, the craftsmen who fashioned those minute gold dragons – two inches long and precise in every scale – which prance across the velvet showcases.

To this Tang capital, already old in refinement, Arabs and Persians arrived by the Silk Route or the southern ports. They came as merchants and mercenary soldiers, and the houses of their Muslim descendants, who call themselves Hui, still cluster in whitewashed lanes. Yet the people looked identical to Han Chinese, and when I ventured into the chief mosque I was surrounded by pagodas, dragon-screens and tilted eaves. Only when I looked closer did I notice that on some memorials Chinese characters gave way to the dotted swing of Arabic, and the prayer-hall enclosed no plump idol but an empty space, inviting a god only in the mind.

Outside, a few caretakers were sweeping leaves along the garden pathways. The chanting of the Koran sounded from a closed room. In one arcade an old man, the skin peeled white about his eyes, was singing in a high, weak voice, while a quorum of ancients seated round him quavered applause. Amongst them the imam of the mosque – a dark, lordly figure – exuded urbane authority. I sidled into talk with him. I was intrigued, I said, by the provenance of his people.

'We arrived in Xian as simple traders', he said, 'and nobody has any record of his ancestry except in his head. Our people came along the Silk Road during the Tang years.' His fingers made a little galloping motion in the air. 'But we stopped speaking Arabic long ago. Even I can only read the classical language of the Koran.'

'But you've been to Mecca?'

'I made the pilgrimage in 1956.'

He was dressed portentously in white cap and blue-grey robes. I played with the idea of his Arab-Persian descent for a while, studying his hirsute chin and tufted eyebrows. But nothing in his face – nor in that of anyone else – betrayed a trace of western Asia. 'You all look Chinese,' I said.

'Yes,' he answered bluntly. 'I can't tell any difference myself, not in any of us – and there are fifty thousand Hui in this city. But I suppose if we hadn't intermarried we would have died out. Still, it's a mystery.'

'In the Cultural Revolution. . . .'

'Oh that.' He smoothed his hands resolutely over his robes. 'The

Red Guards arrived planning to smash up the mosque, but I sat them down and talked to them. I told them this was a historical place of great importance. Then . . .' – even now he looked surprised by the outcome – 'then they just left. They simply went away.' A flicker of his fingers dispelled them. 'The mosque was closed down, of course, and we went into the fields. . . . But nobody touched it.'

A lesser man would have called it a miracle.

*   *   *

Mouli came from a desert town on the borders of Inner Mongolia, to which he was doggedly attached. Alone in his school, he had passed exams into the language college at Xian, and there – a year ago, on a fleeting first visit to China – I had found myself standing beside him in the scrap-iron market by the eastern gate, watching a street opera. Beneath a cloth backdrop hoisted on bamboo poles, I remember, a three-piece orchestra was sending up a shriek of viols and cymbals, while two singers in creased gowns and glass earrings trilled and simpered and trailed their mud-spattered hems across the beaten earth. Amongst the two hundred watching faces, Mouli's was arresting for its look of brooding irony. 'Hideous,' he kept murmuring. 'Frightful.'

Bit by bit the opera lost our attention, and Mouli, speaking in the privacy of English, dropped stray remarks into its pauses. It emerged that he was homesick. Almost all his friends were in the north, he said, in that desert town of 200,000 – a pin-prick on the map of Shaanxi. 'When I'm homesick I declaim poetry. It's a kind of release, like singing. But I have such a terrible voice I don't even sing to myself.' He grimaced at the improvised stage. Even in the street-lamp's flattery, the made-up faces looked besmirched. 'Poetry is best.'

'You write it?'

'I try. But it's like opening your mouth and no sound coming out. In China we say "anger and sorrow make the poet". Perhaps I haven't enough of either.'

But this was not the impression he gave. Moustached and unshaven, dressed with no thought of show, he looked older than his thirty-two years. His laconic bursts of speech expressed strong, controlled feelings. Behind their glasses his eyes appeared sceptical-melancholy, but a thick smear of eyebrows and a sensuous mouth contradicted them.

'You must be quite a hero back at home.'

'In a way.' He looked distantly pleased. 'My old classmates are factory workers and farmers, so they admire my job as a teacher. But I don't think they envy me. You see, I'm still single at thirty-two. They don't believe a man's happy like that. And my mother weeps when I go back. I'm her favourite son, and she always hopes I'll bring back a wife.'

'Will you?'

'I don't know. Not as I feel now. . . .'

Occasionally, rarely, I sensed a time when someone would talk more intimately with a foreigner than with one of his own. It would be like confiding in a star or a tree. We had reached this point now, and drifted out of the crowd and down the street. I probed him gently.

'The trouble started in the Cultural Revolution,' he said. 'It was while I was still in secondary school – I suppose I was only sixteen – and this girl was exiled from Beijing with her parents.' His face had set stubbornly. 'They were big people – he an important bureaucrat and she a doctor. The girl was only thirteen then – frail-looking and very pretty. But little by little we fell in love.'

He turned into a restaurant, where we bought some food-tickets for dried meat and scallion. The meat came in cold, compressed rectangles, like playing-cards. We found a table littered with chicken-bones, which Mouli swept off with his sleeve. Two beggars watched us from the wall.

He became engrossed in remembering. 'This girl was intelligent but very delicate. The damp affected her, and she had a weak heart. In those days we thought the Cultural Revolution would never end, and my relatives told me I was mad to want to marry her, that she'd be no good in the home or in the fields, she was so frail. But I was very stubborn.

'After two years I left school and had to work in a production brigade constructing houses. I can still drive a three-horse cart and could build you a traditional house with my own hands. My home town was so remote that its schools never really closed. So sometimes I would go back, and I watched this girl growing up.'

He spoke wryly, but from time to time his thick glasses and thick brows and hair coalesced in melancholy. Then he looked bearish, wounded. 'After that I struggled into language college. At first our time was wasted in military training and digging an anti-nuclear air-raid shelter. It was the last year of the Cultural Revolution. We had to go in for criticism campaigns too – first against Zhou Enlai, who was already

[267]

dying in hospital, then against others. By the end of the year I didn't know what to think of anybody, or who was meant to be what. I was totally confused. I was still struggling with my work, and couldn't marry, although I felt so much in love.' His food was untouched in front of him. Suddenly he wanted a confidence in return, some token that I did not think him a fool. 'Have you ever felt that? I mean . . . loving a girl you couldn't marry?'

'Yes.' My laughter was like Chinese laughter at tension or sorrow. It reassured him.

He spat scallion on to the floor. 'The girl's parents liked me until they realised what we felt. Then they turned against me. By that time they knew they'd be going back to Beijing. If we'd married, their daughter would have been stuck in Xian or in my home town, which seemed like villages to them. She was their only child. . . .'

One of the beggars, a little mad, came dancing forward on the balls of his feet, cupping his hands in front of him. He hovered at the shoulder of anybody eating, and was requited with leftover morsels or violent shoves. I was relieved when he carried off my deck of compressed cards.

'That was a wretched year for us,' Mouli said. 'At first she resisted her parents, but if old people can't get their way by coercion, they grow pathetic and weep. That's what her mother did. Her mother had always tended her during her illnesses so the girl felt a great duty towards her, and some love. In the end she did as her parents pleaded, and they went back to Beijing.' He said 'Beijing' as if it were a planet. He had never been there. 'So it was her family, not mine, which parted us in the end.'

The beggar was teetering at his shoulder now, but Mouli did not see. He said: 'In a way it was all a matter of class. . . .'

'You mean you were peasant class?'

'Yes.' He laughed, a little bitterly. 'Although they call them "farmers" now.' Then, as if to divest himself of this label, he said: 'Early this year I passed my exams – and became a qualified lecturer.'

'Does she know?'

'I don't write to her. But she has friends who understand about us. They must have told her.' His smile contained pride, and a hint of revenge. 'She's living in Tangshan now, posted to a middle-school.'

It was ironic. While she was working as a low-grade teacher in earthquake-stricken Tangshan, he had risen to a lectureship in the booming capital of Shaanxi; and they had lost touch. It was over. They were chance casualties from the disruption of those disastrous years – a hard-willed ex-peasant and a lonely schoolmistress, who were contained in no statistics.

Mouli laughed harshly, suddenly – laughter at the irony of things, at the self seen as a speck in a giant and rather ludicrous picture. 'Many girls want to marry me now, of course. I've got a position. And twice I've thought: Yes, I think I could marry that one. But then I've drawn back. I don't want to marry. I won't.'

I doubted him. I had never met a Chinese who was voluntarily single. 'Your family will hate it.'

'My father died when I was ten, so I'm used to being independent. And what about you? You must tell me when you get engaged and I'll send you an embroidered quilt – two of them. For weddings we always send two!'

But it was he who wrote first. Six months later, in England, I received a letter saying that he had decided to marry a twenty-six-year-old nurse.

'I remember a classic Chinese poem,' he wrote, 'which can probably explain why I am going to get married. Its general meaning is: "There are hundreds of royal palaces there,/ but most of them are locked or curtained./ It is nearly mid-summer,/ and where should we build our nest?/ Under the thatched eaves, among the smoke,/ the swallows are twittering in pairs." Recently, I often dreamed of my first girlfriend. I feel guilty when I see my fiancée, but I cannot help it.'

All this had been a year ago, and now, when I entered the language institute and located the grim blocks of teachers' dormitories, I did not know what I might find. The corridors were cluttered with bicycles and vegetables; the married staff lived in cramped rooms, one to each couple. I knocked diffidently on Mouli's door. On the far side somebody whispered, then it opened on a face unchanged from the one I remembered. Mouli and Runliang had brightened the narrow space with bookshelves; the symbol for 'double happiness' hung over the double bed. I was surprised, for some reason, to find her handsome. Her hair was parted in the middle, scattering old-fashioned curls around a vivid, high-coloured face.

But she had drowned herself in Mouli. It was impossible to disinter her personality from her love. She had become a soft-voiced slave who smiled at him for approval, pathetically, all the time, until her tall peasant body and glowing colour seemed expended in nothing but mute appeal.

And the appeal went unanswered. Each afternoon, during the next three days, we roamed about Xian together. Once we visited Runliang's parents, once a restaurant, and once they accompanied me to buy protection against the sharpening cold – a quilted overcoat in puritan grey-blue.

'But you can't buy one of *those*.' Runliang was momentarily another person, herself, disgusted. 'They're out of fashion. Those colours are from the Cultural Revolution time. Nobody wears *those* any more.' She herself was dressed in pastel blue with dainty white gloves. She wanted me to buy a jacket lined with fox fur. She was vicariously shopping.

But when we walked along the streets, Mouli would often march in front of her, although he would never have ignored male friends. Then she would slip her arm through his a little desperately; and on the buses, when he turned away from her, the white-gloved hands circled him lightly from behind or held the folds of his overcoat, as if for support, while her cheeks brushed his broad peasant back, he unknowing.

Only when I was alone with him for an hour did I realise how her presence constrained him. I had scarcely seen him smile. But now the dogged endurance which seemed natural to him found its voice. 'I can't feel anything. My friends say I treat her like a servant.'

I said wanly: 'She loves you. The way she looks at you. . . .'

'That's the trouble. That's why we're married. It's she who's in love, she who wanted it.'

'But you made the decision.'

He took off his glasses, as if he didn't want to see. 'Last Friday we had a row. Our first row. I told her that if she talked that way she could go home to her parents.' He added coldly: 'She just wept.'

'She's very warm,' I said, 'she's good-looking.'

He threw back his shoulders and splayed his hands down his chest. 'She's very robust.'

He was dreaming, I knew, of the other, fragile one, back in Tangshan.

The next moment he said: 'I don't talk to any of my friends about this. It's impossible. But I can't get the other girl out of my mind. I keep comparing them.'

'The other one's only better because you're dreaming her,' I said, not knowing. My voice sounded hectoring.

He seemed not to hear. 'She's given up writing to her friends. I'm not even sure where she is now.' He stared down at his hands. 'She's gone.'

He and Runliang had been married less than four months, but while we were together he almost ignored her, so that I became embarrassed and wretched to be with them, and planned to get away. As for Runliang, her expression went dead whenever she was not looking at him, and when she did, she saw only his indifference.

*　　　*　　　*

The burial mound of the first emperor, Qin Shihuangdi, lies twenty-five miles east of Xian.

He was a tyrant of near-mythic stature. By alternative decisiveness and treachery, he led his state of Qin – a rural Sparta on the periphery of civilised China – to devour all the other kingdoms in the fragmented land, and by 221 BC he ruled an empire spreadeagled from the Gobi to the Gulf of Tonkin. He broke down its maze of separating walls and castles, its diversities of script and law and coinage, and knit it into a cultural unity which has never been broken since. His roads and canals cut across the earth at the hands of conscript legions. In the north, stitching together the scattered ramparts of his predecessors, he created the Great Wall against the Huns, building with the forced labour of a million convicts and peasants, most of whom died of exposure and exhaustion.

So the old mosaic of feudal princedoms was transformed into a centralised bureaucracy, administered in districts by civil and military governors. Its presiding philosophy turned from Confucian benevolence to the Machiavellian doctrine of Legalism. It imposed social conformity through harsh laws and a code by which men became answerable for one another's behaviour, watching and informing on one another. So Qin Shiguangdi moulded the country named after him – China – and although his Dynasty of Ten Thousand Years lasted barely fourteen, the country's Confucian paternalism has been steeled by Legalist severity ever since.

But he declined into near-madness. His despisal of tradition turned into a wholesome obliteration of the past, an assault on any voice or memory other than his own. He ordered most of the books in his empire burnt – all philosophy, poetry and history except the annals of his own house. Scholars were conscripted or buried alive. Everything was sacrificed to unity of vision, his vision, so that in a later century Mao Zedong invoked him as a worthy model.

By the time of his death Qin Shihuangdi had become a haunted idolater, searching in vain for the elixir of life. For seventy miles around his capital 270 different palaces had been decorated in the native styles of the regions he had conquered, and furnished with their food and concubines. Now these palaces were linked by covered passageways down which the ageing emperor, terrified of assassination, moved neurotically, continually, never sleeping in the same bed twice.

Yet he died a thousand miles from his capital, after a fruitless voyage searching for the isle of Elysium. For weeks his councillors concealed his death, and issued orders and execution-warrants in his name, while he was carried back to Xian from the coast. Eventually the corpse became so putrid that a wagon of rotting fish was summoned to accompany the closed litter to hide its stench.

He was buried under an enormous tumulus in a mausoleum prepared over thirty-six years of his reign. For two millennia the grass and trees grew over it. Then in 1974 a unit of peasants, sinking a well nearby, broke into a vault where life-size terracotta warriors stood mysteriously to arms. Soon afterwards archaeologists, with increasing astonishment, uncovered a buried army of an estimated six thousand men – archers, infantry, charioteers – mustered to guard the emperor through eternity.

A coach-park signals the spot now. A village of snack-stalls and souvenir kiosks has sprung up, and tourists are photographed astride terracotta horses. The excavations – still scarcely begun – have been covered by a hangar whose glass roof lets in sallow light. Visitors circle the site along gangways at ground level, and look into a pit where the army assembles in column, divided by walls, over a grey-tiled earth.

It is eerily moving. The soldiers mass in files four abreast – more than six hundred men. They seem to march through the earth as if it were their habitat. Their spear-hafts and lacquered bows have disintegrated or been pilfered, leaving their fists to circle nothing.

Separately, no figure is extraordinary. But the individuation of each warrior imparts an unearthly, living quality to the whole. The army has not been portrayed as the brutal machine which a ruler might covet, but rather as it was – a variegated, unsure flood of men, who wait here in independent grimness and fear. Most are thin-chested, their hands small, almost delicate. Their stomachs sag a little over their belts, but the bodies within the armoured shells, one feels, may be malnourished.

Every facial expression is different. There are iron-featured veterans and thin-faced recruits, officer material and cannon-fodder. Beards mark their cheeks and chins like incipient tusks. Moustaches drip and twirl.

Even the armour is diverse. Battalions of archers and crossbowmen in short tunics are backed by phalanxes of heavy infantry whose multi-leaved jerkins descend to the pelvis and drip over their shoulders. In front of wooden chariots which have long ago crumbled, the horse-teams prick their ears. Each stallion is separately modelled, its tail twisted in a bun like the soldiers' hair, while behind them the charioteers' arms rise to the strain of vanished harness, and their fingers twitch on the reins.

Yet these hundreds are only a fraction of the mass. Behind them the torsos of over five thousand more men-at-arms tilt and wade through the coagulated earth, limbs and heads cast up at random, awaiting restoration. Two other chambers have been discovered in trial digs – one containing heavily armoured charioteers and mounted archers; the other a command post. In the brief time before its burial, this stupendous retinue, once sombrely painted in red and green – black armour and pink flesh – must have seemed more permanent than any human multitude. Yet four years later rebel troops robbed the mausoleum, and brought the roofs of the funerary chambers crashing in with fire.

As for the burial-mound itself, it lies unexcavated, and its state is unknown. Contemporary accounts recorded that seven hundred thousand convicts worked to raise the tumulus over a mausoleum planned as a vast and intricate map of the Qin empire. Its plains and mountains were sculpted in copper and precious stones, and scattered with minutely copied cities. Amongst them the rivers wound in channels twelve feet deep, filled with quicksilver and set in motion by machinery so that they flowed into a quicksilver sea. Overhead a copper dome glimmered with a night sky set in pearls. Lamps of seal-fat were placed here to shine for ever, and at the centre, like a spoilt child buried with a monstrous toy, the cadaver of the emperor sailed the rivers in a boat-shaped coffin.

On the sepulchre's completion all his concubines were entombed with him, and the burial-chamber workers were suffocated in the passageways by the descent of stone gates. To deter robbers, concealed crossbows were primed to fire automatically at any intruder; knives sprang from walls, and hidden machines racked the vaults with a chilling thunder. Even now, nobody is sure if the tomb has been violated, and Chinese archaeologists, infinitely patient, give no date when they may enter.

*　　　*　　　*

'What do you want to go to *that* town for?' asked the receptionist. Her face filled with condescension. 'You won't have trouble getting a hotel room *there*, anyway. It's just an old Communist place. I suppose you've been to Shaoshan too?'

'Yes,' I said sheepishly.

She burst into laughter. 'You think you'll see Mao Zedong or something? Nobody goes to those sites any more. You're a better Communist than I am!'

I was setting out for Yenan, in the harsh Shaanxi hills where the Red Army had ended its Long March. Late in 1934 it had slipped out of Nationalist encirclement near the borders of Fujian on the East China Sea, and all the next year the column of soldiers and dependants, critically outnumbered, had fought and feinted its way six thousand miles northwards. Of the ninety thousand who set out, only eight thousand arrived. The rest died in battle, deserted or perished of hunger and cold. But the war-tempered remnant regrouped in Yenan, and until 1947 this was Mao's headquarters against Nationalists and Japanese. After his victory it became, of course, a holy place.

'Don't blame me for it,' the girl said. 'I warned you.'

At dawn my bus from Xian set out to cover the three hundred intervening miles by nightfall. We climbed into hills as porous as old plaster, wrinkled with wadis and blackened by winter scrub. I could have thrust my bare arm into them, I felt, and pulled out their rock. But they were formed only of powder – the aeolian sand of the Gobi – and I was too cold to lift a finger. My breath froze on the window's glass. I squatted in my outsize overcoat like a drab chrysalis. As we ascended, the villages turned to mud. Their terraces were yellow dust. Great ravines appeared, where stifled streams crept, and lorries had dropped off the road five hundred feet.

I wondered about the peasants' lives in this wilderness. Beside me sat an ex-commune official, chain-smoking. In his home village, he said, the people farmed maize and vegetables, but they were too far from the cities. 'The farmers living near towns are doing well – they sell their stuff on the free markets. Vegetables fetch a good price now, and the middlemen make real money – fellows with the use of a truck or two. But remote villages are much the same as they always were, I can tell you.'

'But better since the 1960s?'

'Yes.' He lit one cigarette from another, closing his eyes. He had a sombre, intelligent face. 'But that was a terrible time. In those days we were all ordered to "Learn from Dazhai" – a village which was reclaiming land. In our region that was hopeless. We didn't need more land, we needed water. But instead we all had to learn from Dazhai.' He laughed cynically. We were moving through a land turned grey, as if by pollution. The maize in its fields stood stripped and dead. 'In those years the winters were unspeakable. My uncle's family owned one quilt among seven people. When his son fell ill, they went to the vet, then to the local witch, but they couldn't afford the fee of either. The witch asked ten cents. . . .'

'There's a witch in your village?'

'There are witches everywhere.' His eyes screwed into knowing dots. 'They can't be traced because the local officials won't give them away. Our witch was recently consulted by a family which had fallen sick. She told them to dig in their courtyard, and what do you think?' – he turned a suddenly incredulous face to mine. 'They dug up a corpse!'

Our bus twisted through ever more mangy hills – a carcass-land where white goats trickled. It was too cold to sleep. By early afternoon we were pushing across a plateau severed by canyons. I was reminded that nine-tenths of China was uncultivable – grasslands, desert, mountain. In the past thirty years alone the population had doubled while one-tenth of the farmland had succumbed to urban spread or erosion. In this landscape the statistics became real and cruel. They haunted the thinly watered valleys and invaded the troglodyte villages. The government birth-control plans fell into fierce perspective. By the year 2000 it was anticipated that a hundred million peasants would be unemployed, with tens of million urban youth. The one-child stipulation for the cities had been relaxed to a two-child rule for the farmers, but in both cases extra births were punished by a withdrawal of privileges and eventually by fines. The alternative, perhaps, was starvation.

I glanced at my neighbour. He appeared to be asleep, but a cigarette was smoking happily at his lips. I said: 'Do you have children?'

The shrewd eyes opened. 'Four.'

'So many?'

'It's not many. Four is necessary. Nowadays every household has a piece of land, and we all need help. My elder children take care of pigs and sheep – and of the younger children.'

'What about school?'

'They do that too. But some people say what's the point? Educated people can't make more money. Not now.' He sounded morose. 'It's wrong to limit babies. I've heard about these one-child families in the towns, and the children are growing up to be little emperors. Spoilt. And what do you do if you only have a girl? Confucius said your first duty was to give your parents heirs – to carry on the name. It's terrible to have no son. People die out that way.'

He invoked Confucius as naturally as he might once have parroted a Party directive (but confused him with Mencius). I said: 'So what happens to the girl babies?'

But I knew, of course, what sometimes happened. The custom of killing them is inveterate. In the last century missionaries often came upon baby girls, sometimes still alive, pitched over town ramparts to the rubbish and pariah dogs below.

The man said: 'Occasionally girl babies are abandoned on the town streets, and people adopt them. There's no penalty attached to adopting. But out here everyone wants sons. Girls can't do the same heavy work.' He gestured at the mutilated terraces beyond the window. 'So sometimes, secretly, the girl babies are drowned. . . .'

Towards evening we were lumbering across tablelands faulted over their whole length by a labyrinth of gulleys – an ideal guerrilla stronghold. Their cliffs dangled icicles, and the streams were edged with floes. As we drove into Yenan, I saw that the receptionist had been right. The town looked exhausted. It was strung in dust along a factory-crowded valley, many of its houses scooped out of cliffs. As I alighted, a loudspeaker brayed out an appeal for local criminals to surrender to the Bureau of Public Security, then added an announcement of public executions.

In my morgue-like hotel – the only one to accept me – time had stood still for fifteen years. Across its dining-hall some hundred workers in caps and blue suits turned as one man to stare at me. On the way out their files of dangling cigarettes and crumpled trousers faltered before my table. Two men drew up chairs to watch me eating. One touched my cheeks with his fingertips, as if testing what I was made of.

I resigned myself to a desolate two days. The buildings, the valley, the people, all seemed dimmed by a film of dust. I felt its gauze settling over my eyes, my brain. For hours I tramped about the cave-dwellings from which the Red leaders had conducted eleven years of war. The cold, dry air did nothing to desanctify them. They opened on empty courts in Spartan plainness. The streams beneath them had hardened white. Behind latticed wood façades, whose windows were paned only by ricepaper, the rooms burrowed into the cliffs with scanty furniture on brick floors. Crank-handled telephones stood on the desks. Air-raid shelters disappeared into the loess.

Here Zhou Enlai had worked, said the caretakers; over there Zhu De had darned his socks on a spinning-wheel. At this desk Mao Zedong wrote his essays. Beyond were Liu Shaoqi's quarters, which had ceased to exist after his denunciation – but were now open again.

Journalists who reached this hideout during those years left disparate portraits of Mao. They reported him benign, sophisticated, coarse, sinister, unreadable. Some described him as a slovenly peasant who picked lice from his body and whose tobacco-blackened mouth poured out foul language. Others were unnerved by a long-haired aesthete with high-pitched voice and girlish hands. But his energies exhausted everybody. When not working, he read voraciously, talked or played poker through the night. He owned almost nothing, and dressed in the grey fatigues of a private soldier. He seems to have been subtly isolated – even from those closest to him – by a self-perceived destiny.

Over the Yenan years it was the Communists, not the Guomindang, who harried the Japanese most effectively. Men flocked to them. The intensive indoctrination of their soldiers resembled a religious conversion, and they earned the trust of the peasants among whom they operated. By 1945 they had seeped behind Japanese lines over much of north China, and could field almost a million troops.

But I wandered these shrines almost alone. They were stiffening into history. Some of their rooms were now stacked with caretakers' bric-à-brac: ropes, bedding, old wood. From the wartime photographs on their walls, the celebrated faces – Mao, Zhou, Liu – gazed out still boyish and firm, untroubled by the complexities of peace.

'I remember during the 1960s when hordes of foreigners came, and literally millions of Chinese every year.' The caretaker was openly nostalgic. 'That guesthouse where you're staying was given over to Africans, thousands of them, while Chinese tourists slept in inns all over town, or just dossed down on empty factory floors. Mao was a god then.'

'What do people here feel now?'

'Sad.'

I signed his visitor's book. It showed four Chinese tourists that day. In the Party assembly-hall I found not a soul. Built like a church, it was hung with hammer-and-sickle banners and mildewed portraits of Stalin and Marx. My steps echoed down its aisle. Above the dais medallions of Mao and Zhu De were circled in painted sheaves of Soviet corn. It was rife with certainties now gone.

A small girl had slipped in after me and was running her finger along the visitor's book, trying to decipher what I had written.

'English,' I said.

Her chapped face grinned. She announced with dogmatic pomp: 'My teacher says the times are different all round the world, but that English time is right and Russian time is wrong.' She puffed out her chest. 'I'm pleased. I've seen England on television, and it looks OK.'

'Just OK? Not at all strange?'

She tugged on her pony-tails. 'There was one odd thing. There was this woman who had beautiful earrings. I wanted them. . . .' Her thoughts trailed away. She shuffled her feet under a cracked portrait of Lenin. 'We can't buy earrings like that. But the strange thing was this beautiful woman *smoked*.'

I realised that the smoke fogging every Chinese bus and railway carriage rose exclusively from men. The only women smokers I had seen were the very old, and the few peasants who shared their husbands' pipes. As we walked back into the daylight, I tried to explain the Western custom to the girl – that there was no stigma attached to smoking, that women in the West behaved much as men did, that . . . I floundered into a welter of lying simplicities.

The girl watched me in silence, her eyes overarched already by the feathery brows which are so striking in Chinese women. After a while, perhaps feeling sorry for me, she plucked a sprig from the fragrant pine behind her, and said formally: 'I want to give you this. If you press it in a book – have you got a book? – it won't die.' She pulled another sprig off. 'And this is for your wife. Tell her it's from me.'

That evening a biting wind arose, strewing the darkness with refuse, and swung the hotel windows back and forth to sounds of smashing glass. I sat sleepily in a furnace of central heating, plotting my route north-west to the high grasslands of Qinghai and the fringe of the Gobi. It would be a race against the cold, I thought, the cold which shrivels travel into endurance and empties the landscape.

Someone knocked on my door, and an elderly, unshaven face peered in. 'I am very sorry. . . .' The voice was querulous, musical; it spoke in English. 'I am disturbing you, I think ? . . . my name is Lu . . . I have language problem.'

Somehow he had heard that there was an Englishman in the town, and had bluffed his way past the hotel doorman. He was a post office clerk, he said, and had been charged with translating into English a list of regulations. 'Could you check, sir, if they have accuracy or not?' Furtively, as if it were gelignite, he drew from his overcoat an envelope containing twenty close-written pages, and insinuated them on to my lap.

I started to read: 'If to bear on the under matter small packets it will be written oblique cross symbol which is the elected item by sender, on the back of the despatch note about the handle idea of all items for undeliverable, and added one red transvers line under the words of the line. To Hongkong it will be stuck the label handle ideas for undeliverable and written oblique cross symbol inner square frame. Identical sender will send identical weight to identical receiver for many parcel (except the value of parcel). It will be stuck on the front of parcel for up couplet and stuck on the despatch note for down couplet. Don't allow with red colour to write. . . .'

Lu's eyes pleaded with me. I stared back at him, shell-shocked. The storm groaned outside. Two hours later I was still toiling through corrections to page eleven, guided by his explanations and by stray phrases which floated intact on the quagmire's surface. Gradually I became initiate in the technicalities of the Chinese postal system, in the minutiae of the oblique cross couplet, the handle idea and the undeliverable. Even decoded, they twined themselves in mandarin knots.

How had this English evolved, I asked? Where had he learnt it?

He had studied in secondary school, he said, and now he was teaching himself. He delved into his overcoat again and pulled out two dog-eared primers. 'These books were forbidden to export. . . .' He handed them to me apprehensively as if some ghostly interdict still lay upon them. Perhaps it did.

They had been printed in 1971 and 1975, the later years of the Cultural Revolution, and were intended to prepare primary school pupils to be sent down into the countryside. While Lu pored over the up couplet, the down couplet and the three identicals, I settled at a table to study the primers. They fell open in my hand like cheap survival manuals, and their evangelism – page after suffocating page – still rang across the years. I scanned the first exercises in the 1971 book. It's sentences swam to meet me like parodies: 'Translate: *Why do you study English? We study English for the revolution. . . .* Translate: *Unite and defeat the US aggressors and all their running dogs! . . . Never forget class struggle. . . . One day a little African girl said: "Mamma, I wish to have a Chairman Mao badge." . . .* Fill in the following: *" – four people in my family. We all love Chairman Mao." . . .'

I read the Quotations of Chairman Mao, a panegyric on Yenan, and 'We Owe our Happiness to Chairman Mao'. I became mesmerised. I reached a translation exercise:

'Wang: *We cut wheat with the poor and lower-middle peasants. They gave us lessons in class struggle. We criticised Liu Shao-chi's counter-revolutionary revisionist line together.*

'Li: *The workers and the poor and lower-middle peasants are our good teachers. We must earnestly receive re-education from them.*

'Wang: *Yes, we must learn from them. I'm going to military training. Good-bye!'*

Perhaps I should have laughed. Everybody now knew how the peasants had resented the exiles thrust on them, and how the students had recoiled from peasant squalor. But laughter that evening, in the presence of those soiled books, didn't come. Yenan – and China itself – were still too darkened by those years; and that awesome philosophy, self-perpetuating in enmity, hovered too close, too unaccountable, was perhaps battering at the windows even now with the storm.

When I opened the 1975 primer, nothing had changed. Only the injunction to criticise the Liu Shaoqi line had been turned against Lin Biao (for Liu was long dead).

The man looked up and smiled at my expression, a little wanly. 'Not language,' he said. 'Just politics.'

'It's frightful, isn't it?'

'It was made for those times.'

Turning the last page, I came upon 'Questioning the POWs'. *'We are the Chinese People's Liberation Army,'* I read. *'According to our policy, we treat the POWs well. Now answer my questions: What's your name? Are you an officer? What post? Which unit (. . . company, platoon, squad) do you belong to? Who is your commander? Where is your headquarters? What's your password? What's your mission?'*

I put it down with a faint trembling. A whole generation of schoolchildren had been reared on this, I thought, and I had

[280]

eavesdropped on their past. I glanced covertly at Lu, for some reason feeling guilty, like a child who has steamed open a letter behind his parents' back. (*Now I know what they think of me.*) But Lu had been brought up in another age, in the random chaos before 1949. And he was busy worrying about the stipulations for parcel post.

I glanced back at 'Questioning the POWs' (a translation piece for ten-year-olds). At what target, I wondered, was it aimed? For what English-speaking prisoners, on which front, and at what time? Or was it written in anticipation of nothing real at all, simply an unspecified dream of power?

But the crumpled book – its pages yellowing now – gave no answer.

12. To the Last Gate Under Heaven

WEST FROM XIAN my train penetrated deeper and deeper into the loess country, squirming through an eroded wilderness of scrub and powder. At first the skyline was crossed by telegraph poles, and the smokestacks of half-industrialised towns poked from the valleys. But hour after hour the land seemed to age around us. It softened to the texture of sawdust. The hills fell in pale terraces, like discoloured wedding-cakes. Their earth was carved dust. Through it the millennia-long chafing of rivulets had sunk chasms of disproportionate majesty, sweeping out valleys whose tiers converged in ashen cascades. Everything in sight was smooth, absorbent, dead. Whole villages had been cut into the cliffs, suspending their inhabitants above the fields.

Even in winter this region is tormented by dust storms, whose grains are so small that they can be rubbed like ointment into the skin. As we went north through Gansu province, the dust came seeping through the train's closed windows. It settled on the peasants round me, faded our coats into camouflage, greyed our hair. But outside, the country was quiet as death. The temperature had dropped permanently below freezing. Around walled farmhouses the only movement was the havering of smoke-columns in the air. Frost stifled the fields, and in the canyons the streams had stilled to trickles of ice. The earth was in suspension. Soon mountains lifted from the horizon in huge shadows.

I sat wedged among a family of farmers. We were padded stiff as astronauts. An aisle of trampled pears bisected the carriage, mixed with a grey paste of spittle and cigarette-ash which an attendant with a mop redistributed every two hours.

By nightfall there was no room to stir. People not crammed into the seats lay interlocked in a jigsaw of bodies – old men, women, children – sprawled in the grime of phlegm and discarded food across the corridors, underneath the benches, in the lavatories, kneeling with their foreheads resting on any square inch of seat. Their forearms were thrown up to cover their eyes against the light. In its neon glow this stupefied cargo might have belonged to a cattle-truck bound for Siberia in the 1930s and 40s (or for Qinghai province any time).

I slept bolt upright, cocooned in my *démodé* overcoat, squashed between farmers. During the night the head of the woman beside me slid on to my shoulder, then gradually, with each jolt and swing of the carriage, eased across my chest in a tangle of cropped hair and slumped into my lap. Forestalling her shame, I tilted her gingerly erect again, then shored her up, still asleep, between the arms of her snoring husband.

At some time in the night we pierced the mountains by a mile-long tunnel whose excavation in the early 1950s had left hundreds of labourers dead. I could not sleep. Ahead of us this bitter region of Gansu – a province as large as Texas – made a jagged crescent to Mongolia, while somewhere in the darkness to my left stretched the last, mammoth provinces of the north-west – the Qinghai plateaux and the planetary sands of Xinjiang.

When we reached Lanzhou, the provincial capital, I found an industrial limbo of two million inhabitants. It is the most polluted city in China. The Communists inherited it as a caravan town where the trade routes of western Asia converged on those from inner China and Tibet, and they transformed it by a giant infusion of Soviet-made oil refineries, chemical, machine and textile factories, manned by workers sent from all over the too-populous east. Now the city gave a manufacturing heart to the province. Heaped between its mine-scarred mountains, it was blurred in smoke and dust from end to end. Sometimes its avenues vanished wholesale into the air's opacity; at others, they splintered through downtown alleys, squeaky with trams; and further out, the Yellow River, still young before its long detour north and east, grumbled muddily behind the city's back under an assortment of bridges.

I walked here in unaccountable exhilaration. According to local dictum, the temperature is so erratic that the inhabitants wear furs in the morning and silks in the afternoon. But I didn't see any of either. Instead, the noon sun shed a brief mildness. On the far riverbank some jaded temples and a pagoda stood, and a mosque – the first to look the part – pushed a dome and four hesitant minarets into the smog.

Islam has a grim past here. The Hui peasants rebelled against the Chinese in 1862, and the western provinces were racked by a decade of war. They rose again in 1894, and were not suppressed before quarter of a million people lay dead. I found Hui still living in the old sector of

Lanzhou: about fifty thousand. Their faces looked as Chinese as those in Xian, but they wore embroidered Turkic caps tipped at un-Islamic angles, and their wives went in diaphanous black wimples, as if some slovenly order of nuns had taken to the streets.

The wind, by evening, seemed to be blowing a flurry of razor blades. My zest disappeared. The passers-by suddenly looked anxious, brutalised. I noticed the victims of industrial accidents and burns. I hunted for shelter. Even in this cold a night-soil collector was pushing his leaky cart among the alleys. He advanced it on thin rubber wheels like an old-fashioned pram, stopping outside each courtyard to hoist his buckets in a cloud of stench. 'Do well in sanitation. Build up Socialist Civilisation', ordered a sign in the road beyond, and nearby a hoarding read: 'Cherish Youth and Make Good Use of Your Time'.

I was savouring the innocence of these, when the elderly man huddled beside me suddenly said: 'My father was a graduate of Cambridge University.'

'*What?*'

'My father . . .'

He spoke incongruously in Mandarin. Between his frayed cap and upturned collar I saw a faltering smile and a pair of sensitive, wide-set eyes. Even in its bulky overcoat his body looked fragile, and his face was pared and delicate – the kind of face that got kicked in during the Cultural Revolution.

'. . . my father graduated in geography.'

I asked in astonishment: 'And what do you do?'

'I?' He considered this pronoun apologetically. 'I'm a building labourer.'

His hands, I now saw, emerged rugged from the overcoat sleeves, their skin callused, their nails broken.

'I build walls. I'm a bricklayer. I've done that for more than thirty years.' He seemed to flinch. 'It's cold here.'

We marched towards his home. In the *hutong* entrance we passed the head of his street-committee – a big, genial man who clasped his shoulder. 'What's up, Old Wang?'

'I've asked this foreign guest to my home.'

The committee man shook my hand. 'You'll be all right with Old Wang,' he said.

We entered a courtyard where tiles were sliding from the cottage roofs like rotten skin. I said: 'Do you have to get permission to ask me in?'

But Old Wang didn't know. 'I've never asked a foreigner in before.'

The tiny yard was occupied by sodden baskets, two bicycles and the communal water-tap. Thirty years before, he had come from Beijing with his wife and baby, and bought the cottage for a pittance. Now the whole alley was choked with his descendants, with sons who worked in the salt industry, in electrics factories and printing works, while Old Wang had retired to two back rooms with his youngest daughter and a grandson.

The rooms were almost naked. A single light bulb hung in the doorway between them. An umbrella and a pair of scissors dangled from a nail. In one room stood two iron beds and a chest-of-drawers. In the other were some chairs and a rusty stove heaped with detachable pipes for a vent in the ceiling. The stove was fed by briquettes which burnt toxically for hours. But it had gone out. Wang was wheezing lightly, breathlessly. 'I have to attach these pipes to the ceiling or I get a headache.' Either the noxious fumes, or the pollution outside, had spattered his lungs with bronchitis. 'But this is a good area,' he said. 'We're peaceful. A lot of districts get thieves.'

He had arrived in 1950, when jobs were scarce in Beijing. 'I wish I could have followed my father. It would have pleased him. But I . . . hadn't the ability.' His eyes winced and glowed all the time he spoke. 'My father worked as a professor in Changchun in Manchuria, and died there more than thirty years ago. We used to write to one another, but I wasn't with him when he died.' His lungs whined with every breath. 'I came too late. After he'd gone I found this gown and strange hat – what do you call that?' – his hands described a mortar-board – 'and there was a photograph of him graduating with two fellow-students on either side. But I didn't keep them. I was young then. I didn't know what they were.'

His grandson had just returned from school, and crouched beside us, shining-faced. Wang beamed at him. 'That is my role now – looking after him,' he said. 'I sleep here now.' He pointed to the single bed. 'My wife died three months ago.'

That explained the play of hurt over his face, I thought, and perhaps the loneliness which had asked a stranger in. The woman's photograph was on the chest-of-drawers. In front of it stood a home-made ancestral tablet – a sliver of inscribed black wood.

'What does it say?'

'It just gives her name, and says that this is her place.' He patted the top of the chest-of-drawers. That, for him, was where she was now. It was a shadow of the old belief that the soul divides itself between the grave and the memorial tablet. He fingered the paper scrolls scattered around her. 'We call this dead men's money. It's meant for her use after death. Tomorrow I'll burn these at her grave and set off firecrackers.' He smiled a hard, remedial smile. 'That's our custom. It announces our remembrance. . . .'

I wanted to ask him other things, but most were too painful. I said obliquely: 'Do many people believe in an afterlife?'

'Some. Perhaps not many.' He looked down. 'But I do not believe. I cannot believe.' Suddenly his face was contorted by mingled sorrow and bitterness, held in by a heart-rending laughter. 'We Chinese have a saying: "All that is born must die". But that doesn't stop this . . . this . . .' – he turned his forefinger against his body, insinuating it between his torn jacket, drilling inside – '. . . this grief.'

In the naked room, with the single bulb slung in its doorway, his imagined loneliness was unbearable. I wanted to touch him, but remained inert. He seemed beyond pity. He was stricken instead by a terrible acquiescence – not the blinding loss or hope of Christian mourning, but a recognition of the balance and proportion in things. Suddenly his people seemed immeasurably old. Perhaps this, I thought, was why they sometimes seemed able to look on death – and even inflict it – unmoved. They were not less humane than we, merely less illusioned.

But it was only a passing thought.

And I was unnerved to feel a spasm of relief, as if, after so many months, I still retained some childhood idea that the Chinese never grieved or pitied. I had imagined that these simmering questions of suffering and conscience had quietly drowned during the last weeks of my journey. But now, seeing the old man's face, I realised that this wasn't so, because by his sorrow something in me was being obscurely pacified.

'I took her to the military hospital,' he said. 'She was there twenty days. But just the same, she died.'

*   *   *

I found a bus to where the Sanmen dam delays the Yellow River in a fifty-square-mile reservoir, and boats ply to a monastery in the cliffs. It was desolately peaceful. My boat sailed over a surface ice-grey like the sky, creating only an olive-coloured ripple in its wake. The sun was a

[286]

blurred incandescence. All round us the shores showed the unnatural-ness of their artificial waterline. No jumble of rocks or paths disturbed them, no gentling, intermediate slopes. Their hills were the heads of drowned mountains. They lay weakly about us, their colours wrung out.

We turned into a creek circled by 300-foot pinnacles. Sometimes they seemed to lean on one another tiredly. They ended at a bluff where a seventy-foot Buddha, carved by Tang monks, sat in the rock. But it had been hideously restored, plastered smooth. The contours of its torso were defined only by a few folds of gown and girlish nipples. Its limbs were formal cylinders. Even the face, shaped from the living scarp, had been denatured. It wore a look of barbaric hurt, its eyes brutal slits above a nose flattened by wind.

I rummaged through scores of caves. In some the figures kept vestiges of paint. But in others Red Guards had hacked the statues from the walls, and they lay in butchered chunks, like so much old meat, their haloes sloughed in the rock behind them.

But as I floated back over the ghostly reservoir, I realised that even the Cultural Revolution had shuffled into a temporary place in my acceptance. And that evening, when a language professor in Lanzhou exorcised those years in an ebullient burst of humour, I did not inquisition him.

Old Huang was a tubby dynamo. As he sat in his bedroom-study, his shoulders and arms danced in merriment at life's bathos. Every time he rolled back laughing in his chair, his legs dangled free from the floor, and his mouth opened on a leftover pair of buck teeth, like Confucius's. Years ago, he said, he had consulted a religious oracle in Chongqing by drawing sticks. 'And do you know? – it said I'd have eight daughters! Just as if it was teasing me! But that's what I've got! And no son. Hahaha! Disaster! Now they're all married with children – thirty-one altogether – and every one in a good job. There's productivity for you!'

He dashed off a personal history riddled with disasters and resurrections. From each battering decade he had emerged laughing and irrepressible into the next. He had been educated at missionary school almost in imperial times, had studied at Nanjing under Pearl Buck's first husband, then had fled from the Japanese in the 1930s and worked in propaganda for the Guomindang. 'But the oracle said I'd have trouble in 1957 – and sure enough I was sent to prison as a Rightist and Deviationist and various other -ists. No sooner was I out than the Cultural Revolution broke, and it almost put a stop to me. I was forced to be the college dustman. For ten years! Haha! From professor to dustman!' He hooted derisively. 'But guess why they punished me? Guess what they found in my study? Just two *bibles*!' His laughter detonated again. 'But that was quite enough! So I carted dust about.'

'You're a Christian?'

'No, no! Hahaha! Me? I'm a practical man! I enjoyed the bibles for their *literature*. How can you understand English literature without knowing the Bible? So many allusions! Those Proverbs! *As a jewel of gold in a swine's snout, so is a fair woman which is without discretion.*' He clapped his knees in a futile attempt to sober himself. 'The priest at my missionary school did try to baptise me. Don't you want to enter the body of Christ, he asked? But I didn't want to, not in the least. Hahahaha! Poor man, he did look unhappy. . . . Recently I sneaked into church services in Beijing, and they're as dreadful as ever.' He rocked back in his chair again. His legs swung like a child's. 'I can still remember the names of all my teachers, but I can't recall what I did yesterday. . . . As for the students who persecuted me – I forgive them! They were just young. And I'm broadminded!' He waved his arms around the bare room, his books, his photographs of grandchildren. 'The oracle said that in my last years I'd be restored to my old glory. And here I am!'

*   *   *

The frontier of Qinghai – the cold province of labour-camps – ran less than a hundred miles to the west. I climbed on a train to its dour capital of Xining, hoping to reach the inland sea which the Mongolians call Koko Nor. In this region the old imperial control petered out among Tibetan and Mongolian herdsmen who still wander the high grass-lands. It is almost empty. Some of its eastern regions darken into mephitic swamps. In the west its saline marches brim with precious metals and oil scarcely touched.

Outside my window the loess hills were already levelling to a stonier desolation. Ice-bleared pools appeared. The rivers flowed fast and brown along the valley where we went, watering mud villages and leafless windbreaks. Higher up, I heard, snow had already fallen a metre deep.

Everything was changing. Muslim peasants, shaggy in their sheep-skins, sat in my carriage among the Han Chinese, and a few of the

Lamaist Tu people were squatting on the floor with their black-veiled women. Outside, over half the southern horizon, a line of snow-lit mountains hovered. As the sun steered westward to light them, their crests shone in glittering amputation from the earth. It was as if somebody had engraved them on glass. They were the first portent of Tibet.

Opposite me a four-year-old boy reached behind his father's back and vacantly tugged off the ribbon from the pigtail of a young woman. Innocently, he had violated her. She jumped to her feet with a scream of fury. Her hands trembled to her hair. Then she stood above the child and flailed him in staccato bursts of rage. She was ugly, malnourished. But some subtle, yet external, essence had been defiled. She kept fondling her pigtail in disbelief. She held out the ribbon beside it as if something were irreparably broken. Just as her harangue seemed over, she would start again. She went on for fifteen minutes. And all the time she burnt the child with a livid, undeflecting stare.

At first the boy's parents – they looked like Hui peasants – joined in her censure, but little by little, as she continued, they fell silent, then tried to mollify her, then mutely remonstrated. Meanwhile the boy kept his eyes fixed level with her waist. Beneath his abashment, some kernel remained unbroken, and it was perhaps this which so infuriated her. At last her anger turned on the whole family, until all the shock and ignominy of this symbolic rape exploded in racism. 'You're not Han people!' The words rang out with an age-old superiority. 'You can't be Han people! You're some other kind!'

But nobody answered her. They looked away. And soon we were debouching at Xining station under a canvas of Mao greeting China's minority races – vanquished Tibetans, despised Miao, oppressed Hui. They were smiling round him in grateful reverence. At any moment, it seemed, he would raise his hand in papal blessing as his superior wisdom and moral purity led them, all clean in their folk-dress, to the brightness of Revolution.

Xining was a medium-sized town strung along a river valley circled in smokestacks. For centuries it had been a garrison post on the brink of the nomad wilderness, and had traded in wool, deer horn and musk from Koko Nor sixty miles to the west. Even now a third of its people were Muslims. It owned a hideous Catholic church, a near-defunct Taoist monastery, and the largest mosque in the north-west. Tibetan and Mongolian herdsmen, burly in sheepskins and strapped with silver-sheathed daggers, lumbered its streets to trade. Alongside them their women marched in a soiled brilliance of skirts and sashes, the Mongolians' hair coiled in two inky cables, the Tibetans' braided down their backs in a shower of tallowed plaits.

Their spiritual lodestar was the four-hundred-year-old Kumbum monastery, banked up a valley which I reached in an hour's bus-ride. It had been built at the birthplace of Tsong-Khapa, greatest of the reformers of Lamaism, and its monks numbered over five hundred. Among its multi-coloured colonnades, lamas and pilgrims were sticking their coins on magical stones and bells, and decking the pipal trees with wool-tufts as a thanksgiving. I walked here in vague unease. Inside the shrines, the lamp-wicks glimmered on pools of coagulated yak butter. Their stench soured the darkness. I heard the moan of a ritual horn. Painted hangings rustled and dripped from the dimness and altars rose before myriad-headed Hindu godlings. There were statues carved in yak butter, Tantric saints in nests of gilded wood, figures of Dalai and Panchen Lamas from the past, and thrones for those in the present. In front of them the mahogany heads of Tibetan and Mongolian pilgrims coalesced in prayer and a glint of gold rings, their lips shifting in a mechanical *'Om mani padne hum. . . .'* I was awed and indefinably repelled. Girls whose cheeks had been wind-burnt to crimson discs were draping scarves over the thrones. Outside one temple Han sightseers were posing tastelessly for photographs in lama fancy dress. Inside, a gang of Mongolian patriarchs was scooping out yak butter from tins and dolloping it in front of idols and into lamps.

An elderly monk sat in a porch, cradling a puppy. It was the first time I had seen anyone caress an animal in months. I touched its fur.

'You like them?' He looked up with dreamy eyes. 'Do you have these where you come from?'

To Tibetans, I remembered, all creatures were incarnations. In the temple behind us, stuffed and mouldering bears, bison and monkeys leant on the verandas, their coats peeling in moth-eaten shreds. They were kept there, said the monk, because they shared divine powers. He smiled wanly into the puppy's face. I stroked it hesitantly now. In his arms it had become a mystery.

He asked: 'How much money is it to come from your country to my country?'

'You mean . . . ?'

'Tibet.'

I guessed a low figure. 'Have you been to Lhasa?'

'Yes. I got there three or five years ago . . . or ten.' He spoke softly, sleepily. The months and years drifted into incoherence for him.

'And what was it like?'

He lifted his head to the sun. 'Lhasa is beautiful. You can't imagine. . . .'

But in the nearby temples, I could imagine. The crimson and gold prayer-wheels twirled and squeaked under the pilgrims' hands, magically multiplying their devotions, and round the chief shrines the most ardent believers – many of them women – were advancing on their bellies through the dust in linked prostrations. Fifty, a hundred, two hundred times, they measured the earth with their bodies, their gold-bangled arms outstretched before them, then heaved their shoulders forward to their hands, rose again, fell forward again, on and on, braids trailing in the dirt, faces white with dust, their grimed children sauntering after them.

*   *   *

I had seen Tong several times before. His flat-set eyes and high-arched eyebrows stamped him with a look of congenital surprise. In Beijing I had shared a pool with him in the bath-house. Then I had found him trying to repair my hotel elevator. In Kunming, I noticed, he had lost two fingers in an industrial accident. And I had enjoyed his act as a subsidiary clown in the Shanghai circus. It was not that he was following me. Simply he was a type. Near Wuxi he had put on thirty years and a little weight. In Chengdu he had taken it off again. I rather liked him.

And now here he was again in Xining, emerging from a cinema. He came towards me, intent on making contact. He had a thin moustache. 'That film was real crap,' he said. 'You can write it off.'

His Mandarin was full of slangy English, mostly picked up from films. My own was hesitant and puritanical. So we conversed in a *mélange* of vulgarism and formality.

Tong was deathly bored. He worked in industrial chemicals, he said, and had been posted here from Tianjin in the east. The transfer had been desolating – a move from everything he considered civilised into a region synonymous with banishment. He exuded a sense of waste. He belonged to that generation reared during the Great Leap Forward and the Cultural Revolution – 'born in famine, raised in chaos', as they say. I wondered vaguely why he had been sent here. Perhaps he had fallen foul of someone.

'But I'm stuck now,' he said. 'Xining! There's nothing to do. Even Qinghai television is crap. A lot of it's in Tibetan anyway, so you're stuck with the national channel. Our local newspaper's the same. You read the headlines for world news, then chuck it away. It's full of stuff by political officials.'

His laughter was a kind of glittering unrest, which might soon rot into cynicism. I tried to cheer him up. 'What about your work?'

'It's dead boring. But if I tried to change it I'd need my work unit's permission, and they'd refuse. Anyway I've nowhere to go. My only residence permit is for Xining. So I'm trapped. Xining!' He reduced the place to a hiss.

We were trudging through the dark in no particular direction. The cold had emptied the streets. I felt guilty for my freedom. But Tong would not be pitied. He lived in the energy of his anger. He was twenty-seven. He existed on a low government salary, almost in exile. Meanwhile on television, the West tortured him. He touched my arm. 'You don't have any American magazines? *Anything?*' But I had nothing. 'Never mind. It's a relief just talking to you. It's stifling here. . . .'

'There's a bar in my hotel.'

'That hotel's bugged, I reckon. I think the foreigners' hotels in all the big cities are bugged. Not that we Chinese can get into them.' His habitual look of surprise disconcerted me now. Nothing would much surprise him. 'In the old days in Shanghai, you know, dogs and Chinese were kept out of places like that – and now it's just the same.' He described a circle above his head – a gesture of cyclic misery. 'Except perhaps the dogs get in sometimes. Let's go to my flat. There's nothing to do there, but it's better than this.'

It comprised two rooms and a shared bath. He was lucky to be assigned it, he said. He wouldn't get anything better until he married. He flung off his overcoat. Underneath were patched jeans and a printed sweater. 'But how do I meet girls? The only places for dancing here are lousy. The boys just dance with boys, and the girls with girls.'

'Can't you even talk?'

'Yes, but the girls of Xining are the bottom. Really thick – and ugly, like peasants, or like those Tibetan women you see with bright red and black cheeks. I ought to get married soon, but how can I marry one of those?' He looked harshly depressed. 'If I was in Tianjin or Beijing . . . the girls are OK there.'

I said uncertainly: 'Yes.' But even these grim Meccas seemed light-years away. I wondered about him. Had he, at twenty-seven, never even kissed a girl?

I could now decipher the gauche English slogan on his sweater. It read: *Do you like this sweater? It's the hottest item this winter. It's not only functional to keep out the coldness, but also fashionable for both youngsters and athletes.*

The youngster in question slumped on to a chair, and the earnest legend crumpled into nonsense over his chest. I said, 'What will you do?'

'I don't know. Right now I make do with video cassettes. A friend of mine's got a video. He gets these smuggled cassettes from Hong Kong.'

'What sort?'

'Oh, boys and girls, you know.' He made it sound like a children's playgroup. 'Sex.'

I was surprised. Xining was such a backwater. Ten years ago he might have died for this. 'Do many of you watch?'

'No. Just three or four friends. Any more would be too risky. But these cassettes are nothing. I've heard of workers' children in this city – kids of fifteen and sixteen – sleeping together. What else can people do when they can't move around? Things here aren't like with you. Nothing's really changed. This government is the same as all the others – Mao Zedong, Hua Guofeng, Deng Xiaoping – none of them makes us free. In our constitution it gives us freedom of speech, freedom of correspondence, freedom of everything . . . but just try using it.' He got to his feet to check the flat door, jerking it open and closing it soundlessly behind him again. 'To say anything safely against the government you have to be walking alone in the streets. We have a slogan which says the Party is our father and the Motherland our mother. But what a father! Euuh! I'd rather be an orphan.' His mouth soured into disgusted laughter. 'How can you love a father who beats you up half the time?'

The abyss between ruled and ruler had never seemed so great. Half a century and a whole flowered and faded ideology separated them. Tong was smoking angrily. He had outgrown even his name – a literary synonym for 'Red'. 'It's not as if the system is even honest. Even towns like this are full of "back-door" people – freelance fellows earning twice what I do. And there's a network of corrupt officials right to the top. The posh Party children get all the privileges. The Party blabs that the West is corrupt and Capitalist, then they send their children to study there. Why?' He crushed out one cigarette, lit another. 'It's hopeless. There's nothing we can do. I think this whole system is useless. Look at South Korea – richer than the North. Why? Look at West Germany – richer than East Germany. Why? Why is Japan so rich? And here it's thirty-five years since Liberation and we're still pathetic. A few of us may be better off, but most are wretched. And we're meant to be grateful!' He glanced round at his blotched walls dribbling loose plaster, pitted with nail-holes for vanished scrolls or posters. In protest or hope, he had done nothing to the place since his arrival. To clothe it would make it more permanent.

'This is just about the worst province you can be sent to,' he said. 'It's the place for criminals, chock-full of labour-camps. The area round Golmud, where the Kazakhs are, is full of them, I've heard – prisoners working in the fields and zinc and copper mines. How many? I don't know. Nobody knows. I've never even heard a figure. Some of the criminals go way back. Twenty, thirty years, maybe – even more. . . .'

Not only criminals were exiled here, but political and conscientious offenders. Next morning, a few miles out of Xining, my bus passed a huge, blank-walled compound encircled by guard turrets. Their soldiers were armed and faced inwards. A minute later they were gone, and we were climbing where green rivers raced out of the hills, mottled by ice-floes.

Somewhere over the tablelands before us spread the Gulag of China. Vast, walled enceintes, it is said, scatter this desolation – self-contained countries where 'reform through labour' goes forward in a regime of physical hardship, confessions, informings, political indoctrination and struggle sessions. In some camps the prisoners are packed ten or twelve to a cell; they can barely turn over at night. Brutish bullying is the norm, and sometimes torture. In 1979 convicts became so desperate that they rioted, and had to be suppressed by the army.

Their numbers are never published. But throughout China, it is estimated, over a hundred thousand political prisoners languish – ten times the number in the Soviet Union. For even dissidence is collective here. In each new storm of policy, those too deeply tainted by a past clique or attitude have been interned *en masse*. So the camps hold the detritus of countless half-disowned campaigns, a whole mournful history. With each shift of political direction, thousands are shriven and released. But others replace them; and others stay on. Ageing Guomindang soldiers and bureaucrats waste away beside 'historical counter-revolutionaries' arrested in the purges of the 1950s, and victims of the 1964–5 'Socialist Education' and the 'Four Clean-ups' campaigns. Leftover 'rightists' imprisoned during the 1957–8 debacle of the Hundred Flowers movement linger beside Cultural Revolution 'leftists', Red Guards, supporters of the 'Gang of Four', 'democracy movement' activists, Party officials fallen foul of the 1983 Rectification Campaign, Roman Catholic priests. . . .

Our road spiralled through defiles out of the valley. Snow was falling in a light, flurrying dust. In my bus, Han soldiers and farmers crowded together with lean-faced Kazakhs and families of Hui and Tu. Sandwiched among Tibetan herdsmen, I shared apples and boiled eggs but no word of language with them. Swollen in their hides, they blocked the bus with skinned and upended sheep, stiff as trolleys.

All morning we ascended, jammed among the carts of Mongolian nomads. A lorry had skidded into the cliff-face, stacked with frozen sheep's carcasses, victims of the early snows. Then the road lifted into uplands over ten thousand feet, mottled with ashy grass. Yaks browsed along the snow-fields. Their sickle-shaped horns, together with the quaint sag of their necks and countervailing humps, made a prehistoric strangeness in the valleys.

We continued west into the afternoon. Far to the south, like the landscape of another time, the whole skyline was littered with snowpeaks. We had arrived on the tablelands of Qinghai-Tibet, starved of monsoons by the Himalaya, and now deforested: the cold heart of Asia. Among those first ranges lay the sources of the Yellow River. Ahead of us, out of sight, the Kunlun mountains lifted – home of the Jade Emperor and the Mother-Queen of the West. The Yangtze and the Mekong rose at their feet.

As for Koko Nor, it was so saline that no plant mellowed its shores. The hills cradled it in death. Its waters were polished the same blue as the sky. The sky might have been inverted and spilt into the hills.

I climbed off the bus near an isolated fishing settlement. Its boats had been beached. I walked towards it alone. The rustle of a wind arose, and a desolate twitter of birds in the grass. The peaks were a glistening wasteland, and the lake so huge – the largest in China – that its western banks were invisible seventy miles beyond.

The fishermen were huddled indoors against the cold. At this altitude they sat idle six months of the year. The lake, they said, was reverenced by the surrounding nomads, and herdsmen along the shores had reported an aquatic monster. Its body undulated like a serpent's but its face, apparently, was that of an old man, and tapered to a waterlogged beard.

I wondered if the fishermen were ex-prisoners. Convicts are often refused permission to return to their home provinces, and are settled in this region they hate. But the fishermen said they had been coaxed from the Shandong seaboard by high wages. They seemed numbed by winter and waiting. They found me a bed in an empty guesthouse, and left me alone.

I roamed along the shore. The air's stillness made the cold bearable. The lake's edges were crusted with ice, which the lisp of the water had undermined. Its grey sand was scattered with pink stones. But no sea-monster appeared, and no sign of the naval units which are said to train here in secret. Over the withered slopes the snow had gone and the grasses sprouted in waist-high tussocks. The emptiness infiltrated my mind. Sky and water were as blank as one another. The lake was carved in the nakedness like an abstract idea. It might have belonged in the third day of Creation, at that instant before plants or beasts had been willed into life, or man complicated things, or any serpent broke the surface.

*   *   *

Two days later I was back in Lanzhou. Winter had hardened, and nobody loitered in the streets now. When I went to visit the ebullient Professor Huang, I found that he had left for the south. So I turned to my journey's end. Ever since the early 1950s a railway had curled along the Gansu corridor, slaloming among the debris of the Great Wall where it petered to the west. Five hundred miles and eighteen hours would bring me to where the fortress of Jiayuguan put a full stop to the old Chinese world.

But on my last evening in Lanzhou, on a distant introduction from England, I tracked down Professor Yu. For months I had been carrying in my rucksack a gift for his blind daughter.

The austerity of people's flats no longer surprised me, and I climbed an outside staircase in a slashing wind. Often families seemed merely to be encamped in their rooms – so many townsmen were aliens where they lived. But Yu's family had lived here for three generations. His ancestors had been accused of bribery and exiled from Wuxi by the last of the Qing emperors. His wife was half Russian – her face plumped by a Slavic fullness – for her father had worked in the Siberian gold mines and married a local girl.

I had brought their daughter a folding white stick, but as Yu extended his hand to me, I realised that his own sight was failing. His stubby fingers missed mine altogether. He laughed sadly in apology. He was stocky in baggy trousers and corduroy shoes. He led me uncertainly to the sitting-room. A sofa in crimson velveteen stood on a concrete floor spotted with paint. We sat down awkwardly. The only ornaments were a miniature rock in a tray of water, a calendar featuring demure girls, and a scroll inscribed with a poem by Li Bai: 'See the waters of the Yellow River. . . .'

He apologised for his ill-preparedness. It was a long time since he had entertained a guest, he said, because of his health. 'This eye has gone blind' – he touched it with his fingertips – 'and now the left one's going too.'

'Is it hereditary?'

'No. My daughter had eye cancer when she was just two years old, and lost her sight then. My blindness is different. My left eye failed because of a detached retina, and that strained the right one.'

He spoke a fluent, idiomatic English, whose timbre mellowed whenever he talked of his daughter. For his own blindness he had no tone of voice. 'It happened very suddenly. Two months ago I woke up feeling I was underwater. Things kept looming in and out of focus. My retina was bleeding. Even now, when I look at you' – he extended a hand – 'I can't see half of you at all, and the other half is waving about.'

But only the lazing of his left eyelid betrayed that anything was wrong. The rest – the sunken creases shutting in his gaze, the small features lost in jowls – belonged to his sixty-two years. It was a warm face, secure. He said: 'It's hard to think of never seeing the countryside again. This is a harsh province, as you know, but beautiful. In the Gansu corridor you can see the Qilian mountains above the desert. That's very wonderful. And the pass beyond Jiayuguan where the Great Wall ends – you see the snows high up. And in Xinjiang there's Heaven Lake.' He glanced involuntarily at the window's rectangle of sky. 'I'd care to see Heaven Lake again.'

He was like a man talking about death. This was a kind of death.

'But what I most miss is novels. I used to read for four hours every day. I loved the Russian stories – Turgenev especially – and Hardy's *The Mayor of Casterbridge*, and the Chinese classics I read in childhood – *Journey to the West*, *The Dream of Red Mansions*, *Outlaws of the Marsh*.'

Already this rich disparity of images – the bandits of *Outlaws of the Marsh*, the hills above Heaven Lake and Casterbridge – seemed to be both hurting and consoling him.

But perhaps he would recover.

'My daughter's in Beijing at a school for the blind,' he said. 'She's learning English and braille – in Roman lettering, because it can't be done in Chinese characters. She's very quick. Her teacher told me that he made a complicated joke in English class and there was this solitary sound of laughter – my daughter.' His face crumpled with affection and pride. Now his sightless eye was scarcely more closed than the other – and both looked bright and deceptively alive. 'She still remembers things which she saw as a baby. She remembers my face and her mother's – or our faces as we were then, fourteen years ago.' He paused, struck by the strangeness of this – that to the blind, people do not age. He felt his face. 'We took her to Beijing Zoo, and she remembers the tiger she saw, and the elephant and a certain snake, for some reason. She remembers colours. But because she could once see, I think it's sadder for her, knowing what she's missing.' He might have been talking of himself too. 'But it makes her more intelligent. She understands what the physical world is like.'

Then there came one of those moments which fell into the sombre landscape of my journey with a flash of intimacy. Tentatively, I gave Yu the white stick for his daughter. I did not know what he would feel. Perhaps it was he, very soon, who would need it.

He grasped and unfurled it. It was neat, light.

'She can fold it up and put it in her bag,' I said. 'But perhaps she has one already.'

'Not like this. Not like this.' He clasped it against him and smiled with an intense, flooding warmth. 'Oh thank you!' He looked overcome, hid it away in a drawer. '*Thank you.*'

Above his momentarily turned back, I saw the scroll poem by Li Bai on the wall. I remembered:

> See the waters of the Yellow River
> Leap down from Heaven,
> Roll away to the sea
> and never turn again. . . .

The next moment his wife had entered with dinner – minced lamb, marinated fish, bamboo-shoots, toffeed apples, sweet vermouth, which she disparaged in Russian. She would not sit with us. Yu lifted each morsel hesitantly to his mouth, focusing it sideways like a bird. Only after I had pressed him over his failing eyesight did he confide its cause.

'During the Cultural Revolution,' he said, 'many teachers in my college were subjected to "struggle". It was a fearful period. Most of us admitted to things we'd never done, just to make an end. My wife and I had relatives in Russia, so we were accused of being spies.' He thrust his arms behind him. 'I was held like this and subjected to hours of beating and shouting, many times. But I refused to say anything. I kept telling myself: *I've loved my country. I've never betrayed it. This can't go on.* I never uttered. That's probably why I was sent to prison for two years. My wife, too. I was beaten about the head so often. . . .' His fingers fluttered against his eyes.

I wondered who these students were who had battered him. But I realised, with muffled surprise, that I was no longer deeply perplexed. Perhaps I had been too long in his hard land, I thought, with its terrible obediences, its mass of unredeemed poor. My acceptance, even to me, was a little chilling, as if my understanding (if that is what it was) might be the beginning of indifference.

He said: 'The worst students were the ambitious ones and the pupils who got low marks – the stupid or lazy ones, the ones we hadn't favoured. They wanted revenge.'

He spoke with no outrage, as if half in collusion with the cruelty visited on him. He forgave the rank-and-file of his persecutors as he might have forgiven ants which had bitten him. It was not, after all, their fault. It was the social organisation. They were misled. They had only done what was expected. It was the personal humiliation which hurt, and the waste of it all.

Then the hardy optimism of his people resurfaced. 'But now everything has changed, just as I knew it would. We've got our sanity back. The whole country is in revolution again, but it's a fruitful one.' He was buoyant. 'You've seen how poor our soil is here – only good for one crop a year. But already our free markets are booming.' He twirled his chopsticks. 'Three years ago I wouldn't have dared even talk to you. But today I can ask you to my house and give you supper!'

But what about those old wounds, I asked? His own college, I knew, was split from top to bottom by the enmities engendered in those years.

'Who can tell?' His smile steadied. 'But the Cultural Revolution won't return. Not like that. You see, *everybody* suffered then. I think we all feel shriven in a way, exhausted. . . .'

* * *

In my train to Jiayuguan there was scarcely room to sit on the floor, and the cold was so intense that people's breath blinded the windows to frost-patterns inside.

For a few miles we followed the Yellow River before it looped under a bridge and was gone. Then night came. Padded and scarved, passengers slept where they were, heaped among their bundles as if in camp, their children sprawled loose over their knees. Every time the train stopped, a new influx sent a tremor of suffocation through the mass. I found a space in the bridge between two carriages, where my quilted overcoat enclosed me like an eiderdown, and tried to sleep. I was crushed among Hui farmers, who sang to themselves in small, toneless voices, propped against one another's backs and shoulders, or asleep on their feet like horses. Women brought their babies to urinate down the joint between the carriages beside us, holding them proudly steady. The urine froze within seconds.

I woke to morning and a changed country. The Qilian range had retreated southward behind a ravelin of snowy foothills, and to the north stretched a sandy, level plain – the southern rim of the Gobi. The mountains dropped into it with a frozen brilliance. I half expected them to sizzle. But the desert was as cold as they were. An intermittent dust of grey stones covered it, and here and there the wind had swept it into a liquid tumult of dunes. All around us, the horizon was closed by the shaped splendour of those mountains, or by nothing at all. It was the end of one wilderness and the start of another. Our engine smoke divided them with a pink streamer in the early sun.

We reached Jiayuguan at midday. It was a bungaloid steel town, built for the desert to howl in. I was the only person in my hotel. I gnawed through a near-inedible meal, my head full of the fortress I had glimpsed in the desert close by. In my restaurant the suggestions book had last been inscribed a month before by a lone Japanese: 'The service was dreadful. Nobody even spoke to me.'

I marched to the fort in cold excitement. It had been rebuilt by the Ming in 1372, and dubbed the 'Impregnable Pass under Heaven', and for two millennia, under almost all dynasties, its site had marked the western limit of the Great Wall. From here, since the early years of the Roman Empire, the Silk Road had linked China to the Mediterranean. Even now it invited a journey westward through the Muslim oases of Xinjiang, but the snows and the enormous fort – the traditional terminus of China – dissuaded me.

Massed foursquare on the desert's edge, the slope of its bastions lent it an Assyrian austerity. But as I approached, its ramparts erupted into a delicacy of coloured gate-towers, like a funfair inside a prison, and beyond them a little open-air theatre, now restored, had been painted with women and animals in an absurd, defiant sweetness of civilisation at the end of the world.

I climbed its ramparts into the wind, my eyes streaming. To the south, the pass which it defended opened between the black folds of the Mazong range and the white of the Qilian mountains. To the west the Great Wall crossed the desert in isolated scarps and beacon-towers. For a moment, restored to its thirty-foot height, it wrapped the fortress in an outer curtain, then faltered southward a few more miles to its end.

But to the north the Gobi – the drowner of cities – spread void under the colourless sky. A mauve band dissolved its horizon. This was the feared hinterland of the Chinese mind, a chaotic barrenness racked by demons and the ever-lingering nomad. From where I stood, a flying crow, hunting for civilisation, would spread its wings a thousand miles south-west across Qinghai and Tibet before alighting hopelessly on Everest. If instead it endured a thousand miles due west, it would plummet into the wilderness of Taklimakan far short of the Afghan frontier; and northward, after crossing Mongolia, it might wander Siberia for ever.

Into any region beyond the Great Wall, disgraced Chinese were banished in despair. Jiayuguan was 'China's Mouth'. Those beyond it were 'outside the mouth,' and its western gate – a vaulted tunnel opening into the unknown – used to be covered with farewell inscriptions in the refined hand of exiled officials. Local people called it the Gate of Sighs. Even if the outcasts survived among the surly Mongols, they would die beyond the reach of any heaven. Demons would torment them in their sandy graves, and Buddhists be condemned to an eternal cycle of barbarian reincarnations.

It was early evening when I started across the sand the last few miles to the Wall's end. I withdrew my head into my overcoat like a tortoise. The wind flayed every chink of exposed skin. In front of me the rampart had long since shed its gloss of tamped clay, and was blistered to earth innards. Often the desert had overwhelmed it, pulling a pelt of stones and camel thorn over the parapets until the sand slid down the far side and subsumed them. Ahead, the Qilian ranges were divorced from the plain by haze – a glistening mirage. I could understand why Yu loved them.

I had been walking for two or three miles. The light was fading. The only life was a pair of Bactrian camels browsing on nothing. In the approaching mountains I saw no trace of ramparts, no sign where the Wall went.

Suddenly the land dropped sheer beneath my feet. In its canyon, two hundred feet deep, wound a concealed river – an ice-blue coldness out of nowhere. It must have started as a glacial torrent, but over millennia it had sliced the earth clean. The ground looked so unstable I was afraid to approach the edge. I found myself shivering. All colour had been struck out of it, except for mineral greys and blues. Under the Wall's last, broken tower the river moved to its end in the Gobi through the steel-grey earth under the white mountains.

Index

Amoy, *see* Xiamen
Anhui province, 50, 51, 121, 134
Aurelius, Marcus, 254

Bai people, 218
Beidaihe, 69–71, 76
Beijing (Peking), 1, 3, 4ff., 67, 88, 129,
  138, 164, 182, 258, 267, 268, 285,
  288, 291, 292, 298; *hutong*s, 5–7;
  Tiananmen Square, 7, 36, 61; For-
  bidden City, 7, 14, 28–32, 36, 53;
  Fragrant Hills, 11; Wangfujing Street,
  13; nuclear shelters, 13–15; Summer
  Palace, 14; Coal Hill, 14; bath-house,
  15–17; kindergarten, 21–3; Zoo,
  23–8, 224, 298; Monument to the
  People's Heroes, 36; Tomb of Mao
  Zedong, 36–7; Lama Temple, 38–43;
  marriage introduction bureau, 43–5;
  Democracy Wall, 45; Great Wall
  Hotel, 51–3, 168; Temple of Heaven,
  53–4; Altar of Heaven, 54–6; tradi-
  tional medicine college, 56–8; Altar of
  Moon, 58–61
Beijing Opera, 147, 189–90
Binglingsi, 286–7
Bodhidarma, prince, 258, 259
Bohai Gulf, 72
Britain, 52, 54, 130, 134, 141–4, 152,
  173, 195, 221–2, 234, 278
Buck, Pearl, 287
Bulang people, 219
Burma, 1, 77, 211, 218, 222, 223, 225,
  241
Burma Road, 211

Caishiji, 109–11
Cambodia, 223

Canton (Guangzhou), 2, 52, 77, 172,
  173, 175ff., 215, 235; Pearl River,
  175–6, 178, 181; nursery, 177;
  Cathedral, 177–8; Shamian, 178;
  White Swan Hotel, 178; restaurants,
  182–6; Cultural Park, 188–90;
  market, 190–2
Changchun, 285
Changsha, 194, 195, 198
Chengdu, 228, 234–8, 291
Chiang Kai-shek, 89, 176, 239, 248
China Sea, 77, 141, 165, 176, 274
Chongqing, 106, 144, 213, 238–40, 287
Confucius, 36, 79–85, 99, 100, 112, 130,
  145, 159, 163, 199, 251, 261, 271, 276
Cultural Revolution, 2, 3, 8, 11, 25–8,
  33–5, 41, 45–7, 59, 93–6, 97–9, 123,
  124, 132, 134, 139, 142, 145, 147–9,
  161, 163, 165, 186, 189, 196, 198, 199,
  200, 220, 234, 238, 251, 257, 259, 261,
  265–6, 267–8, 270, 279–81, 287, 291,
  295, 299–300

Dai people, 211, 218, 219, 220–1, 222,
  223
Dai Ailian, 33–6
Dalai Lama, 39, 290
Dazhai, 275
Deng Xiaoping, 293
Dengming, computer scientist, and the
  author, 17–21
Dian, Lake, 215, 218
Dream of Red Mansions, The, 297

Emei, 230
Emei, Mount, 230–4; Baoguo monastery,
  230

Feng, honeymooner, and the author, 215-17
Fo, Dogs of, 31
France, 138, 142, 177, 247
Fujian province, 109, 117, 165, 167, 173, 274

Ganenbang, 223-5
'Gang of Four', 35, 94, 98, 142, 295
Gansu province, 282, 283, 296, 297
Gobi desert, 1, 2, 42, 75, 193, 247, 271, 274, 278, 300-2
Golden Triangle, the, 223
Golmud, 294
Grand Canal, 14, 77, 127, 129-31, 215
Great Leap Forward, the, 197, 198, 201, 238, 253, 291
Great Wall, the, 1, 14, 65-6, 68, 72-7, 247, 264, 271, 296, 297, 301-2
Guangdong province, 173
Guangxi province, 210
Guanyin, Goddess of Mercy, 123, 126-7, 163, 177, 224
Guilin, 204-9; Li river, 205-7
Guiyang, 210
Guizhou province, 210
Guo, Party Secretary, and the author, 45-51, 151
Guomindang, 80, 89, 132, 277, 287, 294

Han dynasty, 264
Hangzhou, 14, 129, 162-3
Hani people, 219, 224
Hanoi, 218
Harbin, 104, 105, 212
Heaven Lake, 297, 298
Hefei, 114, 115
Henan province, 263
Himalaya Mountains, 1, 78, 193, 234, 295
Hong Kong, 39, 52, 141, 144, 166-7, 175, 176, 179, 193, 195, 210, 213, 234, 258, 293
Hua, ex-convict, and the author, 212-14
Hua, factory singer, and the author, 102-8
Hua Guofeng, 198, 293

Huang, professor, and the author, 287-8, 296
Huangpo river, 141, 143
Hui sect, 265-6, 283-4, 289, 295, 300
Hunan province, 129, 174, 182, 194
Huns, 76, 271

I Ching, 247
India, 124, 126
Inner Mongolia, 3, 56, 75, 248, 264
Irrawaddy river, 218

Japan, 89, 106, 144, 152, 155, 176, 195, 204, 212, 236, 239, 240, 248, 258, 263, 274, 277, 287, 294, 300
Jardine, Matheson Co., 67, 142
Jews of Kaifeng, 252
Jialing river, 238, 239, 240
Jiang Qing, 33, 34, 197, 198, 202
Jiangsu province, 248
Jianming, commercial traveller, and the author, 109-18
Jiayuguan, 75, 76, 296, 297, 300-1
Jinghong, 219, 220, 221, 222
Jiuhuashan, 77, 115, 117, 118ff.
Journey to the West, 297

Kaifeng, 247, 250-3, 254
Karakoram Mountains, 1
Kazakh people, 195, 294, 295
Khmer Rouge, 223
Koko Nor, 288, 289, 295-6
Kong Demao, 82-3
Korea, 76, 264, 294
Korean War, 2, 90, 201, 214
Kublai Khan, 28, 218
Kumbum monastery, 290-1
Kunlun Mountains, 295
Kunming, 210-18, 220, 226, 291

Lanzhou, 283-4, 287, 296
Lao She, 134
Laos, 77, 211, 218, 223
Legalism, 271
Lenin, V. I., 37, 187, 278
Lhasa, 290, 291
Li Bai, 109-11, 297, 298

Li Guangxiu, 215
Li Yun, tax official, and the author, 174–5, 179–81
Lijun, honeymooner, and the author, 215–17
Lin Biao, 80, 280
Lingyin temple, 163
Little Red Book, the, 36, 81, 96
Liu Shaoqi, 108, 196, 201, 252–3, 277, 280
Liuyin, unemployed, and the author, 59–61
Long March, the, 155, 274
Lu, postal clerk, and the author, 279–81
Luoyang, 7, 247, 253–7, 260, 264

Macao, 170, 175
Manchu dynasty, 30, 31, 62, 66, 89, 234
Manchuria, 1, 73, 105, 212, 214, 285
Mao Zedong, 3, 7, 17, 26, 30, 33, 35, 36–7, 45, 80, 81, 95, 96–7, 99, 132, 155, 164, 170, 176, 180, 182, 187, 194–202, 234, 251, 252–3, 272, 274, 277, 278, 280, 289
Mazong Mountains, 301
Mekong river, 1, 77, 218, 219, 222–3, 295
Mencius, 28, 276
Miao people, 289
Ming dynasty, 53, 62–6, 76, 89, 123, 151, 208, 238, 258, 264, 300
Ming Tombs, 62–6, 217
Mongol dynasty (Yuan), 163, 218
Mongolia, 1, 39, 40, 78, 244, 283, 288, 289, 290, 295, 301
Mouli, teacher, and the author, 266–71
Muslims, 288, 289, 301; *see* Hui

Nanjing, 77, 85, 87ff., 102, 109, 127, 241, 244, 287; history, 89; mausoleum of Sun Yatsen, 89–91; hospital, 91–2; high school, 93–5; Cockcrow Temple, 95–6; Yangtze bridge, 96–7; Protestant church, 97; seminary, 97–100; funerary monument, 100–1
Northern Wei dynasty, 255

Opium Wars, 142, 167
Ordos desert, 248
Outlaws of the Marsh, 198, 297, 298

Panchen Lama, 290
Peking, *see* Beijing
Perfect Emperors, the, 55
Polo, Marco, 4, 131, 162
Puxian, bodhisattva, 232

Qilian Mountains, 297, 300, 301, 302
Qin empire, 271, 273
Qin Shihuangdi, emperor, 76, 264, 271–4
Qinghai province, 247, 278, 283, 288, 292, 294, 295, 301
Quemoy, 165, 168, 171, 173
Qufu, 79–85; palace, 79–81, 83; library, 82; Apricot Altar, 82; Hall of Great Perfection, 82; Forest of Confucius, 83–5

Red Detachment of Women, The, 33, 36
Red Guards, 7, 26, 49, 80–2, 84, 98–9, 108, 120, 132, 147–9, 220, 223, 230, 257, 266, 287, 295
Red river, 218
Responsibility System, agricultural, 164–165, 238, 274–5
Romance of the Three Kingdoms, The, 198
Runliang, Mouli's wife, 269–71

Salween river, 218
Sani people, 218
Sanmen dam, 286
Shaanxi province, 264, 266, 269, 274
Shandong province, 296
Shanghai, 2, 52, 54, 77, 85, 90, 138ff., 215, 235, 241, 254, 292; Nanjing Road, 138; fashion, 140; beauty salon, 140–1; Bund, 141–3; Cathay Hotel, 143; youth palace, 145–6; 'The Great World', 146; music conservatory, 146–148; church, 148–50; arts and crafts institute, 150; Academy of Traditional Painting, 150–1; Jail, 152–6; circus,

Shanghai—contd
156–7, 291; chemist, 157–8; mental
hospital, 158–61
Shanhaiguan, 68, 71–5, 76
Shaolin monastery, 257–60, 162, 262
Shaoshan, 180, 182, 194–202, 274
Sichuan province, 78, 202, 227, 228,
229, 235, 238, 239, 243
Silk Road, the, 75, 252, 265, 301
Simao, 218
Singapore, 141, 172–3, 180, 241
Song dynasty, 74, 88, 96, 128, 162, 163,
250, 251
Special Economic Zones, 168
Stalin, J., 3, 198, 238, 278
Sun Yatsen, Dr, 89–91, 176
Suzhou, 102, 114, 127, 131–7; Humble
Administrator's Garden, 135; Lion
Forest Garden, 136; Master of the
Fishing Nets Garden, 136–7

Tai, Lake, 128, 134
Taiping Heavenly Kingdom, 89, 252
Taiwan, 67, 77, 80, 82, 154, 165
Taklimakan depression, 1, 301
Tang dynasty, 71, 74, 88, 109, 132, 162,
243, 250, 251, 255, 257, 258, 260,
264–5, 287
Tangshan, 35, 68–9, 268, 270
Taoism, 217, 258, 260–1, 289
Thailand, 219
Tian Mountains, 1
Tian Qi, emperor, 66
Tianjin, 68, 69, 291, 292
Tibet, 1, 32, 39, 40, 42–3, 78, 231, 233,
234, 241, 248, 283, 288, 289, 290, 292,
295, 301
Titsang, God of Hell, 120, 123
Tong, chemist, and the author, 291–4
Tonkin, Gulf of, 218, 271
Tsong-Kapa, 290
Tu people, 289, 295

Uighur people, 195
United States, 47, 54, 73, 90, 134, 139,
142, 144–5, 148, 155, 158–60, 213,
237–8, 240, 244, 255

USSR, 7, 13, 35, 54, 67, 95, 100, 134,
187, 212, 213, 229, 234, 238, 244,
251–2, 283, 294

Vietnam, 112, 211, 218, 223, 244

Wan Li, emperor, 63–4
Wang, bricklayer, and the author, 284–
286
Wei river, 264
Weidong, teacher, and the author, 202–
203
Weigi, friend of author, 101–13, 105–
107
White-haired Girl, The, 33, 36
Wu, professor, and the author, 144–5,
158
Wuhan, 221
Wuhu, 115–18
Wuxi, 114, 127, 128–31, 291, 296
Wuyi Mountains, 166

Xiamen, 167–73; The Sea Paradise, 168–
170; Gulangyu island, 170–2
Xian, 247, 254, 264–6, 268, 270, 271,
272, 274, 282, 284
Xigun, municipal worker, and the author,
235–8
Xihui, economics student, and the
author, 85–7, 115
Xining, 288, 289–94
Xinjiang province, 75, 283, 297, 301
Xishuangbanna, 218

Yang, professor, and the author, 56–8
Yangshuo, 207
Yangtze river, 2, 17, 23, 41, 78, 87–8,
96–7, 109, 110, 111, 114, 118, 127,
162, 221, 227, 229, 238, 239–42, 295;
Gorges, 243–6; Gezhouba dam, 246
Yellow river, 3, 75, 78, 129, 162, 247–8,
250, 264, 283, 286, 295, 297, 298, 300
Yellow Sea, 68
Yenan, 247, 274–8, 280
Yi people, 211
Yu, professor, and the author, 296–300,
302

Yulong, schoolgirl, and the author, 103, 105, 107–8
Yunnan province, 93, 211, 218

Zhengzhou, 247, 248–50, 254, 263

Zhou, schoolmaster, and the author, 132–4
Zhou Enlai, 7, 33, 35, 80, 155, 176, 196, 267, 277
Zhu De, 35, 196, 277, 278
Ziyang, and the author, 39–43